PROFILES IN BELIEF

Profiles in Belief

THE RELIGIOUS BODIES
OF THE UNITED STATES AND CANADA

VOLUME I

ROMAN CATHOLIC

OLD CATHOLIC

EASTERN ORTHODOX

By ARTHUR CARL PIEPKORN

HARPER & ROW, PUBLISHERS

NEW YORK, HAGERSTOWN

SAN FRANCISCO, LONDON

1817

FIRST EDITION

Designed by Sidney Feinberg

Library of Congress Cataloging in Publication Data

Piepkorn, Arthur Carl, 1907–1973.
  Profiles in belief.
  Includes bibliographies and index.
  CONTENTS: v. 1. Roman Catholic, Old Catholic,
Eastern Orthodox.
  1. Sects—North America. I. Title.
BR510.P53 1977   200'.973   76–9971
ISBN 0–06–066580–7 (v. 1)

79 80 81 10 9 8 7 6 5 4 3 2

Contents

Foreword by Martin E. Marty   xi
Editor's Preface   xiii
Introduction by Harry J. McSorley   xv

PART I
PRE- AND NON-CHALCEDONIAN CHURCHES

1. The Church before Chalcedon   3

   A Formative Period: From the Council of Nicaea (325) to the
        Council of Constantinople (381)   3
   The Church of the East and of the Assyrians   4

2. The Non-Chalcedonian Churches   13

   The Syrian Orthodox Church of Antioch in the United States and
        Canada   13
   The Syrian Orthodox Church of Malabar in the United States   16
   The Armenian Church   16
   The Armenian Diocese of North America Under the Catholicate of
        all Armenians at Holy Etchmiadzin   20
   Prelacy of the Armenian Apostolic Church of America   20
   Coptic Orthodox Church, Diocese of North America   21
   Ethiopian Orthodox Church in the United States of America   23

PART II
EASTERN ORTHODOX CHURCHES

3. Eastern Orthodoxy   31

   The Division between the East and the West   32
   History   34
   Eastern Orthodoxy in Russia   36
   Worldwide Eastern Orthodoxy   38

v

Eastern Orthodox Theology   38
The "Mysteries"   44
Noneucharistic Worship, the Calendar, and Canon Law   48
Eastern Orthodox Missions   50
Eastern Orthodoxy and Other Christian Denominations   50
Eastern Orthodoxy in North America   52

4. Eastern Orthodox Churches in the United States and Canada   61

The Orthodox Church in America   61
*Patriarchal Parishes of the Russian Orthodox Church in the United
    States and Canada*   62
The Russian Orthodox Church Outside of Russia   63
Greek Orthodox Archdiocese of North and South America   64
Hellenic Traditionalist Orthodox Diocese of Astoria, New York   66
Holy Greek Orthodox Church of America   66
The Antiochian Orthodox Christian Archdiocese of North America   67
The Ukrainian Orthodox Church of the United States of America   69
The Ukrainian Greek-Orthodox Church in Canada   70
*The Ukrainian Orthodox Church of America (Ecumenical
    Patriarchate)*   71
La Santa Iglesia Católica Apostólica Ortodoxa de Puerto Rico   71
*The Ukrainian Autocephalous Orthodox Church in the United
    States of America*   71
[Holy] Ukrainian Autocephalic Orthodox Church in Exile   72
The Byelorussian Autocephalic Orthodox Church   73
*Byelorussian Orthodox Parishes under the Jurisdiction of the
    Ecumenical Patriarch*   74
The American Carpatho-Russian Orthodox Greek Catholic Diocese   74
*The Holy Orthodox Church in America (Eastern Catholic and
    Apostolic)*   75
Eastern Orthodox Catholic Church in America   76
Estonian Orthodox Church in Exile   77
American Finnish Orthodox Mission   78
*The Bulgarian Eastern Orthodox Church (Diocese of North and
    South America and Australia)*   78
*The Bulgarian Eastern Orthodox Church (Diocese of the United
    States of America and Canada)*   79
The Serbian Orthodox Community in America   80
*Serbian Orthodox Church in the United States of America and
    Canada*   80
*Serbian Orthodox Diocese in the United States of America and
    Canada*   80
*Macedonian Orthodox Churches, Diocese of America, Canada, and
    Australia*   81

The Romanian Orthodox Community   82
The Romanian Orthodox Missionary Episcopate in America   82
The Romanian Orthodox Episcopate of America   82
Western Hemisphere Romanian Orthodox Missionary Episcopate
of Canada   83
The Albanian Orthodox Archdiocese in America   83
The Albanian Orthodox Diocese of America   84

5. Churches Deriving Their Orders from Eastern Orthodox and Other
Eastern Sources   90

The American Catholic Church (Syro-Antiochian)   92
The African Orthodox Church   92
The Church of Antioch, Malabar Rite   94
The Archdiocese of New York of the American Catholic Church   95
The Holy Orthodox Catholic Patriarchate of America   96
The Orthodox-Catholic Church of America   96
Christ Catholic Church of the Americas and Europe   97
Byelorussian (White Ruthenian) Patriarchate of St. Andrew the
Apostle, the First-Called   98
The Diocese of Brooklyn and New Jersey of the Autocephalous
Greek Orthodox Church of America (Newark, New Jersey)   99
Universal Shrine of Divine Guidance of the Universal Faith
(Apostolic Universal Center)   100
American Orthodox Catholic Church   101
The American Synod of the Holy Orthodox Church   102
Ukrainian Autocephalic Church of North and South America   103

6. The Russian Old Believers   108

Priestist Old Ritualists   110
The Old Orthodox Church (Russian Old Believers, Pomortsi)   111
Other Bezpopovtsy   113

PART III
THE CHURCH IN THE WEST:
THE FIRST FIFTEEN CENTURIES

7. Theological and Ecclesiastical Leadership   119

Theologians   119
Councils   129
The Bishops of Rome   137

8. Dogma and Doctrine   148

Creeds   148
Specific Doctrines   153

9. Worship and Church Life   165

    Liturgy and Worship   165
    Religious Life   167
    Missions   170
    Canon Law   171
    Advocates of Reform   173

PART IV
THE ROMAN CATHOLIC CHURCH

10. From the Council of Trent to Vatican II   179

    The Council of Trent   179
    The Counter-Reformation   182
    The Seventeenth and Eighteenth Centuries   184
    The Nineteenth Century   186
    Into the Twentieth Century   190
    Vatican Council II   191
    Developments since Vatican Council II   194

11. Movements within Roman Catholicism   203

    Roman Catholic Modernism   203
    The Biblical Movement   204
    The Liturgical Movement   205
    *Changing Roman Catholic Attitudes toward the Ecumenical
      Movement*   206
    The Lay Movement   207

12. Theology and Doctrine   211

    Roman Catholic Theology Today   211
    Theological Degrees of Certainty   212
    God and the Universe   213
    Creation   215
    Angels and Demons   216
    Predestination   217
    Revelation and Dogma   218
    Human Beings and Sin   223
    Christ and Mary   226

13. Nature and Function of the Church   239

  The Church   239
  Bishops, Cardinals, and Priests   241
  The Communion of Saints   244
  Religious Freedom   247
  Religious Education and Catechetics   248
  The Religious   248
  The Priesthood of the Faithful   250
  The Impact of the Ecumenical Movement on the Roman Catholic
    Doctrine of the Church   251
  The Pope   254
  The Roman Catholic Church and Non-Christians   256
  The Roman Catholic Church and Secret Societies   258
  Roman Catholic Missions and Missionary Practice   259
  Roman Catholicism in the United States and Canada   263

PART V
CHURCHES DERIVED FROM
POST-TRIDENTINE ROMAN CATHOLICISM

14. The Old Catholic Communion in Europe   279

  Polish National Catholic Church of America   280

15. Other Churches Claiming Old Catholic Orders   286

  The North American Old Roman Catholic Church (Brooklyn,
    New York)   286
  The North American Old Roman Catholic Church (Chicago,
    Illinois)   287
  The Old Catholic Church in America   288
  North American Province of the Old Roman Catholic Church   288
  Evangelical Orthodox Church in America (Nonpapal Catholic
    Establishment, Diocese of the Western States)   289
  The Old Catholic Church in North America   290
  Old Roman Catholic Church in Europe and North America
    (English Rite)   290
  The Ontario Old Roman Catholic Church   291
  The Old Roman Catholic Church (Orthodox Orders)   292
  The Orthodox Old Roman Catholic Church, II   293
  Ultrajectine Ordinariate, Holy Catholic Church (Old Roman
    Catholic Church, Incorporated; The [Roman] Catholic Legation
    [of Utrecht])   294

*The Brotherhood of the Pleroma and Order of the Pleroma,
Including the Hermetic Brotherhood of Light (Formerly the
Brotherhood and Order of the Illuminati); Pre-Nicene Catholic
(Gnostic) Church*   294
The Liberal Catholic Movement   296
*The Liberal Catholic Church, Province of the United States and
Province of Canada*   299
International Liberal Catholic Church   301
The Liberal Catholic Church (Miranda, California)   302

16. The Renovated Church of Jesus Christ   311

Index   317

Foreword

"One book is about one thing—at least the good ones are." Eugene Rosenstock-Huessey's famous dictum may seem inappropriate in the eyes of readers who might casually come across the present work. That it is a "good book" will be immediately apparent, even to the casual user. But that it is "about one thing" may seem less obvious at first.

Arthur Carl Piepkorn's good and even great work seems to be about many things. It concerns itself with profiles of the many beliefs of millions of Americans who are separated into hundreds of religious bodies. Many of them, it may safely be presumed, will not even have been known by name to most readers before they acquaint themselves with the table of contents. Never before within the covers of several volumes in a single series will the student of American religion have been able to find convenient and reliable access to so many different religious groups. How can one in the midst of such variety think of Piepkorn's book as being "about one thing"?

The answer to that question, on second thought and longer acquaintance, could well be, "Easily!" For here is a single-minded attention to the one thing that is supposed to be at the heart of almost all of these religious groups, their beliefs. The telephone book includes many names, but it is "about one thing," and no one will mistake its purposes or its plot. So with Piepkorn's presentation of *The Religious Bodies of the United States and Canada*. It is precisely what its precise author's title claims it to be: *Profiles in Belief*.

Profile: it is a side view, an outline, a concise description. This book offers such an angle of vision. No individual can speak from within all these denominations and movements. To invite a separate speaker from each tradition would be to convoke a new Babel of tongues. Here we have something coherent and believable, the voice of a single informed observer. He establishes the "side view" and then invites criticism and approval by a member of each group to check on the accuracy of the portraits. This process assures evenness in tone and consistency in proportion without sacrificing either fairness or immediacy. While the description inevitably has had to grow long because of the number of groups presented, even its several volumes will be seen to be but an outline, something concise.

Beliefs: these by themselves do not constitute or exhaust all that a religion is or is experienced to be. For a full description the student will want to learn about social contexts and environments, about behavior patterns and practices of individuals and groups. But since these external marks purportedly grow out of the group's shared set of formal meanings and values and since these, in turn, derive from root beliefs, somewhere and somehow it is important to gain access to such beliefs. Had we all world enough and time it is possible that the knowledgeable could establish for themselves the profile of a large number of these religious bodies. But with the industry and intelligence for which he was noted, Dr. Piepkorn devoted years to the task of assembling the data for others. His profiles can be ends in themselves or instruments for further research. Of one thing we can be sure: they will force all thoughtful readers to take the beliefs more seriously than before.

Arthur Carl Piepkorn was a confessional Lutheran, but he does not use the confessional stance as a means of ranking the value of beliefs. Instead, that stance turned out to be the means of assuring readers that the author knew the importance of beliefs, knew what it was to confess a faith, was aware of the intellecutal power that can reside in a religious tradition. If, as a book title of some years ago asserts, "beliefs have consequences," the opposite was also true for Piepkorn. He could look at behavior and practice and step back, in effect saying, "consequences also have beliefs."

This is not the place to read the narrative of American religion, be enthralled by anecdote, or ramble with a sage author dispensing practical advice. This is a very formal guide to belief systems. As an ecumenist of note, Dr. Piepkorn came to be empathic about others' beliefs. As a military chaplain he had practical experience encountering people of faiths remote from his own in the American and Canadian contexts. As a teacher he knew how to get ideas across. As a confessor he valued faith. His book is certain to be a classic.

A classic is, among other things, a book behind which or around which one cannot easily go. Once it has appeared and come into common use it is a measure or benchmark for others. While the official title of this series is likely to endure, it is probably destined to be referred to in shorthand as "Piepkorn." If so, as the standard reference in the field, the designation will be a fitting tribute to the person who prepared himself well and spared himself not at all for the writing of this life work.

MARTIN E. MARTY
The University of Chicago

Editor's Preface

Death is almost always tragic. Not the least tragic in Arthur Carl Piepkorn's death was that his almost-finished magnum opus had not yet been published. At the request of his widow, Miriam Södegren Piepkorn, it became my responsibility to arrange for its publication. For me that was opportunity to pay tribute to a respected colleague, valued counselor, and dear friend and to assure that the results of years of scholarship would be available to others.

The material in this first volume in a series on religious bodies in the United States and Canada had been completed by the author and was ready for publication. Written a year or two before the author's death in December 1973, the material required some editing in order to bring statistical information up-to-date and to take account of recent major developments in some churches. I assumed the task of editing the material for publication.

Fully aware that I was handling the work of a master, I took pains to change only what was necessary to bring the material up-to-date. I tried to be as meticulous as the author in discovering and verifying data. I made first-hand contacts with officials of the churches described in the volume when published sources were not available to me. I take full responsibility for any inaccuracies or omissions in the material.

Of course, the major emphasis of the book is the beliefs of Christians gathered in a variety of churches related to the Eastern Orthodox and Roman Catholic traditions. Beliefs are more enduring than membership statistics or organizational structure. The description of beliefs in this volume is pure Piepkorn.

In the extensive notes which he has provided, the author has paid tribute to innumerable people who provided information for this volume. If he were writing the preface, the author no doubt would have included a list of other acknowledgments. I am aware that James Geisendorfer of Minneapolis, Minnesota, was especially helpful to the author in providing material on little-known ecclesiastical organizations, as several notes in this volume attest. I regret that I cannot single out others whom the author would have wanted to thank in this public manner for their helpful contributions. Except one, his wife Miriam. To her, for her persevering patience and her encouraging support for a project whose breadth and detail consumed so much of her husband-scholar's time and energy, this book is affectionately dedicated.

As Arthur Carl Piepkorn himself would have concluded, *pax et gaudium*.

JOHN H. TIETJEN
Seminex, St. Louis, Missouri

Introduction

Many memories of Arthur Carl Piepkorn came to mind as I read this impressive volume. The one that best recalled Piepkorn the scholar was situated in Washington, D.C., in September, 1968. The occasion was the Lutheran–Roman Catholic Theological Dialogue on the sacrament of the Eucharist. During the discussion of the concept of transubstantiation, someone raised the question: Does the Eastern tradition have any counterpart to this idea? Modestly allowing a few seconds of silence to pass, Piepkorn responded: "The Greek Fathers and theologians have traditionally used five verbs to describe the change or transformation of the elements—*metaballō, metapoieō, metarrhythmizō, metaskeuazō,* and *metastoicheioō.*" This prompted the remark of one of the dialogue partners—a Roman Catholic biblical scholar who was no mean linguist himself: "Arthur Carl, you're the only person I know who could tell us something like that."

Now *we* know. Those facts, figures and insights concerning comparative theology and ecclesiology that regularly amazed those who knew Piepkorn were not odd tidbits stored up in a pedantic section of this first-rate scholar's mind. They, and thousands more, were all part of a grand design that is finally beginning to emerge with the appearance of this first volume of *Profiles in Belief,* an unprecedented encyclopedic treatment by one man of the religious bodies of the United States and Canada. This is not the place to compare Piepkorn's work with the earlier single-volume studies covering similar ground with varying degrees of accuracy, objectivity, thoroughness and value. It is the place to thank Harper & Row for their role in the major publishing event, as well as John Tietjen for admirably bringing off the difficult editorial task of working with a manuscript still unfinished in some parts and requring updating others. Although the editor assures us that this first volume is virtually "pure Piepkorn," I am sure he and many of us wish we could have what we do not have—Piepkorn's own preface and introduction. Only there would we be able to learn definitively of Piepkorn's objectives, intentions and methodological assumptions and techniques.

Quite clearly this work promises to stand on its own scholarly merits as the definitive reference work on the religious bodies of the northern part of North America. But will it have even more significance than this? As I write these words during the annual Week of Prayer for Christian Unity, I cannot help but think of the value of this volume for ecumenism.

First of all, it lays bare in a shocking, yet scholarly way the scandalous fact of Christian division in the United States, in Canada and throughout the world. Accustomed as Americans and Canadians are to thinking of divided Christianity mainly in terms of the division between Protestantism and Roman Catholicism and of the divisions within Protestantism, this volume instructs us about the divisions between Eastern and Western Christianity which antedate the sixteenth century and which not only persist, but also continue to give rise to new divisions. Thus Piepkorn can list thirty-one different "Eastern Orthodox" churches in the United States and Canada—not all of which are in communion with one another—as well as twelve other churches derived from the foregoing bodies. While reading this sad tale of division we learn, for example, that caution must be used in speaking about the Patriarch of Antioch —there are at least five of them! There is a correspondingly bewildering list of churches emanating from the Roman Catholic Church since the eighteenth century. Recalling the distinction between sinful division and legitimate diversity, which has been commonplace in ecumenical discussions since the 1954 Evanston assembly of the World Council of Churches, one finds in this volume divisions which may have resulted from sinfulness, often on more than one side, while other divisions might better be understood as psychopathological, felonious, or simply bizarre in origin.

Second, reflecting his own commitment to Christian unity, Piepkorn gives rightful attention (in chapters 4, 12 and 14) to the same kind of commitment that is becoming increasingly prominent in both Eastern Orthodoxy and the Roman Catholic Church. Christians on all levels of those churches are dissatisfied with anything less than full communion with one another because of their new awareness that the very credibility of Jesus is linked in the New Testament (John 17, 21–23) to unity among his followers.

Third, the very existence of a series of volumes such as this is an asset to the ecumenical task. The *Decree on Ecumenism* (art. 9) of the Second Vatican Council states: "We must get to know the outlook of our separated brethren. Study is absolutely required for this, and it should be pursued in fidelity to truth and with a spirit of good will. Catholics who already have a proper grounding need to acquire a more adequate understanding of the respective doctrines of our separated brethren, their history, their spiritual and liturgical life, their religious psychology and cultural background." I take it for granted that any church committed to Christian unity, or any religious body concerned with better relations with its religious neighbors would be able to express the same desire relative to its own membership. I also take it as beyond dispute that Piepkorn has pursued his study "in fidelity to truth and with a spirit of good will." A more difficult question is: Has Piepkorn acquired an "adequate understanding of the respective doctrines" of the separated brethren about whom he has written in this volume? Putting the question another way: Would the churches described here recognize their beliefs in Piepkorn's description of them?

Responding as a Roman Catholic theologian only with reference to Piepkorn's lengthy treatment of Roman Catholicism, I have to say that, with one notable exception, and leaving aside a number of relatively minor points which one would more properly note in a review article, Piepkorn has presented an extraordinarily able account, not only of the doctrines of the Roman Catholic Church with the broad range of theological interpretations attached to them, but also of Roman Catholic history, and spiritual and liturgical life, if not its religious psychology and cultural background. In short, even though they might wish to recast phrasings or supply different emphases (I find, for example, an under-emphasis of Catholic social teaching and activity), Roman Catholics would, by and large, recognize their belief and their life in Piepkorn's description of it. And that is the decisive ecumenical test for an undertaking of this kind.

The notable exception is that Roman Catholics would not recognize that their church came into being in the sixteenth century as a descendant of the "Church in the West" of the first fifteen centuries, as the titles of Parts III and IV suggest. Chapter 11 begins with the sentence: "Modern Roman Catholicism can at least in a sense be said to have been born at the Council of Trent" of the mid-sixteenth century. I find this quite acceptable because of the qualifier "modern" and the further limitation "at least in a sense." But I find no prior section in the volume entitled Early or Medieval Roman Catholicism, not even in Part III.

Piepkorn's footnote to the sentence cited above explains that he is using "Roman Catholic" as a denominational and confessional designation, and "Catholic" to describe the traditional faith and practice of "historic Christianity generally." I see two difficulties here. First, this concept of "Catholic," which recalls that found in the unofficial German translation of article VII of the *Apology of the Augsburg Confession* ("*Ich gläube ein katholick, gemeine, christliche Kirche*"), is too formal and general. It lacks theological, as distinct from historical, content and fails to deal with the problem of orthodoxy and heresy. Thus Arians and Donatists, not to mention the living churches treated in this book which do not accept the teaching of Ephesus or Chalcedon, all belong to "historic Christianity generally." This means that all of them can or could have been considered "Catholic" along with the churches which accepted the first four ecumenical councils. It also suggests that the teaching of those councils concerning Jesus Christ is not integral to being "Catholic," something which the Fathers of the Church, the apologists of the Augsburg Confession and modern churches which lay claim to catholicity would dispute.

The second difficulty has already been mentioned, namely that felt by Roman Catholics who can accept that name as a confessional designation, but not if this is seen as implying that their church came into being in the sixteenth century or that it is not a specific form of "historic Christianity generally." Roman Catholic consciousness and faith includes the belief that the very nature of the ministry conferred on Peter according to the New Testament requires that it be operative in the church of every age, that the Bishop of Rome has historically been the bearer of that ministry, and that Christians not in communion with that bishop are lacking a ministry Christ intended his church to have. Roman Catholics thus see their church beginning in the New Testament and developing throughout the centuries—not always in a purely evangelical manner, to be sure, but with a continuity palpably signified by the succession of the bishops of Rome, some of whom were genuine rocks of faith during times of crisis, others who were stumbling blocks at best, and most, like Peter, a mixture of both.

Roman Catholics would thus feel much more at home, for example, with the statement in Frank S. Mead's *Handbook of Denominations in the United States**: "For the first 1500 years, up to the time of the Protestant Reformation, the Western world was almost totally Roman Catholic." Such an observation is not found in Piepkorn's treatment of the first 1500 years of the Western Church. Perhaps the reason for this can be found in the peculiar manner in which the role of the bishops of Rome is portrayed during that period—primarily to account for the controversy about the papacy in the sixteenth century, and not as an account of the way Roman Catholics see the papacy developing. As a result, Piepkorn's account tends to be one-sided. By stressing minimalizing interpretations of or ambiguities in early texts relating to the papacy and by depicting—quite fairly to be sure—medieval abuses of the papal office, along with late medieval criticism of it, he succeeds well in showing how the stage was set for the widespread rejection of the papacy in the sixteenth century. But has he accounted for the fact that, even today, millions of Christians are still able to recognize the Bishop of Rome as the holder of a ministry designed to serve the church throughout the world? The more scholarly among these millions are aware of the lacunae in the historical evidences for the claims made for the papacy, but they are also aware that there is often more than one scholarly way of reading the same evidence, and more than one way of stating those claims.

Moreover, for Roman Catholics, the most important historical evidence for the Petrine ministry that has been exercised by the Roman bishops is not the patristic testimony, but that of Scripture. And it is here that I think it is both possible and appropriate to allow Piepkorn to update Piepkorn. The editor tells us that Piepkorn's manuscript for this volume was completed a year or two before his death. But so much was happening in the world of ecumenical dialogue during that period on the very question under discussion,

* Revised and enlarged edition, 1956; p. 187.

and Arthur Carl Piepkorn was personally very much engaged in that dialogue. Barely two months before his death he was able to approve with his colleagues on the U.S.A. Lutheran–Roman Catholic theological dialogue the landmark statement on the Petrine ministry. In that document, *Papal Primacy and the Universal Church*, one finds Piepkorn joining with New Testament and patristic scholars in saying: "The line of development of such [Petrine] images [in the New Testament] is obviously reconcilable with, and indeed favorable to, the claims of the Roman Catholic Church for the papacy. The same may be said of some images of Peter which appeared in early patristic times."* There are, of course, many other questions to be asked concerning the Petrine ministry and the papacy. But I have cited this rather revolutionary consensus of Lutheran and Roman Catholic scholarship to show that my one major complaint with Piepkorn's presentation of Roman Catholicism is not an irremediable one.

Profiles of Belief may well become a classic. That it will be a challenging work, above all for the members of the various churches and religious bodies described in it, is clear even from this first volume. Reviewers from each religious body will be challenged above all to evaluate Piepkorn's performance with regard to their own body and to propose modifications for subsequent editions. Perhaps it is not too much to hope that future editions will record ever deeper communion among the churches and the religions. That will surely add to Arthur Carl Piepkorn's joy in the Kingdom of God.

HARRY McSORLEY
St. Michael's College, University of Toronto

---

* Ed. P. Empie and T. Austin Murphy (Minneapolis: Augsburg Publishing House, 1974), p. 41.

PART I

PRE- AND NON-CHALCEDONIAN CHURCHES

1. The Church before Chalcedon

A Formative Period:
From the Council of Nicaea (325) to the Council of Constantinople (381)

The first creed, or symbol, that an ecumenical council decreed was the Creed of the 318 Fathers of Nicaea in 325. It read:

We believe in one God, Father, All-ruler, maker of everything visible and invisible.

And in one Lord Jesus Christ, the son of God, begotten[1] unique out of the Father, that is out of the being of the Father; God out of God, light out of light, genuine God out of genuine God; begotten, not made; identical in being with the Father; the one through whom the universe was made, the things in heaven as well as the things on earth; for us human beings and for our salvation come down and incarnated, become man, executed,[2] risen on the third day, gone up into heaven, and coming to judge the living and the dead.

And in the Holy Spirit.

The catholic (and apostolic) church condemns those who say that there was a "then" when there was no son of God, and that he was not before he was begotten, and that he was made out of the things that are not, or who allege that he is out of a different hypostasis[3] or being [from that of the Father] or that he is a creature or mutable or subject to change.

The second creed, or symbol, that an ecumenical council decreed was the Creed of the 150 Fathers of Constantinople. Tradition and the bulk of contemporary scholarship attribute it to the second ecumenical council, held at Constantinople in 381. It is commonly, but inaccurately, called the Nicene Creed or, slightly less inaccurately, the Niceno-Constantinopolitan Creed. With minor variations it is used by all Christian churches in the United States and Canada that profess to trace their history directly or indirectly to the church of the first two ecumenical councils. In its original form the Creed of the 150 Fathers of Constantinople reads:

We believe in one God, Father, All-ruler, maker of heaven and earth, of everything visible and invisible.

And in one Lord Jesus Christ, the unique son of God, begotten[4] out of his Father before all ages; light out of light, genuine God out of genuine God; begotten, not made; identical in being with the Father; the one through whom the universe was made; for us human beings and for our salvation come down from heaven and endowed with flesh out of Holy Spirit and the Virgin Mary, and made a human being; crucified on our behalf under Pontius Pilate and executed[5] and buried; and risen the third day according to the Scriptures; and gone up into heaven; and seated at the right hand of the Father; and coming again with glory to judge both the living and the dead; of whose kingly rule there shall be no end.

And in the Holy Spirit, the lordly and life-giving one; proceeding out of the Father; jointly adored and jointly glorified along with the Father and the Son; the one that spoke through the prophets.

In a single holy catholic and apostolic church.

We confess a single baptism for the forgiveness of sins.

We await the resurrection of the dead and the life of the coming age. Amen.

While those church bodies in the United States and Canada—of both the Eastern and the Western traditions—that trace their ancestry back directly or indirectly to the established church of the Roman Empire accept the dogmatic decisions of two to five additional ecumenical councils (Ephesus, 431; Chalcedon, 451; Constantinople II, 553; Constantinople III, 680–681; and Nicaea II, 787), and while the Non-Chalcedonian Christians accept the third ecumenical council (Ephesus, 431), the breakup of Christendom as it has come down to our time began in the fifth century.

The Church of the East and of the Assyrians

Among the church bodies of North America the Church of the East and of the Assyrians traces its history back beyond the most ancient ecclesiastical schism, which divided the church in the East from the church of the fifth-century Roman Empire and its modern descendants.

The Church of the East claims apostolic origins. The existence of a Christian community at Urfa (Edessa) is historically demonstrable as early as the second century. According to traditions committed to writing in the fourth century, Christianity was brought to Urfa by the apostles SS. Peter, Thomas, and Bartholomew, as well as by St. Addai and his disciple St. Mari.

Some fathers of the Church of the East describe both St. Addai and St. Mari as among the seventy-two disciples sent out by Christ, while others identify St. Addai with St. Thaddeus the Apostle. In the official "Table or Tree of Life of Apostolic Succession of the Catholicos-Patriarchs of the East" the first name after St. Mari's is that of Abris, "relative of the virgin Mary," and the third name is that of James I, "relative of Yosip [that is, Joseph] the Carpenter," husband of Mary.[6]

Politically, the early Aramaic-speaking Church of the East was in territory under Parthian rule. In 226 the Sassanians or Persians came to power, an event of major significance for the Church of the East because of the Sassanians' endemic and inveterate hatred of the Roman Empire. Just as the persecution of Christianity as an illicit religion by the Roman emperors had won for the Christians of the East at least a limited measure of tolerance under Sassanian rule, so the conversion of the Roman Emperor Constantine to the Christian faith immediately made the loyalty of the Christians of the eastern regions suspect to their overlords. For a century, from Sapor II in the 330s to Yezdegerd the Wicked in the 440s, persecutions went on intermittently in the East. Under Sapor one of the martyrs was Shimun-bar-Sabbai, the Catholicos (the designation for the metropolitans of Seleucia-Ctesiphon from 280 on). Under Yezdegerd 150,000 Christians were executed at one time at Kirkuk in modern Iraq, according to tradition.

Because of the prevailing political situation the Church of the East was not represented at the third ecumenical council held at Ephesus in 431. That council decided against the Byzantine patriarch Nestorious because he rejected the title of *theotokos* ("Mother of God") for the Blessed Virgin Mary —although he was willing to concede her the title of "Mother of Emanuel"— and because he insisted that she be called nothing more than *christotokos* ("Mother of Christ"). The council also unjustly charged him with having taught that there are two persons in Jesus Christ as well as two natures.

Subsequently the Church of the East not only refused to join in the condemnation of Nestorius but protected disciples of his who fled into Persian territory. When the emperor Zeno closed the famed Christian college at Urfa in the 480s, the teachers fled to Nusaybin [Nisibis], where they were permitted to establish a no less influential center of learning. Because of the posture of the Church of the East toward Nestorius and his disciples, its members came to be known as Nestorians to Christians in the Roman Empire.

In 484 Barsoma, one of the teachers of Nusaybin, succeeded in committing the Church of the East to a formula which attempted to resolve the Christological problem by affirming the eternal and inseparable union in Christ of the two natures (*kyane*), the divine and the human, in two hypostases (*qnume*), and in one person (*parṣūpa*).[7] This disassociation from the Christology of the church in the Roman Empire had the merit of emphasizing to the Persian overlords that there was a difference between the Christianity of their subjects and the Christianity of the Roman imperial church. Nevertheless, the difference over Christology led to a move toward reconciliation with the Church of the Roman Empire and to formal acceptance of the Chalcedonian formula by the Church of the East during the catholicate of Awa I (536–552), a distinguished administrator and a convert from Zoroastrianism.[8] The rapproachement failed when Constantinople posthumously condemned two teachers whom the Church of the East had admitted to its canon of saints, Theodore of Mopsuestia and his mentor

Diodore of Tarsus. The Muslim conquest in the early seventh century made further efforts at reconciliation between the Church of the East and the Church in the Roman Empire impossible.

Unparalleled missionary expansion ultimately carried the Church of the East across all of Asia from Arabia to the Pacific Ocean. The expansion is traceable back at least as far as the beginning of the fourth century, when the Catholicos sent Bishop David of Basra to India as a missionary. The persecutions of the fourth and fifth century helped to scatter the members of the Church of the East. By the mid-sixth century their congregations were found in Ceylon, India, Burma, Thailand, and Indochina. In the early seventh century the Church of the East penetrated China, where the stone stele at Hsian-Fu, erected in the late eighth century, shortly after the catholicate of Khnanishu II (died 778), is one of the most important documents pertaining to the missionary outreach of the Christian faith in the Orient.[9]

In the fifth century the Catholicos of Seleucia-Ctesiphon took the title Catholicos-Patriarch of the East. The monastic life of the Church of the East was placed on a firm foundation especially through the efforts of Auraham of Kashkar (491–596), founder of the great monastery on Mount Izla near Nusaybin, and of Bawai the Great (569–628). Bawai's great theological work, *The Book of the Union*, is the definitive statement of the Christology of the Church of the East during this period.

After the completion of the Arab conquest of Persia in 651 the Christians of the Church of the East received reasonably good treatment at the hands of the Muslims most of the time, punctuated by periods of persecution. With the removal of the catholicatial see from Seleucia-Ctesiphon to Baghdad in the catholicate of Khnanishu II, the Catholicos-Patriarchs became political figures of considerable prominence for a number of centuries.

During the early Mongol period, before the Mongols had decided definitively for Islam and were disposed to be friendly toward Christianity, the Church of the East achieved the zenith of its extent and influence. But it shared in the general decline and eclipse of Asiatic civilization that followed in the wake of the Tatar invasions of the late 13th and 14th centuries.

The East Syrian core of the Church of the East survived precariously in the mountains of Kurdistan and Azerbaijan and around the shores of Daryācheh-ye Rezā'īyeh (Lake Urmia). After the sack of Baghdad by Hulagu Khan the seat of the Catholicate was established at first within the headquarters of the conqueror; then it moved to Marāghe in Iran, finally to Al-Qosh, near Mosul. The Catholicos Eshuyo Shimun VIII,[10] who ruled from 1538 to 1551, transferred it first to Azerbaijan, then to Qudshanes. It was about this time that political developments cut off communication between the metropolitan of Malabar and the Catholicos Patriarch of the East and that the course of events began which finally diverted all of the St. Thomas Christians of the Malabar Coast to Roman Catholicism or to the Syrian Orthodox Church of Antioch.

In 1553 a segment of the Church of the East in the Middle East accepted the authority of the Bishop of Rome[11] and thereby paved the way for the ultimate establishment in 1828 of the Roman Catholic Chaldean Rite as a Roman Catholic community parallel to the Church of the East. Its prelate, who resides at Mosul, has the title of Patriarch of Babylon.

Proselytization of members of the Church of the East by other denominations was undertaken on a considerable scale during the nineteenth century. Between 1874 and 1907 a segment of the Roman Catholic Malabarese Rite in India withdrew from papal authority and placed itself under the Catholicos-Patriarch of the East, who is represented in India by a metropolitan. Since World War I the Church of the East and the "Assyrian"[12] nation of which it is the religious embodiment have been the victim of Near Eastern power politics.

Individual "Assyrians" began to come to the United States as early as the mid-1700s, but immigration in fairly large numbers did not begin until after World War I. Those who had belonged to Russian Orthodox, Roman Catholic, or Presbyterian congregations in the Middle East were usually absorbed into the counterpart communities in North America. Until 1940 immigrant members of the Church of the East maintained their religion as best they could with the minimal episcopal supervision that the church could supply. In that year the Catholicos-Patriarch of the East moved his "patriarchal cell" to the United States; he established himself first in Chicago, then in Modesto, California, and finally in San Francisco. In addition to the congregations in the United States and the congregations on the Malabar Coast of India, there are organized congregations of the Church of the East in Syria, Lebanon, Iran, Iraq, and the Union of Soviet Socialist Republics. The world-wide membership of the Church of the East is variously estimated at 60,000 to 500,000, depending on the meaning of membership.

The international headquarters of the Church of the East are at 3939 Lawton Street, San Francisco, California. There are seven churches and missions in the United States with an estimated 10,000 members.

Since the early fifth century the Church of the East has recognized the ecumenical councils of Nicaea (325) and Constantinople (381).

"The Creed of the 318 Fathers who assembled in the city of Nicaea, in the days of King Constantine, because of the blasphemy of Arius"—in reality the Niceno-Constantinopolitan Creed—reads in the form that the Church of the East confesses it:

> We believe in one God, the Father Almighty, Maker of all things, visible and invisible. And in one Lord Jesus Christ, the Son of God, the only-begotten and first-born of all created, begotten of His Father before all worlds and not made, very God of very God, of one essence with His Father; by whose hands the worlds were established and everything was created; who for us men and for our salvation came down from heaven and was incarnate by the Holy Spirit and became man, and was conceived and born of the Virgin Mary; he suffered

and was crucified in the days of Pontius Pilate; he was buried and he rose again on the third day as it is written and ascended into heaven and sat down on the right hand of His Father; and He shall come again to judge the dead and the living. And in one Holy Spirit, the Spirit of truth, who proceeds from the Father, the life-giving Spirit, and in one holy [and] apostolic catholic church; and we confess one baptism for the remission of sins; and the resurrection of our bodies, and the life for ever and ever. Amen[13]

The Church of the East continues to affirm its traditional Christology. A typical liturgical formulation occurs in the matins hymn by Bawai the Great that is sung from Advent to the Epiphany, *Brikh khannana* ("Blessed is the Compassionate One"):

> One is Christ, the son of God
> Worshipped by all in two natures,
> In His Godhead begotten of the Father,
> Without beginning, before all time,
> In His manhood born of Mary,
> In the fulness of time, united in a body (*bpaghram kaydha*).
> Neither the Godhead is of the nature of the mother
> Nor the manhood of the nature of the Father.
> The natures are preserved in their selves (*baqnó mayhón*)
> In one person (*parṣūpa*) of one sonship.[14]

The Church of the East rejects the designation "Mother of God (*yaldath alaha*)" for the Blessed Virgin Mary and insists on "Mother of Christ (*yaldath mshikha*)" instead.[15]

Since the thirteenth century at least it counts seven sacraments: "(1) The priesthood, which is the ministry of all the other sacraments; (2) holy baptism; (3) the oil of unction; (4) the oblation of the body and blood of Christ; (5) absolution; (6) the holy leaven, namely, the 'King'; [and] (7) the sign of the life-giving cross."[16]

The priesthood has nine ranks that correspond to the angelic hierarchies: Patriarchs, metropolitans, and bishops are the counterparts of the cherubs, seraphs, and thrones (in that order); archdeacons, vicars general (or episcopal visitors or archpriests),[17] and priests are the counterparts of virtues, dominions, and powers; deacons, subdeacons, and lectors are the counterparts of principalities, archangels, and angels. The patriarch is above human judgment.[18] The Church of the East holds rigorously to the doctrine of apostolic succession of the episcopate and teaches that apart from the apostolic succession "there are no sacraments, no church, and no operation of the Holy Spirit."[19] Since the sixth century celibacy is expected of those in bishop's orders.

Baptism is administered by threefold immersion, usually forty days after birth, and is followed by the "seal," or chrismation ("drawing the sign of the living cross [with] the holy ointment on the forehead of the recipient of baptism"),[20] and the first holy communion. The church is conceived of as the company of all baptized persons.

Individual confession in the presence of the priest alone is permitted, but not generally practiced. Individual absolution is imparted on request or when the priest deems it necessary, and a general absolution is imparted to the whole congregation before the administration of the holy communion.

The Church of the East teaches that in the sacrament of the Holy Communion the true body and blood of Christ are received through faith[21] under the form of leavened bread and wine. Communicants fast before receiving the holy communion. They drink the sacramental blood of Christ directly from the chalice. As an oblation the sacrifice of the eucharist is identical with the sacrifice of the cross and not a repetition of it.

The holy leaven (*malka*, that is, "King") reflects the tradition that SS. Addai and Mari brought with them to the East a portion of the original bread which Christ consecrated at the last supper in the cenacle. By leavening the flour from which the sacramental bread is made with a part of a loaf consecrated at a previous celebration, the eucharists celebrated in the Church of the East today are seen as in a continuous material succession with the first eucharist.

In the sign of the cross the thumb and the first two fingers are joined to represent the Trinity; touching his mouth the worshiper says "Glory," touching his forehead he says "to the Father," touching his breast he says "to the Son," and touching in succession his right and left shoulders he says "and to the Holy Spirit."

The Blessed Virgin Mary and the saints (among them Nestorius) are venerated, and their intercessions are solicited. The faithful departed are remembered in prayer. Images and icons are forbidden, and the only licit object of veneration is a simple cross. The decalog is divided into four and six commandments, the Our Father (at the end of which the doxology is always said) into three or ten sections.

The Eastern Syriac form of the Peshitta version of the Bible, which contemporary scholarship assigns to the fourth century but which the Church of the East regards as the original from which the Greek Bible was translated, is used; the Old Testament apocrypha are accounted noncanonical. The primary liturgy is the fourth-century rite named after SS. Addai and Mari and attributed by the Church of the East to St. James of Jerusalem.

Anchorites and hermits observe seven periods of prayer daily, but the common people are obligated to only four: At early dawn, just before sundown, after supper (or before retiring), and at night; women are excused from the obligation of the night prayer.

Fasts play a prominent role in the calendar of the Church of the East: The 25 days of Advent, the three-day Ninevite Fast (which begins 21 days before the First Sunday in Lent), the 50 days of Lent, the 50 days after

Pentecost, the 50 days of the "Prophet Elijah's Fast" (September 8 to October 20), the 15 days of St. Mary's Fast (August 1–15), and all Wednesdays and Fridays throughout the year. Advent, Lent, and the Ninevite Fast are especially insisted upon. The faithful whose health permits are expected when fasting to refrain from all flesh meat, fish, milk products (including ghee), eggs, and similar food of animal origin; during the periods of fasting they are restricted to one vegetarian meal a day.

NOTES

1. It is difficult to reproduce the force of the Greek original in English, especially since English has no active past participle. In the Greek original "begotten," "made," "come down," "incarnated," "executed," "risen," "gone up," and "coming" are all participles that modify "Jesus Christ." The only relative clause is "through whom the universe was made," the only adjectives "unique" and "identical in being (homoousion)."

2. The Greek verb used here means "to suffer." In contexts like this it has the technical meaning of "to suffer death," that is, "to be executed."

3. Hypostasis is the substance, subsistent principle, or essential nature of anything. At this point in church history it was a synonym of being ("essence"). Before the end of the fourth century it had changed its meaning when Christian theologians used it; it was no longer a synonym of being, but the term that differentiated the Father and the Son and the Holy Spirit within the Trinity and that English-speaking theologians, following the Latin persona, call a "person" of the Trinity.

4. See note 1 above. In the Creed of the 150 Fathers of Constantinople "begotten," "made," "come down," "endowed with flesh," "made a human being," "crucified," "executed," "buried," "risen," "gone up," "seated," and "coming again" are all participles that modify "Jesus Christ." In the third paragraph of the Creed of the 150 Fathers of Constantinople, "life-giving one," "proceeding," "jointly adored," "jointly glorified," and "the one that spoke" are all neuter participles modifying "the Holy Spirit."

5. See note 2 above.

6. Iskhaq Rehana, "Table or Tree of Life of Apostolic Succession of the Catholicos-Patriarchs of The Church of the East, Namely, Those Who Served on the See of Khuhy in Seleucia-Ctesiphon, Babylon," in (Mar) O'dishoo, The Book of Marganitha (The Pearl) on the Truth of Christianity, translated by Eshai Shimun XXIII (Ernakulam, Kerala, India: Mar Themotheus Memorial Printing and Publishing House, 1965), pp. 109-110.

7. Qnuma reproduces the Greek hypostasis (in Hebrews 10:1 of the Peshitta translation, for instance); it means "solid existence, substance (as distinct from a shadow), self," and is used to describe the three hypostases of the Trinity. Parṣūpa is a transliteration of the Greek prosōpon, literally "face," the equivalent of the Latin persona; in the theological language of the Greek church fathers prosōpon is a synonym of hypostasis. On the differentiation between qnuma and parṣūpa in the thought of the Church of the East, see the excerpt from The Harmonious Texture by a contemporary of Odishu, Rabban Yokhanan Bar-Zubi, in O'dishoo, pp. 82-91.

8. William Ainger Wigram, The Assyrians and Their Neighbours (London: G. Bell and Sons, 1929), pp. 56-57. The acceptance of the Chalcedonian decree has never been formally rescinded.

9. For the text of this important document, see James Legge, The Nestorian Monument of Hsi-an Fu in Shen-Hsi, China, Relating to the Diffusion of Christianity in China in the Seventh and Eighth Centuries, with the Chinese Text of the Inscription, a Translation, and Notes, and a Lecture on the

Monument (New York: Paragon Book Reprint Corporation, 1966, a reprint of the 1888 London edition), and P. Yoshio Saeki, *The Nestorian Monument in China*, 2nd printing (London: SPCK, 1928). See also Frits Vilhelm Holm, *My Nestorian Adventure in China: A Popular Account of the Holm-Nestorian Expedition to Sian-Fu and Its Results* (New York: Fleming H. Revell Company, 1923). The stele summarizes the chief tenets of the "Luminous [or Illustrious] Religion" and chronicles the progress of Christianity in China from 635 to 781. The creedal statement emphasizes the Trinity and the Incarnation, but says nothing specific about Christ's crucifixion and resurrection. There are indications of a considerable degree of accommodation and even of assimilation to the popular religions of China in the form in which it presents Christianity. For a general survey and appreciation of the missions of the Church of the East, see John Stewart, *Nestorian Missionary Enterprise: The Story of a Church on Fire* (Edinburgh: T. and T. Clark, 1928). The tradition of the Church of the East places the penetration of China in the fifth century.

10. Since the catholicate of Shimun III (1369–1392), all but two of the acknowledged catholicoi-patriarchs have borne the name Shimun (Simon); since the sixteenth-century catholicate of Eshuyo Shimun VIII, each catholicos-patriarch has prefixed Shimun with another name. The 119th catholicos-patriarch, Eshai Shimun XXIII, began his rule in 1920 and died in 1975. His successor has not yet been chosen.

11. Some members of the Church of the East had gone to Cyprus and there had accepted the authority of the bishop of Rome and the Latin Rite in 1340.

12. This designation, popularized by Anglicans, became common only in the nineteenth century.

13. *The Liturgy of the Holy Apostolic and Catholic Church of the East,* trans. Eshai Shimun XXIII (Chicago: The Patriarchate of the East, 1949), pp. 9-10.

14. Cited in V. K. George, *The Holy Apostolic and Catholic Church of the East and Mar Nestorius* (Ernakulam, Kerala, India: Mar Themotheus Memorial Printing and Publishing House, 1960), p. 46.

15. The Church of the East nevertheless holds the Blessed Virgin Mary in high honor, affirms her perpetual virginity, and calls her by such titles as Second Heaven, the Arc of Light, and the Mother of Light and Life (*Messianic Teachings of the Holy Apostolic and Catholic Church of the East* [*Yulpana m'shikhay d'eta qaddishta washlikhayta o'qathuliqi d'mathnkha*], trans. from Malayalam by M. P. Francis [Erankulam, Kerala, India: Mar Themotheus Memorial Printing and Publishing House, 1962], p. 31).

16. O'dishoo, p. 45.

17. The Syriac is *piryadota*, that is, the Greek *periodeutēs* ("once called *Corepiscopa*," that is, the Greek *chōrepiskopos*). "He may do all the services that a priest does. In addition to these he may visit the villages as the representative of his bishop and preach to them. He could also direct and send priests to other places where necessary" (*Messianic Teachings*, p. 64). The Adam who erected the Hsian-Fu stele was a "presbyter and chorepiscopos, and pope (*papas*) of China" (Legge, p. 3).

18. "Under no circumstances may a man say that the Catholicos of the East can be judged by those under him or by patriarchs like himself. He will be the judge of all those under him and his own judgment will be reserved to Christ" ("Decree from the Synod of Mar Dadishu the Catholicos [424 A. D.]," quoted in *Rules Collected from the Synhados [Canonical Law] of the Church of the East and Patriarchal Decrees* [San Francisco, Calif.: The Holy Apostolic and Catholic Church of the East, 1960], p. 7).

19. *Sermon Delivered by His Holiness, Mar Eshai Shimun XXIII, Catholicos Patriarch of the East, on Sunday, August 22, 1954, in the Cathedral of Mar Sargis, Chicago, Illinois* (Chicago: The Patriarchate of the East, 1954) 16-page multilithed document), p. 7. Nevertheless the Church of the East belongs to the World Council of Churches.

20. *Messianic Teachings*, p. 76.

21. This formulation probably reflects nineteenth-century Anglican influence. In the thirteenth century Mar Odishu wrote: "Through this divine command [Christ's words of institution] the bread is changed into His Holy Body and the wine into His Precious Blood and they impart to all who receive them in faith and without doubting the forgiveness of sins, purification, enlightenment, pardon, the great hope of the resurrection from the dead, the inheritance of heaven and the new life" (O'dishoo, pp. 56-57). The translator glosses the word "changed" with this footnote: "The change which the author refers to, however, is not physical, but rather [refers] to the power inherent in this Holy Sacrament for the remission of sins of them that partake it in true faith" (p. 56. note).

BIBLIOGRAPHY

Badger, George Percy. *The Nestorians and Their Rituals*. Ed. by John Mason Neale. 2 vols. Farnborough, Hampshire, England: Gregg International Publishers, 1969. A reprint of the 1852 edition.

Joseph, John. *The Nestorians and Their Muslim Neighbors: A Study of Western Influence on Their Relations*. Princeton, N.J.: Princeton University Press, 1961.

Leroy, Jules. *Monks and Monasteries of the Near East*. Translated by Peter Collin. London: George G. Harrap and Company, 1963. Chap. 7, "On the Borders of Kurdistan," pp. 152-188, is devoted primarily to the Church of the East, especially its monastic tradition.

Liturgical and Sacramental Hymns and Praises of the Holy and Apostolic Catholic Church of the East. Modesto, Calif.: The Patriarchate of the East, 1957. A 26-page mimeographed brochure containing transliterated texts of hymns (one of them with a translation by Eshai Shimun XXIII) for Palm Sunday and Easter.

The Liturgy of the Holy Apostolic and Catholic Church of the East. Trans. Eshai Shimun XXIII. Chicago: The Patriarchate of the East, 1949. A 79-page typescript brochure that provides the transliterated Syriac text and an English text in parallel columns.

Luke, Harry Charles. *Mosul and Its Minorities*. London: Martin Hopkinson and Company, 1925. Chapters 4-7, pp. 44-103.

(Mar) O'dishoo. *The Book of Marganitha (The Pearl) on the Truth of Christianity*. Trans. from the Aramaic original by Eshai Shimun XXIII. Ernakulam, Kerala, India: Mar Themotheus Memorial Printing and Publishing House, 1965. The author was the metropolitan of Nusaybin (Suwa) and Armenia at the end of the thirteenth century.

Messianic Teachings of the Holy Apostolic and Catholic Church of the East (Yulpana m'shikhay d'eta qaddishta washlikhayta o'qathuliqi d'mathnkha). Trans. from the Mayalam version of a lost Syriac original by M. P. Francis. Revised edition. Ernakulam, Kerala, India: Mar Themotheus Memorial Printing and Publishing House, 1962. This is the authorized English-language catechism of the Church of the East.

Wigram, William Ainger. *The Assyrians and Their Neighbours*. London: G. Bell and Sons, 1929.

———. *An Introduction to the History of the Assyrian Church*. London: SPCK, 1910.

2. The Non-Chalcedonian Churches

The non-Chalcedonian[1] churches are a group of national churches that refused to accept the christological definition formulated by the Council of Chalcedon in 451. As a result a breach developed between these churches and the rest of Christendom. The churches that comprise this group are the Syrian Orthodox Church, the Armenian Orthodox Church, the Coptic Orthodox Church, and the Abyssinian (or Ethiopian) Orthodox Church.

The Syrian Orthodox Church of Antioch in the United States and Canada

The Syrian Orthodox Church of Antioch in the United States and Canada[2] is the North American segment of the Christian community that acknowledges the spiritual authority of His Holiness, the patriarch of Antioch and All the East, who now resides at Damascus.

In the fifth century a large segment of the church in Syria, along with most of the Christians of Egypt and Armenia, refused to accept the Creed of Chalcedon (451) with its teaching that the "one and the same Christ, the Son, the Lord, the Only-Begotten, must be acknowledged in two natures, unconfusedly, immutably, indivisibly, inseparably, and without the difference of the natures being taken away by such union, but rather the peculiar character of each nature being preserved and the two being united in one Person and Hypostasis, not separated and divided into two persons, but one and the same Son, the Only-Begotten, God the Word, the Lord Jesus Christ." Instead they affirmed—as the Syrian Church of Antioch still does—that Christ's "true Godhead and His true manhood were in Him essentially united, He being One Lord and one Son, and that after the union took place in Him He had but one nature incarnate, was one Person, had one Will, and one Work." The Incarnation, they said and the Syrian Church of Antioch still says, involves a "natural union of persons, free of all separateness, intermixture, confusion, mingling, change, and transformation."[3]

In the fierce controversy that continued after the Council of Chalcedon, the Chalcedonian party coined the term "Diaphorites" to label their Syrian adversaries, while the Syrian opponents of the council's definition called the Chalcedonians "Melkites."[4] In the midst of the turmoil, Patriarch Theodosius of Constantinople and Patriarch Anthimus of Alexandria, with the approval of Empress Theodora I and of Al-Harith, monarch of the Arab kingdom of Ghassan east of the Jordan, consecrated to the episcopate in Constantinople a zealous Syrian monk Jacob, or James, nicknamed Baradeus ("the Ragged", d. 578) and a Ghassanian monk, Theodore. The sympathies of the empress, like those of the two patriarchs, were with the Syrian opponents of Chalcedon. The nickname "the Ragged" refers to the beggar's clothing that the wandering monk-prelate wore as a disguise to escape arrest while for more than thirty years he went about from Egypt to the Euphrates consecrating bishops (including his own successor as Syrian patriarch of Antioch), ordaining priests, and making deacons and thus establishing throughout the region a hierarchy that paralleled the hierarchy which accepted Chalcedon. From around the seventh century on, the name "Jacobite"[5] became a derogatory term for the Syrian opponents of Chalcedon, which they themselves categorically reject. They argue that Jacob Baradeus neither founded their church nor initiated a new faith or dogma. Both proponents and the opponents of Chalcedon have consistently designated themselves as "Orthodox," as the Syrian Orthodox Church of Antioch still does.

After the Arab conquest of Syria in the seventh century many Syrians became Muslims. Subsequent internal conflicts had a deleterious effect upon the Syrian Church. Nevertheless, under the Abbasid caliphate (750–1258) it expanded its influence until it had churches and missions across Asia from Cyprus to China; the twelfth and thirteenth centuries mark the zenith of the Syrian Orthodox Church of Antioch. In the late fourteenth century it suffered severely in the Mongol invasion of Persia and Mesopotamia under Timur.

The efforts of the Western Church to bring the Syrian Orthodox Church of Antioch under the authority of the Roman see go back to the fifteenth century, and the brief reconciliation of the Syrian Orthodox Church of Antioch with the West at the Council of Florence in 1442 was one step in the direction of this goal.

In 1665 the Syrian bishop of Jerusalem, Gregory (Abd al-Jalil al-Mawsili; d. 1671), arrived on the Malabar coast of India as the delegate of the Syrian patriarch, Abd al-Masih I, and spent six years among the members of the ancient Christian community there. He indefatigably opposed the efforts of the European Roman Catholic missionaries to enforce the union with Rome that the Synod of Diamper had decreed in 1599 and succeeded in confirming the authority of the Syrian patriarch of Antioch over a considerable segment of the Malabar community. But here too internal dissensions and schisms (including the separation of the Mar Thoma Church in 1889 and the catholicos group in 1911) and conflicts with the Syrian patriarch of Antioch paved the way for the establishment of a Malankarese Rite Roman Catholic Church in 1930. In 1958 the catholicos group and the patriarchal group were reunited in the Syrian Orthodox Church of Malabar.

In Syria itself the Roman Catholic Church was successful in varying degrees in making converts from the sixteenth century on, and since 1783 a rival Roman Catholic Syrian patriarchate has been in continuous existence.[6] The Syrian patriarch of Antioch—who always takes the name Ignatius in honor of St. Ignatius of Antioch (35?–107?)—claimed "about a million of believers" as his spiritual subjects.[7]

The Syrian Orthodox Church of Antioch in the United States and Canada has ten parishes with an estimated 35,000 faithful. Its headquarters are at 293 Hamilton Place, Hackensack, New Jersey.

Apart from its understanding of the Incarnation, the faith of the Syrian Orthodox Church of Antioch differs little from that of Eastern Christendom generally. It accepts the dogmas of the first three ecumenical councils of Nicaea, Constantinople, and Ephesus; teaches that there are nine choirs of angels; affirms that the Blessed Virgin Mary maintained her virginity after Christ's birth; confesses the creed without the phrase that affirms the procession of the Holy Spirit from the Son; and holds that at death the souls of the righteous go to Paradise and the souls of the wicked to the lowest abyss.[8]

Grace in general is defined as "a heavenly gift freely bestowed on man by God in His bounty and mercy and by the merits of Christ, by which he is sustained in working out his salvation," and justifying grace as "a quality dwelling within the soul imparting righteousness to it, that is, it makes man holy and worthy of eternal life."[9]

A perfect sacrament is defined in terms of the material elements, the forms, and the administering priest. The number of sacraments is fixed at seven (with chrismation in place of the Western confirmation).[10]

Baptism is by threefold immersion. In the Holy Eucharist (*Qurbono*) a miraculous sanctification takes place in that the bread and wine are transformed or transmuted into the body and blood of Christ. "Christ appointed this sacrament to make a sacrificial offering of Himself to God His Father in our stead, and to give us spiritual sustenance which we could assimilate and live thereby." Its purpose is "to glorify God, to render Him thanks, and to beseech Him to grant us mercy and pardon for the living and the dead."[11] The Holy Communion is to be received under both species. Anointing is a sacrament "by which the sick receive healing of the soul and rest of body."[12] The ties of marriage are loosed only by the death of one of the parties.

The Syrian Orthodox Church of Antioch divides the Decalogue into tables of four and six commandments. The faithful are to hallow the Sabbath (Sunday) by refraining from all work, by attendance at the Holy Eucharist, and by performing acts of devotion and service. Sin is original ("which embraces all mankind as an inheritance from the disobedience of our father, Adam") or present; present sin is deadly ("punishable by eternal death") or accidental ("it does harm to our spiritual lives").[13]

The faithful are obliged to say ten *kaumas* of prayer in the morning and five in the evening.[14] Worshipers "may also hail the Virgin Mary, beseeching her intercession and that of the saints."[15] The honor paid to the saints is described as limited and is explicitly differentiated from worship. Rather, it is respect paid to them because they are God's beloved and his pure ones and to their likenesses because these are a blessed and beneficial reminder of the saints' lives.[16]

The divine liturgy of the Syrian Church of Antioch is the Antiochene-type Syrian Liturgy of St. James. The priesthood of the church is married; bishops are normally chosen from monastic ranks.

The Syrian Orthodox Church of Malabar in the United States

A growing congregation of members of the Syrian Orthodox Church of Malabar meets every Sunday and on church holidays for the celebration of the divine liturgy in the Lampman Chapel of Union Theological Seminary in New York City. Most of the 150 members are students, diplomatic personnel, and professional people, but many are permanent residents. Periodically services are provided to Malabar Orthodox Christians in Philadelphia, Washington, and Chicago. As occasion demands, the language of the service is Malayalam, Syriac, or English. The Syrian Orthodox Church of Malabar mission in the United States intercommunicates with all the other Non-Chalcedonian Christian communities in North America, notably the Syrian Orthodox Church of Antioch in the United States and Canada, but the mission itself functions directly under the Syrian patriarch of Antioch. The vicar-in-charge of the mission is Dr. K. M. Simon, 12 Edwin Street, Ridgefield Park, New Jersey.[17] (For the history of this group of Christians in India, see above, p. 14.)

The Armenian Church

Armenian tradition traces Christianity in Armenia back to the apostles SS. Thaddeus and Bartholomew. As early as the second century Greek and Syrian missionaries were penetrating the country. The powerful preaching of the Armenian-born convert, St. Gregory[18] the Illuminator (240?–332), resulted in the baptism of King Tiridates III (238?–314) in the last quarter of the third century. In this way Armenia became in 301 the first nation to adopt Christianity as its national faith.

Around the beginning of the fifth century the Armenian Church became an independent national church, the monastery at Etchmiadzin became briefly the seat of its catholicos, and Armenian displaced Syriac and Greek as the ecclesiastical language. From 428 to 633 Armenia was divided between the Eastern Roman Empire and Persia. The catholicos Sahak (387–436) approved the decisions of the Council of Ephesus in 431. Because of the war with Persia in 451 the Armenians were not represented at Chalcedon. At the Synod of Dvin (505/506) the Church of Armenia took its place among the Non-Chalcedonian churches. The decisive document is the letter of Catholicos Papken (490–516) to the Syrian supporters of Chalcedon in Persia; the letter affirms the decisions of the councils of Nicaea, Constantinople I, and Ephesus and the Henotikon of Emperor Zeno; it rejects Nestorianism and, on the ground that the Council of Chalcedon was a Nestorianizing assembly, it also rejects the decisions of that council. But the Armenian Church also rejected Eutyches and Severus. The difficulty seems to some extent to have been a semantic one; the controversies came to center about highly technical terms that did not always admit of precise translation into another language, so that there was room for considerable misunderstanding. At the same time the Armenian Church had scholars who were very well versed in Greek. Another factor—although it too must not be overemphasized—was the strongly nationalistic Armenian tradition and the reluctance of the country to identify itself too closely either with the Roman Empire or with Persia.

The reconciliation with the church in the Roman Empire that seemed likely in the mid-seventh century was a casualty of the Muslim conquest. Armenia recovered its independence in the mid-ninth century, only to lose it again in the tenth to the forces of the Eastern Roman Empire, who attempted in vain to enforce a union of the Churcrh of Armenia with Constantinople. In the eleventh century the Seljuk Turks conquered the country. To escape their oppressors many of the Armenians fled to Cilicia (Lesser Armenia). Here they set up a kingdom in 1075, and in 1293 the catholicate[19] was transferred to Sis. Efforts at reunion both with the Western Church and with Eastern Orthodoxy in the twelfth century failed. Liturgical issues between the Armenians and the Syrians that threatened to bring about a breach within the Non-Chalcedonian fellowship during this period were adjusted without a schism. The "reunion" with the West in 1439 was short-lived.[20]

The Mameluke conquest of Asia Minor in the late fourteenth century opened the way to make Armenia proper the focus of Armenian Christianity again. In 1441 the national council decreed the return of the catholicate to Etchmiadzin. The incumbent, Gregory IX Musabegian, refused to make the move, and a new line of catholicoi of Etchmiadzin began in 1441 with Kirakos Virapesti. The Catholicate of Cilicia (transferred in 1921 to Antelias, four miles north of Beirut, Lebanon, of which it is now a suburb), and the now extinct Catholicate of Aghthamar (1311–1895) on an island in Van Gölü, along with the Armenian Patriarchate of Jerusalem (the title of which goes back to 622 according to tradition, and which the Mamelukes reestablished in 1311) and the Armenian Patriarchate of Istanbul (established in 1461 by the Ottoman Turks to govern the Armenians in their domains) continued to coexist with the restored "mother" see of "Holy" Etchmiadzin. The catholicos of Etchmiadzin has the honorific title of Supreme Patriarch and Catholicos of All Armenians. The catholicos at Antelias is Catholicos of the Great (or Eminent) House of Cilicia. Both have the style of His Holiness, just as both patriarchs have the style His Beatitude.

Centuries of repression and persecution climaxed in a series of bloody genocidal massacres of the Armenians in Turkey between 1895 and 1915. They claimed more than 600,000 lives; indeed, one estimate has 1,500,000 Armenians die in 1915–1916 alone. In addition, over 100,000 Armenian women were kidnaped and forced into Turkish harems. The only survivors were those who managed to escape to other countries and the decimated remnants who had been deported to Syria and Lebanon, then under Turkey, and whom the British army rescued in the course of its victorious march on Syria and Palestine.

The authority that the Russian tsar had exercised over the Catholicate of Etchmiadzin since the 1830s passed into the hands of the Soviet government after World War I. The right of all Armenians, including those outside the Soviet Union, to participate in the free election of the supreme patriarch and catholicos of Etchmiadzin was recognized in the selection of Vasken I in 1955.

The Creed of the Armenian Church[21] reflects the Eastern form of the Niceno-Constantinopolitan Creed:

I. We believe in one God, the Father Almighty, Maker of heaven and earth, of things visible and invisible. II. And in one Lord Jesus Christ, the Son of God, begotten of God the Father, only begotten, that is, of the substance of the Father; God of God, Light of Light, very God of very God; begotten and not made; of the self-same nature of the Father; by whom all things in heaven and on earth, visible and invisible, came into being. III. Who for us men and for our salvation came from heaven and was incarnate, was made man, was perfectly begotten of the holy Virgin Mary by the Holy Spirit, by whom He took body,[22] soul and mind and everything that is in man, truly and not in semblance. IV. He suffered and was crucified and was buried. V. And he rose again on the third day. VI. And ascended into heaven with the same body and sat at the right hand of the Father. VII. He is to come with the same body and with the glory of the Father, to judge the quick and the dead, of whose kingdom there is no end VIII. We believe also in the Holy Spirit, the uncreated and the perfect, who spake in[23] the law and in the prophets and in the Gospels, who came down upon the Jordan, preached to[24] the apostles, and dwelt in[25] the saints. IX. We believe also in only one catholic and apostolic church. X. In one baptism to repentance for the remission and forgiveness of sins.[26] XI. In the resurrection of the dead. XII. In the everlasting judgment of souls and bodies, in the kingdom of heaven and in the life eternal.

As for those who say, "There was a time when the Son was not," or "There was a time when the Holy Spirit was not," or that They came into being out of nothing, or who say that the Son of God and the Holy Spirit be of different substance[27] and that They be changeable or alterable, such doth the Catholic and Apostolic Holy Church anathematize.

The Armenian Church accepts as the orthodox doctrine about the person of Christ the formula of St. Cyril of Alexandria: "One is the nature of the divine Word incarnate."[28] The union of the Godhead and the manhood are "without confusion, without change, and indivisibly." Christ is "without mother from the Father and without father from the Mother."[29]

It holds that Adam's descendants fell with him and that "the whole of mankind became miserable and guilty," with this "inherited sinfulness or original sin in corrupting all generations of mankind."[30]

The salvation of human beings is a free gift of God, achieved by Christ's offering himself as a pure and holy sacrifice on behalf of the sinners who had affronted the divine righteousness and thus taking upon himself the punishment of the sins of all mankind.[31]

The thirty-nine books of the Old Testament and the twenty-seven books of the New Testament are written by divine inspiration.[32]

The Armenian Church divides the commandments as other Eastern Christians do, four in the first table and six in the second. It does not understand its second commandment to forbid the making of representations of Christ and of the saints or the veneration of such representations.[33] It prohibits prayers to the saints, since God alone can give grace and mercy, but it permits the faithful on earth to request the prayers and intercessions of the saints.[34]

The Armenian Church administers six sacraments: baptism by threefold immersion, confirmation or chrismation with holy chrism solemnly blessed by the catholicos,[35] the Eucharist, penance, matrimony, and orders. The anointing of the sick has fallen into disuse in practice, but the rite has been preserved in the service-books.[36] The minor orders are the offices of doorkeepers, readers, exorcists, acolytes, and subdeacons; the major orders are the diaconate, the priesthood, and the episcopate. The Eucharist, celebrated only on Sundays and feasts, is a mystery in which the Holy Spirit brings about a change after which "the outward appearance of the bread and wine still remain the same, yet in reality they are the body and blood of Jesus Christ."[37] The sacrifice of the Eucharist is the same as the sacrifice of the cross in essence and power, but the form or manner of offering it to God is different. The church offers this sacrifice to God for the living and the faithful departed to worship and thank him, to obtain forgiveness, and to ask the grace and power of the Holy Spirit necessary for our salvation.[38]

As in other Eastern churches, the clergy are of two kinds, married and celibate. The married clergy are responsible for the spiritual direction of the people and for the administration of the sacraments. The celibate clergy are trained for scholarly activity[39] and for administrative functions; the bishops are chosen from the celibate clergy. The laity possesses a great deal of power in the Armenian Church. The parishoners elect their parish priests by direct vote; a bishop cannot ordain a candidate to the priesthood on his own initiative, nor can he refuse to ordain a candidate who meets the canonical requirements. In the election of dignitaries, such as primates, patriarchs, and catholicoi, at least two-thirds of the electoral colleges consist of lay elements.

The Armenian Diocese of North America Under the Catholicate of All Armenians at Holy Etchmiadzin

The first Armenians to come to North America appear to have been students, who began arriving from the 1830s on to attend American universities. The real tide of Armenian immigration began in the 1880s, as the Armenians of Asia Minor fled before the heightening Turkish oppression. The first Armenian church in North America was built at Worcester, Massachusetts, in 1889. The catholicos of Etchmiadzin erected the Diocese of the Armenian Church of North America for his spiritual subjects in the New World in 1898. In 1927 he erected a Western Diocese for the states of California and Arizona. A schism over political issues divided the Armenian community in North America in 1932/1933; after more than three decades of self-rule without episcopal oversight, the parishes that had withdrawn from the jurisdiction of the Catholicate of Etchmiadzin placed themselves under the catholicos of Cilicia in 1956. The catholicos of Etchmiadzin put the churches in South America into a separate diocese in 1938.

The two North American dioceses are on a par with each other and both stand directly under the Catholicate of All Armenians at Holy Etchmiadzin. Both are members of the National Council of the Churches of Christ in the United States of America. Armenian is still used almost exclusively in the liturgy, but where the congregation is predominantly English-speaking, the Gospel and the sermon are in that language. To ensure a regular supply of adequately trained priests the two dioceses established the Armenian Theological School at Evanston, Illinois, in 1962.

Together the two dioceses have sixty churches in the United States and claim 450,000 communicants among the 600,000 Armenians in the United States. The headquarters of the Eastern Diocese of North America are in New York City, those of the Western Diocese in Hollywood, California.

Prelacy of the Armenian Apostolic Church of America

The Cilician catholicos died in 1952. A delay in the election of his successor provided the occasion for an effort by the new catholicos of Etchmiadzin to capitalize on divisions within the Catholicate of Cilicia and to restrict the authority of the Antelias catholicate. Vasken's attempt to prevent a scheduled election in 1956 failed, and the Cilician electoral assembly chose Zareh Payaslian, bishop of Aleppo, as catholicos by a vote of 36 to 4 (with fourteen electors, including the clerical elector and the lay elector authorized to the Catholicate of Etchmiadzin, absenting themselves or abstaining). Subsequently an assembly of bishops convoked at Cairo by Vasken declared the election defective and made acceptance of its restrictions on the Antelias catholicate the prerequisite of recognition. Thereupon the *locum tenens* of the Antelias catholicate, assisted by another bishop of the jurisdiction and by a bishop of the intercommunicating Syrian Orthodox Church of Antioch delegated by the patriarch of the latter body, "consecrated" (that is, enthroned) Zareh as catholicos. Zareh acted promtly to provide guidance to Armenian communities in Greece, Iran, and Kuwait over whom the catholicos in Etchmiadzin had not exerted or had not been able to exert direct control.[40] In 1956 the self-governing North American churches that had been out of fellowship with the catholicos of Etchmiadzin since 1932/1933 placed themselves under Zareh's jurisdiction. Vasken withheld recognition from Zareh during the latter's lifetime, but when Archbishop Khoren Paroyan, the present catholicos of Cilicia, succeeded Zareh after the latter's death in 1963, Vasken accorded him prompt recognition. Personal meetings of the two catholicoi have helped to lessen the tension between the two catholicates.

The present archbishop of the Prelacy of the Armenian Apostolic Church of America is the Most Reverend Karekin Sarkissian, who assumed the office in 1973. A Western Diocese was established in California in 1972. National headquarters are at 138 East 39th Street, New York, New York. The prelacy includes twenty-seven parishes in the United States and one in Canada, with a total membership of about 130,000.[41] The churches of the prelacy hold the same faith and use the same liturgy that their co-religionists under the catholicos of Etchmiadzin hold and use. Like the other dioceses of the Antelias catholicate, they recognize the catholicos of Etchmiadzin as supreme in his own jurisdiction; they regard Etchmiadzin as the "mother see"; and they accord the catholicos of Etchmiadzin a primacy of honor (but not of administrative authority) in the Church of Armenia .

Coptic Orthodox Church, Diocese of North America

Christianity came to Egypt at a very early date. Tradition associates its beginnings in Alexandria with the evangelistic activity of St. Mark. Paleographically datable papyri from the period of Trajan and Hadrian point to the existence of a Christian community in the Nile valley in the first and second centuries. Egyptian Christianity enters the clear light of history in the days of Demetrius of Alexandria, around 180, but the state of theological development implies a long tradition of reflection and discussion before his time. The large number of converts among the Egyptian people led to the translation of the Bible into two Coptic (that is, Egyptian) vernaculars in the third century. By the beginning of the fifth century the country had become almost totally Christian.

Among the distinguished Egyptian theologians of the primitive church are St. Clement of Alexandria, Origen, St. Athanasius, and St. Cyril of Alexandria. In a sense Egypt was the seedbed of Christian monasticism, under the leadership of men like St. Anthony of Egypt and St. Pachonium. The monastic tradition came to flower in the Desert Fathers and the great fifth-century Coptic theologian and author, St. Shenûte (Sinuthius) (d. 466?).

In the fourth-century christological controversies the Copts supported the view of the patriarch of Alexandria, Dioscurus (d. 454), who taught that while there were two natures in Christ before the Incarnation there was afterward only the one nature of the Incarnate Word having the properties of both natures. When the Council of Chalcedon in 451 deposed Dioscurus, the vast majority of the Coptic Christians rallied behind him. For the next two centuries the imperial government attempted to reunite the Copts with the church of the empire either by supporting with force the "Melkite"[42] patriarchs of Alexandria and their hierarchy or by devising compromise formulas like the Henoticon of 482 or the "Three Chapters" Edict of Justinian in 543–544.[43] The Coptic community resisted both force and blandishments. It learned to organize its structures without governmental assistance and developed a degree of hardihood that enabled the Coptic community to maintain itself in the face of the Muslim conquest of Egypt in the seventh century.

Although the new regime meant liberation from imperial efforts to force Chalcedonian Christianity on the Copts, the missionary zeal of the Muslims came to represent an even greater threat. From 725 to 830 the Copts revolted periodically and unsuccessfully. (This period also marks the completion of the Coptic theological system.) The continuing Muslim pressure resulted in the martyrdom or flight of many Copts and the conversion of a few to Islam; by 900 the Copts had become a minority in Egypt. (The larger families of the polygamous Muslims were also a factor.) At the turn of the millennium came the persecution of the mad caliph, el-Hakim (996–1021), who reportedly burned 3,000 churches.

The expansion of Egyptian hegemony over the Near East under the later Abbasids facilitated contact between the Copts and the like-minded Syrian and Armenian churches. From the mid-thirteenth century to the Turkish conquest of Egypt in 1517 the Mameluke overlords exerted unremitting pressure on the Copts. They imposed new restrictions, destroyed church buildings, and suppressed the Christian education of the laity and the training of the clergy. The consequence for the Copts was a material loss of theological substance and a radical decline in size. The church in Nubia was utterly eradicated; the number of sees in Egypt dropped to twelve, and cloisters to 13; the ratio of Copts in the total population declined to a tenth (possibly even a twelfth). Arabic displaced Coptic as the language of people; this was not wholly an unmixed evil, since it permitted better communication with the Syrian Christians, who also had perforce dropped Syriac in favor of Arabic. Toward the end of this period there is evidence of theological penetration from the West, even though indirectly, in the fixing of the number of sacraments at seven.

The dark days of Turkish domination, which began in 1517, came to an end in 1798. Determined efforts to unite the Coptic church to the Roman see in 1442 (the bull *Cantate Domino* of Eugenius IV) and in 1594 had failed, but in 1740/1741 a schism in the Coptic ranks finally took place when the Coptic bishop of Jerusalem, Athanasius, with a small number of followers, accepted the authority of the Roman Catholic Church; this is the origin of that denomination's small Coptic Rite. In the mid-nineteenth century the reformatory effort of the Coptic Pope Cyril IV came to an abrupt end with his death. During the fifty-three-year pontificate of Cyril V (1874–1927), the Coptic Church achieved relative freedom of worship when the British occupied Egypt after the battle of Tell-el-Kebir in 1882, and the Coptic laity acquired a considerable measure of power in the church. The present century has seen a significant revival of Coptic theological learning and literary productivity. Since 1928 the synod elects the patriarch.

The Church of Ethiopia achieved its constitutional freedom from the Coptic Church in 1946 after 1,300 years of dependence, and in 1959 it elected the first patriarch of its own. The two churches remain in communion with one another, and the lively interest of the former emperor of Ethiopia in his Coptic co-religionists provided the Copts with valuable help in their dealings with successive Egyptian governments. Since the beginning of the century the number of Copts in Egypt has more than doubled.

The Coptic liturgy is that named after St. Mark. The Coptic calendar, which begins in September, is noteworthy for its five fasts, the three-day pre-Lenten "Fast of Nineveh," the fifty-five-day Great Fast of Lent, the Fast of the Apostles after the Ascension Day, the Fast of the Virgin from August 7 to August 21, and the forty-two-day Fast of the Nativity preceding Christmas.

In 1962 Coptic immigrants to North America organized the Coptic Association of America to serve the Copts in New York City and to work for the provision of pastoral care to all Copts in North America. The next year Cyril VI (b. 1902), the 116th pope of Alexandria, ordered negotiations with the Coptic Association, looking to its sponsorship of a priest in North America; and in 1964 Father Marcos Abdel-Messih, later known as Father Marcos Marcos, was ordained for this work in St. Mark's Cathedral, Cairo. He began his work in Toronto, which had the largest concentration of Copts on the continent. The Diocese of North America of the Coptic Orthodox Church, with headquarters now at 35 Bedele Avenue, Willowdale, Ontario, Canada, was erected in 1965, and in 1967 a second mission with its own priest was begun at Montreal. Since then fourteen additional church centers have been established, two of them in Canada and twelve in the United States. The total number of adult Copts in North America known to the clergy of the diocese is between 10,000 and 15,000.[44]

Ethiopian Orthodox Church in the United States of America

According to tradition, the treasurer of Queen Candace, whom St. Philip the Evangelist baptized, brought the gospel to Ethiopia in the first century. In the mid-fourth century the king of the 300-year old kingdom of Axum, Aizanas, converted to Christianity after the example of Emperor Constantine. Ethiopic church history connects with this important development the names of two brothers, SS. Frumentius and Aedesius of Tyre. St. Athanasius himself consecrated St. Frumentius as bishop of Axum. The affectionate title of Abuna ("Our Father") that the people gave to St. Frumentius survives as the official style of the Ethiopian patriarch; St. Frumentius is also known as "Abba salama [that is, "Father of peace']' the Light-Bearer." His energetic proclamation of Alexandrian orthodoxy sealed Ethiopia against the penetration of Arianism. At least some historians regard the influential "Nine Roman [that is, Byzantine] Saints," a group of monks who came to Ethiopia, apparently from Syria, around 500, as Non-Chalcedonians. At all events, the transfer of the Non-Chalcedonian Patriarchate of Alexandria to Cairo around 640 made the Ethiopian Church wholly dependent on it. As a result the Ethiopian Church accepts the doctrinal decisions of the first three ecumenical councils but rejects the creed of Chalcedon. Like the Coptic Church, the Ethiopian Church affirms that Christ is perfect in his deity and perfect in his manhood, and that the deity and the manhood is united in him in a complete union of essence, hypostasis, and nature. After the Incarnation he is God incarnate, one nature out of two natures, with the one nature possessing the properties of both natures.

Dependable historical information about Christianity in Ethiopia from the beginning of the eighth to the end of the twelfth century is hard to come by; the continuing struggle against Islam seems to have wholly engaged the energies of the Ethiopian Church. The thirteenth century saw a religious and literary renaissance in both the Coptic community and Ethiopia. About this time the rule began to be enforced that required the bishops and patriarchs of the Ethiopic Church to be Copts. The late Middle Ages saw the beginning of a theological controversy between the Unionists and the Unctionists that has never been definitively settled. Both hold to the unity of the divine and human natures in the one incarnate nature of Christ, but the Unionists held that the divine-human nature of Christ had been present in him throughout his earthly life and was merely perfected by the anointing of the Holy Spirit, while the Unctionists asserted that the man Jesus became the natural Son of God by the anointing of the Holy Spirit, which completely absorbed the human nature through divinizing it. A third party arose, which denied that Christ ever *received* an anointing, but that he himself is simultaneously the Anointer, the Anointed, and the Anointing.

Efforts at bringing the Ethiopian Church into union with the Roman see began in the middle of the thirteenth century. The acceptance of the Union of 1441–1442 at the Council of Ferrara-Florence by the Ethiopian participants was disavowed by the Ethiopian emperor. In the sixteenth and seventeenth centuries the Portuguese made renewed efforts to bring about the submission of the Ethiopian Church to the bishop of Rome, and even the Ethiopian emperor briefly accepted the Roman Catholic faith, but the attempt was finally unsuccessful.[45]

The first native Ethiopian bishops in centuries received consecration in

1929; in 1951 Abuna Basil became the first native Ethiopian patriarch. The total membership of the Church of Ethiopia is estimated at 17 million.

Ethiopian church buildings have paintings but no sculptured images; since the fifteenth century an altar of the Blessed Virgin Mary is an invariable feature of every Ethiopian church building. The services of the Ethiopian Church are conducted in Ge'ez, although the language is not generally understood by the worshipers; the Divine Liturgy is noteworthy for its fourteen anaphoras. The biblical canon of the Ethiopian Church includes a number of books that the rest of Christianity classifies as apocryphal or pseudepigraphic, among them the Book of Enoch, the Ascension of Isaiah, and the Shepherd of Hermas. Ancient Jewish influence is evident in the Ethiopian observance of Saturday, in the practice of circumcision, in the use of the sacred dance in worship, and in the distinction between clean and unclean foods. The secular clergy are married; the chanting of the church offices and the teaching in the schools is in the hands of lay clerks, called *dabtaras.*

The patriarch, Abuna Theophilos, deposed in the revolution that removed Emperor Haile Selassie, established the Ethiopian Orthodox Church in the United States of America in 1959 when he was bishop of Harar. It has a single congregation, claiming 2,000 members, under the jurisdiction of Abba Laike Mendefro, whose headquarters are at 140 W. 176 Street, Bronx, New York.[46] There is another Ethiopian Orthodox community in Toronto, Canada, consisting of sixty to seventy families. Served for a time by a priest from the West Indies, the community is presently leaderless.[47]

NOTES

1. The churches of this group reject the term "Monophysite" as a description of themselves.
2. Although the Syrian Church of Antioch on the North American continent once called itself the Assyrian Orthodox Church, since 1952 it has officially rejected the designation "Assyrian" as being a modern English label for the "Nestorian" communion known as the Holy Apostolic Catholic Church of the East (and of the Assyrians). See Ignatius Ephrem I, *The Syrian Church of Antioch: Its Name and History,* Arabic and Syriac original and English translation on opposite pages (Hackensack, N.J.: The Archdiocese of the Syrian Church in the United States and Canada, 1952).
3. Severius Ephrem Barsoum (Ignatius Ephrem I), *The Shorter Catechism of the [As]Syrian Church,* trans. from the 3rd edition by Elias S. Sugar (West New York, N.J.: [As]Syrian Apostolic

Church of the Virgin Mary, 1950), pp. 5-6.
4. From the Syriac *melk,* "king," the equivalent of the Roman emperor's Greek title *Basileus.* "Melkites" thus are "the king's men," the party loyal to and supported by the Roman emperor. "Diaphorites" (that is, "Distinguishers") was a term applied to the so-called Niobites.
5. It occurs as early as Timothy the Presbyter of Constantinople (6th/7th century), *Peri diaphoras tōn proserchomenōn* (Migne, *Patrologia graeca,* 86, 72C); Antiochus the Monk (d. after 619), *Homilia 130* (89, 1848C); and Anastasius of Sinai (d. after 700), *Hodēgos,* 8 (89, 129A).
6. The seat of this patriarch of Antioch is now in Beirut, Lebanon.
7. Severius Jacob, "The Syrian Church—Yesterday and Today," in Ignatius Ephrem I, *The Syrian Church of Antioch,* p. 30. The Syrian Orthodox

Church of Malabar numbers about 600,000. Non-Syrian scholars estimate the number of the remaining faithful subject to the patriarch of Antioch at from 70,000 to 200,000.

8. Severius Ephrem Barsoum, *The Shorter Catechism,* pp. 4-14.
9. Ibid., p. 15.
10. Ibid., p. 19. The influence of medieval Western scholastic theology is apparent both in the understanding of grace and in the doctrine of the sacraments.
11. Ibid., p. 23.
12. Ibid., p. 28.
13. Ibid., pp. 40-41.
14. In its simplest form a *kauma* consists of the Sign of the Holy Cross and the Trinitarian Invocation, followed— the worshiper kneeling—by "Holy, holy, holy, Lord God Almighty, the heavens and the earth are full of Thy praises. Glory be in the highest." Thereupon the worshiper addresses the Trisagion prayer to the Incarnate Word: "Holy art Thou, O God. Holy art Thou, Almighty One. Holy art Thou, O Immortal. O Thou who wast crucified for our sakes, have mercy upon us." (This is said three times in three prostrations, the worshiper crossing himself.) The Trisagion prayer continues: "O our Lord, have mercy upon us. O our Lord, show us Thy compassion and be merciful unto us. O our Lord, receive our worship and our prayers, and have mercy upon us. Blessed be Thou, O Creator. Glory be to Thee, O Christ the King, who showest mercy on Thy sinful servants." The *kauma* concludes with the Our Father (ibid., p. 18). For a guide to more elaborate worship in the Syrian Church of Antioch, see Severius Ephrem Barsoum (Ignatius Ephrem I), *The Golden Key to Divine Worship, with Commentary on the Ritual of the Syriac Church,* trans. James E. Kinnear (West New York, N.J.: n.p. [available from the Syrian Church of Antioch in the United States and Canada, Hackensack, N.J.], 1951).
15. Severius Ephrem Barsoum (Ignatius Ephrem I), *The Shorter Catechism,* p. 19.
16. Ibid., p. 32.
17. Letter from the Reverend K. M. Simon, M.A., D.D.
18. The Armenian Church is sometimes called "Gregorian" after St. Gregory.
19. On the analogy of the French *Catholicossat* the term "catholicosate" sometimes is used in English.
20. Some of the Armenians who had immigrated to Polish Galicia accepted the authority of the Roman see in 1635 and received an archbishop of their own at Lemberg. In 1742 a schism in the Cilician catholicate resulted in the establishment of a rival catholicate under Roman Catholic authority (the Roman Catholic Church's Armenian Rite) at Kraim in what is now Lebanon; in 1928 its headquarters moved to Beirut.
21. Here quoted according to Khoren Narbey, *A Catechism of Christian Instruction according to the Doctrine of the Armenian Church,* trans. Psack Jacob, ed. Tiran Nersoyan, 2nd printing (New York: Diocese of the Armenian Church of North America, 1964), pp. 5-6. The alternative renderings in notes 22 through 27 have been suggested by the Reverend Kourken Yaralian, pastor, Armenian Apostolic Church of the Holy Trinity, Fresno, California, a parish belonging to the Prelacy of the Armenian Apostolic Church of America, in a communication dated November 22, 1967.—The Armenian Church sees the creed abridged in the doxology of St. Gregory the Illuminator: "As for us, we shall glorify Him who was before the ages, worshipping the Holy Trinity and the One Godhead, the Father, the Son, and the Holy Spirit, now and forever and unto the ages of ages. Amen" (Narbey, p. 7).
22. Or: thus he assumed flesh.
23. Or: through.
24. Or: through.
25. Or: among.
26. Or: In one baptism, in repentance, in the remission and forgiveness of sins.
27. Or: essence.
28. Narbey, p. 5: "There is but one person in Christ, that of God, and . . . this divine Person took manhood in the womb of the Blessed Virgin Mary."
29. Ibid., p. 21. See Tiran Nersoyan, *The Christological Position of the Armenian Church* (New York: Diocese of the Armenian Church of America, 1962) (12-page tract).
30. Narbey, p. 27.
31. Ibid., pp. 29, 61.

32. Ibid., pp. 32-33. The Synod of Partav defined the canon in 768. The Old Testament apocrypha are considered deuterocanonical; they are retained in the Armenian Scriptures for "their purity of morals" and are regarded with reverence, but not as part of the inspired canon (ibid., pp. 35-37). The Scriptures are to be read by all the faithful (ibid., p. 38).

33. The Armenian Church does not encourage the use of icons and, except for pictures of the Mother of God and the Holy Child, representations of Our Lord and of the saints are rare. Instead of an iconostasis, Armenian churches have a curtain.

34. Narbey, pp. 112-113.

35. Ibid., p. 186. The catholicos of Etchmiadzin uses "the revered relic (the right arm) of St. Gregory the Enlightener" in blessing the confirmation chrism as well as in other acts of blessing.

36. Ibid., p. 187n.

37. Ibid., p. 202.

38. Ibid., pp. 208-209.

39. A vartapet is a celibate priest to whom the bishop gives, with special prayers and blessings, the authority to teach the faith; as a sign of office he carries a doctoral staff (ibid., p. 190).

40. See *The Catholicate of Cilicia: Her Place and Status in the Armenian Church* (Antelias, Lebanon: The Catholicosate of Cilicia, 1961) (39-page brochure). There have been previous schisms involving the two catholicates, notably one in the seventeenth century

and another in the nineteenth.

41. Letter from M. Cheteyan, secretary of the Prelacy, 138 East 39 Street, New York, New York.

42. From the Syriac, *melk*, "king," that is, the imperial Basileus.

43. The Fifth Ecumenical Council (553), held at Constantinople, condemned the edict. The modern Coptic Church holds that the non-Chalcedonian formula "one nature of the Incarnate Word" and the Chalcedonian Creed "express the same meaning and the same theological fact" to a great extent, but that the non-Chalcedonian formula is more biblical and less dangerous. See Waheeb Atalla Girgis (Pakhoum A. El-Moharraky), *The Christological Teaching of the Non-Chalcedonian Churches* (Cairo, Egypt: The Coptic Orthodox Theological University College, n.d.) (16-page pamphlet).

44. Letter from the Reverend Marcos Marcos, Diocese of North America, Coptic Orthodox Church.

45. Since 1930 the Roman Catholic Ethiopic Rite has had a native-born Ethiopian hierarchy. Currently the 50,000 members of this rite are divided between two exarchates, one in Ethiopia itself, the other (the larger of the two) in Eritrea.

46. Communication from Abba Laike Mendefro.

47. Communication from the Reverend Marcos Marcos, Diocese of North America of the Coptic Orthodox Church, Toronto, Ontario, Canada.

BIBLIOGRAPHY

Chakmakjian, Hagop A. *Armenian Christology and the Evangelization of Islam: A Survey of the Relevance of the Christology of the Armenian Church to Armenian Relations with Its Muslim Environment*. Leiden: E. J. Brill, 1965.

Daoud, Marcos, translator-editor. *The Liturgy of the Ethiopian Church*. Addis Ababa, Ethiopia: Berhanenna Selam Printing Press, 1954.

Jones, Arnold Hugh Martin, and Monroe, Elizabeth. *A History of Ethiopia*. Oxford: Clarendon Press, 1955.

Leroy, Jules. *Ethiopian Painting in the Middle Ages and during the Gondar Dynasty*. Trans. Claire Pace. New York: Frederick A. Praeger, 1967.

Mercer, Samuel Alfred Browne. *The Ethiopian Liturgy: Its Sources, Development, and Present Form*. Milwaukee, Wis.: The Young Churchman Company, 1915.

Narbey, Khoren. *A Catechism of Christian Instruction according to the Doctrine of the Armenian Church*. Trans. Psack Jacob, ed. Tiran Nersoyan. 2nd printing in the United States of America. New York: Diocese of the Armenian Church of North America, 1964.

O'Leary, De Lacey Evans. *The Ethiopian Church: Historical Notes on the Church of Abyssinia*. London: SPCK, 1936.

Ormanian, Malachia. *The Church of Armenia: Her History, Doctrine, Rule, Dis-*

cipline, Liturgy, Literature, and Existing Condition. Trans. G. Marcar Gregory. 2nd edition by Terenig Poladian. London: A. R. Mowbray and Co., 1955.

Samuel, Athanasius Yeshue, ed.-trans. *Anaphora: The Divine Liturgy of Saint James, the First Bishop of Jerusalem, According to the Rite of the Syrian Orthodox Church of Antioch, Trans-* lated *from* [the] *Original Syriac.* Hackensack, N.J.: Athanasius Yeshue Samuel, 1967.

Sarkissian, Karekin. *The Council of Chalcedon and the Armenian Church.* London: SPCK, 1965.

———. "The Ecumenical Problem in Eastern Christendom," *Ecumenical Review* 12 (1959/1960): 436-454.

PART II

EASTERN ORTHODOX CHURCHES

---

3. Eastern Orthodoxy[1]

Three more ecumenical councils followed the break between the established church of the Roman Empire and the Non-Chalcedonian churches.

The Fifth Ecumenical Council (Constantinople II, 553) condemned the "three chapters" and thereby reaffirmed Chalcedon. Emperor Justinian had previously condemned the "three chapters" in an edict of 543/544—the works of the Antiochene theologian and exegete Theodore of Mopsuestia (350?–428) for their allegedly unorthodox views on the Incarnation of Christ; the writings of Theodoret of Cyrrhus (393?–458?) against St. Cyril of Alexandria (375?–444) for what was seen as a "Nestorianizing" tendency in them; and the letter that Ibas of Edessa (d. 457) sent in 433 to the Persian bishop Mari, in which Ibas took a mediating stand between the Nestorian position and that of St. Cyril. Justinian's action was apparently designed to mollify the Non-Chalcedonians and to reconcile them to the imperial church by a show of anti-Nestorian zeal. Vigilius of Rome (d. 555) refused to approve the edict on the ground that it contradicted the decisions of Chalcedon, but in 548 he reluctantly concurred under imperial pressure in the condemnation of the three chapters, then withdrew his assent. In 554 he declared his adherence to the decision of the Fifth Ecumenical Council, although a serious schism in the West was the result.

The Sixth Ecumenical Council (Constantinople III, 680–681) condemned Monothelitism, a doctrine derived from the correspondence of Honorius of Rome (d. 638) with Sergius of Constantinople (d. 638), in which the bishop of Rome imprudently affirmed "one will" (*hen theléma*) in Christ and rejected the expression "two wills" as likely to provoke controversy. Monothelitism was thus a mediating stance between the position of the Non-Chalcedonian churches and orthodoxy. The Sixth Ecumenical Council confirmed the decisions of a synod held at Rome in 679, rejected Monothelitism, and asserted the existence of two wills in Christ, a divine will and a human will, as an integral part of the Catholic faith.

The Seventh Ecumenical Council (Nicaea II, 786–787) settled the iconoclastic controversy, which came to a head in 726 when Emperor Leo III the Isaurian (680?–741) declared that all images were idols and ordered their destruction. The edict was followed by the systematic persecution of the "iconodules" (that is, those who venerated icons). The persecution continued under Emperor Constantine V Copronymus (718–775). It abated to a degree under Leo IV the Khazar (749–780) and was ordered stopped by his widow, the empress-mother Irene (752?–803) as regent for Constantine VI (770–798?). In 784 St. Tarasius (d. 806) was (uncanonically, since he was a layman) elected patriarch of constantinople. Together with the empress-mother Irene, he persuaded Hadrian I of Rome (d. 795), to send legates to what became the Seventh Ecumenical Council. It defined that the "venerable and holy images (*eikonas*)" of Christ, of the Theotokos ("she who gave birth to God"), of the angels, of all saints, and of holy men (*hosiōn andrōn*) were to receive "reverent veneration" (*timētikēn proskynēsin*), but not the "genuine worship based on our faith" (*kata pistin hēmōn alēthinēn latreian*) that is reserved for God alone.

The Division between the East and the West

Church historians put the date of the definitive break between the established church of the Byzantine Empire and the established church of the Western Roman Empire at various points on a continuum that runs from the ninth century to the fifteenth, possibly even the seventeenth. Schisms between Constantinople and Rome were nothing new; between the First Ecumenical Council in 325 and the Seventh Ecumenical Council in 787, Constantinople and Rome had been in mutual schism intermittently for a total of 203 years.

Some church historians see the definitive break as occasioned by the mutual excommunications exchanged by St. Photius (810?–895?), patriarch of Constantinople, and St. Nicholas of Rome.[2]

Since the sixteenth century it has been conventional to see the definitive break precipitated by the action of Cardinal Humbert of Silva Candida (d. 1061) in depositing on the altar of the Cathedral of the Holy Wisdom in Constantinople just before the Divine Liturgy began on July 16, 1054, a bull anathematizing Michael Cerularius (1000?–1058), patriarch of Constantinople, and his supporters in the name of a bishop of Rome, St. Leo IX (1002–1054), who three days short of three months dead. Michael replied to Humbert by excommunicating "the impious document and its authors."[3]

Other church historians date the definitive break in 1204, when the Western armies of the inglorious Fourth Crusade sacked Constantinople.

Still others relate the definitive break to the Eastern repudiation of the union of Lyons that the representatives of the Eastern Roman emperor Michael VIII Palaeologus (1225?–1282) signed in 1274.

In the same vein another school of church historians traces the definitive break to the initially lonely but unwavering refusal of St. Mark (Eugenicus) of

Ephesus (1391?–1445) to sign the capitulation to Rome that commanded the subscriptions of all the other Greek hierarchs at Florence in 1439.

Indeed, some modern scholars have come to think of the schism as "a gradual, fluctuating, disjointed process, perhaps not consummated until the end of the fifteenth century and perhaps only reaching its present form about 1650."[4]

In any case, whatever the date one chooses, the definitive separation was long in coming.

Some of the factors that ultimately led to it are older than the establishment of Christianity in the Roman Empire. The administrative division of the empire into eastern and western parts, ruled by coequal imperial Augusti, goes back to Diocletian and thus antedates by a generation the peace of the church (313) under Emperor Constantine (whom Eastern Orthodoxy deems a saint).

With the decline of Greek in the West and the general victory of Latin and with the emergence of the clergy in the West as almost the only literate class for centuries, a linguistic barrier was added to the profound cultural and psychological differences that separated the Greek East and the Roman West.

The growing ties that linked the highest church leadership of the West with the Frankish monarchs climaxed in the coronation of Charlemagne (742–814) by Leo III (d. 816) in St. Peter's Church in Rome on Christmas Day, 800. This de facto revival of the Western empire increased the political tension that already existed. At the other end of the Mediterranean, the growing Eastern orientation of Byzantine policy and the ever greater identification of church and empire in the East contributed, along with the iconoclasm of the Byzantine emperors of the seventh and eighth centuries, to the dissolution of links with the West.

The intensifying insistence of the bishop of Rome on his superiority over all other bishops was incompatible with the Eastern idea of the parity of the historic patriarchates, even though the East was always ready to acknowledge the historic role of the patriarch of the West as the first among equals.

The barbarous behavior of the Western crusaders after their capture of the Christian capital of Constantinople in 1204, followed by the sixty-year-long Latin empire in the East, made hatred of the West something that Easterners imbibed with their mother's milk.

Theological and ceremonial differences between the churches exacerbated the waxing disunity. The churches of the East and the West differed on the very nature of theology. They differed in their doctrine of human beings; "the injury done to the image of God in man" by Latin theology was one of the Eastern gravamina. Increasingly after the fifth century the East insisted that the invocation (*epiklēsis*) of the Holy Spirit upon the bread and wine of the Eucharist accomplished the sacramental change, while the West attributed the eucharistic miracle to the recitation of the words of institution. In the Western addition of the words "and the Son" (*Filioque*) to the statement of the Creed of the 150 Fathers of Constantinople that the Holy Spirit proceeds from the Father, the East professed with swelling emphasis from the eighth century onward to see both a divisive trinitarian heresy and an indefensible unilateral alteration of the creed of the Catholic Church. The idea of a penal purgatory, the evolving insistence on the immaculate conception of the Blessed Virgin Mary in many parts of the late medieval West, obligatory clerical celibacy, and the theory of indulgences from the eleventh century onward were in Eastern eyes further evidence of Western heterodoxy.

Such ritual issues as using leavened or unleavened bread for the Eucharist (and for the *antidōron* [see below p. 45] of the East), the age at which an infant was brought to baptism, fasting or eating on Saturday, priestly beards or clean-shaven priestly cheeks, singing Alleluia throughout the year or abandoning its use during the weeks before Easter, and the shape of ecclesiastical vestments and ornaments were all convenient ritual differences that immediately identified a co-religionist or an adversary to the simple faithful.

History

The first seven ecumenical councils—all of them held in the East—are part of the common tradition of East and West. So are the great theologians and fathers, St. Pachomius (290–346), St. Anthony the Greek (251?–356), St. Athanasius (296?–373), St. Basil of Caesarea (330?–379), St. Gregory of Nyssa (330?–395) and St. Gregory of Nazianzus (329–389), St. John Chrysostom (347?–407),[5] St. Cyril of Jerusalem and St. Cyril of Alexandria (375?–444), St. Maximus the Confessor (580?–662), and St. John of Damascus (675?–749?) are only a few of the more prominent names on an almost endless roster.

The spread of Islam from the seventh century onward reduced the influence of Eastern Christianity in much of the Middle East. Jerusalem fell to the Arabs in 657 (not to be liberated until 1099), and the Arab siege of Constantinople in 717 was an ominous portent that cast its shadow across more than seven centuries.

The eighth century saw a mounting conflict between the Byzantine government and the church—represented chiefly by the monks—and in the ninth century a forty-year resurgence of imperially endorsed iconoclasm did not come to an end until 843, when Theodora, the queen-mother regent, ordered discontinuance of the persecution of the "iconodules." The triumph of the church over the iconoclastic emperors in 843 is still commemorated on the first Sunday in Lent in Eastern Orthodox churches as the "Sunday of Orthodoxy."[6] It was a triumph for the monks as well.

The centuries that followed are the era of the "Byzantine theocracy," with empire and church linked in a tension-filled intimacy. At its best this relation created a unique Byzantine humanism. At its worst it ended in the subjection of the church to the state[7] or, more rarely, the subjection of the state to the church.

The official theology that began to develop in Constantinople in the tenth century and that persisted until the end of the empire tended to look backward and to stress creativity less than the faithful transmission of culture and tradition. The most noteworthy contributions of the early Middle Ages within Eastern Orthodoxy were in the areas of liturgy and of ascetic and moral theology. In the former realm the influence of St. John of Damascus and of St. Theodore Studites (759–826) remained strong. In the latter realm the memorable names are those of St. Symeon the New Theologian (949–1022) and St. Gregory Palamas (1296–1359); it is to St. Gregory Palamas that Eastern Orthodoxy owes its unique understanding of "grace." Byzantine church music underwent extensive development in this period; in the course of time it exerted a marked influence not only on Slavic church music but also on the later plain chant of the West.

While the expansion of Islam and the schisms that separated the church of the Byzantine Empire from the Non-Chalcedonian churches and the Church of the East were containing (and even constricting) Eastern Orthodoxy in Asia and Africa, the Eastern Orthodox mission to the Slavic peoples began. The initial evangelization of the western Slavs by the two brothers, SS. Constantine (826–869), who took the religious name of Cyril when he became a monk in Rome just before his death, and Methodius (815?–885), was undertaken with the joint approval of both Constantinople and Rome, but it was short-lived in its immediate effect. The mission to the Bulgars was more immediately successful. Defeated by the imperial forces, the Bulgar Khan Boris I (d. 903) allowed himself to be baptized on the battlefield in 869 as a condition of peace. Political considerations forced him into a brief association with Rome, but he turned once more to Constantinople and secured the assistance of St. Clement of Ohrid, one of St. Methodius's disciples, in establishing Eastern Orthodoxy in the kingdom of Bulgaria. The outreach to the Slavs touched Serbia in the ninth century, but it is St. Sava (1176?–1235?) who is revered as the father of both Serbian Eastern Orthodoxy and the Serbian state. Even the conquest by the Ottoman Turks did not succeed in rooting out Eastern Orthodoxy in the Balkans.

After the fall of Constantinople in 1453[8] (and of Athens in 1456), the Turks recognized the ecumenical patriarch as the *millet pasha*, the political and religious leader of the Christians in the Ottoman Empire. The period that followed was largely one of systematic humiliation and programmatic persecution for Eastern Orthodoxy. Even when the Turkish Empire began to decline, the situation became, if anything, worse; thus during a seventy-three-year period in the eighteenth century the sultans replaced the ecumenical patriarch forty-eight times. The oppression came to a climax with the martyrdom of Ecumenical Patriarch Gregory V on Easter 1821.

The Turkish conquest of the Balkans had as a side effect the Hellenization of the leadership of the Balkan Eastern Orthodox community by the ecumenical patriarchs. The Patriarchate of Trnava in Bulgaria was suppressed in 1394.

The Bulgarian Eparchy of Ohrid, established in 1018, retained its independence until 1776, when Ecumenical Patriarch Samuel I, who had eliminated the Serbian patriarchate at Péc the year before, completed the "unification," that is, the Hellenization, of the Eastern Orthodox Church in the
Balkans. A similar fate befell the Eastern Orthodox Arabs in the patriarchates
of Jerusalem, Antioch, and Alexandria.

The reformations of the sixteenth century had a palpable impact on
Eastern Orthodoxy. The Lutherans—from Philipp Melanchthon to the
Tübingen theologians who initiated a correspondence with Ecumenical Patriarch Jeremiah II (d. 1598)—began to court the approval of a church which
they saw as genuinely Catholic but which sturdily refused to acknowledge
the supreme authority of the bishop of Rome.[9] The post-Tridentine Roman
Catholic Church began a programmatic penetration of Eastern Orthodoxy
by every available means, not least the considerable theological, educational,
and diplomatic resources of the Society of Jesus. Reformed ideas likewise
succeeded in penetrating the Eastern Orthodox community. The confession
of faith of no less a dignitary than Ecumenical Patriarch Cyril Lucaris (1572–
1638) himself bears the clear imprint of Genevan theology.[10]

The church of Greece became autocephalous in 1833, and a rise of religious nationalism accompanied the rise of political nationalism in the
Turkish Empire in the 1860s and 1870s.

Eastern Orthodoxy in Russia

Eastern Orthodoxy in Russia has its own history, which begins officially
with the baptism of St. Vladimir (956–1015) of Kiev in 988 and which may
go back in fact to the ninth century. Although efforts were made to install
Russian metropolitans in Kiev as early as the eleventh century, the Eastern
Orthodox church in Russia during the Kievan period was strongly dependent
on Constantinople. Native monasticism, however, took early root. St. Anthony established the Caves (Pechersk) Cloister at Kiev in 1051, but St.
Theodosius (d. 1074), the first monastic saint to be canonized by the Russian
Orthodox Church, commonly rates as the real founder of Russian monachism.

The Tatar conquest of Russia in the 1230s shifted the political and ecclesiastical center of gravity to the cities of Vladimir and Suzdal until the church
leadership established itself at Moscow early in the fourteenth century. The
power of the state over the church grew with the waxing influence of the
Muscovite monarchs, and the Eastern Orthodox Church in Russia entered
into a "dark ages" of its own. During this era the authentic Orthodox tradition
was perpetuated chiefly by the monks, among whom St. Sergius (1320–1392)
of Radonezh was particularly eminent.

The movement of Eastern Orthodoxy in Russia toward independence
from the domination of Constantinople gained a great deal of impetus from
the almost unanimous capitulation of the Greek hierarchs to the bishop of

Rome at the Council of Florence. The Russian Church became autonomous in fact in 1448, when Grand Prince Basil II (d. 1462) convened a council of bishops in Moscow that elected Bishop Ioan of Ryazan' (St. Jonas) the metropolitan of All Russia without the permission of the ecumenical patriarch. At the same time the council professed obedience to the mother church of Byzantium, "except for the present recently-appeared disagreements." With what the Russians regarded as the lapse of Old Rome into heterodoxy and with the obvious judgment of God on New Rome when the Turks captured it in 1453, they began more and more to think of Moscow as the divinely chosen Third Rome, the embodiment of the ancient Byzantine theocratic ideal.

In 1589 Ecumenical Patriarch Jeremiah II (d. 1598) elevated the Muscovite metropolitan Job to the rank of patriarch. Once the Russian Church had thus achieved patriarchal status and autonomy, it felt the pressure of Roman Catholic, Lutheran, and Reformed influence. The first permanent *unia* (Russian for "union," from which the word "uniat[e]"—formerly used to describe Eastern Rite Roman Catholics—derives) of a significant segment of Eastern Orthodox bishops with Rome took place in Poland-Lithuania under royal pressure at Brest-Litovsk in 1596. Under the influence of the eminent but strongly Latinizing metropolitan of Kiev, Peter Moghila (1597–1647), Roman Catholic theological methodology triumphed, and Peter's confession of faith required extensive reworking before it became generally acceptable in Eastern Orthodox circles.

The seventeenth century also saw the tragic internal rupture that goes by the name of the *Raskol* ("separation"). This resulted in the expulsion of the Old Believers from the Russian Orthodox Church. To a significant extent, the Old Believer movement was a visceral reaction of conservative elements in the Russian Church to the newer Greek and Western influences that seemed to be importing confusing and demoralizing changes into the church's life and faith.

The eighteenth and nineteenth centuries saw the rise of a variety of dissident movements in Russia, some native in origin, but many of them the direct or indirect result of Western denominations.

The progress of Peter the Great (1682–1725) in the direction of Western political absolutism involved the suppression of the Patriarchate of Moscow and its replacement with the Holy Synod. The change in effect reduced the church to a department of the government. The patriarchate was restored only after the revolution of 1917.

An effort by the communist regime in the Union of Soviet Socialist Republics in 1922 to establish a rival, wholly state-controlled religious community, the Living Church (the moderate wing of which evolved into the Renovated Church), had completely failed by the end of the decade.

A by-product of the rise of communism in Eastern Europe has been the return—sometimes voluntary, sometimes forcible—of Eastern Rite Roman Catholics in communist-controlled territory to Eastern Orthodoxy.

Worldwide Eastern Orthodoxy

Currenly worldwide Eastern Orthodoxy has from 60 to 90 million practicing members, of whom all but about 15 percent are in communist-ruled countries. Four of the ancient Eastern Orthodox jurisdictions are predominantly Greek, the Patriarchate of Constantinople, the churches of Greece and of Cyprus (the latter independent since 431), and the autocephalous Church of Sinai (which consists of a score or so of monks and about eighty laymen in St. Catherine's Monastery). As archbishop of Istanbul and the patriarch of New Rome, the ecumenical patriarch (at least ideally) is the highest spiritual authority in Eastern Orthodoxy. As the "first among equals" among the eight patriarchs,[11] he has the authority to call all pan-Orthodox meetings. The ecumenical patriarch has jurisdiction over Turkey, Crete, some Aegean islands, the worldwide Greek diaspora, some Slavic emigrant jurisdictions, Mount Athos, and the Eastern Orthodox Church of Finland. The patriarchates of Antioch and of Jerusalem are predominantly Arab. The former is currently torn by the rivalry that exists between a Moscow-oriented "Damascus faction" and a westward-looking "Beirut faction." The Patriarchate of Alexandria is a mixture of Greek, Arab, and African Eastern Orthodox Christians; its jurisdiction extends to the Eastern Orthodox Church of Uganda and the latter's mission in Kenya. The patriarchates of Moscow, Serbia, Bulgaria, and Romania, and the Eastern Orthodox churches of Macedonia, Georgia, Albania, Poland, Czechoslovakia, the People's Republic of China, and Japan, as well as the mission in Korea, are all national churches.

Eastern Orthodox Theology

Eastern Orthodoxy affirms its living continuity with the apostolic church,[12] with the church of the ecumenical councils, with the Fathers of both the East and the West until the eighth century, and with its own succession of Fathers and teachers since. Its objective it finds in the words of St. John of Damascus: "We keep the tradition just as we have received it."

Tradition for Eastern Orthodoxy is the total witness of the Holy Spirit within the living church, the sum of the preaching, polity, worship, ascetic practice, and art that Eastern Orthodoxy has inherited.[13] The existence of an Eastern Orthodox tradition does not, of course, preclude the possibility of the existence of relatively valid local and regional traditions.

In Eastern Orthodoxy's appreciation of this bequest from the past, a growing degree of careful discrimination, especially in those parts of the world where Eastern Orthodoxy has had to come to terms with other Christion communions, is gradually replacing a somewhat uncritical acceptance and at times overzealous defense of its inheritance.

Within the tradition so understood, Eastern Orthodoxy gives primacy to the sacred Scriptures, to the Creed of the 150 Fathers of Constantinople, and to the doctrinal definitions of the seven ecumenical councils. It attaches a lesser degree of authority to the writings of the Fathers, and a still more limited authority to what it sometimes calls its symbolical books.

Eastern Orthodoxy requires its faithful, its clergy, and its theologians to accept and understand the sacred Scriptures "in accordance with the interpretation which was and is held by the Holy Orthodox Catholic Church of the East."[14] The authoritative text of the Old Testament is that of the Septuagint version; Eastern Orthodoxy regards the differences between this Greek version and the Hebrew text as changes that the Holy Spirit inspired. It counts thirty-nine "protocanonical" books in the Old Testament. It counts in addition ten "deuterocanonical" books on a lower footing than the protocanonical documents; the deuterocanonical books are the ones that some other Christian communions call the Old Testament apocrypha. For Eastern Orthodoxy the sacred Scriptures are an icon of Christ.[15]

Of comparable authority is the Creed of the 150 Fathers of Constantinople (commonly called the Nicene Creed), which Eastern Orthodoxy sings at every celebration of the Eucharist and daily at compline.[16]

When a council has come to be deemed ecumenical, that is, one whose doctrinal decisions are accepted as binding upon all the faithful, Eastern Orthodoxy regards its doctrinal decisions as irreformable and infallible, but a decision that a regional council of the bishops of one or more national churches hands down or that an individual bishop includes in his confession of faith can be wrong. Broadly, the authority of such a regional or individual pronouncement is in proportion to the extent to which it commands permanent acceptance in the Eastern Orthodox community. No definitive canon of authoritative pronouncements of the Eastern Orthodox faith exists, but most lists would include:

1. St. Photius's encyclical letter of 866/867
2. The first letter of Michael Cerularius to Peter of Antioch, 1054)
3. The decisions of the councils of Constantinople of 1341 and 1351 on the Hesychast Controversy[17]
4. The encyclical letter of St. Mark of Ephesus of 1440/1441
5. The confession of faith (1455/1456) of Ecumenical Patriarch Gennadius II (George Scholarios) (1400?–1468?)
6. The replies of Ecumenical Patriarch Jeremiah II to the theologians of the University of Tübingen (1573–1581)
7. The confession of faith (1625) of Metrophanes Kritopulos (d. 1641), patriarch of Alexandria
8. The acts of the Council of Istanbul (which the Greeks have continued to call Constantinople) of 1638
9. The acts of the Council of Iaşi (Jassy) of 1642
10. The confession of faith (1638) of Peter Moghila (1597–1646), metropolitan of Kiev, as revised by the Council of Iaşi of 1642

11. The acts of the Council of Istanbul of 1672

12. The acts of the Council of Bethlehem-Jerusalem of 1672

13. The confession of faith (1672) of Dositheus (1641–1707), patriarch of Jerusalem,[18] as ratified by the Council of Bethlehem-Jerusalem of the same year, and formally approved in 1721 by all the Eastern Orthodox patriarchs

14. The acts of the Council of Istanbul of 1691

15. The answers of the Eastern Orthodox patriarchs to the Anglican Nonjurors (1716/1725)

16. The encyclical letter of the Council of Istanbul of 1722 to the Eastern Orthodox Christians of Antioch

17. The confession of faith of the Council of Istanbul of 1727

18. The encyclical letter of the Council of Istanbul of 1836 "against the Protestant missionaries"

19. The encyclical of the Council of Istanbul of 1838 against the Latin innovations

20. The reply of the Eastern Orthodox patriarchs to Pius IX (1848)

21. The reply of Ecumenical Patriarch Gregory VI to Pius IX (1868), declining the invitation to attend the First Vatican Council

22. The reply of the Synod of Istanbul to Leo XIII (1895)

23. The five encyclical letters of the ecumenical patriarchate between the years 1920 and 1952 on Christian unity and the ecumenical movement

24. The decision of the Eastern Orthodox Assembly in Moscow "against Papism" (1948)

Among the Fathers, Eastern Orthodoxy accords special reverence to the "Three Great Hierarchs" (SS. Basil the Great, Gregory of Nazianzus, and John Chrysostom) and, from later centuries, to SS. Maximus the Confessor, John of Damascus, Theodore Studites, Symeon the New Theologian, Gregory Palamas, and Mark of Ephesus.

Eastern Orthodoxy criticizes Western Christendom for being cataphatic, that is, for being too prone to the making of formal dogmatic definitions, and sees itself as more "apophatic," that is, more reluctant to try to reduce theological mysteries to dogmatically defined concepts. It enshrines its belief at many points less in creedal affirmations than in the words, actions, and gestures of the liturgy, the divine office, and private worship.

The Eastern Orthodox doctrine of God presents him as both transcendent and immanent. It makes an important distinction between God's being and his energies. His being is unapproachable, according to Eastern Orthodox theology, but his energies, which are God himself, permeate all creation and import divinizing grace and divine light to Christians. The Father, the Son, and the Holy Spirit constitute a unity as well as a union, with each hypostasis dwelling in the other two by a perpetual movement of love. Eastern Orthodoxy tends to think of the Trinity in terms of the "social analogy"; the standard Eastern Orthodox iconic representation of the Trinity depicts the three angelic visitors to Abraham under the terebinths of Mamre. At the same time Eastern Orthodoxy sees the principle of the unity of the Godhead in the person of the Father, who begets the Son and from whom the Holy Spirit proceeds. Many of its theologians would accept the formula that the Holy Spirit proceeds from the Father *through* the Son, but Eastern Orthodoxy unanimously believes that Western Christendom errs in affirming that the Holy Spirit proceeds from the Father *and* the Son. Thereby, Eastern Orthodoxy holds, the West rejects the biblical witness, unilaterally alters an ecumenical creed, emphasizes the oneness of God at the cost of his threeness, confuses the hypostases of the Trinity, destroys the balance between unity and diversity, makes God too much an abstract being and too little a concrete personality, and subordinates the Holy Spirit to the Son. Ultimately, in the eyes of Eastern Orthodoxy, the Filioque is responsible for what Eastern Orthodoxy sees as the West's distorted doctrine of the church as a mundane institution and for Roman Catholic centralization of authority in the hands of the pope.

In its doctrine of human beings, Eastern Orthodoxy tends to be somewhat more optimistic about people than the classic theologies of the West, with their indebtedness to St. Augustine. Eastern Orthodoxy differentiates in each human being the image or icon of God—the human being's rationality and freedom—from the likeness of God—the human being's similarity to God through virtue. As the icon of God a human being who knows himself knows God; for the same reason each human being is infinitely precious in God's sight.

Eastern Orthodoxy rejects every doctrine of divine grace that seems to it to limit the freedom of human choice; looking at the entire process of salvation, it describes the relation between God's grace and the human being's freedom of choice as cooperation or synergy. The grace of God invites everyone, Eastern Orthodoxy holds, but it compels no one. But by accepting and guarding the free gift of divine grace a human being acquires no claim on God and earns no "merit." Indeed the concept of "merit" as it evolved in the West, especially after St. Anselm, is wholly alien to Eastern Orthodoxy. At the same time, Eastern Orthodoxy holds that, while a human being cannot merit salvation, the biblical doctrine that "faith by itself, if it has no works, is dead," implies that he must labor for salvation.

In Eastern Orthodox thinking there is a mysterious unity of the human race through which, as a result of the original sin of disobedience of the first human beings, all their progeny come into a world in which sin prevails everywhere. In this environment it is easy to do what is wrong and difficult to do what is right. The mind of human beings has become so darkened, and through desire (the counterpart of "concupiscence" in the West) the power of their wills has become so weak, that divine grace no longer acts on them from within, but only from without, and they cannot hope to attain the likeness of God. Even though the native sinfulness of each human being does not destroy the rationality and the freedom that is the image of God in him, it gravely wounds him and limits the scope of the freedom of his will. Human beings, Eastern Orthodoxy holds, inherit Adam's corruption and mortality, but not his guilt. Each human being is guilty to the extent that he imitates Adam through his own free choice.

The sinfulness and the sins of human beings, according to Eastern Orthodoxy, have created a barrier between them and God that none could tear down by one's own effort. To open the way to reunion with himself, God in his love for human beings (*philanthrōpia*) came to them. As the second Adam, Jesus Christ reversed the effect of the first Adam's disobedience. He showed human beings what the true likeness of God is. Through his redemptive and victorious sacrifice he put the likeness of God within reach of human beings. Eastern Orthodoxy stresses that Christ is at once true God and true man, one person in two natures, inseparably but without a mixture of the two, with two wills and two energies. Eastern Orthodoxy sees the glory of Christ's Godhead as manifested especially in his transfiguration and his resurrection. It links Christ's resurrection with his crucifixion in a single action that in both stages reveals the victory of God incarnate over his and humanity's enemies.[19]

The work of Christ and the work of the Holy Spirit are reciprocal in Eastern Orthodox theology. "The Word took on human flesh," it recalls St. Athanasius as saying, "that we human beings might receive the Spirit." St. Seraphim of Sarov says that "the true aim of the Christian life is the acquisition of the Holy Spirit."

Eastern Orthodoxy uses the term *theōsis* (literally translated into English as "deification" or "divinization") to describe the salvation and redemption that is the final goal of the Christian life. As used in Eastern Orthodoxy, *theōsis* implies a human participation in the divine nature in the sense of union with the divine energies (not the divine being). It is a way of affirming that human beings "become God" by grace or status not by nature, and each one retains fully the personal characteristics of his created nature without any pantheistic absorption into God. The complete *theōsis* of Christians will take place at Christ's final self-manifestation, when the inward glory of the Spirit's presence will fully transfigure their bodies as part of the transformation of the entire material creation.

Eastern Orthodox theology thinks of the church in a trinitarian fashion as the image of the Trinity, as the body of Christ, and as the continuation of Pentecost. It is visible, in that it comprises empirical worshiping communities on earth, and invisible, in that it also comprises the faithful departed and the angels. It is human, in that its members are sinful human beings, and it is divine, in that it is the body of the divine Word incarnate.

By the grace of God, Eastern Orthodox theology affirms, the Eastern Orthodox communion is the single true and infallible church, the one holy catholic and apostolic church of the creed.

The Eastern Orthodox churches are hierarchically structured. They have bishops that stand in an apostolic succession, priests, deacons, and lesser orders. But Eastern Orthodoxy also recognizes that the people of God have a prophetic and priestly service to perform. It acknowledges that members of the laity may possess spiritual gifts; in this connection it points to the *staretsi* of Russia, the influential spiritual directors who had no place in the formal hierarchical structure of the church, and to the Eastern Orthodox tradition, which makes the teaching of theology as much a lay[20] as a clerical vocation.

Eastern Orthodoxy holds that the faithful departed continue to be members of the single family of God even after physical death. Accordingly, Eastern Orthodox Christians pray for the faithful departed and ask the faithful departed to pray for them.

A saint in the technical sense is one whom an autocephalous church in whose midst the individual's remains repose has canonized. But even in recent times a spontaneous cultus has sometimes developed without formal canonization. St. John of Kronshtadt (1829–1908), formally canonized to date only by the Russian Orthodox Church Outside of Russia, and the New Martyrs of the Bolshevik revolution are cases in point.

Eastern Orthodoxy gives the Virgin Mary a uniquely preeminent position —"higher than the cherubim, more glorious than the seraphim."[21] It venerates her as Theotokos ("the one who gave birth to God"), as ever-virgin, as *panagia* ("all-holy"), and as pure (in the sense that she never committed an actual sin).[22]

The veneration (*proskynēsis*) of the icons of the saints (and of the Godhead) bulks large in Eastern Orthodox piety. But Eastern Orthodox theologians make a careful distinction between *latreia* (adoring worship of God), on the one hand, and *hyperdouleia* (the veneration accorded the person of the Theotokos) and *douleia* (the veneration accorded to saints, to relics, and to icons, even icons of Christ and the Theotokos), on the other.

Eastern Orthodoxy awaits the great *apocatastasis* ("restoration")[23] or *anakephalaiōsis* ("summing up, renewal") at the end of time, when God will fully redeem and transform the material universe at Christ's appearing and will create a new heaven and a new earth.

The essence of heaven Eastern Orthodoxy sees as the complete union in body and in spirit of the members of the redeemed community with God. The essence of hell is less a punitive imprisonment by God than a self-incarceration, with an accompanying spiritual anguish, brought about through the misuse of one's free choice. On the question of the ultimate salvation of all intelligent creatures both patristic opinion and contemporary Eastern Orthodox theological opinion cover a range of views. To say that all must be saved would be deemed heresy, but Eastern Orthodoxy would allow for the hope that all may be saved.

A parallel variation exists on the question of the "intermediate" state of the faithful departed between death and the final judgment. Eastern Orthodoxy commonly teaches a particular and partial judgment of each human being at the moment of death, when his everlasting destiny is irrevocably determined. Individual Eastern Orthodox theologians, especially in the past (Peter Moghila and Dositheus, for instance), have held an opinion close to the Roman Catholic view of a penal purgatory, although Eastern Orthodoxy as such has never followed them on this point and few, if any, Eastern Orthodox theologians hold this view today. Most would deny that the faithful departed suffer at all. Some would hold that they may suffer, but that this is a cleansing rather than an expiatory suffering, since Christ, as the Lamb of God that takes away the sin of the world, is the only atonement and satisfaction for believers. A third group would leave the entire matter open.

The Mysteries

The chief channels of divine grace in Eastern Orthodox theology are the "mysteries," sometimes called in English by the Western designation "sacraments."

Since the fifteenth century Eastern Orthodoxy counts seven mysteries. Some Eastern Orthodox theologians hold that Christ personally instituted all seven, others that he instituted baptism and the Eucharist immediately and the others mediately through his apostles.

Baptism is administered in the Eastern Orthodox communion by threefold immersion (except in an emergency, when affusion is permitted) with the formula: "The servant of God [Christian name] is baptized in the name of the Father, Amen, and of the Son, Amen, and of the Holy Spirit, Amen." Baptism is normally imparted in infancy and is seen as conferring the forgiveness of both original sinfulness and all actual transgression. The normal minister is a bishop or priest, in an emergency a deacon or any baptized Christian. Eastern Orthodox theologians are divided on the validity of baptism administered in other Christian communions; most theologians presume the validity of such baptisms, but others call for administration of baptism to applicants for Eastern Orthodox church membership even if they have already been baptized in the Roman Catholic, Lutheran, Anglican, or Reformed communities, on the ground that the heterodoxy of these denominations renders the validity of that baptism dubious. Eastern Orthodoxy recognizes the validity of the "baptism of blood" (that is, martyrdom), but the Roman Catholic notion of "baptism by desire" is foreign to Eastern Orthodoxy.

Immediately after baptism the newly baptized person, regardless of age, receives chrismation (from *chrisma*, "anointing"), the counterpart of the medieval Western rite of confirmation. The officiating minister, normally a priest, traces the sign of the cross with *myron* ("myrrh"), a special ointment made of olive oil blended with forty sweet-smelling additives and consecrated by a bishop who heads an autocephalous church, on the candidate's forehead, eyes, nostrils, mouth, ears, breast, hands, and feet, saying at each anointing,

"The seal of the gift of the Holy Spirit." By baptism the candidate has been made a member of Christ, Eastern Orthodoxy teaches; by chrismation he receives the gift of the Holy Spirit and becomes a "laic," a member of the *laos* ("people") of God. Chrismation also serves as the sacrament of reconciliation for returning apostates and—normally—for the reception of Christians from other communions whose previous baptism is deemed valid.[24]

Immediately after receiving baptism and chrismation, the new member, again regardless of age, receives Holy Communion.

In parish churches the Eucharist, or the Divine Liturgy, is celebrated (always chorally and with incense, if at all possible) every Sunday and on festivals. Although the rites in use in Eastern Orthodoxy are longer and more complex than the normal eucharistic rite of the West as it has survived among Roman Catholics, Lutherans, and Anglicans, for instance, the basic structure is the same:

1. an office of preparation, in which the elements are readied for their use
2. the *synaxis* ("assembly"), of which the climax is the "little entrance" of the gospel, followed by the *trisagion* ("three times holy")[25] and the lessons from the sacred Scriptures; and
3. the Eucharist proper, beginning with the "great entrance" of the "holy gifts" (that is, the eucharistic elements), the litany of supplication, the kiss of peace, and the creed; continuing with the eucharistic prayer, the "fraction" (that is, breaking of the consecrated bread), and the communion of the clergy and the lay communicants; and ending with the thanksgiving, the blessing, and the distribution of the *antidōron* (literally, "return-gift"), that is, a piece of bread that has been blessed but not consecrated, to all the worshipers.

The normal eucharistic rite on Sundays and festivals is the Liturgy of St. John Chrysostom. The basically identical but somewhat longer Liturgy of St. Basil the Great is used ten times a year. The Liturgy of St. James the Brother of the Lord is used only on his feast day, October 23, and only in a few places in the Eastern Orthodox world. In the Liturgy of the Presanctified Gifts on the Wednesdays and Fridays in Lent and on Monday, Tuesday, and Wednesday in Holy Week, there is no consecration and the celebrant communicates himself and the faithful from elements consecrated on the preceding Sunday.

The language used in divine worship in Eastern Orthodox churches is the national vernacular of the respective country or community, although in the ancient Byzantine form in the case of the Greek Rite and in Old Church Slavonic in the Russian and some other Slavic rites.[26]

Eastern Orthodoxy holds that after the prayer of consecration the bread and the wine have in reality become the body and the blood of Christ, but that the way in which this takes place is a mystery.[27]

The role of the prayer of invocation (*epiklēsis*) of the Holy Spirit in contrast to the repetition of the words of institution was at one time a theological issue between the East and the West. But contemporary Eastern Orthodoxy holds that the whole prayer of the anaphora is necessary for the consecration of the elements. While the *epiklēsis*, the invocation of the Holy Spirit upon the elements does not by itself effect the consecration, and the repetition of the words of institution is not merely a nonessential and incidental adiaphoron.

Eastern Orthodoxy consecrates the Holy Communion under the forms of leavened bread and fermented grape wine and administers the sacrament by giving to each communicant a small piece of the consecrated bread in a spoonful of consecrated wine from the chalice.

According to Eastern Orthodox theology the Eucharist is a sacrifice as well as a sacrament, although no one theory of the nature of the eucharistic sacrifice is universally and exclusively held by theologians. There is agreement that Christ is both the real priest and the victim; that the eucharistic congregation under the liturgical leadership of the bishop or priest offers the sacrifice to the entire Trinity; that, on the one hand, the Eucharist is not a bare or imaginary representation of God's act in Christ on the cross and that, on the other hand, it is neither a new sacrifice nor in any sense a repetition of the once-and-for-all sacrifice that comprises Christ's Incarnation, his holy life, his obedience to his Father, his last supper, his crucifixion, and his exaltation; and that in some sense Christ and the Holy Spirit make this once-and-for-all sacrifice of Christ present before God and before the celebrating eucharistic congregation. As the act of the congregation, the Eucharist (from *eucharistia,* "thanksgiving") is a sacrifice of praise and gratitude, the unbloody "spiritual worship" (*lokigē latreia*) of the participating Christians; as a making present again of the saving sacrifice of Christ it is "propitiatory" (*hilastērios*). "What is yours from you we offer to you in behalf of all (*kata panta*) and for all,' the Eastern Orthodox liturgy declares.

Canon law requires Eastern Orthodox Christians to go to confession at least once a year and receive Holy Communion at least four times a year, preferably during the four great fasts. Communicants—who receive the consecrated elements standing—must abstain totally from food and water from the midnight before. The relative infrequency of communion by Eastern Orthodox laypeople in the past is slowly giving way to a trend toward weekly reception of Holy Communion.

Eastern Orthodoxy reserves the consecrated eucharistic elements for the communion of the sick and the dying,[28] but there is no public veneration of the reserved sacrament outside the Divine Liturgy.

Sins that an Eastern Orthodox Christian who has attained the age of reason has committed after baptism are forgiven in the mystery of confession (*exomologēsis*) or repentance (*metanoia*). Both the penitent and the priest, whose role is seen as that of a witness and servant of God rather than that of a judge in a tribunal, stand upright in the open church before a stand with a cross and an icon of Christ (or the Book of the Gospels) on it, or, in the Greek church, before the icon of Christ in the iconostasis, with the priest a step behind and to one side of the penitent. The Greek form of absolution is deprecative ("May God forgive you"); under Western influence the Slavic branches of Eastern Orthodoxy adopted the indicative form of absolution ("I forgive you") from the seventeenth century onward. At the priest's discretion he may—but need not—impose an *epitimion* (literally, "penalty"); this is not an integral part of the rite. He may also give such spiritual counsel as he deems appropriate. Except in the case of frequent communicants, Eastern Orthodox penitents commonly make their confessions and receive absolution before each Communion.

In Eastern Orthodoxy the bishop, priest, and deacon are in major orders; the offices of subdeacon, reader, and acolyte are among the minor orders that have survived. Ordinations always occur during the Divine Liturgy and only one person at a time can be ordained to a given order. The bishop is the only minister of ordination.[29] Eastern Orthodox theologians general regard the the consent of the eucharistic assembly—voiced by the acclamation *axios* ("worthy")—as essential. A minimum of three bishops (in emergencies two, never one) is required to consecrate a bishop. Since the sixth century, Eastern Orthodox bishops have been celibates or widowers who have taken monastic vows. The election of bishops from the ranks of the married as well as of the unmarried clergy is being strenuously urged in some quarters of the Eastern Orthodox community in North America. Parish priests are almost universally married men; almost all of the celibate clergy have taken monastic vows before ordination.[30] Once ordained a deacon, a clergyman, celibate or widowed, cannot marry and continue to exercise his office.[31]

The higher administrative grades of bishop confer no additional spiritual power. In the oldest Eastern Orthodox usage, a metropolitan is a bishop whose see city is a provincial capital and an archbishop is a bishop of special eminence whose see city is not a provincial capital; the distinction is no longer uniformly preserved and modern usage varies.

The spiritual gift that an Eastern Orthodox husband and wife require for their life together they receive formally through the mystery of matrimony. The priest is the minister. The exchange of rings and consent takes place in the preliminary engagement office; the mystery proper is the office of coronation. While marriage is conceived of as ideally a lifelong union, Eastern Orthodoxy permits termination of a marriage on scriptural grounds through the issuance of a divorce by a church tribunal and allows a second or even a third (but never a fourth) marriage afterward. Canonically the only ground for divorce is adultery, often interpreted in practice as anything that "adulterates" a marriage. Artificial methods of birth control are officially banned in the Church of Greece and in the jurisdictions directly under the ecumenical patriarch.

The last of the seven mysteries is the "oil of prayer" (*euchelaion*), administered in church where feasible and preferably by more than one priest. The anointing has as its primary purpose the recovery of the sufferer and the transformation of spirit that enables him to accept his suffering and to re-evaluate his personal spiritual life and his relation to God. Where recovery does not follow, the mystery is seen as a source of spiritual strength that prepares the patient for death.

Noneucharistic Worship, the Calendar, and Canon Law

In addition to the Divine Liturgy, the chief daily services in Eastern Orthodoxy are the dawn office (*orthros*) and the evening office (*hesperinos*). The midnight office, prime, terce, sext, none, and the "after-supper" office are the minor offices. Like the Divine Liturgy, the services of the divine office are sung and are in the national vernacular.

Eastern Orthodoxy lays great stress on private prayer and it has produced a vast library of devotional works.[32] It also encourages the thoughtful reading of the Bible and of the devotional works of older and more recent writers, but it has not systematized discursive meditation ("mental prayer") as Western spirituality has done.[33]

The services for the Christian year in Eastern Orthodoxy fill over twenty volumes.[34] The ecclesiastical year begins on September 1. The "feast of feasts" is Easter. The "twelve great feasts" are the birth of the Theotokos (September 8); the exaltation of the lifegiving cross (September 14), kept as a strict fast; the presentation of the Theotokos (November 21); the birth of Christ (December 25); the theophany or epiphany of Christ (January 6), which commemorates his baptism; the presentation of Christ (February 2); the annunciation of the Theotokos (March 25); the entry of Christ into Jerusalem (Sunday before Easter); his ascension (fifth Thursday after Easter); Pentecost (the seventh Sunday after Easter); the transfiguration of Christ (August 6); and the falling asleep of the Theotokos (August 15).[35]

The four major fasts—carried out with great rigor and severity by Western standards—are Lent (seven weeks before Easter); the Apostles' feast (from the second Monday after Pentecost, whenever it falls, through June 28); the fast of the falling asleep of the Theotokos (August 1 through 14); and the Christmas fast (November 15 through December 24).

In 1923 an Interorthodox Congress at Istanbul proposed the replacement of the Julian ("old") calendar with the Gregorian ("new") calendar. During the next few years the patriarchates of Constantinople, Alexandria, and Antioch, and the churches of Greece, Cyprus, and Poland introduced the Gregorian calendar, not without some resistance and a degree of reluctance in a few places that has not been wholly overcome down to the present.[36] The Patriarchate of Jerusalem, the churches of Russia, Serbia, and Bulgaria, and all but one of the monasteries on Mount Athos clung to the old calendar. Thus part of the Eastern Orthodox community keeps Christmas on December 25, new style, while the rest of the Eastern Orthodox world keeps it on January 7, new style. But practically the whole Eastern Orthodox community (the Eastern Orthodox Church in Finland is the most noteworthy exception) still reckons Easter according to the ancient Alexandrian practice approved at the First Ecumenical Council in 325. According to this procedure, Easter falls each year on the first Sunday after the first full moon that happens on or after the spring equinox or, if this Sunday should fall in the Jewish Passover, on the first Sunday after the first full moon after the Jewish Passover.[37]

An important part of both public and private worship in Eastern Orthodoxy is the veneration of icons. These are seen as ways through which God reveals himself to men and through which the worshiper acquires a vision of the spiritual world. Although technical competence and artistic creativity are not depreciated, the painter of icons must exercise his art within rules prescribed by tradition. Byzantine iconography thus exhibits a specifically spiritual representation and character all its own.

Eastern Orthodoxy early developed a more or less typical form of church architecture(often called "Byzantine") which the tendency toward conservatism has helped to preserve, although with national variations. In North America there has been a degree of assimilation of Eastern Orthodox church architecture to Western models and practices. This has gone so far as to admit even pews and organs. But one characteristic feature has been almost universally retained. This is the icononstasis, a screen with from one (normally two) to as many as five ranks of icons that separates the altar chamber from the *solea* (that is, the space between the altar and the nave). The Royal Gate (or Holy Doors), with a separable curtain behind them to close the aperture for certain parts of the rite, pierces the screen in the center and there are doors at either side near the walls. On the Holy Doors the four evangelists frequently appear.

Since the Middle Ages the arrangement of the icons has become fairly stereotyped, but many variations occur. Flanking the Royal Gate to the worshiper's right is an icon of Christ, to the worshiper's left an icon of the Theotokos with the infant Jesus. The second icon on the worshiper's right is usually St. John the Baptist. The second icon on the worshiper's left is usually the saint whose name the particular church bears. On the south and north doors respectively are normally icons of the archangels SS. Gabriel and Michael. If there are panels for icons beyond the south and north doors they are sometimes of SS. George (fourth century?) and Demetrius (d. 232?). In the second tier of icons the Last Supper is conventionally depicted over the Royal Gate; it is sometimes flanked by icons of the apostles, sometimes by representations of events in Christ's life and in the life of the Theotokos. In the latter case, the third tier may contain icons of the twelve apostles, a fourth tier patriarchs and prophets of the Old Covenant. A representation of the crucified Christ, flanked by St. John the Apostle and the Theotokos, stands at the top of the iconostasis above the center.

The canon law of Eastern Orthodoxy represents an attempt to apply the teachings of the faith and their implications to the daily life of Christians. Like the doctrine of the church, Eastern Orthodox canon law is drawn from disciplinary decisions of the ecumenical councils, regional councils, and individual bishops. The better-known collections are those of Theodore Balsamon (1140?– after 1195) and John Zonaras (twenfth century). The standard modern commentary is the *Pedalion* ("rudder") that St. Nicodemus of the Holy Mountain published in 1800. There is a great need for a revision of canons, since many have become obsolete, while new and modern situations are simply ignored.

Eastern Orthodox Missions

The frequently made charge that Eastern Orthodoxy is not a missionary community is less than wholly true and fair. For centuries Islam effectively inhibited the Eastern Orthodox community from evangelizing Muslim territory, but the tradition of missionary effort that began with the outreach to the Slavs over a millennium ago has never wholly ceased to assert itself, although its intensity has waxed and waned. In European and Asiatic Russia there was unbroken missionary activity from 1237 down to the first decades of the present century. Eastern Orthodox missionary activity began officially in China in 1715 (although it may go back as far as 1658), in Alaska in 1794, and in Korea in 1898. The first indigenous convert to the Eastern Orthodox mission in Japan received baptism at the hands of Nicholas Kassatkin (1836–1912) in 1869. In 1882 Russian Eastern Orthodoxy began missionary work among the Arabic-speaking Muslims of Syria. In 1948 the Greek archdiocese of North and South America began a Latin American mission in Mexico. Eastern Orthodoxy has succeeded in making a limited number of converts from among the religiously uncommitted throughout its diaspora from Western Europe to Australia. In these territories it has likewise attracted a not inconsiderable number of Christians of other denominations, primarily from among the Eastern Rite communities of the Roman Catholic Church in the Western world[38] and to a more limited degree from that denomination's Latin Rite, but also from non-Roman-Catholic denominations, notably the Anglican communion. Of special interest is the Eastern Orthodox community in Uganda, which the patriarch of Alexandria formally recognized in 1946. It received its original impetus from a segment of the United-States-based African Orthodox Church in Uganda that broke away from the parent body and subsequently sought admission to Eastern Orthodoxy. In 1955 the Uganda community established a mission in Kenya. There is also a mission in Tanzania sponsored by the Eastern Orthodox Church of Greece.

Eastern Orthodoxy and Other Christian Denominations

Its conviction that Eastern Orthodoxy is the only true church has inhibited the participation of some segments of Eastern Orthodoxy in the ecumenical movement. At the same time the ecumenical patriarchs have manifested a deep interest in ecumenism since the beginning of the present century, and increasingly Eastern Orthodox jurisdictions have affiliated with the World Council of Churches (where Eastern Orthodoxy has displaced the Lutheran community as the largest single denominational bloc) and in North America with the national councils of churches in the United States and in Canada. In its participation in the organized ecumenical movement, Eastern Orthodoxy has taken the position that it is the church of the creed and that it is in the organized movement "to bear witness as the true church to the truths of the Catholic faith."[39]

Relations between Eastern Orthodoxy and the Non-Chalcedonian churches have been increasingly friendly in recent years and conferences looking toward some kind of reunion are under way.

The entry in 1898 of a Persian diocese of the Church of the East into the Eastern Orthodox Church of Russia has suggested to the Eastern Orthodox that some kind of parallel accommodation could be achieved between Eastern Orthodoxy and the entire Church of the East.

In spite of many points of agreement between the Roman Catholic Church and Eastern Orthodoxy, real progress toward reunion has been very slow, even after Vatican Council II and the Pan-Orthodox Congress at Rhodes in 1964. Eastern Orthodoxy sees the major issues as the supreme ordinary jurisdiction and infallibility of the pope, the words "and the Son" in the creed, and the difference in the normal mode of baptism. At the practical level some of the knottier problems are mixed marriages, Roman Catholic "proselytizing," and the existence of Roman Catholic churches that are counterparts to Eastern Orthodox jurisdictions.

Since 1874 representatives of Eastern Orthodoxy and the Old Catholic Church of Utrecht have been holding periodic conferences. There have been no practical results to date. Since 1932, when the Old Catholics entered into formal intercommunion with segments of the Anglican community, the issue has been bound up with the question of Anglican and Eastern Orthodox relations.

Informal efforts at effecting intercommunion between Eastern Orthodoxy and the Anglican community go back over a century, and a number of official conferences have been held since 1930 between representatives of both communities. While a number of Eastern Orthodox jurisdictions have since 1922 given carefully qualified recognition to the validity of Anglican ordinations, the practice of Eastern Orthodox bishops to whom Anglican clergymen have applied for admission to their respective branches of the Eastern Orthodox communion has consistently been to receive such applicants as laymen and to ordain them. Eastern Orthodoxy sees as the chief barriers to intercommunion with the Anglican community the heterogeneous comprehensiveness of Anglicanism, the (in Eastern Orthodox eyes) intolerably equivocal character of Anglican doctrinal formulations—notably on the sacraments and on the church—and the broad spectrum of interpretations that these formulations admit in practice. Here and there Eastern Orthodox leaders still raise the charge of Anglican "proselytizing."

Lutheran interest in Eastern Orthodoxy goes back to the sixteenth century. Particularly since World War II semiofficial and lately official contacts have been initiated in both Europe and North America.[40]

Eastern Orthodox discussions above the local level with the Presbyterian and Reformed community and with other Western Christian denominations besides those noted[41] had been almost wholly within the broader framework of the organized ecumenical movement.

Eastern Orthodoxy in North America

Eastern Orthodoxy came to the North American continent with the Russian traders and colonists who began to arrive in Alaska after 1741; missionary work among the Eskimos and North American Indians began there in 1794. John Veniamonov (1797–1879) became known as the Apostle of Alaska. In 1858 the Holy Synod of Moscow established an auxiliary see at Sitka; it became an independent missionary see with the sale of Alaska to the United States in 1867. In 1872 it was transferred to San Francisco, in 1905 to New York, which became the headquarters for the archbishopric of North America. Until 1917 the Eastern Orthodox Church of Russia was the only canonical representative of Eastern Orthodoxy at the episcopal level in the United States and Canada.

After 1917 Moscow was no longer able to exercise effective control over its North American establishment, and one national church after another established its own jurisdiction. A hopeful plan of Archbishop (later Patriarch) Tikhon (Vasily Ivanovich Belyavin) in 1905 for the establishment in America of a single Eastern Orthodox exarchate of national Eastern Orthodox churches with their own bishops, each independent in his own field, foundered. The spread of communism in Europe after World War II exacerbated an already difficult situation.

Today Eastern Orthodoxy in the United States and Canada is divided by national, ideological,[42] and sometimes personal rivalries. All too often competing hierarchs have engaged in unedifying raids on one another's jurisdictions. Factionalism has likewise manifested itself at the level of interjurisdictional cooperation in practical matters, such as youth work. The process of acculturation is reinforcing the generally felt desire for a greater measure of oneness and the recognition of the theologically anomalous character of the situation of Eastern Orthodoxy in North America, but progress is slow. At the same time the effort to secure public recognition of Eastern Orthodoxy as a separate category of Christianity is achieving some success.

The Standing Conference of Orthodox Bishops in the Americas, organized in 1960, brings together a majority, but not all, of the Eastern Orthodox church bodies in the United States and Canada. Its headquarters are at 8–10

East 79 Street, New York, New York. Its membership comprises the primates of the Albanian Orthodox Diocese in America; the American Carpatho-Russian Orthodox Greek Catholic Diocese; the Antiochian Orthodox Christian Archdiocese of New York and All North America; the Bulgarian Eastern Orthodox Church; the Greek Orthodox Archdiocese of North and South America; the Orthodox Church in America (formerly the Russian Orthodox Greek Catholic Church of America); the Romanian Orthodox Missionary Episcopate in America; the Serbian Orthodox Church in the United States of America and Canada; the Ukrainian Orthodox Church of America; and the [Holy] Ukrainian Autocephalic Orthodox Church in Exile. Canonical and jurisdictional issues stand in the way of membership by other Eastern Orthodox church bodies.

A number of activities are being carried out on a joint basis within the Eastern Orthodox community, including organization of Pan-Eastern Orthodox campus fellowships, the joint endorsement of candidates for chaplains' commissions in the armed services, and many local cooperative efforts. Local Eastern Orthodox federations of priests or parishes or both exist in many metropolitan communities; these tend to be more inclusive than the Standing Conference of Orthodox Bishops in the Americas.

NOTES

1. It is difficult to find a wholly satisfactory name for what throughout this volume is referred to as Eastern Orthodoxy. "The Holy Eastern Catholic and Apostolic Church" is cumbersome. The Non-Chalcedonian churches and the Church of the East are also Eastern. "Orthodox" is a predicate that appears in the official name of many church bodies, and none of them willingly concedes its exclusive applicability to another communion or church; the same is true of "Holy," "Catholic," and "Apostolic." "The Greek Church" was intelligible enough in the Middle Ages, although it failed to take cognizance of the increasing number of Eastern Orthodox Slavs from the seventh century on, but "Greek Orthodox" has become a narrowly national description. "Greek Catholic" is open to criticism from the Eastern Orthodox point of view, since it has become the name of those Eastern Rite Christians who have accepted the authority of the bishop of Rome. With a due sense of the limitations of "Eastern Orthodoxy," the present volume uses this combination to designate those Christians who profess to stand in the tradition that accepts the doctrinal definitions of the first seven ecumenical councils and that (ideally at least) regards the ecumenical patriarch of Istanbul as the ranking hierarch among the autonomous and autocephalous churches which constitute the Eastern Orthodox communion.

2. The Council of Constantinople that St. Photius and John VIII sponsored jointly in 879–880 and that Western Christians accounted an ecumenical council as late as the eleventh century ended this schism.

3. Paul VI and Ecumenical Patriarch Athenagoras I lifted these mutual excommunications as "a gesture of good will" in 1965. Their actions would appear not to have affected subsequent and more comprehensive anathemas on both sides, and they have not escaped extensive criticism within Eastern Orthodoxy.

4. So, for example, Gervase Matthew, quoted in George Every, *Misunderstandings between East and West* (Richmond, Va.: John Knox Press, 1966), p. 9.

5. Eastern Christianity evangelized the

Gothic tribes in the Balkan peninsula and southern Russia during the third and fourth centuries and an Ostrogothic bishop participated in the First Ecumenical Council in 325. Eusebius of Nicomedia (d. 342?) consecrated Ulfilas, a young priest of Cappadocian ancestry who had been born among the Goths, as "bishop of the Christians in the land of the Goths" around 341. St. Basil the Great took particular interest in the Gothic mission and St. John Chrysostom provided the Goths in Constantinople with a church of their own where services were conducted in Gothic.

6. Ancient custom discountenances the use of three-dimensional statues in Eastern Orthodox churches, but icons and bas-reliefs have been regarded as permissible since the Seventh Ecumenical Council (787).

7. The modern term "Caesaropapism" that has been coined to describe the subservient relation of the church authorities to the government in the Byzantine Empire is one about which Eastern Orthodox Christians are understandably sensitive. The careless use of the term overlooks the fact that "even in those times when the church was prepared to recognize the supreme right of imperial supervision over itself, the patriarch as guardian of the discipline of the church was able to excommunicate the emperor" (Norman Baynes and H. St. L. B. Moss, eds., *Byzantium: An Introduction to East Roman Civilization* [Oxford: Clarendon Press, 1948], p. 276). Commenting on the term "Caesaropapism," Runciman asserts: "The emperor was an august figure whose sacred rights were respected and who in a struggle with the patriarch would usually have his way. But neither he nor the patriarch, for all their splendour, could live securely in his high office if he lost the sympathy of the Christian people of Byzantium" (Steven Runciman, *The Great Church in Captivity: A Study of the Patriarchate of Constantinople from the Eve of the Turkish Conquest to the Greek War of Independence* [Cambridge, England: University Press, 1968], p. 74). See also Deno John Geneakoplos, *Byzantine East and Latin West: Two Worlds of*

Christendom in Middle Ages and Renaissance—Studies in Ecclesiastical and Cultural History (New York: Harper & Row, 1966), chap. 2, pp. 55-83.

8. Steven Runciman, *The Fall of Constantinople 1453*, 3rd printing (Cambridge, England: University Press, 1969), is a vivid chronicle of this epochal event. The exodus of Greek scholars from Byzantium to the West had important consequences for the fifththeenth-century Renaissance.

9. For an English translation of the first exchange between the Tübingen theologians and the ecumenical patriarch, see George Mastrantonis, "The Correspondence of the Tübingen Theologians and Jeremiah II on the Augsburg Confession and a Translation of the First Answer of the Ecumenical Patriarch Jeremiah II to the Lutheran Theologians of Tübingen in 1576" (St. Louis, Mo.: Unpublished master of sacred theology thesis, School for Graduate Studies, Concordia Seminary, 1969).

10. For a patently partisan modern appraisal of Cyril Lucaris from a Reformed point of view, see George A. Hadjantoniou, *Protestant Patriarch: The Life of Cyril Lucaris (1572–1638), Patriarch of Constantinople* (Richmond, Va.: John Knox Press, 1961). Ever since the publication of Cyril Lucaris's confession of faith, there have been Eastern Orthodox apologists who have declared that the confession was not written by the patriarch himself but by others who used his name. On this point a distinguished contemporary Eastern Orthodox historian observes: "The original manuscript of Loukaris is preserved by the Library of Geneva and suffices to prove that the *Confession* is indeed authentic. Ancient and recent claims to question its authenticity are nothing more than pious attempts to save the good name of the patriarch" (John Meyendorff, *The Orthodox Church: Its Past and Its Role in the Church Today,* trans. from the French by John Chapin [New York: Pantheon Books, 1962], p. 93, n. 10).

11. His patriarchal seat has been located at the Phanar in Istanbul since 1601. The presence of the titular head of

Eastern Orthodoxy in the capital of Turkey during an era of delicate Turco-Greek political relations and of no less delicate political and ideological relations between the communist and noncommunist worlds has frequently evoked internal and international repercussions in the recent past.

12. The ecumenical patriarch of Istanbul claims a local succession that goes back to the traditional establishment of the church in Byzantium in 38 by St. Andrew the Apostle, the First-Called. See Francis Dvornik, *The Idea of Apostolicity in Byzantium and the Legend of the Apostle Andrew* (Cambridge, Mass.: Harvard University Press, 1958), pp. 138-299.

13. Many Eastern Orthodox theologians express appreciation of the canon of Catholicity set up by St. Vincent of Lérins (fifth centnury): "That is genuinely Catholic that has been believed in all places and at all times by all [Christians]." In this connection, see Georges Florovsky, "The Function of Tradition in the Ancient Church," *Greek Orthodox Theological Review* 9 (1963–1964): 181-200.

14. From the promise that a new member of the Eastern Orthodox communion must make, quoted in Timothy Ware, *The Orthodox Church* (Baltimore, Md.: Penguin Books, 1963), p. 208.

15. Since the Seventh Ecumenical Council, Eastern Orthodoxy has required the same veneration for the Book of the Gospels (*Euangelion*) that it prescribes for the holy icons.

16. Eastern Orthodoxy does not use the other two "catholic" creeds of the West, the so-called Apostles' Creed and the Athanasian Creed, although it has adopted the *Te Deum laudamus* ("We praise you as God").

17. Hesychasm, from the Greek *hesychia* ("rest"), designates a method of spirituality developed on Mount Athos and vindicated by St. Gregory Palamas against its opponents. Through meditation, contemplation, deliberate quieting of body and of mind, and certain positions of the body, the practitioner of this method seeks to see the uncreated divine light that enveloped Christ at his transfiguration (which Eastern Orthodox tradition assigns to Mount Tabor) and therewith to achieve supreme bliss. In this connection, see John Meyendorff, *A Study of Gregory Palamas,* trans. George Lawrence (London: The Faith Press, 1964).

18. John H. Leith, ed., *Creeds of the Churches: A Reader in Christian Doctrine from the Bible to the Present* (Garden City, N.Y.: Doubleday & Company, 1963), pp. 485-517, provides an easily accessible English version of this important Eastern Orthodox confession.

19. See Savas Agourides, "Salvation according to the Orthodox Tradition," *The Ecumenical Review* 21 (1969): 190-203.

20. Noteworthy examples are the late Vladimir Lossky and the contemporary ecumenical theologian Nikos Nissiotis.

21. One of the best-known Eastern Orthodox acts of devotion to the Theotokos is the Acathist Hymn ("the hymn of not sitting down"), traditionally ascribed to the Monothelite patriarch of Constantinople, Sergius (d. 638), who is supposed to have written it in praise of the miraculous intervention of the Theotokos in delivering the city from the Avars and Slavs in 626. (It has also been ascribed to George Pisides, to the Byzantine patriarch St. Germanus [634?–733?], to St. Photius, and, with a considerable degree of intrinsic probability, to the prolific Greek hymnographer St. Romanus Melodus [d. 556?]). It takes its name from the fact that it is sung standing up. It consists of twenty-four stanzas, each beginning with a letter of the Greek alphabet.

22. Eastern Orthodoxy commonly teaches that the Theotokos was born with original sin but that God cleansed her from it at the annunciation. The encyclical of St. Photius (867), the confession of faith of Metrophanes Kritopulos (1625), and the reply of Ecumenical Patriarch Gregory VI to Pius IX (1868) formally reject the doctrine of the immaculate conception of the Blessed Virgin Mary. The great majority of Eastern Orthodox theologians regard the immaculate conception of the Blessed Virgin Mary as "a theological heresy of the Roman church," biblically untenable, contrary

to Eastern Orthodox tradition and theology, and a concept that vitiates the Eastern Orthodox teaching about redemption and the Eastern Orthodox understanding of the relation of the Theotokos to her son and to the church. Even those Eastern Orthodox theologians who accept the immaculate conception of the Theotokos and her bodily assumption into heaven after her death concede that these tenets are not definable as dogmas.

23. Although not in the universalist sense that Origen (185?–254?) gave to the term.

24. The Eastern Orthodox Church of Russia usually makes an exception in the case of Roman Catholics and admits them to membership on a simple profession of faith without chrismation.

25. To be differentiated from the *Ter sanctus* ("Holy, Holy Holy") that follows the eucharistic preface. The Trisagion reads: "*Holy* God, *holy* [and] mighty, *holy* [and] immortal, have mercy on us."

26. The transition of Julian Joseph Overbeck (1824–1905), a Roman Catholic who had become a Lutheran, to Eastern Orthodoxy in London in 1865 gave impetus to the ultimate creation of an Eastern Orthodox Western Rite. (A recent discussion of his significance is Wilhelm Kahle, *Westliche Orthodoxie: Leben und Ziele Julian Joseph Overbecks* [Leiden, Holland: E. J. Brill, 1968].) Some Eastern Orthodox jurisdictions in the West have established such Western Rite affiliates. In North America the Western rites of the Syrian Antiochian Orthodox Archdiocese and of the Russian Orthodox Church Outside of Russia have between them a total of seven parishes and missions from coast to coast (letter from the Reverend Joseph Salkeld, ed., *Orthodoxy*, 7 Old Wagon Road, Old Greenwich, Connecticut). Some of these have attracted both clergymen and layfolk from Western denominations, chiefly the Roman Catholic and Episcopal churches. A case in point is the American Orthodox Church of the Redeemer, 11890 Magdalene Avenue, Los Altos Hills, California, begun in the early 1960s by a group of about one hundred members of the Pro-

testant Episcopal Church of St. Mark, Palo Alto, who followed their rector, Canon Edwin F. West (d. 1965), out of the Protestant Episcopal Church. Canon West was ordained an Eastern Orthodox priest in 1963. (The present writer acknowledges gratefully the kindness of the Reverend Paul H. D. Lang, pastor emeritus, Trinity Church, Palo Alto, who interviewed Canon West's successor, Archimandrite Theodore Kiece Micka, on behalf of this writer.) Western Rite communities retain all their Western rites, devotions, and customs which are not contrary to the faith of Eastern Orthodoxy and which logically derive from Western usages that antedate the eleventh century. A typical form of the Divine Liturgy used in Western Rite parishes and missions is that contained in *The Missal for Use of Orthodox* (Mount Vernon, N.Y.: Society of St. Basil, 1963) (36-page pamphlet); in it the invocation of the Holy Spirit is inserted in the otherwise almost unaltered Gregorian canon of the Roman Rite. On the Western Rite movement, see William Sutfin Schneirla, Alexander Turner, and David F. Abramtsov, *Western Rite Orthodoxy* (Mount Vernon, N.Y.: The Basilian Fathers, n.d. [after 1960]) (27-page illustrated brochure). Since 1969 the bimonthly journal *Orthodoxy* has concerned itself primarily with Eastern Orthodox Western Rite matters.

27. Traditionally Eastern Orthodox theologians used five verbs and their cognate abstract nouns to describe the change or transformation—*metaballō, metapoieō, metarrhythmizō, metaskeuazō,* and *metastoicheioō*. In the seventeenth century *metousiōsis*, the literal-etymological equivalent of the Latin *transsubstantiatio*, entered the Eastern Orthodox theological vocabulary under the influence of Roman Catholic neo-scholasticism. But Eastern Orthodoxy holds that this term is only one of a number of equally applicable synonyms and has no unique propriety, and that its use is in no sense an attempt to explicate the eucharistic mystery.

28. On Thursday of Holy Week annually the parish priest soaks a quantity of consecrated bread in the consecrated wine, allows the bread to dry out,

breaks it into small particles, and deposits it in the tabernacle.

29. He may delegate his power in a case of necessity to an archpriest (or protopope) or to an archimandrite (the head of a monastery, usually of larger size) only for the ordination of a reader.

30. Ordained monks are called "hieromonks."

31. Unlike the West, Eastern Orthodoxy knows only one order of monks and nuns. Their number is relatively fewer than in the Roman Catholic community.

32. For examples, see *Early Fathers from the Philokalia,* trans. E. Kadloubovsky and G. E. H. Palmer (London: Faber and Faber, 1953); Lorenzo Scupoli, *Unseen Warfare: Spiritual Combat and Path to Paradise,* ed. Nicodemus of the Holy Mountain, revised by Theophan the Recluse, trans. Kadloubovsky and Palmer (London: Faber and Faber, 1963); George P. Fedotov, ed. *A Treasury of Russian Spirituality* (New York: Sheed and Ward, 1948); and Tito Colliander, *The Way of the Ascetics,* trans. Katharine Ferré, ed. R. M. French (New York: Harper & Brothers, 1960). Thomas Hopko, "Orthodox Spirituality," in Jordan Aumann, Hopko, and Donald Bloesch, *Christian Spirituality East and West* (Chicago: Priory Press, 1968), pp. 101-162, is an informed and competent survey of the relation of theology, the liturgy, and prayer to the spiritual life in Eastern Orthodoxy.

33. The "Jesus Prayer" ("Lord Jesus Christ, [Son of God,] have mercy on me [a sinner]") is a very old Eastern Orthodox devotion that has become widely appreciated in the West, in part through versions in Western European languages of the anonymous nineteenth-century work, *The Candid Narrations of a Pilgrim to His Spiritual Father,* trans. into English by R. M. French as *The Way of a Pilgrim,* revised edition (London: SPCK, 1954).

34. The Epistolary (*Apostolos*); the Book of the Gospels (*Euangelion*); the Psalter; *Oktoechos* ("eight-tone book"), containing the variable parts of the service from the first Sunday after Pentecost (Sunday of All Saints) through the week preceding the Sunday of the Tax-Collector and the Pharisee (that is, the week of the tenth Sunday before Easter); *Triōdion* ("Three-ode Book"), containing the variable parts of the services from Sunday of the Tax-Collector and the Pharisee through the Saturday of Holy Week; *Pentekostarion,* containing the variables of the services from Easter through the week of Pentecost; a *Mēnaion* (from *mēn,* "month"), containing the variable parts of the services for the immovable commemorations, for each month, beginning in September; *Horologion,* containing the recurring portions of the ecclesiastical office through the year; *Euchologion,* containing the texts of the eucharistic rites, the invariable parts of the divine office, and the prayers used in the administration of the sacraments and various quasisacramental rites; *Hieratikon,* containing the text and ceremonial directions for the priest's conduct of the commonly used services with the *Archihieratikon* containing the text and ceremonial directions pertaining to episcopal functions; and *Typikon,* the manual that indicates how the services are to be recited during the church year, with tables of precedence of commemorations that fall on the same day.

35. Other important commemorations include the Protection (*skepē*) of the Theotokos (October 1); St. Nicholas the Miracle-Worker (December 6); the conception by St. Anne of the Theotokos (December 9); the circumcision of Christ (January 1); the Three Great Hierarchs (January 30); All Saints' Day (first Sunday after Pentecost); the birth of St. John the Baptist (June 24); SS. Peter and Paul (June 29); and the beheading of St. John the Baptist (August 29), kept as a strict fast.

36. The Palaioimerologitai (Old-Calendarites) of Greece, for instance, are an illegal religious community in that country, subject to persecution, but in many parts of Greece they have their own bishops, priests, monasteries, and publications, and succeed in thriving.

37. Thus the Eastern Orthodox Easter may fall up to five weeks later than the Western Easter. In 1964, when the

vernal equinox fell on March 20, the next full moon March 27, and the beginning of the Jewish Passover fell on the first full moon after the Jewish Passover fell on a Sunday, April 26, the Western Christian community kept Easter on Sunday, March 29, and Eastern Orthodoxy kept Easter on Sunday, May 3.

38. The American Carpatho-Russian Greek Catholic Diocese in North America is a case in point. See in this connection, Alex Simirenko, *Pilgrims, Colonists, and Frontiersmen: An Ethnic Community in Transition* (New York: The Free Press of Glencoe, 1964). This is a sociological examination of the dynamics of social and cultural change that accompanied the formation and transformation of the Russian community in Minneapolis. Between 1877 and 1891 the community completed its shift in allegiance from the Roman Catholic Church to Eastern Orthodoxy—the first community in the United States to make the transition—and for fifteen years it was the only training center for Russian-speaking Eastern Orthodox priests in the United States.

39. In this connection, see (Metropolitan) Nikodim, "The Russian Orthodox Church and the Ecumenical Movement," *The Ecumenical Review* 21 (1969): 116-129, and Leonidas Contos, *Guidelines for the Orthodox in Ecumenical Relations* (Brooklyn, N.Y.: Standing Conference of Canonical Orthodox Bishops in the Americas, 1966) (31-page pamphlet).

40. The Pan-Orthodox Conference held at Geneva in 1968 made important decisions not only about the "holding of a Great and Holy Council of the Holy Orthodox Church of the East," which it made "its chief objective and direct effort," but also about the dialogues going on between Eastern Orthodoxy and the Roman Catholic, the Anglican, the Old Catholic, the Non-Chalcedonian, and the Lutheran churches. See *Unity Trends,* vol. 2, no. 6 (February 1, 1969), p. 10.

41. A minor point on which Eastern Orthodoxy agrees with Judaism and the Reformed and Anglican traditions against the Roman Catholics and the Lutherans is in the division of what Roman Catholics and Lutherans call the second commandment into two commandments ("You shall have no other gods before me" and "You shall not make for yourself a graven image") and the combination of what Roman Catholics and Lutherans count as the ninth and tenth commandments into a single precept.

42. Where one group in a divided Eastern Orthodox ethnic community is loyal to the mother church in a communist-dominated country in Europe and the other group has broken its administrative ties with the mother church, communism frequently becomes an issue (or at least a pretext). The independent group may charge the other group with communist sympathies or with being blind to the fact that the communist government in the motherland is using the leadership of the mother church for its own ideological-political ends. With explicit reference to this writer's question as to what the view of responsible officers in the United States Department of State is "of the degree of peril of communist subversion through the Albanian, Bulgarian, Russian, Romanian, Serbian, and Ukrainian [Eastern Orthodox] communities [in the United States] that maintain spiritual and canonical ties with the national [Eastern] Orthodox churches of their respective motherlands," Mr. William B. Macomber, Jr., assistant secretary for Congressional relations, Department of State, wrote under date of March 31, 1967, to the Honorable Thomas B. Curtis, the then representative of the Second Congressional District of Missouri: "The Department is aware of the divisions which exist within some Eastern religious groups. We are aware also of efforts made from time to time in the past by certain Eastern European governments to utilize their national Orthodox churches in furtherance of their policies. We do not believe, however, that such activities represent a major danger to the security of the United States."

BIBLIOGRAPHY

Andrews, Dean Timothy. *The Eastern Orthodox Church: A Bibliography*. 2nd edition. New York: Greek Archdiocese of North and South America, 1957.

Armstrong, A. H., and Fry, E. J. Barbara, ed. *Rediscovering Eastern Christendom: Essays in Commemoration of Dom Bede Winslow*. London: Darton, Longman, and Todd, 1963. The authors of the essays are Eastern Orthodox, Anglican, and Roman Catholic.

Bashir, Antony, ed. *Studies in the Greek Orthodox Church*. 3rd edition. N.p.: n.p., 1960.

Benz, Ernst. *The Eastern Orthodox Church: Its Thought and Life*. Trans. from the German by Richard and Clara Winston. Garden City, N.Y.: Doubleday & Company, 1963.

Bogolepov, Aleksandr Aleksandrovich. *Toward an American Orthodox Church: The Establishment of an Autocephalous Church*. New York: Morehouse-Barlow Company, 1963.

Bratsiotis, Panagios. *The Greek Orthodox Church*. Trans. Joseph Blenkinsopp. Notre Dame, Ind.: University of Notre Dame Press, 1968. Trans. from the German edition of 1966.

Calian, Carnegie Samuel. *Icon and Pulpit: The Protestant-Orthodox Encounter*. Philadelphia: The Westminster Press, 1968. Baptized in the Eastern Orthodox community, the author writes from the point of view of a Presbyterian professor of theology.

Callinicos, Constantine N. *The Greek Orthodox Catechism: A Manual of Instruction on Faith, Morals, and Worship*. Revised edition. New York: Greek Archdiocese of North and South America, 1960.

Catechism of the Christian Doctrine of the Holy Eastern Orthodox Catholic and Apostolic Church. 7th edition. Brooklyn, N.Y.: Syrian Antiochian Orthodox Archdiocese of New York and All North America, 1960. A 56-page archiepiscopally authorized manual of instruction.

Congar, Yves. *After Nine Hundred Years*. New York: Fordham University Press, 1959. A Roman Catholic view of the East-West schism.

Demetrakopoulos, George H. *Dictionary of Orthodox Theology*. New York: Philosophical Library, 1964.

Every, George. *Misunderstandings between East and West*. Richmond, Va.: John Knox Press, 1966.

Fedotov, George P., comp.-ed. *A Treasury of Russian Spirituality*. New York: Sheed and Ward, 1948. An anthology covering nine centuries from St. Theodosius to St. John of Kronshtadt and Alexander Yelchaninov (1881–1934).

Geanakoplos, Deno John. *Byzantine East and Latin West: Two Worlds of Christendom in Middle Ages and Renaissance —Studies in Ecclesiastical and Cultural History*. New York: Harper & Row, 1966.

Hapgood, Isabel Florence. *Service Book of the Holy Orthodox-Catholic Apostolic Church*. Revised edition. New York: Association Press, 1922.

Holzhausen, John von. *The Book of Orthodox Common Prayer of the Holy Orthodox Eastern Catholic and Apostolic Church*. Toledo, Ohio: Theophany Publications, 1964.

Istavridis, Vasil T. *Orthodoxy and Anglicanism*. Amsterdam: Erasmus, 1966.

Kokkinakis, Athenagoras. *Parents and Priests as Servants of Redemption: An Interpretation of the Doctrine of the Eastern Orthodox Church on the Sacraments of Matrimony and Priesthood*. New York: Morehouse-Gorham Company, 1958.

Kourides, Peter T. *The Evolution of the Greek Orthodox Church in America and Its Present Problems*. New York: Cosmos Greek-American Printing Company, 1959.

Lossky, Vladimir. *The Mystical Theology of the Eastern Church*. London: James Clarke and Company, 1957.

———. *The Vision of God*. Trans. by Asheleigh Moorhouse. London: The Faith Press, 1963. A patristic introduction to the Palamite resolution of the antinomy between the inaccessibility of God and the participation of human beings in his nature.

Mastrantonis, George. *Divine Liturgy of St. John Chrysostom of the Eastern Orthodox Church*. New York: Greek Orthodox Archdiocese of North and South America, 1966.

———. *A New-Style Catechism on the Eastern Orthodox Faith for Adults*. St.

Louis, Mo.: The OLOGOS Mission, 1969.

——. *What Is the Eastern Orthodox Church?: Selected Fundamentals on Its Origin, Teachings, Administration, and History.* 6th edition. St. Louis, Mo.: OLOGOS, 1956. A concise and very useful 42-page brochure by a learned parish priest.

Maximos IV Sayegh (Saigh), *The Eastern Churches and Catholic Unity.* New York: Herder and Herder, 1963. The late author was an Arab Roman Catholic Eastern Rite patriarch.

Meyendorff, John. *The Orthodox Church: Its Past and Its Role in the World Today.* Trans. John Chapin. New York: Pantheon Books, 1962.

——. *Orthodoxy and Catholicity.* New York: Sheed and Ward, 1966.

Meyendorff, John; Afanassieff, Nicholas; and others. *The Primacy of Peter.* London: The Faith Press, 1963.

Nassar, Seraphim, ed. *Book of Divine Prayers and Services of the Catholic Apostolic Church of Christ.* New York: The Blackshaw Press, 1938.

Orthodox Spirituality, by a Monk of the Eastern Church. London: SPCK, 1961.

Ostrogorski, Georgije. *History of the Byzantine State.* Oxford: Basil Blackwell, 1968.

Pelikan, Jaroslav J. *The Christian Tradition: A History of the Development of Doctrine.* Vol. 2: *The Spirit of Eastern Christendom (600–1700).* Chicago: University of Chicago Press, 1974.

Philippou, Angelos J., ed. *The Orthodox Ethos: Essays in Honour of the Centenary of the Greek Orthodox Archdiocese or North and South America.* Oxford, England: Holywell Press, 1964.

Rinvolucri, Mario. *Anatomy of a Church: Greek Orthodoxy Today.* New York: Fordham University Press, 1966. An objective survey of Eastern Orthodoxy in modern Greece, with an important chapter on "The Phanar and World Orthodoxy" (pp. 148-166) and an appended "Report on the Orthodox Church in Bulgaria."

Runciman, Steven. *The Great Church in Captivity: A Study of the Patriarchate of Constantinople from the Eve of the Turkish Conquest to the Greek War of Independence.* Cambridge, England: University Press, 1968.

——. *The Orthodox Churches and the Secular State.* New York: Oxford University Press, 1973.

Schmemann, Alexander. *The Historical Road of Eastern Orthodoxy.* Trans. Lydia W. Kesich. New York: Holt, Rinehart and Winston, 1963.

——. *Sacraments and Orthodoxy.* New York: Herder and Herder, 1965.

Serafim, Archimandrite. *The Quest for Orthodox Church Unity in America.* New York: Saints Boris and Gleb Press, 1973.

Shaheen, Michael, trans.-ed. *The Divine Liturgy.* Toledo, Ohio: Toledo Archdiocese. 1967.

Sherrard, Philip. *The Greek East and the Latin West.* New York: Oxford University Press, 1959.

Stroyen, William B. *Communist Russia and the Russian Orthodox Church 1943–1962.* Washington, D.C.: Catholic University of America Press, 1967. A sociological analysis by a Russian Orthodox priest who is also a chaplain in the United States Air Force.

Suput, Ray R. "Eastern Orthodoxy in a Descriptive and Bibliographical Outline," in *American Theological Library Association—Summary of Proceedings* 16 (1962): 116-135.

Tarasar, Constance, ed. *Orthodox America, 1794–1976: Development of the Orthodox Church in America.* New York: Orthodox Church in America, 1975.

Upson, Stephen H. R. *Orthodox Church History.* 3rd edition. Brooklyn, N. Y.: Syrian Antiochian Archdiocese, 1960.

Verghese, Paul. *The Joy of Freedom: Eastern Worship and Modern Man.* Richmond, Va.: John Knox Press, 1967.

Ware, Timothy ([Father] Kallistos). *The Orthodox Church.* Baltimore, Md.: Penguin Books, 1963.

Zernov, Nicolas. *Eastern Christendom: A Study of the Origin and Development of the Eastern Orthodox Church.* New York: G. P. Putnam's Sons, 1961.

4. Eastern Orthodox Churches in the United States and Canada

The Orthodox Church in America

Formerly known as the Russian Orthodox Greek Catholic Church of America, or Metropolia, the Orthodox Church in America traces its origins to a mission established by monks of the Russian Orthodox Church in Alaska in 1794. In 1870 the Russian Orthodox Church formed the Diocese of the Aleutian Islands and Alaska, which in 1900 became the Diocese of the Aleutian Islands and North America.

In 1917 the reforming All-Russian Council revived the Patriarchate of Moscow, which Peter the Great had suspended, and elected Metropolitan Tikhon of Moscow who earlier had been Archbishop in America, as All-Russian patriarch. The basic tendency of this council was the restoration of *sobornost*—the active participation of the whole church, bishops, clergy, and laity, in every aspect of the church's life, in contrast to the centralized bureaucracy that had previously ruled the Russian church.

The efforts of the Bolsheviks to destroy the Russian church had serious consequences for the church in America. Financial support was no longer available for missionary work, and a new wave of refugees came to America. In 1919 the Russian Church in America held its first national council (*sobor*) in Pittsburgh; the second followed in 1924 at Detroit. This second sobor took two important steps. Following literally the decisions of the All-Russian Council of 1917–1918 it elected as its primate Metropolitan Platon, a senior bishop of the Church in Russia and former head of the American diocese during the seven years before World War I. It also declared the autonomy of the Russian Church in America.

Theophil, the second head of the Metropolia, in 1935 effected a practical understanding and intercommunion with the Russian Orthodox Church Outside of Russia, from which the latter's attempt to depose Platon as American metropolitan had separated the Metropolia. The American sobor ratified this Provisional Agreement in 1936. In 1938 Theophil opened St. Vladimir's Theological Seminary, now located at Crestwood, New York, one of the most influential centers of Orthodox theological learning in the Western hemisphere.

In 1946 the Cleveland sobor of the Metropolia again terminated its relationship with the Russian Orthodox Church Outside of Russia. The latter was unwilling to recognize the patriarch of Moscow in any way under the present circumstances; the Metropolia was willing to accept him as spiritual father provided he recognized the Metropolia's autonomy, which he at that time refused to do.

On April 10, 1970, His Holiness Alexis, patriarch of Moscow and All Russia, with the approval of the Sacred Synod of the Russian Orthodox Church granted the Metropolia the status of the Autocephalous Orthodox Church in America, thus bringing an end to decades of separation of the members of the Metropolia from the patriarchate in Russia. The Russian Church agreed to remove its ecclesiastical jurisdiction in the United States and Canada, dissolving the American Exarchate of the Russian Orthodox Catholic Church though granting its parishes and priests the right to continue under the direct supervision of the Russian patriarch.[1]

The decree of the Russian patriarch not only granted total self-government to the Metropolia but established it as the instrument of unity for all Orthodox Christians in America, as is clearly expressed in its new name, the Orthodox Church in America. Pointing to its status as the original missionary church of Orthodoxy in America, the Orthodox Church in America claims the right to be the unifying instrument for all Orthodox in America and is at present inviting "all of the national Orthodox church 'jurisdictions' in America to join with it in unity."[2] These claims have not been recognized by most Orthodox Churches whose primates are members of the Standing Conference of Canonical Orthodox Bishops in the Americas.[3]

The jurisdiction of the Orthodox Church in America extends throughout North and South America. Its headquarters are at Syosset (Box 25A), New York. It has nine dioceses in the United States and one in Canada with 469 parishes and an inclusive membership of one million. Its primate is His Beatitude, Metropolitan Ireney, archbishop of New York and metropolitan of All America and Canada. The Romanian Orthodox Episcopate (since 1960) and the Albanian Archdiocese (since 1971) are under its canonical jurisdiction but enjoy full administrative autonomy. Since 1972 the Orthodox Church in America has been active in Mexico through a special exarchate composed of one bishop, nine priests, and eleven communities.[4]

Patriarchal Parishes of the Russian Orthodox Church in the United States and Canada

The troubled career of All-Russian Patriarch Tikhon led to his imprisonment at the hands of the Soviet government. He died in 1925, and Metropolitan Peter of Krutica became patriarchal vicar. He too went to prison, and Metropolitan Sergei of Nizhni-Novgorod took over the administration of the church and tried to make peace with the Soviet government. Imprisonment was his lot also, but after his liberation he succeeded in securing legal recognition for the church. With the increased freedom that World War II brought to the Russian Church, the government allowed the election of new patriarchs.

In 1933 the Moscow patriarchate sent Metropolitan Benjamin Fedchenkov to assert its authority over the Russian Orthodox churches of America, divided in their allegiance at the time between the Russian Church Outside of Russia established in 1921, and the American Metropolia, which had declared its autonomy in 1924. Although his mission had very limited success, he established the American Exarchate of the Russian Orthodox Catholic Church with headquarters in New York. Subsequent efforts of Archbishop Aleksei of Jaroslavl in 1945 and of Metropolitan Gregory of Leningrad in 1947 to persuade the Metropolia to place itself under the authority of the All-Russian patriarch were unsuccessful.

In April 1970 negotiations were completed which granted autocephalous status to the Metropolia, which changed its name to the Orthodox Church in America. The agreement called for the dissolution of the American exarchate, though parishes and clergy which chose not to transfer to the new autocephalous church were permitted to remain in the Russian patriarchate with a vicar bishop of the patriarch of Moscow as the ruler. Parishes of the former exarchate met in August 1970 and resolved "to continue under the Omophor of the Moscow Patriarchate," though pledging to cooperate with the autocephalous Orthodox Church in America. By unanimous vote it was decided that the new name for the group would be Patriarchal Parishes of the Russian Orthodox Church in the U.S.A.[5] The parishes in Canada have a similar designation.

In August 1970 Bishop Makary was named vicar bishop for the parishes in the United States and Canada. His successor since January 1975 has been Bishop Job. His headquarters are at 15 East 97 Street, New York, New York. He is responsible for forty-one churches with a membership of 51,000 in the United States and twenty-four churches and missions with 8,000 to 10,000 members in Canada. In the past five years three priests and two parishes have transferred from the patriarchate to the Orthodox Church in America.[6]

The Russian Orthodox Church Outside of Russia

After the Bolshevik Revolution some of the bishops of the Russian Church attempted to establish a supreme church administration in southeastern Russia. But the advance of the Bolsheviks drove them out of the country. In November 1920 the refugee bishops organized the Supreme Church Administration for Churches Outside of Russia in Istanbul with the approval of the ecumenical patriarch. At the invitation of the patriarch of Serbia it moved to Yugoslavia soon afterward. In 1921 twelve of these bishops, along with priests and representatives of the laity, held a sobor (council) in Sremski Karlovci, Yugoslavia. Here they established the headquarters of the temporary supreme church administration for the faithful of the Russian Orthodox Church outside the Soviet Union, under the terms of a ukase that the patriarch of Moscow, Tikhon, had issued in 1920. During World War II the headquarters of this body moved to Munich, Germany; in 1950 it went to New York.

From 1927 to 1935/1936 and again from 1946 on, the North American fraction of the Russian Orthodox Church Outside of Russia and the Russian Orthodox Greek Catholic Church of America (the Metropolia) existed as separate ecclesiastical entities, divided by their respective attitudes toward the patriarch of Moscow. The Russian Orthodox Church Outside of Russia refuses to recognize the Patriarchate of Moscow in any way on the ground that the Soviet government completely controls the patriarchate.

The headquarters of the Russian Orthodox Church Outside of Russia are at 75 East 93 Street, New York, New York. Five dioceses in the United States count 116 churches, missions, and monasteries with a total membership of 73,000 in sixteen states and the District of Columbia. New York, California, and New Jersey have the largest number of churches. In Canada one diocese administers twenty-two churches, missions, and monasteries in five provinces, with a total membership of 13,000.[7]

In 1958 a group of clergy and faithful withdrew from the Romanian Orthodox Missionary Episcopate in America and placed themselves under the jurisdiction of the Russian Orthodox Church Outside of Russia, which erected the Western Hemisphere Romanian Orthodox Missionary Episcopate of Canada for them. Similarly, a group of clergy and faithful withdrew in 1963 from the Bulgarian Eastern Orthodox Church on this continent and placed themselves under the Russian Orthodox Church Outside of Russia. The latter body consecrated the leader of the withdrawing group to the episcopate and erected the Diocese of the United States of America and Canada of the Bulgarian Eastern Orthodox Church for him and his followers.

Since 1965 ten priests of the Greek Orthodox Archdiocese of North and South America and of the two Syrian Eastern Orthodox jurisdictions in North America have reportedly transferred their allegiance to the Russian Orthodox Church Outside of Russia, partly in protest against the ecumenical activities of the Greek and Syrian jurisdictions.[8]

In 1968 the synod of bishops of the Russian Orthodox Church Outside of Russia established a Western Rite, administered by a Western Rite Commission of two bishops and two priests. The Western Rite has parishes in Georgia, Pennsylvania, and Connecticut. Since 1969 it has published the biomonthly *Orthodoxy* in the interest of Eastern Orthodox Western Rite affairs generally.

Greek Orthodox Archdiocese of North and South America

A small colony of Greek merchants founded the first Greek Orthodox church in North America at New Orleans, Louisiana, in 1864. The extension of Greek Orthodoxy throughout the country came with the rising tide of immigration from Greece during the last decades of the nineteenth century and the first two decades of the twentieth. Six out of every ten of the present-day Greek communities and churches were firmly founded by 1920, in spite of the fact that most of the immigrants came to North America with the intention of returning to their native land.

Until 1908 the Greek Orthodox churches in North America came under the direct jurisdiction of the ecumenical patriarch at Istanbul. For the decade preceding 1918 the Holy Synod of the Church of Greece exercised jurisdiction over them, but it was unable to provide the quality of leadership or the kind of organization that the situation demanded. The first step toward improvement came when the Metropolitan Meletios, whom the ecumenical patriarch sent to North America in 1918, established a synodical council as a central source of authority for the Greek parishes and missions. When Meletios became ecumenical patriarch, one of his first official acts was to restore ecclesiastical jurisdiction over the Greek churches in North America in his own see; later that year he formed the churches and missions of North and South America into an archdiocese governed by a patriarchal exarch. The political confusion that divided Greece during the remainder of the third decade of this century was reflected in Greek-American church life. In 1930 the metropolitan of Kerkyra (Corfu), Athenagoras, became archbishop of North and South America; during the next eighteen years he succeeded in unifying the Greek communities of the New World under the control of the archdiocese. When Athenagoras became the ecumenical patriarch in 1949, Archbishop Michael (d. 1958), a brilliant scholar and linguist, succeeded him; during his pontificate the Greek Orthodox Archdiocese of North and South America joined the National Council of the Churches of Christ in the United States of America and the World Council of Churches. His successor, Iakovos (James), previously metropolitan of Melita and the representative of the ecumenical patriarch at the central office of the World Council of Churches at Geneva, was the first American citizen to be selected to head the Greek Orthodox Church in the Americas. The meetings of Eastern Orthodox bishops in the United States which he initiated led in 1960 to the establishment of the Standing Conference of Canonical Orthodox Bishops in the Americas.

As hemispheric exarch of the ecumenical patriarch, the Greek Orthodox archbishop of North and South America also exercises direct spiritual supervision over the American Carpatho-Russian Orthodox Greek Catholic Diocese and the Ukrainian Orthodox Church of America (Ecumenical Patriarchate), although these jurisdictions function in total independence of the Greek archdiocese and their bishops as members of the Standing Conference.

The archdiocese is organized into eleven districts, each under a bishop or archbishop. One district covers Canada and Alaska; one is for South America; another is for Central America; and eight districts cover the United States. The archdiocesan headquarters are at 10 East 79 Street, New

York, New York. The archdiocese reports 443 churches and missions in the United States and thirty-six churches and missions in Canada with an inclusive membership of 1,770,000.[9]

In addition to the jurisdictions represented in the Standing Conference, the Greek archdiocese is in communion with the Estonian Orthodox Church in North America, the Russian Orthodox Church Outside of Russia, and the Antiochian Orthodox Christian Archdiocese of New York and All North America.

Hellenic Traditionalist Orthodox Diocese of Astoria, New York

The introduction of the Gregorian (new style) calendar in place of the Julian (old style) calendar that the Interorthrodox Congress at Istanbul proposed in 1923 evoked very strong opposition in Greece. There, the groups who adhered to the Julian Calendar—the *Palaioimerologitai*, or "Old Calendarists"—broke off communion with the official church and in consequence suffered severe persecution as an illegal movement, although the Julian Calendar monasteries on Athos remained in communion with the Ecumenical Patriarch in Istanbul and the Church of Greece.

In 1952 an archimandrite of Mount Athos, Petros Astyfides, came to the United States to bring the Greek Julian Calendar immigrants together in a single jurisdiction. By 1962 he had made sufficient progress to warrant his consecration to the episcopate by two prelates of the Russian Orthodox Church Outside of Russia, Archbishop Leonty of Santiago and Bishop Serphim of Caracas. Bishop Petros is Exarch of the Traditionalist (Old Calendar) Orthodox Church of Greece. His diocese is in full communion with the Russian Orthodox Church in Exile.

Except for the difference in keeping the calendar, the Hellenic Traditionalist Orthodox Diocese of Astoria, New York, is at one with the rest of Greek Orthodoxy. The number of Greek Orthodox Christians following the Julian calendar cannot be determined since the church accepts any Orthodox laymen, whether Old Calendarist or not, though one estimate places the number at 25,000. The five churches and missions of the diocese in Michigan and New York in the United States, and in Montreal, Canada have a total of 10,000 adherents. The services in these churches and missions are in Greek.[10]

Holy Greek Orthodox Church of America

In 1961 the Reverend Theodore S. Kyritsis, St. George's Church, Port Arthur, Texas, resigned from the Greek Orthodox Archdiocese of North and South America as a result of differences with his ecclesiastical superiors, placed himself under the jurisdiction of the Hellenic Orthodox Church of America, and became pastor of St. George's Church in Memphis, Tennessee. After the Archdiocese of North and South America had deposed Kyritsis in 1962, other like-minded priests and members of their flocks associated themselves with him, among them the congregation of the downtown Church of the Holy Annunciation (Evangelismos) in Philadelphia, Pennsylvania. In September 1964, at Philadelphia, they constituted themselves an independent jurisdiction under the name the Autocephalous Greek Orthodox Church of America and elected Photios, the former metropolitan of Paphos on the island of Cyprus, as archbishop, and Theoklitos Kantaris of Salamis, bishop of the Greek Orthodox Diocese of New York and pastor of the Church of St. Nectarius in Astoria, as auxiliary. The enthronement of Photios followed in October, but he later resigned his post and was reconciled to the Greek Orthodox Archdiocese of North and South America. In 1969 archbishops Hrihoriy and Hennadios of the Ukrainian Autocephalous Church in the United States of America consecrated the Very Reverend Archimandrite Spyridon to the episcopate to provide the Holy Greek Orthodox Church of America with a bishop of its own.[11]

Kyritsis later returned to the jurisdiction of the Greek Orthodox Archdiocese of North and South America under His Eminence Archbishop Iakovos. Those who had established the independent jurisdiction incorporated it under the name Holy Greek Orthodox Church of America and later placed it under the jurisdiction of the Patriarchate of Alexandria and its exarchate in the United States. The present presiding bishop is the Most Reverend Theoklitos Heliopolis, who serves at Saint Athanasios Greek Orthodox Cathedral, 6557 S.W. 33 Street, Miami, Florida.[12]

The doctrine and practice of the Holy Greek Orthodox Church of America is identical with that of other Greek Orthodox jurisdictions, although its canons give the laity a role in the selection of its prelates and provide that the funds of the local churches are to remain under the control of the local congregation. The jurisdiction is in communion with the Serbian Orthodox Diocese in the United States of America and Canada (Libertyville, Illinois) and with the Ukrainian Autocephalous Church in the United States of America (Chicago, Illinois). It also has an Australian affiliate.

The six churches and missions in the United States that belong to the jurisdiction have an estimated 2,000 members. The Monastery of the Holy Virgin in Alaska associated itself with the Holy Greek Orthodox Church of America in 1967.

The Antiochian Orthodox Christian Archdiocese of North America

The Antiochian Orthodox Christian Archdiocese of North America is an American daughter-church of the Arabic-speaking Eastern Orthodox Patriarchate of Antioch at Damascus, Syria.[13] It came into being through two missions to Syrian and Lebanese immigrants who in Asia had been under the Syrian Orthodox patriarchate.

The Syrian mission of the Russian Orthodox Church goes back to 1892; in 1904 Archimandrite Raphael Hawaweeny (d. 1915), the overseer of the mission, became the first Eastern Orthodox bishop of any nationality to be consecrated in the United States.

The mission of the Antiochian patriarchate began in 1914 when the patriarch sent the metropolitan of Seleucia and Baalbek to the United States to found additional parishes for Antiochian Orthodox Christians.

In 1936 both missions united. In the election which followed, the majority of the American churches chose Archimandrite Anthony Bashir (1898–1966), whom the personal representative of the Antiochian patriarch consecrated in New York on April 19, 1936. In 1940 the patriarch elevated Bishop Bashir to the rank of metropolitan archbishop of New York and All North America. During his thirty-year-long pontificate his church body led all the Eastern Orthodox bodies in North America in the extension of English-language work among the faithful. In 1969 it adopted the name, the Antiochian Orthodox Church in New York and All North America.

At the time of the union of the Russian and patriarchal missions in 1936, a group of midwestern Antiochian Orthodox parishes, the membership of which consisted chiefly of immigrants from Aita, Lebanon, selected Archimandrite Samuel David (d. 1958) as their bishop. Three Russian bishops consecrated him on the same day that Anthony Bashir was consecrated. Bishop David established his see in Toledo. Relations between the two Antiochian Orthodox groups were very tense for some time. Communion was restored in 1954, when the Holy Synod granted the Toledo jurisdiction canonical recognition and elevated its bishop to the rank of metropolitan archbishop. After Metropolitan Samuel David's death in 1958 no successor was elected until 1962, when the synod chose Michael Shaheen, an American-born and American-trained priest of the Antiochian Orthodox Archdiocese of New York, and Patriarch Theodosios consecrated him as metropolitan of the Antiochian Orthodox Archdiocese of Toledo (Ohio) and Dependencies in North America.

In August 1961, by the authority of the patriarch in Damascus, Archbishop Bashir incorporated into the then Syrian Antiochian Orthodox Church the American Orthodox Church after an eight-year period of probation. This body, formally organized in 1940, consisted of three congregations of English-speaking converts to Orthodoxy.[14] The Syrian archbishop gave the head of the English-speaking group the rank of mitred archpriest in the Syrian Antiochian Orthodox Church and made him vicar-general of a new Western Rite vicariate. In addition, English-speaking priests of the Syrian Antiochian Church were authorized to use the texts of Western rites, "purified of their heterodox elements" and revised to conform to Eastern Orthodox theological standards, to furnish their churches in Western fashion (without the iconostasis, for instance), and to wear the traditional Western liturgical vestments.[15] In 1967 the Most Reverend Maurice Francis Parkin, primate of the Old Catholic Church (Philadelphia, Pennsylvania), also known as the Old Catholic Church of the West, together with three of his priests, was received into the Antiochian Orthodox Western Rite.[16] The Very Reverend W. S. Schneirla is presently administrator of the Western Rite.

In 1966 the Lebanese-born, American-trained priest Philip Saliba received consecration in Damascus as Archbishop Bashir's successor. Like Archbishop Bashir, the prelate is a member of the Standing Conference of Canonical Orthodox Bishops in the Americas.

The patriarch of Antioch recognized both the New York and the Toledo archdioceses as canonical and as directly under his jurisdiction. On August 19, 1975, the Holy Synod of the Patriarchate of Antioch and All the East united the two archdioceses into one, the Antiochian Orthodox Christian Archdiocese of North America. Metropolitan Philip of New York is now primate and Metropolitan Michael of Toledo is auxiliary archbishop. The new archdiocese comprises 105 churches with a membership of 150,000.[17] The headquarters are at 358 Mountain Road, Englewood, New Jersey.

The Ukrainian Orthodox Church of the United States of America

Tradition has St. Andrew the First-Called carry the gospel to the area about Kiev. The mission of SS. Methodius and Cyril certainly touched the Ukraine. The first Christian ruler over the Kievan state was St. Olha (Olga; d. 969), the grandmother of St. Volodymyr the Great (Vladimir; d. 1015), who accepted baptism himself around 986 and in 988 commanded the Christianization of his entire nation. In the fifteenth century part of the Ukrainian national church came under the Moscow patriarchate and the process was completed in the late seventeenth century. The Russian Revolution of 1917 and the struggle for Ukrainian independence led to a rebirth of the Ukrainian church. In the Cathedral of the Holy Wisdom in the city of Kiev in that year the Ukranian priests, deacons, and laity, after three days of fasting and after the Russian Orthodox bishops had refused to consecrate a Ukrainian hierarchy for them, declared the Ukrainian Orthodox Church autocephalous and independent of Moscow. They chose a metropolitan of their own, Vasyl Lypkyvskiy, on whom the entire body of priests laid their hands. He then with other clergy laid hands on Nicolai Bretzkiy and another priest and so the Ukrainian hierarchy was reestablished. Both Vasyl and Nicolai were among the thirty-four Ukrainian Orthodox bishops who, together with over 2,000 priests and many laypeople, met martyrdom in the communist persecution of 1921-1931.[18]

The Ukrainian Orthodox Church of the United States of America had already been organized in 1919. It consisted of Ukrainian Orthodox immigrants and of immigrants who in those parts of the Ukraine that were under non-Russian political rule had belonged to the Ruthenian Rite of the Roman Catholic Church and who had elected to return to Eastern Orthodoxy when the liberty that they had in the New World allowed them to do so.

Metropolitan Jovan (John) Theodorovich, who came to the United States in 1924, had been consecrated to the episcopate in 1921 at Kiev by Metropolitan Vasyl and Bishop Nicolai. Some other Eastern Orthodox prelates in the United States—including the members of the Standing Conference of Canonical Orthodox Bishops of the Americas—withheld recognition from the Ukrainian Orthodox Church of the United States of America on the ground that Metropolitan John did not have authentic episcopal orders. To regularize his status, Metropolitan John submitted to reconsecration in 1949 at the hands of the late Archbishop Christopher Pentapolis and Archbishop Mstyslaw S. Skrypnyk, then president of the consistory and now metropolitan of the Ukrainian Orthodox Church in the United States of America. In 1962 Metropolitan John forbade his clergy to participate in any sacred rite with priests subject to prelates belonging to the Standing Conference of Canonical Orthodox Bishops in the Americas.

The Ukrainian Orthodox Church in the United States of America is in full communion with the Ukrainian Greek-Orthodox Church in Canada and it has maintained cordial relations with the Serbian Orthodox Diocese of the United States of America and Canada headed by Bishop Dionisije.

The faith and practice of the Ukrainian Orthodox Church in the United States of America are identical with the faith and practice of other Eastern Orthodox Christians, except that the Ukrainians adhere more strictly than some other Eastern Orthodox Christians to the rule that the only music permissible in the church is vocal and that instrumental music must not be employed.

Currently the jurisdiction reports 105 churches in twenty-two states and the District of Columbia, with an inclusive membership of 100,000. The sobor (assembly) meets every three years. The address of the headquarters is South Bound Brook, New Jersey.

The Ukrainian Greek-Orthodox Church in Canada

The Ukrainian Greek-Orthodox Church in Canada became self-governing in 1918. Canada reportedly has about 500,000 citizens of Ukrainian extraction. The Ukrainian Greek-Orthodox Church in Canada originally drew its membership both from Eastern Orthodox immigrants and from those who in the Ukraine had been Ruthenian Rite Roman Catholics and who returned to Orthodoxy in large numbers in the New World. The headquarters are at 7 St. John's Avenue, Winnipeg, Manitoba. The Canadian hierarchy administers 300 local congregations and missions, with an overall membership estimated at 150,000. The future clergy of the church are trained at St. Andrew's Theological College, Winnipeg, on the campus of the University of Manitoba. The only Ukrainian Orthodox institution of its kind in the world, the college also trains candidates for the Ukrainian Greek-Orthodox priesthood in the United States, Great Britain, and Western Europe. In North America the Canadian church is in communion with the

Ukrainian Orthodox Church of the United States of America.[19] The Very Reverend D. Luchak is chairperson of the church's Presidium.

The Ukrainian Orthodox Church of America (Ecumenical Patriarchate)

The Ukrainian Orthodox Church of America (Ecumenical Patriarchate), whose head is a member of the Standing Conference of Canonical Orthodox Bishops, was organized in 1928. The following year the body elected Joseph A. Zuk, a former Ruthenian Rite Roman Catholic priest who had converted to Eastern Orthodoxy, as administrator. In 1932 he was consecrated the first bishop. After his death in 1934 he was succeeded by Metropolitan-Primate Bohdan T. Shpilka, who was consecrated by order of the ecumenical patriarch in Istanbul in 1937 and who presided over the affairs of the church until November 1965. Under Metropolitan Bohdan's administration, the Ukrainian Orthodox Church of America provided episcopal supervision for a number of Orthodox communities in America with constituencies too small in number to warrant the erection of their own dioceses, among them the American Orthodox Finnish Mission (now independent) and the Santa Iglesia Católica Apostólica Ortodoxa de Puerto Rico. The church recruited a number of energetic young clergymen, some of whom work full-time at secular occupations in order to support themselves. The death of Metropolitan Bohdan brought about a serious crisis in the church body. In September 1965 the Very Reverend Demetrius Sawka published a document in which Metropolitan Bohdan designated him as administrator of the Ukrainian Orthodox Church of America, but the legality of the appointment was challenged after the death of the primate. In December 1966 Andrei Kuschak was named bishop. In the interim the church suffered severe attrition. The *sobor* (assembly) meets on call. The jurisdiction reports twenty-three churches and missions in the United States and Canada with a total membership of 30,000.[20]

La Santa Iglesia Católica Apostólica Ortodoxa de Puerto Rico

Eastern Orthodoxy has been represented in Puerto Rico since 1962 by La Santa Católica Apostólica Ortodoxa de Puerto Rico, headed by a Very Reverend Hegumen and Legate under the jurisdiction and supervision of the Ukrainian Orthodox Church of America. Two active missions (Rio Piedras and Sabana Llana) have attracted 300 adherents. The church uses the Byzantine (Greek) Rite in the Spanish language.[21]

The Ukrainian Autocephalous Orthodox Church in the United States of America

In spite of thirteen years of bitter communist persecution from 1923 to 1936, the ancient faith lived on in the hearts of the Ukrainian people, and when the opportunity presented itself during World War II a revival of

Ukrainian Orthodoxy took place. Among those chosen for consecration to the episcopate was Hrihoriy (Gregory) Osiychuk. Two duly consecrated bishops of the Ukrainian Orthodox Autocephalous Church, Nicanor Abramovych, now the metropolitan of the Ukrainian Orthodox Autocephalous Church in Europe and Australia with his seat in Karlsruhe, Germany, and the late Ihor (Igor) Huba, who died in 1966 in New York as one of the two bishops of the Ukrainian Autocephalic Orthodox Church in Exile, made their way from the western Ukraine to Kiev in 1942 and consecrated Hrihoriy. In 1945 the Union of Soviet Socialist Republics reestablished its power over the Ukraine and once more began to persecute the Ukrainian Autocephalous Church. Hrihoriy remained a bishop of the Ukrainian Autocephalic Orthodox Church in Exile until 1947, when he withdrew from the council of the church held at Aschaffenburg, Germany, and helped to organize the so-called Sobornopravanaya ("council-ruled") Church, which claims to be the only true successor of the Kiev autocephaly of 1921. The conflict was composed in 1955 and intercommunion was reestablished. All the priests of the Sobornopravnaya Church finally left Western Europe.

Hrihoriy arrived in the United States in 1950 and established the archdiocesan headquarters in Chicago, Illinois. There are twenty-three churches and missions in the United States and eleven in England, as well as scattered congregations in Brazil, Argentina, and Australia. The total membership in the United States is estimated at about 5,000.

The services of the church are in Ukrainian. A Western Rite administration, the parishes of which celebrate the liturgy "according to contemporary norms and culture," has its headquarters in Cleveland, Ohio. An effort in the early 1960s to federate the Ukrainian Autocephalous Orthodox Church, the Ukrainian Orthodox Church of America, and the [Holy] Ukrainian Autocephalic Church in Exile, with each retaining its own name, charter, bylaws, and traditions, failed.[22]

The Ukrainian Autocephalous Church in the United States of America maintains fellowship with the Serbian Orthodox Diocese of the United States and Canada, and Archbishop Hrihoriy participates in the latter body's consecrations. In 1969 he and Archbishop Hennandios consecrated a bishop for the Holy Greek Orthodox Church of America, a jurisdiction composed of clergy and laypeople who had withdrawn from the Greek Orthodox Archdiocese of North and South America.

[Holy] Ukrainian Autocephalic Orthodox Church in Exile

Refugee bishops, clergy, and laypeople who fled from the Ukraine after its recovery by the Soviet Union at the end of World War II organized the [Holy] Ukrainian Autocephalic Orthodox Church in Exile in 1954. It traces its line of episcopal succession to the Orthodox Church of Poland, which the Ecumenical Patriarch in Istanbul recognized as autonomous and autocephalous in a special constitution (*tomos*) in 1924.

The headquarters of the [Holy] Ukrainian Autocephalic Orthodox Church in Exile are at the Cathedral of the Holy Trinity, 185 South Fifth Street, Brooklyn, New York. It has ten churches and missions in the United States with a total membership of 3,100, and two in Canada with a total membership of 200. The churches use Ukrainian almost exclusively in their worship.

The Byelorussian Autocephalic Orthodox Church

Byelorussia, or White Russia, is the much-fought-over territory that lies between Poland on the west, Lithuania on the north, the Ukraine on the south, and Muscovite Russia on the east. Since 1291 when Byelorussian Orthodoxy achieved autonomy for the first time with the establishment of the metropolitical see of Novogrudok (ratified in 1316 by Ecumenical Patriarch John XIII Glykys), its history has been one of alternating periods of independence and of subjection to an alien hierarchy. The two eras during which the Byelorussian Orthodox Church was autocephalous for the longest periods were from 1415 to 1596 (when, under Metropolitan Camblak, Byelorussian Orthodoxy achieved autonomy for the second time) and from the reestablishment of the Byelorussian hierarchy by Ecumenical Patriarch Theophilos in 1620 to the final absorption of Byelorussia into Russia in 1795. Following the communist takeover after World War I, the First Council of Minsk proclaimed the Byelorussian Orthodox Church under Metropolitan Melchizedek autocephalous in 1925, but in 1927 Soviet authorities deported the bishops to Siberia and by 1930 the short-lived independence of the church had come to an abrupt end. During the German invasion of Byelorussia in World War II, the Second Council of Minsk once more proclaimed the autonomy of the Byelorussian Orthodox Church in 1942. This phase ended with the submission of Metropolitan Pancieleimon (Pantaleimon) to the Russian Church in 1946. In 1948 refugee Byelorussian bishops gathered in Constance, Germany, and proclaimed the Byelorussian Autocephalic Church in Exile, with Archbishop Sergei (Siarhiey) Okhotsenko as its primate. In 1950 the first Byelorussian Orthodox community in the United States was organized; in 1951 Bishop Vasili Tamashchyk, whom Sergei had consecrated in Germany in 1949, became prelate of the diocese of Europe and North (and South) America, while Sergei retained jurisdiction of the diocese of Australia. In 1958 Sergei elevated Vasili to the rank of archbishop.

In 1968 internal tensions within the North American part of Vasili's jurisdiction and the efforts of some within the church to bring it into union with the Roman Catholic Church led Sergei to divide the United States and Canada into three independent eparchies. Archbishop Vasili retained responsibility for New York and New Jersey, while Sergei, assisted by a Ukrainian prelate, consecrated Michael Matsukyevich of Toronto as titular bishop of Polacak for the Canadian eparchy and Alexander Kryt of Cleveland (under the name of Andrey) as titular bishop of Grodno and Navahradak (Novogrudok) for the midwestern eparchy.[23] The three North American prelates and Metropolitan Sergei form the church's Holy Synod, although some tensions continue to exist among them.

Except for the nationalistic stress on Byelorussian traditions and the uniform use of Old Slavic in its services, the faith and worship of the Byelorussian Autocephalic Orthodox Church is like that of other branches of Eastern Orthodoxy.

The archdiocesan headquarters are at 401 Atlantic Avenue, Brooklyn, New York. Several years ago there were eight parishes and missions in New Jersey (New Brunswick), Ohio (Cleveland), New York (Brooklyn), Michigan (Detroit), Illinois (Chicago and Rockford), and Canada (Toronto), with a total membership of about 2,000.[24] Recent repeated efforts to gather information from the archdiocese have been unsuccessful.

Byelorussian Orthodox Parishes under the Jurisdiction of the Ecumenical Patriarch

Among the Byelorussian refugees from the communist terror of 1945 was a small group that found temporary asylum in Regensburg, Germany. Here they organized the Church of St. Evfrasinia (Euphrosyne) of Polotsk.[25] When they later moved to Michelsdorf and Bucknang within Germany and finally, in 1951, to South River, New Jersey, they took their church with them. Under the leadership of the Very Reverend Protopresbyter Nikolay Lapitzki, their pastor, they placed themselves under the jurisdiction of the ecumenical patriarch in Istanbul, who exercises his episcopal oversight over them through his North American exarch, the Greek Orthodox archbishop of North and South America. Two other Byelorussian Orthodox parishes, one in Toronto, Ontario, the other in Chicago, similarly placed themselves under the ecumenical patriarch in 1951 and 1958, respectively. A fourth congregation, in New York City, initiated services in 1969. The pastor of the South River parish provides administrative liaison between the four churches and Archbishop Iakovos. The total membership of the four parishes is estimated at 4,500.[26]

The American Carpatho-Russian Orthodox Greek Catholic Diocese

The Union of Brest-Litovsk in 1596 established the Roman Catholic Ruthenian Rite to provide religious ministrations for the forcibly converted populations of Eastern Europe that had passed from Russian to Polish-Lithuanian and Hungarian political control. In 1646 the union succeeded in recruiting its first priests in Carpatho-Russia. While the Ruthenian Rite preserved most of the forms of Eastern Orthodoxy, the treatment that the Latin Rite Roman Catholic rulers accorded their Ruthenian Rite subjects created lasting resentment.

Carpatho-Russian immigrants of the Ruthenian Rite came to the United States in growing numbers during the last two decades of the nineteenth century and the Roman Catholic Church created parishes and ultimately dioceses for them. At the same time it carried on an energetic program of increasing Latinization. A particularly sore point—although not the only one—was the question of married priests. A movement back to Eastern Orthodoxy had begun among Oriental Rite Roman Catholic immigrants as early as 1891. The increasing restrictions which the American Roman Catholic hierarchy imposed on the utilization of married priests—whose wives and children continually affronted Latin Rite Roman Catholics trained to expect a celibate clergy—greatly accelerated the movement back to Eastern Orthodoxy among the immigrants.

In 1936 some forty seceding Ruthenian Rite parishes elected the Right Reverend Orestes P. Chornock of Bridgeport, Connecticut, to head their movement. The next year they chose him as their bishop-elect and appealed for canonical recognition to the ecumenical patriarch in Istanbul. In 1938 the latter consecrated Chornock and named him bishop of the Carpatho-Russian Orthodox Diocese, with headquarters at Johnstown, Pennsylvania. In 1966 the ecumenical patriarch elevated Chornock to the dignity of metropolitan and later in the year gave him an assistant bishop in the person of another convert, the former chancellor of the Roman Catholic Byzantine Rite Diocese of Pittsburgh, John R. Martin.

The Carpatho-Russian Diocese functions directly under the ecumenical patriarch and is wholly independent of other Eastern Orthodox jurisdictions in North America; its bishop is canonically responsible for all phases of the spiritual supervision and administration of the diocese. As the exarch of the ecumenical patriarch in the Americas, the archbishop of the Greek Orthodox Archdiocese of North and South America canonically intercedes for the diocese when it seeks the appointment of a new bishop; he is also entrusted by the ecumenical patriarch with the new bishop's consecration.

The American Carpatho-Russian Orthodox Greek Catholic Diocese has seventy churches with an estimated membership of 100,000.[27] The diocese jealously safeguards its traditional Eastern Orthodox faith and practice, even though it still reveals some traces of its past association with the Roman Catholic Church, such as the retention of the title of monsignor for proto-priests.

The Holy Orthodox Church in America
(Eastern Catholic and Apostolic)

The Holy Orthodox Church in America, founded and incorporated in 1934, traces its line of episcopal succession back to the Russian Orthodox Church and to its consecration in 1927 of Aftimios Ofeish as archbishop of an autocephalous North American Pan-Orthodox Church, a position from which he was deposed following his marriage in 1933. In 1932 Aftimios, assisted by Bishops Sophronios Beshara and Joseph A. Zuk of the Ukrainian Orthodox Church of America, consecrated Ignatius William Albert Nichols (d. 1946), a former Protestant Episcopal clergyman, to the episcopate. Nichols, assisted by Bishop Ambrose Raines, in turn consecrated George Winslow Plummer (d. 1944), a former Roman Catholic priest and the founder of the Holy Orthodox Church in America, in 1934. In 1936, Plummer and Nichols consecrated Theodotus Stanislaus De Witow (Witowski) as archbishop-primate.

The Holy Orthodox Church describes its rite, faith, and traditions as rooted in the Eastern Orthodox community. It proposes to interpret the Bible and the holy mysteries under the guidance of the Holy Spirit in terms of the spiritual concepts and truths that the spiritually awakened men of the past received or rediscovered. Over against the claims of the bishop of Rome, it recognizes Christ as the only head of the church. It lays great stress on spiritual healing, with prayers for the sick and afflicted who desire such intercessions at both regular and special services.[28]

The archbishop-primate participated in the consecration of the first bishop of the American Orthodox Catholic Church, Walter (Vladimir) Propheta, and his subsequent elevation to archbishop.

The Holy Orthodox Church of America has its headquarters at 321 West 101 Street, New York. Its churches have been reduced from four to the one church in New York City as a result of the death of its archbishop and its priests. The Divine Liturgy is celebrated once a month by a visiting bishop.[29]

Eastern Orthodox Catholic Church in America

In 1905 the Russian archbishop of America, Tikhon, proposed to the Holy Synod of Russia the formation in America of "an entire exarchate of national Orthodox churches with their own bishops," each of whom was to be independent in his own field of work. As the first step in this program, Tikhon consecrated Raphael Hawaweeny to head the Syrian Orthodox mission. Raphael's successor was Aftimios Ofeish, a hieromonk whom Tikhon's successor, Evdokim, assisted by Alexander Nemolovsky, bishop of Canada and the Aleutian Islands, and Stephen Dzubai, bishop of Pittsburgh, consecrated in New York on April 30, 1917. In 1927 Platon Rozhdestvensky, archbishop of the Russian American Metropolia, presumably with the concurrence of the patriarchal *locum tenens* in Moscow, Sergei, approved the planned formation of the North American Synod of the Holy Eastern Orthodox Catholic and Apostolic Church in North America, with Aftimios as bishop of Brooklyn. Platon withdrew his support, however; the other bishops refused to recognize the letters of peace of Aftimios; the ecumenical patriarch declared Aftimios in schism. When Aftimios married in 1933 the Russian bishops deposed him and he retired. Thereupon Bishop

Sophronios Beshara, whom Aftimios had consecrated in 1932, proceeded with the original synodal plan. Upon the death of Sophronios, John Chrysostom More-Moreno, whom Sophronios and Archbishop-Exarch Benjamin had consecrated in 1933, established the Eastern Orthodox Catholic Church in America, with himself as archbishop-president.

In principle the local churches of the Eastern Orthodox Catholic Church in America retain ownership of their local property and use the English language exclusively in worship and religious education. In line with Eastern Orthodox custom, the body has adapted the inherited liturgical practices of Eastern Orthodoxy to the requirements of the American scene. It publishes the *American Review of Eastern Orthodoxy*. Its headquarters are in Fern Park, Florida, where it maintains the Three Hierarchs Seminary.[30] Three churches have a total membership of 327.

Estonian Orthodox Church in Exile

The Estonian Orthodox Church emerged as a national church after Estonia's War of Liberation in 1920. Two years later it seceded from the Patriarchate of Moscow and in 1923 the ecumenical patriarch in Istanbul received the Estonian Orthodox Church as an autonomous church directly subordinate to him. In 1940 the Union of Soviet Socialist Republics occupied Estonia and the following year the Estonian Church was compelled to affiliate with Moscow once more. A few months later the German occupation of Estonia gave the Estonian Orthodox metropolitan, Archbishop Aleksander of Tallinn (1872–1953), another opportunity to secede from Moscow and attach the Estonian Church to the ecumenical patriarch. When the Union of Soviet Socialist Republics reoccupied Estonia in 1944, Aleksander fled to Sweden, where he reorganized his fellow exiles as the Estonian Orthodox Church in Exile. The Estonian Orthodox population that remained in Estonia was again subordinated to the Moscow patriarchate in 1945 and remains so. From 1953 to 1956, when Archpriest Jüri Välbe (1880–1961) was consecrated to head the Estonian Orthodox Church in Exile with the title of bishop of Ravenna, Archbishop Athenagoras of London served as *locum tenens*. With Välbe's consecration the ecumenical patriarch placed the Estonian Church in Exile under the oversight of the West and Central European Exarchate. Upon Välbe's death, Athenagoras again became *locum tenens*.

In 1949 the Very Reverend Sergius Samon established the first congregation of the Estonian Church in Exile in North America at Los Angeles. Later other congregations were established in San Francisco, Chicago, and New York, as well as in Toronto, Montreal, and Vancouver, Canada. The North American headquarters of the church are at Los Angeles, California. The total number of Estonian Orthodox Christians in the United States and Canada is estimated at about 3,400.[31]

American Finnish Orthodox Mission

In 1955 the Very Reverend Denis W. Ericson founded the only canonical Finnish Orthodox mission in the United States at Lansing, Michigan. It serves a scattered membership of more than 700 baptized persons. When feasible, the administrator conducts services in other communities. English is the language of all services.

Like the Eastern Orthodox Church of Finland, the mission follows the Gregorian calendar for all holy days, including Easter. Otherwise it conforms fully to the conventional Eastern Orthodox patterns of teaching and worship. The primate of the Ukrainian Orthodox Church of America (Ecumenical Patriarchate) provided the mission with episcopal oversight until 1968, when the mission withdrew from the Ukrainian body and became independent.[32]

The Bulgarian Eastern Orthodox Church
(Diocese of North and South America and Australia)

The oldest Bulgarian Orthodox church in North America, located at Madison, Illinois, dates back to 1907. With the increasing immigration of Bulgarians, chiefly from Macedonia, to the New World, the Holy Synod in Sofia established a Bulgarian Orthodox mission in North America to care for the spiritual and cultural needs of these immigrants. In 1938 the Holy Synod erected a bishopric in New York and sent Bishop Andrey Velichky to administer it. When the United States entered World War II, Bishop Andrey, as an enemy alien, returned to Bulgaria. In 1942 the Holy Synod in Sofia sent him to the Ecumenical Patriarchate in Istanbul to begin the negotiations that led in 1945 to the healing of the schism that had existed between the Bulgarian Orthodox Church and the ecumenical patriarch ever since 1872. The ecumenical patriarch also elevated the Bulgarian Orthodox diocese in the New World to the status of a Metropolia, with jurisdiction over all the Bulgarian Orthodox faithful in the Americas and in Australia.

Archbishop Andrey returned to the United States in 1945. In 1947 the Bulgarian Eastern Orthodox Diocese of America, Canada, and Australia was incorporated under the laws of the State of New York and the constitutional assembly proceeded to elect Archbishop Andrey as its prelate, whereupon the Holy Synod declared his election null and void and the exarch of Bulgaria dismissed Archbishop Andrey from all his duties. Andrey and the diocese ignored the order. In 1962 the Holy Synod in Sofia recognized the American-Australian Metropolia and canonically proclaimed Andrey as metropolitan. In 1963 Archbishop Andrey and the Bulgarian metropolitan of Nevrokop, Archbishop Peiman, undertook a joint visitation of the Bulgarian parishes in North America. In 1972 the Holy Synod divided the church into the New York and Akron dioceses.

The church lists eighteen churches and missions in the United States and one in Canada with an estimated total membership of 105,000. Bishop Joseph is its present metropolitan. Headquarters are at 312 West 101 Street, New York, New York.

The Bulgarian Eastern Orthodox Church
(Diocese of the United States of America and Canada)

The constitutional assembly of 1947 that elected Archbishop Andrey as bishop of the Bulgarian Orthodox Diocese of America, Canada, and Australia also declared: "We are an inseparable part of the whole Bulgarian Eastern Orthodox Church, but as long as a Communist regime exists there in Bulgaria, we will not accept any orders from the Holy Synod, but will remain only in spiritual ties." In March 1963 at a diocesan assembly held at Detroit, Michigan, representatives of eighteen churches and missions charged Archbishop Andrey with violating the quoted ruling of 1947, renounced his authority over them as prelate, and elected Archimandrite Kyrill Yonchev of Oregon (a suburb of Toledo, Ohio) as their new bishop. The Holy Synod of the Orthodox Church Outside of Russia took the churches and missions represented at the assembly under its canonical protection, and in August 1964 Archimandrite Yonchev was consecrated at the Russian Orthodox Monastery of the Holy Trinity, Jordanville, New York, and installed as prelate of the Bulgarian Orthodox Diocese in the United States of America and Canada.

The diocese describes as its fundamental guideposts "the Holy Scriptures, the rules and precepts of the Apostles [that is, the Apostolic Canons], the canons and the decisions of the ecumenical and regional councils, the exarchate constitution of the Bulgarian Eastern Orthodox Church" and its own 1964 diocesan constitution. The constitution declares that "as long as the supreme governing board (the Holy Synod) of the Bulgarian Eastern Orthodox Church is controlled by the Communist government of Bulgaria, and is incapacitated on that account to make free decisions, the Bulgarian Eastern Orthodox Church, Diocese of the United States of America and Canada, shall not accept any administrative orders and directions from there." The diocese lays claim to all the structures, cemeteries, and religious organizations of the original Bulgarian-Macedonian Orthodox Mission in America and of the Bulgarian Orthodox Diocese in America of 1938. It acknowledges the contributions made "by the Bulgarians from Macedonia." It deems it the duty of its members "to profess their faith in the Lord freely and to pray to Him in their own mother tongue, the Bulgarian language."[33]

The headquarters are at 519 Brynhaven Drive, Oregon, Ohio. The jurisdiction comprises twenty-one churches and missions in the United States and five in Canada, with an estimated total membership of 12,925. There are also adherents in Western Europe.[34]

The Serbian Orthodox Community in America

The Serbian Orthodox Church in America grew out of the immigration from the Balkans that began around 1890 and that led to the founding of parishes, in 1893–1894, in Jackson, California; Galveston, Texas; and McKeesport, Pennsylvania. The Russian Orthodox Church established a Serbian Orthodox Diocese in American and Canada in 1917, with Archimandrite Mardarije Uskokovich as administrator. In 1921 the reestablished Serbian Holy Synod in Belgrade accepted jurisdiction over the North American diocese, and in 1926 the Serbian patriarch consecrated Archimandrite Mardarije as bishop, with his seat at St. Sava's Monastery—named after the thirteenth-century first archbishop of the independent Serbian church—in Libertyville, Illinois.

Serbian Orthodox Church in the United States of America and Canada

With the continuing growth in the number of parishes, both Bishop Dionisije Milivojevich, who headed the diocese from 1940 on, and the diocesan assemblies appealed several times to the Serbian patriarch and the Holy Synod in Belgrade to elevate the North American diocese to a metropolitanate and to elect two or three auxiliary bishops. Instead, the church authorities in Belgrade in 1963 abolished the North American diocese and in its place erected three new dioceses—the Diocese of the Eastern United States and Canada (of which Cleveland ultimately became the see city), the Diocese of the Mid-West United States (with Chicago as see city), and the Diocese of the Western United States (with Los Angeles, actually suburban Alhambra, as its see city.)[35] A schism resulted. The three dioceses that form the Serbian Orthodox Church in the United States of America and Canada have a common constitution, a common interdiocesan church assembly, a common church council, a central board of religious education, and a bishops' council consisting of the three diocesan ordinaries. Although it is administratively self-governing, the Serbian Orthodox Church in the United States of America and Canada maintains hierarchial and spiritual ties with the Serbian Orthodox patriarch and Holy Synod in Yugoslavia.[36] The bishop of the Mid-West United States diocese represents the Serbian Orthodox Church in the United States and Canada in the Standing Conference of Canonical Orthodox Bishops in the Americas. The three American dioceses list seventy-four churches in the United States and Canada, with an estimated total of 50,000 members. The national headquarters are at 5701 North Redwood Drive, Chicago, Illinois.

Serbian Orthodox Diocese in the United States of America and Canada

In the process of reorganizing the American diocese, the Holy Synod of Belgrade summarily suspended Bishop Dionisije for alleged misconduct. He refused to accept both the reorganization and his own suspension. Supporters rallied around him, and delegates from a majority of the Serbian churches and missions all over the United States and Canada assembled in November 1963 in what they described as a continued session of the Tenth Church-National Assembly of the Serbian Orthodox Diocese in the United States and Canada. The assembly proclaimed the North American diocese "completely autonomous" under the continuing leadership of Bishop Dionisije as long as "Yugoslavia is in the Communist slavery."[37]

Suits at law resulted to test the rights of both bodies to the possession of the property of the church. The Supreme Court of Illinois found that Bishop Dionisije had been improperly removed and defrocked by the Holy Synod of Belgrade and that the mother church's reorganization of the diocese was invalid. However, on appeal the United States Supreme Court in June 1976 reversed the Illinois court's decision, asserting that when hierarchical religious organizations create tribunals for adjudicating disputes over internal discipline and government, civil courts must accept the tribunals' decisions as binding and may not interpose their own judgment.[38]

Bishop Dionisije had led his followers into communion with the Ukrainian Orthodox Church of the United States of America and the Autocephalous Greek Orthodox Church of America.[39] In 1975 the Serbian Orthodox Diocese placed itself under the jurisdiction of the Patriarchate of Alexandria, as His Beatitude Nicholas VI, patriarch of Alexandria, recognized Serbian Bishop Ireney, assistant to Bishop Dionisije, as a canonical hierarch of Eastern Orthodoxy.[40] Bishop Dionisije claims for his jurisdiction fifty-five churches and missions in the United States and Canada with a total membership of 75,000.[41] The headquarters of the diocese are at St. Sava's Monastery, Libertyville, Illinois.

Macedonian Orthodox Churches, Diocese Of America, Canada, and Australia

Estimates place the number of North Americans of Macedonian background and Eastern Orthodox faith at 150,000. In the past these Macedonians have tended to gravitate to Bulgarian Eastern Orthodox parishes. Following World War II, the Serbian patriarch German revived the ancient Macedonian archdiocese of Ohrid, combined it with the metropolitanate of Skoplje, and proclaimed himself patriarch of Serbia and Macedonia. In 1960 he began a mission among the Macedonians of North America with the establishment of the Macedonian Orthodox Church of SS. Peter and Paul in Gary, Indiana. In 1963, at the invitation of the parish, Archbishop Dositei of Ohrid came and consecrated the parish's first church building. In 1967 Dositei was proclaimed metropolitan of the Macedonian Orthodox Church. Other Macedonian Orthodox churches are located in Columbus, Ohio; Syracuse, New York; and Toronto, Canada. Their total membership in North America is approximately 500 families. All function under the Archbishopric of Ohrid and Macedonia, Skoplje, Yugoslavia, with the Most Reverend Kiril as bishop of America, Canada, and Australia. Plans call for the early establishment of additional missions in a number of other North American cities.[42]

The Romanian Orthodox Community

The first Romanian Orthodox parishes in Canada came into being in 1901, the first parish in the United States in 1904. Following a number of unsuccessful attempts over a period of more than twenty years to secure a diocese for the Romanian Orthodox population of the Western hemisphere, the Romanian Orthodox patriarch in Bucharest approved the establishment of the Romanian Orthodox Missionary Episcopate in America in 1930. The first bishop, Policarp Morusca, arrived from Romania in 1935. In 1939, while he was back in Romania attending the meeting of the Holy Synod, World War II broke out and he was never able to return to his see. In 1947 the Romanian Orthodox Church Congress rejected Bucharest's nominee to replace Bishop Policarp, Antim Nica, and decreed full administrative autonomy for the diocese. The next few years saw a schism develop.

The Romanian Orthodox Missionary Episcopate in America

A group of priests and laymen, assembled in Detroit in 1950 as the Romanian Orthodox Missionary Episcopate in America, chose an Akron priest, Andrei Moldovan, as its bishop-elect and the Holy Synod in Romania proceeded to elevate him to the episcopal dignity the same year. The vacancy that followed his death in 1963 was filled in 1966 when the diocesan assembly elected Victorin Ursache, a theological professor at St. Tikhon's Seminary in South Canaan, Pennsylvania, as bishop. The Greek archbishop of North and South America, assisted by two archbishops of the Patriarchate of Jerusalem, consecrated him in August 1966 in the Romanian cathedral at Windsor; later in the same month the representative of the Romanian Orthodox Synod enthroned him in the Detroit cathedral of the diocese. The act of enthronement confirmed the autonomous status of the diocese while maintaining canonical and dogmatic ties with the Romanian mother church. Victorin now has the rank of archbishop and is a member of the Standing Conference of Orthodox Canonical Bishops in America. His headquarters are at 19959 Riopelle Street, Detroit, Michigan, and his authority extends to twelve churches and missions in nine states, nineteen churches and missions in five Canadian provinces, one parish in Venezuela, and three parishes in Australia. The overall membership of the diocese is estimated at 35,000.[43]

The Romanian Orthodox Episcopate of America

In 1951 the Church Congress, representing a majority of the parishes of the North American Romanian Orthodox community, formally rejected

Andrei Moldovan as its bishop and severed all relations with the church authorities in Romania.[44] Thereupon it elected a former concentration-camp inmate and displaced-person lay publicist and theologian, Viorel Trifa, to take episcopal oversight of the diocese as the vicar of Bishop Policarp, who had been in enforced retirement in Romania since 1948. At his consecration by three prelates of the Ukrainian Orthodox Church of the United States of America in 1952 the bishop vicar took the name of Valerian. A series of court decisions between 1952 and 1960 confirmed the right of the episcopate to elect its own bishops. Valerian's episcopate has been a period of recovery and reconstruction, marked by the increasing use of English in both worship and religious education. In addition to the five North American deaneries, four in the United States and one in Canada—comprising forty-four churches and missions with an estimated 50,000 communicants—his jurisdiction includes parishes in South America, Australia, and Europe. Bishop Policarp died in 1958, and in 1960 the diocese, convinced that the future of Orthodoxy in North America depended on close relations among the various Orthodox bodies, placed itself under the canonical jurisdiction of the Russian Orthodox Greek Catholic Church of America, but without sacrificing its administrative autonomy, and Valerian received conditional reconsecration as bishop of Detroit and Michigan at the hands of the late Metropolitan Leonty and two of his archbishops. He has since been elevated to the rank of archbishop. Headquarters of the diocese are at 2522 Grey Tower Road, Jackson, Michigan. The Church Congress, which meets every three years, elects the Episcopate Council of eight lay members and four clergymen, presided over by the bishop, to serve as executive organ of the Congress and to resolve all administrative problems.

Western Hemisphere Romanian Orthodox Missionary Episcopate of Canada

In 1958 a group of Romanian Orthodox priests and laypeople withdrew from the Romanian Orthodox Missionary Episcopate in America and placed themselves under the jurisdiction of the Russian Orthodox Church Outside of Russia, which erected the Western Hemisphere Romanian Orthodox Missionary Episcopate of Canada for them.[45] The residence and office of the bishop, the Right Reverend Teofil Ionescu, for many years pastor of the Romanian Orthodox Church of the Holy Archangels in Paris, are in Detroit, Michigan, but the cathedral, St. George's, is in Windsor, Ontario. The jurisdiction has two centers in the United States and four in the Canadian provinces of Ontario and Quebec. The total membership is estimated at 2,150.[46]

The Albanian Orthodox Archdiocese in America

The Albanian Orthodox Archdiocese in America traces its beginnings to 1908, when the Russian archbishop of North America, Platon Rozhdestvensky, ordained Fan (Theophan) Stylian Noli to the priesthood and authorized him to conduct services in the Albanian language. To this end Noli translated the Divine Liturgy of Eastern Orthodoxy from the Greek into the language of his ancestors and began using it in his ministry to the Albanian immigrants of Boston.[47] In 1918 he became administrator of the Albanian Orthodox Church in America and the next year was elected acting bishop. The chaotic Orthodox ecclesiastical situation in the United States at the time delayed his consecration. With the emancipation of Albania in 1920, Noli was drawn into politics and served as a representative in the Albanian parliament from 1921 to 1924. Always a churchman in spite of his status as a lawmaker, he participated in 1923 in a synod that declared the Orthodox Church of Albania autocephalous and was himself chosen to head the church under the ancient title of metropolitan of Durazzo, Gora, and Shapata, primate and exarch of All Illyria, of the Western Sea, and of All Albania. His plans to devote himself wholly to his ecclesiastical functions were frustrated by the outbreak of a popular revolution against the regime of Armed Zog. Noli joined the rebels and when they drove Zog out in June of 1924, the archbishop became premier for six months, until Zog returned at the head of a White Russian mercenary army. Noli fled on Christmas Eve, 1924, only to spend eight years in Germany waiting impatiently for a visa that would permit his return to the United States. In 1932 he was readmitted and devoted himself for the rest of his life to the Albanian Orthodox Archdiocese in America. From 1950 on his administration concentrated increasingly on two emphases, concern for the next generation, which prompted him to promote with vigor the transition from the Albanian to the English language, and the unification of American Orthodoxy.[48] Shortly before his death in 1965 he arranged for the consecration of his successor, Stephen V. Lasko, by the Holy Synod of the Autocephalous Orthodox Church of Albania.

The archdiocesan headquarters are at 523 East Broadway, Boston, Massachusetts. Fifteen churches claim a membership estimated at 40,000.

The Albanian Orthodox Diocese of America

Late in 1949 the ecumenical patriarch in Istanbul declared that the Albanian authorities had deposed Archbishop-Metropolitan Christopher Kissi of Durazzo and Tirana, the primate of the Autocephalous Orthodox Church of Albania, contrary to Eastern Orthodox canon law and had refused canonical recognition to his then recently enthroned successor, Paisi Voditza. When the Albanian Archdiocese in America continued in communication with the new Albanian primate, a small group of clergymen and laypeople withdrew from the archdiocese the next year and petitioned the ecumenical patriarch to appoint and consecrate as their bishop Mark I. Lipa, a fellow Albanian cleric who resided in Istanbul. The ecumenical patriarch acceded to their request and consecrated their candidate as titular bishop of Lefka. Upon Bishop Lipa's arrival in Boston, the American-Albanian Orthodox Episcopacy was established in that city on December 31, 1950. It took its present name in 1956. The diocesan headquarters are at 54 Burroughs Street, Jamaica Plain, Massachusetts. The diocese consists of ten churches, with a total membership estimated at 5,150. The bishop stands directly under the ecumenical patriarch and is a member of the Standing Conference of Canonical Orthodox Bishops in the Americas.[49]

NOTES

1. Archimandrite Serafim, *The Quest for Orthodox Church Unity in America* (New York: Saints Boris and Gleb Press, 1973), pp. 78-91.
2. Pamphlet entitled *Autocephaly,* published by the Orthodox Church in America.
3. Archimandrite Serafim, *Quest for Orthodox Church Unity,* pp. 87-89.
4. Letter from the Reverend Leonid Kishovsky, assistant to the chancellor, Orthodox Church in America.
5. Archimandrite Serafim, *Quest for Orthodox Church Unity,* pp. 85-89.
6. Letter from Archimandrite Serafim, secretary to Bishop Job, 15 East 97 Street, New York, New York.
7. Letter from the Right Reverend Bishop Laurus, secretary, the Russian Orthodox Church Outside of Russia, 75 East 93 Street, New York, New York.
8. Communication from the Reverend Neketas S. Palassis, presbyter, St. Nectarios American Orthodox Church (Russian Orthodox Church Outside of Russia), 9223 20th Avenue Northeast, Seattle, Washington. Father Palassis left the Greek archidiocese, he said, because it "is becoming Roman Catholic in its administration [and] Protestant in its faith" (*The Vineyard,* published at Brooklyn, New York, by the Brotherhood of St. Mark of Ephesus, vol. 1, no. 1 [lent 1968], p. 8).
9. Communication from Greek Orthodox archdiocesan headquarters, New York City.
10. Communications from the Right Reverend Petros, bishop of Astoria, 22-68 26th Street, Astoria, Long Island City, New York.
11. Communications from the Very Reverend Theodore S. Kyritsis, 1189 North Parkway, Memphis, Tennessee.
12. Communication from the Most Reverend Theoklitos Heliopolis.
13. The Eastern Orthodox patriarch of Antioch ("The Most Blessed Patriarch of the Great City of God, Antioch, and of All the East") claims 350,000 spiritual subjects, of whom it is estimated that one quarter live in North, Central, and South America. The Eastern Orthodox patriarch of Antioch, who is in communion with the ecumenical patriarch in Istanbul, is to be carefully distinguished from a number of other patriarchs of Antioch, among them the Non-Chalcedonian Syrian Orthodox patriarch of Antioch at Damascus, the Roman Catholic Syrian Rite patriarch of Antioch at Beirut, the Roman Catholic Maronite patriarch of Antioch at Aleppo, and the Roman Catholic Melkite patriarch of Antioch, Alexandria, and Jerusalem with residences at Damascus and Cairo.
14. Peter F. Anson, *Bishops at Large* (New York: October House, 1964), pp. 502-506, discusses the American Orthodox Church and the antecedents of its archbishop, Alexander Turner. Both before and after the absorption of the American Orthodox Church into the Antiochian Orthodox Church, the Society of Clerks Secular of Basil, who staffed the American Orthodox Church, published a small but scholarly review, *Orthodoxy.* Since 1969 it has been published in the interest of Eastern Orthodox Western Rite affairs by a Western Rite priest of the Russian Orthodox Church Outside of Russia, the Reverend Joseph Salkeld.
15. The eucharistic rite prescribed in *The Missal for Use of Orthodox* (Mount Vernon, N.Y.: Society of St. Basil, 1963) is an English translation of the Latin Rite of the Roman Catholic Church. The most significant changes are the omission of "and from the Son" in the creed, the substitution of inter-

cessions for the patriarch of Antioch, the metropolitan, the Holy Synod of Antioch, and the president of the United States for the intercessions offered for the pope and his local episcopal representative in the prayer *In primis,* and the introduction of the *Epiklēsis* between the prayers *Supra quae* and *Supplices*: "And we beseech thee, O Lord, to send down thy Holy Spirit upon these offerings, that he would make this bread the precious body of thy Christ and that which is in this cup the precious blood of thy Son, our Lord Jesus Christ, transmuting them by thy Holy Spirit. Amen. Amen. Amen" (p. 15). Father Turner states that the translation of the canon of the Mass derives—somewhat astonishingly—from the version made by the Puritan reformer Miles Coverdale (1488–1568), bishop of Exeter under Edward VI and Elizabeth I, and printed in John Foxe's *Acts and Monuments* (letters of the Right Reverend Alexander Turner; for the text in Foxe see *The Acts and Monuments of John Foxe,* Book X, "The Preface to the Reader," ed. Stephen Reed Cattley, 6 [London: R. B. Seeley and W. Burnside, 1838], pp. 362–368).

16. Bishop Parkin had been consecrated in 1950 by the Most Reverend Richard Arthur Marchenna, metropolitan of the Province of North America of the Old Roman Catholic Church. After Parkin declared himself independent of Marchenna, he became a member of the Orthodox Catholic Patriarchate of America. This writer gratefully acknowledges the assistance of the Reverend Gary T. Schubert, pastor, Nazareth Church, Philadelphia, Pennsylvania, who interviewed Bishop Parkin on this writer's behalf.

17. Letters from officials of both former archdioceses in New York and Toledo.

18. On the period 1921 to 1936, see Mitrofan Yavdas, *Ukrainian Autocephalous Orthodox Church: Documents for the History of the Ukrainian Autocephalous Orthodox Church,* trans. Leonid Poliansky and others, ed. Edward A. McMurray and others (Munich: Peter Beley, 1956).

19. Letter from the Very Reverend D. Luchak, 7 St. John's Avenue, Winnipeg, Manitoba, Canada.

20. *Yearbook of American and Canadian Churches 1975* (Nashville: Abingdon Press, 1975), p. 97.

21. Letter from the Very Reverend George J. Owen, legate and hegumen for the Holy Catholic Apostolic Orthodox Church of Puerto Rico. In 1965 the exarch of the Russian Orthodox Catholic Church in America (Patriarchal Exarchate) appointed the acting chancellor of the exarchate administrator of the Orthodox Communities in Puerto Rico and the Spanish-speaking Orthodox in New York City.

22. Letter from the Reverend Alexander Bykowetz, secretary to Archbishop Hrihoriy. This writer gratefully acknowledges the assistance of Mr. Dennis Ahl, then seminarian assistant at Jehovah Church, Chicago, Illinois, and of the Reverend William A. Borkenhagen, pastor of the Church of the Lord Jesus, Chicago, who interviewed Archbishop Hrihoriy on this writer's behalf. St. Vladimir's Ukrainian Orthodox Church, Los Angeles, California, formerly the cathedral parish, is now an independent Ukrainian Orthodox church that stands outside all of the existing Ukrainian jurisdictions or bishops. To perpetuate in the United States the ideological principles of the Kievan autonomy of 1921 as it understands them, the rector of St. Vladimir's Church organized the Brotherhood of Metropolitan Vasil Lypkivsky in 1958. (Letter from the Reverend Peter M. Mayevsky, pastor, St. Vladimir Ukrainian Orthodox Church, 4025 Melrose Avenue, Los Angeles, California.)

23. *Byelaruski Holas* (Toronto, Ontario, Canada), vol. 18, no. 16 (whole number no. 159) (April 1968), p. 2; letter from Bishop Andrew Kryt, 3517 West 25 Street, Cleveland, Ohio.

24. Communication from Archbishop Vasili Tamashchyk, archbishop of the Byelorussian Autocephalic Orthodox Church.—In connection with the gathering of information about the Byelorussian Autocephalic Orthodox Church, the present writer gratefully acknowledges the assistance of the Reverend Daniel G. Jurcovic, pastor of St. Paul's Church, Toronto, Ontario, Canada; the Reverend John Klein, M. S., pastor of the Church of SS. Peter and Paul, Lorain, Ohio; Mr. Quinn Mehlos, then seminarian assist-

ant at St. Mark's Church, Cleveland, Ohio; and Mr. David M. Schaefer, then seminarian assistant at Immanuel Church, New York City.

25. St. Euphrosyne was the daughter of Prince Svyatoslav of Polotsk and a widely traveled Byelorussian nun who died in 1173. Of the twelve women canonized by the Eastern Orthodox Church in what is now Russia, she is the only unmarried saint. (*Butler's Lives of the Saints,* ed. Herbert Thurston and Donald Attwater, 2nd printing [New York: P. J. Kenedy and Sons, 1962], pp. 2, 377).

26. Letters from the Right Reverend Protopresbyter Nikolay Lapitzki, 178 Whitehead Avenue, South River, New Jersey; the Reverend Oleg Mironovich, pastor, St. George's Byelorussian Orthodox Church, 1500 North Maplewood Avenue, Chicago, Illinois; and the Reverend Yakov Kuzmicki, pastor, St. Ephrasinia's Byelorussian Greek-Orthodox Church, 1008 Dovercourt Road, Toronto, Ontario, Canada.

27. *Yearbook of American and Canadian Churches 1975,* p. 28.

28. *The Holy Orthodox Church in America, Published with the Permission of the Primate, Theodotus, Archbishop* (New York: Metropolitan Synod of the Holy Orthodox Church in America, n.d.) (4-page pamphlet).

29. Information supplied by the senior deaconess, widow of the late Archbishop Theodotus.

30. *The Eastern Orthodox Church in America* (undated pamphlet); letter from the Right Reverend Gregory R. P. Adair, ruling bishop of the Eastern Orthodox Catholic Church in America.

31. "Summary," in Martin Juhkam and others, eds., *Eesti Apostlik Ortodoksne Kirik Exsiilis 1944–1960* (Stockholm: Eesti Apostliku Ortodoksse Kiriku Kultuurfond, 1961), pp. 197-211. The present writer gratefully acknowledges the assistance of Mr. Stephen Wolfe, then seminarian assistant at Faith Church, Inglewood, California, in securing information about the Estonian Orthodox Church in Exile from Father Sergius.

32. Letters from the Very Reverend Denis W. Ericson, administrator, American Finnish Orthodox Mission, P. O. Box 174, Lansing, Michigan.

33. *Constitution, Bulgarian Eastern Orthodox Church, Diocese of the United States of America and Canada* (Toledo, Ohio: Bulgarian Eastern Orthodox Church, Diocese of the United States of America and Canada, 1964), pp. 1-3.

34. Letters from Bishop Kyrill and from the Very Reverend George Nedelkoff, pastor of St. Nicholas' Macedono-Bulgarian Eastern Orthodox Church, Fort Wayne, Indiana, and secretary, diocesal spiritual council, Bulgarian Eastern Orthodox Church, Diocese of the United States of America and Canada. The present writer gratefully acknowledges the assistance of the Reverend Edgar M. Luecke, pastor of the Church of the Prince of Peace, Oregon, Ohio, and the late Reverend Max C. Weissbach, pastor of St. Paul's Church, Niagara Falls, Ontario, Canada, in securing information about the Bulgarian Eastern Orthodox Church, Diocese of the United States of America and Canada, and the counsel of Father Nedelkoff in drafting this section.

35. Two of the new bishops were American citizens, the third a Canadian citizen.

36. The Serbian Orthodox Church in the United States and Canada energetically rejects the charge of "pro-Titoism" that its opponents level against it. It in turn levels countercharges of malfeasance and of illegal and uncanonical actions against the Serbian Orthodox Diocese in the United States of America and Canada and its primate. See, for instance, Djoko Slijepchevich, *The Transgressions of Bishop Dionisije* (Chicago: n. p., 1963).

37. On January 1, 1964, Bishop Dionisije, in a letter to the ecumenical patriarch in Istanbul, charged the Serbian patriarch German with being a schismatic. Bishop Dionisije also asserted that patriarch German had suspended him because of his anticommunist activity and because of an alleged misappropriation of diocesan funds which the regular audit of the diocesan accounts showed to have been correctly handled (Diocesan Register No. 216). The ecumenical patriarch rejected this appeal. Thereupon Bishop Dionisije on March 2, 1966, turned to His Holiness the All-Russian Patriarch Aleksei of Moscow; although Bishop Dionisije

declined to place himself under Muscovite jurisdiction, he pleaded for Patriarch Aleksei's intervention and protection against the Serbian patriarch German and undertook to submit to the decision of Patriarch Aleksei (Diocesan Register No. 280). Some of the documents bearing on the controversy are published in Dionisije [Milivojevich], *Patriarch German's Violations of the Holy Canons, Rules and Regulations of the Serbian Orthodox Church in Tito's Yugoslavia* (Libertyville, Ill.: The Serbian Orthodox Diocese in the U.S.A. and Canada, 1965).

38. *New York Times*, June 22, 1976, p. 22.
39. In Canada one of Dionisije's priests, the Reverend Louis Stojanovich, pastor of the Serbian Orthodox Church of St. Michael the Archangel, Niagara Falls, Ontario, Canada, blessed the new Bulgarian Orthodox Church of St. John of Rila, a congregation which accepts the authority of Bishop Kyrill of Oregon, Ohio (letter from the Reverend Louis Stojanovich).
40. *American Review of Eastern Orthodoxy*, vol. 22, no. 1 (January-February 1976), pp. 2-3.
41. Communications from the Right Reverend Bishop Dionisije, Libertyville, Illinois.
42. Letters of the Reverend Spiro Tanaskoski, pastor of the Macedonian Orthodox Church of SS. Peter and Paul, 5100 Virginia Street, Gary, Indiana, and of Protodeacon Stojan Jankovski, chief of cabinet, Holy Bishops' Synod, Macedonian Orthodox Church, Skoplje, Yugoslavia.
43. The *Romanian Orthodox Missionary Episcopate in America: A Short History* (Detroit: The Romanian Orthodox Missionary Episcopate in America, 1967) (pamphlet), pp. 3-5; *Calendarul Ortodox Credinta pe Anul 1967* (Detroit: The Romanian Orthodox Missionary Episcopate in America, 1966), pp. 34, 37-38, 114, 201-205; letters from the Right Reverend Bishop Victorin.
44. For the text of the resolution, see the mimeographed pamphlet, *The Politics of Patriarch Justinian Marina* (Jackson, Mich.: The Romanian Orthodox Episcopate of America, 1960), pp. 11-13. See also "The Romanian Ortho-

dox Episcopate of America: Historical Background," in *Calendarul Solia pe anul Domnului* (Jackson, Mich.: The Romanian Orthodox Episcopate of America, 1966), pp. 27-28.
45. *Calendarul "Candela" pe Anul Domnului 1959* (Windsor, Canada: The Romanian Orthodox Episcopate of the Western Hemisphere, 1958), pp. 20-21, 63.
46. Communication from the Right Reverend Teofil Ionesco, 768 West Lantz Street, Detroit, Michigan. The present writer gratefully acknowledges the efforts of Mr. Glenn Niebling, then seminarian assistant at the Church of the Epiphany, Detroit, to secure information from Bishop Ionescu for this writer.
47. In 1921, two missionaries of the Albanian Orthodox Church in America used this translation in conducting the first Albanian liturgy in St. George's Cathedral at Korcha, Albania (Fan S. Noli, comp., *Fiftieth Anniversary Book of the Albanian Orthodox Church in America 1908–1958* [Boston: Albanian Orthodox Church in America, 1960], p. 10).
48. The dedications of two books that Noli published in a single year reflect these concerns. *The Eastern Orthodox Pocket Prayer Book* (Boston: The Albanian Orthodox Church in America, 1954) that he compiled is dedicated "to the American Orthodox Church of the future, which will unite all Orthodox groups and enable them to fulfill their evangelic mission in the United States of America for the glory of our Lord and Savior Jesus Christ." The *Eastern Orthodox Catechism* (Boston: The Albanian Orthodox Church in America, 1954) that he translated and arranged is dedicated "to the younger generation of the Eastern Orthodox Church who will take over and carry on her evangelic mission in the United States of America."
49. This writer acknowledges gratefully the help of Mr. Paul W. Krause, then seminarian assistant at the First Lutheran Church in Boston, who interviewed the Right Reverend Mark I. Lipa, bishop of the Albanian Orthodox Diocese of America, on this writer's behalf.

BIBLIOGRAPHY

Eastern Orthodox Catechism. Trans. and arranged by Fan Stylian Noli. Boston: The Albanian Orthodox Church in America, 1954.

Fedorovich, Nicholas. *The Great Prince Saint Vladimir: His Life and Work.* South Bound Brook, N.J.: Ukrainian Orthodox Church of USA, 1957. The second half of this 32-page illustrated brochure contains the author's essay "My Church and My Faith," seven short chapters on the history, faith, and practice of Ukrainian Orthodoxy in the United States and abroad.

Hategan, Vasile. *Fifty Years of the Romanian Orthodox Church in America.* Jackson, Mich.: The Romanian Orthodox Episcopate of America, 1959.

Noli, Fan Stylian, comp. *Eastern Orthodox Pocket Prayer Book.* Boston: The Albanian Orthodox Church in America, 1954.

————. *Fiftieth Anniversary Book of the Albanian Orthodox Church in America.* Boston: The Albanian Orthodox Church in America, 1960.

Wlasowsky, Ivan. *Outline History of the Ukrainian Orthodox Church.* Vol. I: *The Baptism of Ukraine to the Union of Berestye (988–1596).* Trans. M. J. Diakowsky. South Bound Brook, N.J.: Ukrainian Orthodox Church of USA, 1956. This is the first volume in English of a work of which five volumes have appeared in Ukrainian; the complete work traces the history of Ukrainian Orthodoxy to the mid-twentieth century.

5. Churches Deriving Their Orders from Eastern Orthodox and Other Eastern Sources

A number of church bodies in the United States and Canada trace the episcopal succession of their prelates, at least in part, to three individuals who in turn claimed to have derived their own episcopal orders from Eastern sources—Joseph René Vilatte, Julius Ferrete, and Anthony Aneed. These church bodies are not easy to classify in every case. In spite of the source of their episcopal orders, some of these church bodies are by their own choice more Western than Eastern in both theology and liturgy. Again, some of these bodies trace their prelates' lines of episcopal succession not only to one or more of these three persons, but also to other bishops. Indeed, in order to multiply the lines of succession that they incorporate in their own persons, some of the prelates in these bodies have deliberately sought conditioned reconsecration from bishops in other lines of episcopal descent. Accordingly, some of the church bodies in this section could be quite appropriately catalogued under another head. The church bodies here discussed either (*a*) claim to perpetuate organizations founded by one or the other of these three persons, or (*b*) they are explicitly, at least in large part, Eastern in their theological and liturgical orientation, or (*c*) their primates hold membership in one of the two North American synods that link bishops of these successions—the Holy Orthodox Catholic Patriarchate of America, and the Holy Synod of the Orthodox Catholic Churches in America.

Joseph René Vilatte (1854–1920) was a French immigrant to Canada. He left the Roman Catholic Church to become a Methodist in Montreal. He returned to the Roman Catholic Church four times during his life. He returned once more to the Methodist Church. He became a minister in the Congregational Church. He twice entered the Presbyterian Church. At one time his name appeared in the official records of the Protestant Episcopal Diocese of Fond du Lac, Wisconsin, as a candidate for holy orders, and the Protestant Episcopal Church degraded him from its priesthood and excommunicated him, but whether he actually ever became a member of that denomination is debated.

While Vilatte was engaged as a Presbyterian missionary among former

Roman Catholic Belgian immigrants to Wisconsin, he approached the Right Reverend Hobart Brown, Protestant Episcopal bishop of Fond du Lac, Wisconsin, with a view to admission to the presbyterate of that church. Bishop Brown suggested to Vilatte that he seek ordination in the Old Catholic Church. The Old Catholic bishop of Switzerland conferred the diaconate and the presbyterate on Vilatte in 1885. When he was not able to secure consecration to the episcopate from the Old Catholic Church, Vilatte turned to Russian Orthodox Archbishop Vladimir, who extended his church's patronage to Vilatte but did not offer to make a bishop of him. While Vilatte was reported negotiating with the Roman Catholic archbishop of Milwaukee, Wisconsin, with a view to receiving consecration in that church, he learned of the existence of a group of former Roman Catholics on Ceylon. The members of this community had broken with the Roman Catholic authorities and had organized the Independent Catholic Church of Ceylon, Goa, and India. Its leader, Julius Xavier Alvares, had secured episcopal consecration from Mar Paul Athanasius, the Non-Chalcedonian Syrian Orthodox bishop of Kottayam in Malabar. Vilatte went to Ceylon and after some delay Alvares, who called himself Mar Julius I, with the assistance of the Non-Chalcedonian Syrian Orthodox metropolitans of Malabar, consecrated Vilatte to the episcopate under the name of Mar Timotheos as archbishop of North America in 1892.

Subsequently Vilatte consecrated a succession of bishops in England, Italy, and the United States. In the process he violated the canon of the Non-Chalcedonian Syrian Orthodox Church that does not allow one bishop alone to consecrate another bishop. The Non-Chalcedonian Orthodox patriarch of Antioch reportedly excommunicated Vilatte on this ground. The present Non-Chalcedonian Syrian Orthodox Church does not recognize any of Vilatte's consecrations and is not in communion with any of the successors of the bishops that Vilatte consecrated.

In 1920 Vilatte returned to France. In 1925 he was reconciled with the Roman Catholic Church. In 1929 he died in the communion of that church.[1]

Jules Ferrete (d. 1903) appears to have been a French-born convert to Roman Catholicism. In 1850 he was professed as a Dominican, was ordained a priest in Rome in 1855, and was dispatched to Mosul (now in Iraq) as a missionary. A year later he left the Roman Church and for a number of years he worked with the Irish Presbyterian Mission in Damascus. Here he became friendly with Mar Bedros, the Non-Chalcedonian Syrian Orthodox bishop of Homs, who later became the Non-Chalcedonian Syrian Orthodox patriarch of Antioch as Ignatius Peter III. In 1866 Ferrete returned to England, where he claimed that Mar Bedros had consecrated him a bishop earlier that year. In 1874 Ferrete consecrated Richard Williams Morgan, the Anglican curate of Marholm, Northamptonshire, as Mar Pelagius I, archbishop of Caerleon-upon-Usk, and thus initiated what has come to be called the "Ferrete succession."[2]

Anthony Aneed began his ecclesiastical career as a priest of the Roman

Catholic Melkite Rite. After service as secretary to Archbishop Athanasius Sawaya of Beirut, he became a Melkite priest in New York. In 1911, according to Aneed, Archbishop Sawaya visited the United States after Pius X had explicitly forbidden him to do so. In the course of this visit, Archbishop Sawaya allegedly consecrated Aneed as auxiliary bishop of Beirut and exarch of the archbishop of the Melkites in the United States.

In 1942 Aneed broke off all connections with the Roman Catholic Church, formed the now apparently defunct Byzantine American Catholic Church, incorporated it in California in 1944, and took the title of patriarch-president of the Federated Independent Catholic and Orthodox Churches. Among those that he raised to the episcopate were the late Frank B. Robinson of Moscow, Idaho, founder of the now-defunct Psychiana movement, in 1945; Odo Acheson Barry, founder of the now apparently defunct Canadian Catholic Church, as Mar Columba, in 1946; and Nikolai Urbanovich of Winnipeg, Canada, a priest of the Ukrainian Orthodox Church in the United States, in 1949.[3]

The American Catholic Church (Syro-Antiochian)

The American Catholic Church (Syro-Antiochean) is an autonomous American church body organized in 1915, when Joseph René Vilatte consecrated Frederick Ebenezer John Lloyd. Through Vilatte the American Catholic Church (Syro-Antiochian) traces its episcopal succession from the Syrian patriarch of Antioch. It professes to be Catholic in its faith, worship, and discipline. It uses the Western Roman Catholic Rite in the administration of the seven sacraments. Its headquarters are at 1811 Northwest Fourth Court, Miami, Florida. It reports five churches, with an inclusive membership of 495.[4]

The African Orthodox Church

The African Orthodox Church came into being on the flowing tide of American Negro self-consciousness evoked by the activities of Marcus Garvey in the first quarter of the twentieth century. Its founder was an Antigua-born Anglican clergyman and doctor of medicine, George Alexander McGuire (1866–1934). For many years a leader in the Negro work of the Protestant Episcopal Church, in 1913 McGuire went back to his birthplace, English Harbour, where he functioned as a Church of England parish priest for six years. When he returned to the United States in 1919 he began organizing an "Independent Episcopal Church" for Negro Episcopalians who felt that the Protestant Episcopal Church was denying members of their race adequate opportunity within its ranks. McGuire applied for and secured episcopal consecration from Joseph René Vilatte on September 28, 1921. At the first general synod after Bishop McGuire's consecration, the new body adopted the name the African Orthodox Church.

In 1927 the church erected a provincial jurisdiction for Africa and Bishop McGuire became patriarch of the whole church with the title of Patriarch Alexander I. In 1928 he consecrated William F. Tyarks as first bishop of the American Catholic Orthodox Church, only to suspend him in 1932. Tyarks in turn consecrated Cyril John Clement Sherwood in 1930 and in 1932, after Tyarks reportedly denied that he had had a true intention at the first consecration, McGuire conditionally reconsecrated Sherwood. Shortly after this Sherwood founded the American Holy Orthodox Catholic Apostolic Eastern Church (now defunct) although he remained a member of the conclave of bishops of the African Orthodox Church.

Shortly before McGuire's death in 1934 Bishop Reginald Grant Barrow led a group out of the African Orthodox Church and founded the African Orthodox Church of New York. Bishop William Ernest James Robertson (1875–1962) succeeded McGuire, only to have another division take place in the church in 1937. The group that withdrew from Robertson's leadership operated under the McGuire Massachusetts charter. Barrow and his New York church joined them and Barrow became the first primate of the African Orthodox Church of New York and Massachusetts. His tenure of the dignity was brief; Bishop Arthur Stanley Trotman (1869–1945) succeeded him the same year. In 1938 Robertson secured an injunction against three of the officers of the church that Trotman now headed; it prohibited them from representing McGuire as their founder. The same year Robertson was formally elected patriarch with the style of His Beatitude James I.

In 1945 Bishop Robert Arthur Valentine succeeded Trotman. Bishop Frederick Augustus Toote succeeded Valentine in 1954, and Bishop Gladstone St. Clair Nurse succeeded Toote in 1959. In 1962 Robertson died and Bishop Richard Grant Robinson became patriarch as Peter IV. In the same year Nurse consecrated Francis Arthur Vogt for mission work among Caucasians on Long Island.

In 1965 the two branches were reunited with Robinson as patriarch and Nurse as primate. Under Archbishop Nurse, who succeeded Robinson on the latter's death in 1967, the work of reconstruction is going on. Nurse has renounced the title of patriarch and the style of His Beatitude; he has retained the title of primate and the style His Eminence. He is making efforts to correct the somewhat top-heavy organization of the body and to fortify its outreach into the black communities in which it operates.

The African Orthodox Church's thirteen-article declaration of faith accepts the Holy Scriptures as the word of God, along with the traditions and dogmatic decisions of the seven ecumenical councils. It also accepts the Niceno-Constantinopolitan Creed (without the words "and the Son") and affirms the denomination's belief in the Apostles' and Athanasian creeds. It recognizes Christ as the sole head of the church. It affirms belief in the infallibility of the church and in the procession of the Holy Spirit from the Father alone. It honors the Blessed Virgin Mary as the Mother of God and affirms belief in the three hierarchies and nine choirs of angels and in all the saints. It reverences the relics of the saints and holy icons, accepts seven sacraments, and holds "the true doctrine of transubstantiation to be the Real Presence." It sees belief in the "communion of saints" as requiring prayers for the dead and the living, rejects predestination, and declares that both faith and works are necessary for justification. It regards celebration of the divine liturgy as the obligatory central act of the church's worship and affirms both a particular and a general judgment.[5]

At the same time, the worship (with a view to appealing to black Anglicans and Roman Catholics) consists largely of Western formularies; the official hymnal, pending production of the church's own hymnal, is *Hymns Ancient and Modern*; the clergy wear Western-style vestments; and the Roman Pontifical has provided the rite for conferring major and minor orders.

The strict position of the church on divorce is noteworthy. No priest may remarry the guilty party in a divorce action, and the innocent party may remarry only with episcopal permission.

Currently there are eighteen churches and missions in the Atlantic seaboard states, one church in Nova Scotia, and two in Illinois. The total membership of these twenty-one churches and missions and of the four parishes in the Caribbean is estimated at about 5,000.[6] The headquarters of the reunited church are at 122 West 129 Street, New York.[7] The African jurisdiction has its main strength in Kenya and Uganda.

The Church of Antioch, Malabar Rite

In 1915 Joseph René Vilatte, as founder-primate of the American (Old Roman) Catholic Church, consecrated a former Protestant Episcopal clergyman, Frederick Ebenezer John Lloyd, to the episcopate. Lloyd succeeded Vilatte as primate in 1920; in 1923 he consecrated another former Protestant Episcopal clergyman, Gregory Lines, as bishop of the Pacific. In 1927 Lines established a rival branch of the American Catholic Church and consecrated Joseph (Justin) Andrieu Boyle, who subsequently took the name of his natural ancestors as Robert Raleigh, to be his coadjutor; Boyle in turn consecrated a member of the Theosophical Society, Lowell Paul Wadle.[8] Lines returned to Lloyd's jurisdiction, but after the latter's death in 1932, Lines once more seceded from Lloyd's successor, Daniel Cassell Hinton, and established another rival branch of the American Catholic Church. Raleigh headed the American Catholic Church (Lines Succession) until 1965, when he retired in favor of his coadjutor, Netherlands-born Hermann Adrian Spruit, a former Methodist minister and the vice president of the American Ministerial Association, whom the retired Liberal Catholic prelate Charles Hampton, acting in his capacity of bishop of the Old Roman Catholic Church, had consecrated in 1957.

Upon becoming primate of the American Catholic Church (Lines Succession), Spruit redesignated his jurisdiction the Church of Antioch, Malabar Rite, so that the very name might recall the source of Vilatte's episcopal orders.[9]

The Church of Antioch, Malabar Rite, accepts the Nicene-Constantinopolitan Creed, without the phrase "and the Son," and the doctrinal decrees of the seven ecumenical councils. Justification is by faith in Christ's atoning ministry. In its worship it uses the Western Rite, the Western calendar, and Western ornaments. Communion is open to all who love and serve Christ. The seven sacraments are mediating channels for the grace of God to the lives of men. Celibacy of the clergy is not an issue. The jurisdiction makes no pronouncements on birth control and upholds the right of conscientious objection to military service. It teaches that God wills each individual to experience a maximum of health; for that reason it stresses the ministry of healing and cooperates with all agencies that have a similar concern, especially the drugless healing profession. The primate states:

> Strongly influenced by the mystic outreach toward Reality, as reflected in the thought patterns of the East, we profess a diminishing interest in Aristotelian logic. We feel more at home with St. Augustine and perhaps Origen than we do with St. Thomas Aquinas. We confess that the Bible holds all that is needed for salvation and liberation, although we encourage our people to acquaint themselves with the writings of other faiths, inasmuch as a common emphasis can be detected in all the major religions of the world. We leave our clergy free to explore the fields of speculative and mystical theology.[10]

Recent efforts to contact church leaders have been fruitless. Several years ago the headquarters of the jurisdiction were at Santa Ana, California. At that time it had ten congregations and missions in California and Florida with a total membership of 350.[11] Both the Malabar Rite and the Liberal Catholic Rite were in use.[12]

The Archdiocese of New York of the American Catholic Church

This small Afro-American body came into being in 1927. Its first bishop and primate, Metropolitan-Archbishop James Francis Augustine Lashley, traces his episcopal orders to the Syrian Church of Antioch by way of William Frederick Tyarks (who consecrated Lashley in 1928), George Alexander McGuire of the African Orthodox Church, and Joseph René Vilatte. The archdiocese professes the Old Catholic faith with a few exceptions, but is not in communion with the Old Catholic churches of Europe. The sources of its faith are the Holy Scriptures, the accumulated teaching of the Fathers of the church, the final and accepted conclusions of the seven ecumenical councils, and the Synod of Jerusalem of 1692. It administers seven sacraments, uses a ritualistic ceremonial, venerates icons or pictures as sacred things that represent sacred persons, and invokes the intercession of the saints. It reports four churches in the United States, with a membership of 200. The headquarters are at 457 West 144 Street, New York, New York.[13]

The Holy Orthodox Catholic Patriarchate of America

In 1935 a provisional synod was set up for the purpose of combining into an American patriarchate a number of American Orthodox and Old Catholic bodies that were not in communion with any of the canonical jurisdictions of Europe. Out of this provisional organization grew in 1951 the Patriarchal Holy Synod of the Orthodox Catholic Patriarchate of America. The first patriarch was His Holiness Joseph (Klimovich), patriarch of America, whose patriarchal Cathedral of SS. Peter and Paul was in Springfield, Massachusetts.[14] The patriarchate was described as "an indigenous ecclesiastical coalition of different nationalities, different churches and jurisdictions, which are inseparably joined in faith with the great Church of Constantinople and with every Eastern Orthodox Church of the same profession."[15]

The Orthodox-Catholic Church of America

In 1957 Metropolitan-Archbishop Clement Sherwood, patriarchal locum tenens of the Orthodox Catholic Patriarchate of America, assisted by two other bishops of the patriarchal holy synod, consecrated George Augustine Hyde for the renewal and continuation of the domestic missions begun in 1885 by Joseph René Vilatte. In 1960 the community of worker-priests that Bishop Hyde established at Washington, D. C., took the name of The Society of Domestic Missionaries of St. Basil the Great and separated itself from the communion of the Orthodox Catholic Patriarchate on the ground that the Patriarchate was too narrowly Eastern in liturgy, theology, and dogmatic scope. It associated itself with the American Catholic Apostolic Church (Long Beach, California), another branch of the Vilatte succession headed by its archbishop-founder, the late Lowell Paul Wadle.

At the end of 1961, Bishop Hyde's jurisdiction withdrew from communion with Archbishop Wadle because of doctrinal differences and proclaimed itself an autonomous Orthodox Western Rite communion "identical with the Holy Church of Constantinople in our confession and in our doctrine." In 1966 the Western Rite Orthodox Communion took the name Orthodox-Catholic Church of America. By 1967 the liturgical and theological issues that had divided the Orthodox-Catholic Church from the Orthodox Catholic Patriarchate of America had been resolved and Bishop Hyde took his seat as a member of the Holy Synod of the Patriarchate.

The Orthodox-Catholic Church sees itself as representing the Orthodox faith "within the discipline and scope of Byzantine liturgical traditions, but reshaped to the mentality of western culture."[16] Theologically it identifies itself with the Roman Catholic Church and specifically with the Byzantine Rite Roman Catholic community. It asserts that it does not reject the Pope's apostolic office and primacy, but only the narrow, legalistic mentality that has come to rule in the Roman Catholic Church.

The Divine Liturgy, the service book of the Orthodox-Catholic Church of America, combines Western features with a modernized and abbreviated version of the Byzantine liturgy. Orthodox-Catholic churches have no iconostasis, but instead the altars are flanked by stands with icons of Christ and the Mother of God. Statues are not permitted. It published its rite in 1966.

There are twelve churches and missions in Pennsylvania, Maryland, the District of Columbia, South Carolina, Georgia, and Louisiana, organized into three dioceses and comprising 1,300 adult members. Mailing address for the church's publication, *Ortho*, is P. O. Box 1273, Anderson, South Carolina.

Christ Catholic Church of the Americas and Europe

Joseph René Vilatte consecrated Paolo Miraglia Gulotti as Bishop of Piacenza and primate of the Italian National Episcopal Church in 1900. Gulotti in turn reportedly consecrated Joseph Zielonka (d. 1960), who came to North America and in 1913 founded the Polish Old Catholic Church of America. In 1925, while acting as American administrator of the Old Catholic Church of Poland and of the Polish Mariavite Church, Zielonka associated himself with Archbishop William Henry Francis of the Old Catholic Church in America, only to break with him in 1940 and to establish the Old Catholic Archdiocese for the Americas and Europe, which in 1950 was united with the Holy Orthodox Catholic Patriarchate of America.

Upon Zielonka's death, Bishop Peter Andreas Žurawetzky, who had joined Zielonka's body in 1953 as his suffragan, succeeded him in 1961. (Žurawetzky had been a priest in the Ukrainian Orthodox Church of America, and subsequently, from 1940 to 1949, he had functioned under Archbishop Christopher Contogeorge [Kontogiorgios] [died 1949], whom Stylian Fan Noli, the Albanian primate, and Archbishop Sophronios had consecrated, and who claimed to be the American exarch of the Greek Orthodox patriarch of Alexandria.) In 1950 Archbishop Joseph Klimovich, first patriarch of the Holy Orthodox Catholic Patriarchate of America, had consecrated Žurawetzky as bishop of New York, and from 1950 to 1953 Žurawetzky served as secretary of the patriarchate.

In 1961 Žurawetzky redesignated his church body as Christ Catholic Exarchate of the Americas and Europe. An alternative name was Western Orthodox Oecumenical Exarchate, as the head of which Žurawetzky acted as "exarch of the Old Catholics, having in [his] jurisdiction clergymen in North America and abroad."[17] Žurawetzky also uses the title of Patriarch of Miensk and Byelorussia in Dispersion.

Most of the North American clergy of Christ Catholic Church of the

Americas and Europe use the Western Rite in the vernacular, although some, including the primate, normally use the Eastern Rite. The church declares that it "has been unaffected by recent fads in theology, and [that] while its outlook is definitely liberal, it continues to maintain the historic Catholic faith and order."[18]

The church is a member of the Holy Orthodox Catholic Patriarchate of America. Its headquarters are at 946 Leesville Avenue, Rahway, New Jersey. The church body claims twenty-seven churches and missions in the United States with a total membership of 2,200.[19]

An administrator for Canada and All of the British Possessions has from time to time represented the Exarchate in Canada, but there are currently no organized parishes in the dominion.[20]

In 1965 Christ Catholic Church of the Americas and Europe began a mission in Boston. Two years later this mission received a bishop with the elevation of the Reverend Karl Prüter to the episcopate. The jurisdiction claims five churches with a total of 440 members.

Since 1969 a suffragan diocese of the Christ Catholic Church of the Americas and Europe has been the nonterritorial Orthodox Catholic Jurisdiction of the Holy Spirit (Western Rite). It was presided over by the bishop of Glorieta, New Mexico, the Most Reverend Christopher William Jones, whom Žurawetzky together with Bishop Uładysłau Ryžy-Ryski consecrated to the episcopate in August 1969. No information is available on the number of faithful who belong to the jurisdiction. As abbot of the Ecumenical Monastery of Our Lady of Reconciliation, located in Pulaski, Wisconsin, Bishop Jones heads a community of two, including himself.[21]

In 1967 the Most Reverend Peter Andreas Žurawetzky, primate of the Christ Catholic Church of the Americas and Europe, organized the Holy Synod of the Orthodox Catholic Churches in America. The headquarters were at 141 Market Street, Newark, New Jersey. Besides the jurisdictions over which Archbishop Žurawetzky presided, the synod included Archbishop Joachim Souris's Autocephalous Greek Orthodox Church in America, Archbishop Theoklitos Kantaris's Greek Orthodox Diocese of New York, Archbishop Mark Athanasios Karras's Universal Shrine of Divine Guidance in Miami, Florida, and a jurisdiction presided over by the Right Reverend William C. Morgan, Gracewood, Georgia. In 1975 the synod was dissolved by Žurawetzky.[22]

Byelorussian (White Ruthenian) Patriarchate of St. Andrew the Apostle, the First-Called

According to the Most Reverend Uładysłau Ryžy-Ryski, an emigré Byelorussian Reformed minister, he founded the Byelorussian Orthodox Catholic Church (now known as the Orthodoxly-Catholic Byelorussian Christian Church in Dispersion or as the Byelorussian National Catholic Church) in 1958, after he had been licensed as a preacher of the gospel at the Evangelical Center of Theological Studies at Barcelona, Spain. He states that he constituted the synod of the denomination at Princeton, New Jersey, in 1960, after he had taken the degree of Master of Theology at Princeton (Presbyterian) Theological Seminary. The Most Reverend Peter Andreas Žurawetsky, primate of Christ Catholic Church of the Americas and Europe, became the first moderator of the synod. In 1965 the Most Reverend Walter M. Propheta consecrated Ryžy-Ryski as bishop of Laconia, New Hampshire, and the New England states in the American Orthodox Catholic Church (Bronx, New York). At this time Žurawetsky became patriarch of Miensk and All of Byelorussia in Dispersion, with Ryžy-Ryski as apostolic administrator of the Byelorussian Patriarchate of St. Andrew the Apostle, the First-Called, with the rank of archbishop. Ryžy-Ryski has since moved from Laconia to Wren Place, Shrub Oak, New York, where he has established his procathedral and the patriarchal chancery.

Theologically the patriarchate subscribes "to the fullness of the Christian tradition and belief," understood as including the Nestorian tradition,[23] the seven ecumenical councils, Western Catholicity, the Waldensian movement, Lutheranism, and Reformed theology,[24] to the extent that any and all of these "agree with the spirit of the Gospel of our Lord Jesus Christ."[25] It acknowledges as a creedal formulation of this consensus the memorandum read at the Conference of Wilna (Vilnius) of 1599, in which clerical and lay representatives of Eastern Orthodoxy (led by Prince Constantine Ostrogsky) met with leaders of the Czech Brethren (led by Simon Turnovsky) and of the Lutheran and Reformed communities in the territories under the crown of Poland-Lithuania.[26]

For their failure to provide or to demand provision for the religious needs of the non-Russian peoples in the Union of Soviet Socialist Republics, the patriarchate anathematizes the Russian Orthodox Patriarchate of Moscow, the pope of Rome, and the World Council of Churches. It maintains communion with the American Orthodox Catholic Church (New York, New York), Christ Catholic Church of the Americas and Europe, the Paris-based Catholic Apostolic Primitive Church of Orthodox Antioch and of the Syro-Byzantine Tradition (founded in 1953 and headed by Joannes Maria van Assendelft-Altland), the Ecumenical League for Christian Unity (founded in 1937 by Julien Erni of Geneva), and others.

The Patriarchate claims congregations in New York, New Jersey, Illinois, Michigan, Ohio, Ontario, Quebec, Manitoba, England, Belgium, Germany, and Australia, and is the mother church of American World Patriarchates.[27]

The Diocese of Brooklyn and New Jersey of the Autocephalous Greek Orthodox Church of America (Newark, New Jersey)

According to the diocesan seal, the Diocese of Brooklyn and New Jersey of the Autocephalous Greek Orthodox Church of America (*Ellenikē Orthodoxos Ekklēsia Amerikē*) was erected in 1934. At one period the Cathedral of the Holy Resurrection, 675 East 183 Street, New York, now occupied by the American Orthodox Catholic Church, served as its headquarters. The present bishop, Joachim Souris, who uses the style archbishop, received episcopal consecration on June 2, 1951, from the late Russian Archbishop Joseph Klimovich of Springfield, Massachusetts, patriarch of the Orthodox Catholic Patriarchate of America, and the late Greek Archbishop Arsenios. Joachim was a member of the Holy Synod of the patriarchate from 1951 to 1967, when he joined the Holy Synod of the Orthodox Catholic Churches in America. On October 3, 1964, Joachim, who by then had begun to use the style archbishop of the Greek Orthodox Diocese of New York, with the assistance of Archbishop Theodotus de Witow of the Holy Orthodox Church in America (Eastern Catholic and Apostolic) as co-consecrator, imparted episcopal orders to the mitred archpriest Walter (Vladimir) M. Propheta as bishop of New York in the American Orthodox Catholic Church. At present Joachim's jurisdiction, which apparently is not associated with any other Greek Orthodox diocese, seems to consist of a single rented store-front mission at 141 West Market Street, Newark, New Jersey, called the Church of St. Fanourios[28] and Sts. Anargyroi.[29] No information is available about the size of its membership, but it is probably very small.[30]

Universal Shrine of Divine Guidance of the Universal Faith (Apostolic Universal Center)

On July 17, 1966, the Most Reverend Petrus Andreas Žurawetzky, primate of the Christ Catholic Church of the Americas and Europe, and the Most Reverend Joachim Souris, primate of the Autocephalous Greek Ortho-dox Church of America, consecrated Mark Athanasios Constantine Karras (b. 1927), the grandson of a Greek Orthodox priest, to the episcopate. The following day they conferred on him the archiepiscopal dignity, with the title archbishop of Byzantium, a title which, Karras holds, lapsed in 314. In August 1966 Karras founded the Universal Shrine of Divine Guidance of the Universal Faith (Apostolic Universal Center) "to bring to the world a functional and realistic institution of religious nature designed to accept within its fold all religious denominations of persons who believe in the ulti-mate being and power of the Supreme Creator of all existence."[31]

The shrine sees history as divided into three periods: (1) the Judaic period, which offered a regulatory discipline; (2) the Christian stage, which instructed mankind "through the example of moral living"; and (3) the "current period of fulfillment through enlightenment and grace," during which the "third and final part of the Holy Scriptures is now being written by the act of human life as it occurs." It requires of its members only that they "acknowledge the one universal God," although the worshipers repeat the Nicene Creed together in the eucharistic service. Its bishops may marry and women may be ordained to its ministry. The shrine administers the traditional seven sacraments of Eastern Orthodoxy. It holds that the descent of the Holy Spirit upon the eucharistic elements of leavened[32] bread and wine in response to a prayer of invocation transubstantiates them into the body and blood of Christ; and it sees the Eucharist as essentially "a blood-less sacrifice to God." The shrine lays great stress upon divine healing "administered by prayer and the laying on of hands"; the healing act is "tantamount to holy communion of the Christ Spirit within one's body and soul."[33]

The shrine is incorporated in Florida, Illinois, and Indiana. It has its headquarters at 2345 South 21 Avenue, Miami, Florida. There are two congregations, both in Miami, with a total membership of 135.[34] The shrine was in communion with the Holy Synod of the Orthodox Catholic Churches in America presided over by Archbishop Žurawetzky. Recent efforts to contact the shrine have gone unanswered.

American Orthodox Catholic Church

In 1961 Archbishop Peter Andrew Žurawetzky, primate of what is now the Christ Catholic Church of the Americas and Europe, with Archbishop Hubert Augustine Rogers, primate of the North American Old Roman Catholic Church (Brooklyn, New York), and two other bishops of the latter body as co-consecrators, consecrated Robert Schuyler Zeiger as "an Orthodox bishop for Occidentals." In 1962 the American Orthodox Catholic Church formally came into being as a distinct, independent church body with the adoption of a constitution of its own. During the next two years Prime Bishop Zeiger established provincial jurisdictions in San Francisco, Los Angeles, Louisville, Kentucky, and Kansas City, Missouri. Upon his retirement in 1964 Archbishop Homer F. Roebke of Los Angeles succeeded him. In 1965 Roebke, along with the late Archbishop Christopher Maria Stanley (d. 1967) of Louisville, took a considerable segment of the American Orthodox Catholic Church into an identically named church body headed by Archbishop Walter M. Propheta (b. 1912) of New York, in which both Roebke and Stanley became provincial metropolitans. Upon Roebke's withdrawal, Archbishop Colin James Guthrie was chosen prime bishop. In 1969 Guthrie returned the church's official papers to Bishop Zeiger and withdrew to form the Synod of the Holy Orthodox Church.

Propheta, a former priest of the Ukrainian Orthodox Church of America (Ecumenical Patriarchate), had been made a bishop by the primates of the Holy Orthodox Church in America and of the Autocephalous Greek Orthodox Church of America on October 3, 1964. Six months later the primate of the Holy Orthodox Church in America and of the Greek Orthodox Diocese of New York elevated Propheta to the rank of archbishop, and the American Orthodox Catholic Church (New York, New York) came into being as a national denomination. It described itself as "Orthodox but not

Eastern, Catholic but not Papal," and affirms the doctrinal decrees of the seven ecumenical councils.[35] The liturgy that its primate compiled[36] severely shortened and adapted the Eastern Rite and added material from other sources, but the American Orthodox Catholic Church gave its bishops freedom of choice in such matters as rite (Byzantine or Latin), calendar (Julian or Gregorian), ritual, and vestments, as long as they "express nothing inconsistent with the Orthodox faith."[37]

The American Orthodox Catholic Church erected five provinces in the United States of America,[38] a province in the Virgin Islands and Puerto Rico, and a missionary diocese in France, called the French Orthodox Catholic Church.

On May 19, 1970 Bishop Milton A. Pritts of the Denver group incorporated the American Orthodox Catholic Church in the State of Colorado as the mother church of groups by the same name in Canada, Mexico, and the United States. A rapproachement was effected with the New York group under Bishop Propheta in October 1972. Following Propheta's death Lawrence F. Pierre was consecrated archbishop on July 6, 1975. He now serves as the president of the Council of Bishops of the American Orthodox Catholic Church and as archbishop of the United States Diocese. Pritts serves as prime bishop and as archivist of the Grand Synod.[39]

The doctrinal article of the church's constitution (Article I, Section II) states that the church "accepts the general principles of Faith of the One Holy Catholic and Apostolic Church of Christ as expressed in the doctrinal decrees of the Seven Ecumenical Councils, and in the Catholic Creeds. In its organization the church is "comprised of a Grand Synod, and three Archdioceses (Canada, United States, and Mexico) affiliating with other organizations as the Grand Synod shall deem expedient" (Article II, Section II).

Authority is not concentrated in a single person or office but is diffused among a number of basically equal bishops, to whom the church reserves the right to bind and loose for itself in disciplinary (but not in dogmatic) matters. The clergy may marry before or after ordination. Holy Communion is administered under both kinds. Either the Roman or the Byzantine Rite is used for ordinations or consecrations. Services are formal but simple and are held wholly in English. Most of the priests and bishops support themselves by other occupations. Many of its congregations are "house churches."

The chancellery of the American Orthodox Catholic Church is at 6262 East Ninth Avenue, Denver, Colorado. Membership statistics could not be ascertained.

The American Synod of the Holy Orthodox Church

In 1969 Archbishop Colin James Guthrie, prime bishop of the American Orthodox Catholic Church (Denver, Colorado), turned back the corporation papers to the church's founder, Bishop Robert Schuyler Zeiger, and incorporated a new church, the American Synod of the Holy Orthodox Church. Avowedly Orthodox in outlook, the new church established dioceses in Denver, Colorado, Baton Rouge-New Orleans, Louisiana, and Nashville, Tennessee, and took the Society of St. Basil under its jurisdiction. It has sixteen churches and missions with 300 members. Headquarters are at 70 West Sixth Avenue, Denver, Colorado.[40]

Ukrainian Autocephalic Church of North and South America

The headquarters of this jurisdiction are at 2224 Liberty Street, Allentown, Pennsylvania. Its canons permit its bishops to be married. The primate, the Most Reverend Wasyl Sawyna, was reportedly at one time an archdeacon in the Ukrainian Autocephalous Church in the United States of America under Archbishop Gregory (Hrihoriy). Later the Most Reverend Evhen Batchynskiy allegedly consecrated Sawyna a bishop and designated Sawyna as his representative in North America.[41] On Passion Sunday, March 15, 1964, Sawyna, acting jointly with the Most Reverend Orlando Jacques Woodward, Fort Oglethorpe, Georgia, described as "a bishop of the Old Catholic succession," consecrated James Parker Dees to serve as primate of the Anglican Orthodox Church free of the jurisdictions of his consecrators. No information is available on the number of churches, missions, and members that compose the Ukrainian Autocephalic Church of North and South America.[42]

NOTES

1. On Vilatte and the churches that trace their lineage back to him, see Henry R. T. Brandreth, *Episcopi Vagantes and the Anglican Church,* 2nd edition (London: SPCK, 1961), pp. 47-69, 126-129, and Peter F. Anson, *Bishops at Large* (New York: October House, 1964), pp. 91-129, 252-322, 550-551, 556-557.

2. See Brandreth, pp. 70-89, 129-133; Anson, pp. 31-47, 216-251, 546-547, 554-556.

3. See Brandreth, pp. 108-110, 133-134; Anson, pp. 512-514.

4. *Yearbook of the American Churches for 1975* (Nashville: Abingdon Press, 1975), p. 29.

5. Arthur Cornelius Terry-Thompson, *The History of the African Orthodox Church* (New York: African Orthodox Church), 1956, p. 44.

6. Communication from the Most Reverend Gladstone St. Clair Nurse, L.Th., D.D., 68 Harold Street, Boston,

Massachusetts, primate, the African Orthodox Church.

7. This writer acknowledges with gratitude the invaluable assistance of Mr. Roger E. Kuhn, then seminarian assistant at St. Matthew's Church, New York, who personally interviewed the Most Reverend Gladstone St. Clair Nurse, primate of the African Orthodox Church, on this writer's behalf.

8. In 1940 Wadle became coadjutor to Percy Wise Clarkson, a former Protestant Episcopal clergyman whom Hinton had consecrated for the American Catholic Church (Lloyd Succession) in 1933. After Clarkson died in 1942, Wadle took the style of "Primate of the American Catholic Apostolic Church (Vilatte Succession)," with headquarters at Long Beach. At the time of his death in April 1969, Raleigh was "spiritual director" of a corporation which he had had chartered in 1940, the Church

of Antioch and the National Academy of Metapathics, Agoura, California. Reportedly Raleigh had in January 1969 consecrated Joseph Damian Archbishop Hough, Ph.D., M.D., D.D., as archbishop of the Malabar Rite (St. Thomas Christians) with right of succession to the office of exarch of the exarchal see of America, Malabar Succession of Antioch, a title that Hough has added to his title of archiepiscopal legate of the Ultrajectine Ordinariate of the Holy Catholic Church.

9. Since Wadle's death in 1965, the bulk of his followers have reportedly associated themselves with the Church of Antioch, Malabar Rite.

10. Hermann Adrian Spruit, *The Church of Antioch, Malabar Rite* (Santa Ana, California: Church of Antioch, 1967) (pamphlet), p. [2].

11. Communications from the Most Reverend H. Adrian Spruit, Santa Ana, California.

12. *Contact,* August 1967, p. 2.

13. Letter from the Most Reverend James Francis Augustine Lashley, archbishop-primate of Archdiocese of New York of the American Catholic Church; *Yearbook of American Churches for 1975*, pp. 28-29; Lashley, *Questions and Answers on the American Catholic Church Archdiocese* (undated pamphlet).

14. Reportedly he was consecrated in 1935 in the Russian Orthodox Cathedral of St. Nicholas, New York, by Archbishop Nikolai Kedroffsky and Archbishop Arsenios Saltas. Kedroffsky had reportedly been consecrated by Saltas and Christopher Contogeorge, who is described as "the Greek Archbishop of Philadelphia, Pennsylvania, and who later represented the Alexandrian Patriarchate of America." Saltas in turn had been consecrated by Contogeorge and by Albanian Archbishop Fan Stylian Noli. Contogeorge had been reportedly consecrated by Noli and by Archbishop Sophronios of Brooklyn, whom Aftimios Ofiesh had consecrated.

15. *Thirtieth Anniversary Services of the American Holy Orthodox Catholic Apostolic Eastern Church, Sunday, April 28th, 1963, Sts. Peter and Paul Church, 247 East 126th Street, New York, N. Y.* (pamphlet), p. [4].

16. George A. Hyde, "American Orthodox-Catholic Church Maintains Distinction," *Ortho*, Vol. 1, No. 2 (October 1966), 1.

17. Letter from the Most Reverend Petrus Andreas Žurawetzky, D.D., primate, Christ Catholic Church of the Americas and Europe. For a time the Western Orthodox Oecumenical Exarchate included the Byelorussian Reformed Church, founded by Uładysłau Ryży-Ryski, who subsequently became bishop of Laconia, New Hampshire, and the New England States in the American Orthodox Catholic Church (New York, New York) and who is now also administrator of the Byelorussian Patriarchate of St. Andrew the Apostle, the First-Called. In 1961 Žurawetzsky consecrated Robert Schuyler Zeiger, founder of the American Orthodox Catholic Church (Denver, Colorado).

18. *Christ Catholic Church (Diocese of Boston)* (Goffstown, N.H.: St. Willibrord's Press, 1967) (4-page pamphlet), p. 4.

19. Letter from Archbishop Žurawetzky.

20. Among recent appointees is the Most Reverend Waclaw Mateczyk of Hamilton, Ontario, a homepathic doctor and nonmedical health adviser by profession (consecrated in 1964 by Earl Anglin James and John Wilson).

21. *The Canons* (Glorieta, N.M.: Orthodox Catholic Jurisdiction of the Holy Spirit, 1969) (10-page pamphlet); *Monastic Guidelines* (Glorieta, N.M.: Monastery of Our Lady of Reconciliation, 1969) (10-page pamphlet).

22. Letters from the Most Reverend Peter Andreas Žurawetzky, president, Holy Synod of the Orthodox Catholic Churches in America. The present writer's repeated requests to the Right Reverend William C. Morgan for information about his jurisdiction went unanswered.

23. Because Nestorian missionaries are supposed to have participated in the evangelization of the Khazars, whose empire included eastern Byelorussia.

24. On the progress of the Genevan Reformation in Byelorussia-Lithuania during the sixteenth century, see Uładysłau Ryży-Ryski, *The Reformation in Byelorussia* (Princeton, N.J.: N.p., 1961) (67-page mimeographed brochure), pp. 51-53.

25. Letter from the Most Reverend Uładysłau Ryžy-Ryski, Th.M., Litt.D., apostolical administrator, Byelorussian (White Ruthenian) Patriarchate of St. Andrew the Apostle, the First-Called, of the Orthodoxly-Catholic Byelorussian Christian Church in Dispersion.

26. At a joint session of the Evangelical and Eastern Orthodox parties held on May 28, 1599, eighteen articles of faith were read in which, it was declared, both parties agreed: "(1) They believe and confess together that the holy Scriptures of the prophets and apostles are the fountain of truth and of the doctrine of salvation; (2) that God is one in substance, threefold in person; (3) [that] according to the teaching of the Synod of Nicaea these three persons are different, but they have the same essence, and none of them is before or after the others; (4) [that] the epitome (*Inbegriff*) of the apostolic doctrine that is called *symbolum* is the chief content of divine worship and of the true confession; (5) [that] Christ, the Son of the living God, is true God, begotten from eternity in an ineffable fashion by the Father, and true man, born for our salvation of the Virgin Mary; (6) [that] by offering himself this Christ has satisfied by his death for our sins; (7) [that] God is neither the cause nor the author of sin; (8) [that] all men are conceived and born in original sin; (9) [that] all who genuinely repent and convert themselves receive the forgiveness of their sins; (10) that believing Christians must do good works; (11) that Christ himself is the sole head of his church, both the visible [church] and the invisible [church]; (12) [that] in the visible church one stands in need of the ministry of clergymen (*des geistlichen Dienstes*), which functions (*nützet*) through the proclamation of the word [of God] and through the sacraments; (13) [that] marriage is not forbidden to clergymen; (14) [that] children must be brought to holy baptism; (15) [that] the supper of the Lord must be given to all the faithful under both species; (16) [that] the holy Scriptures nowhere speak of a purgatory in which the souls are to cleanse themselves after death; (17) [that] as Christ ascended bodily into heaven, so he sits at God's right hand, from where he will come to judge the living and the dead; (18) [and that] as the bliss of the believers is eternal, so the punishments of the damned are eternal" (Georg Wilhelm Theodor Fischer, *Versuch einer Geschichte der Reformation in Polen* II [Graz: Mittler'sche Buchhandlung (A. E. Döpner) in Posen, 1856], 110-111; see also Walerian Skorobohaty Krasinski, *Historical Sketch of the Rise, Progress, and Decline of the Reformation in Poland and of the Influence Which the Scriptural Doctrine Has Exercised on the Country in Literary, Moral, and Political Respects* II [London: Murray, 1840], 149-150, quoted in Uładysłau Ryžy-Ryski, "An Introduction to the History of the Reformation in Byelorussia and a Documentary Illustration on It" [Princeton, New Jersey: unpublished master's thesis, Princeton Theological Seminary, 1959-1960], appendix, p. xxxvi). It is not clear who drafted this document. Several articles point to a Reformed author. In any case, Turnovsky proposed that in connection with other doctrines, where the Eastern Orthodox and the Evangelicals disagreed with one another, annual synods, to be convoked alternately by the two parties, should attempt to achieve agreement. On the ground that they had no authority to engage in doctrinal negotiations, the Eastern Orthodox theologians refused to discuss theological issues; the most that they promised to do was not to write or speak against the efforts at unification (Fischer, II: 111-112).

27. Letters from Archbishop Ryžy-Ryski.

28. To the Reverend Constantine Andrews, pastor of the Greek Orthodox Church of St. Nicholas, St. Louis, Missouri, this writer owes the information that the Great Martyr (*Megalomartys*) St. Fanourios the New Convert (*Neophytos*) of Rhodes, commemorated in Eastern Orthodoxy on August 27, is known only from an icon found on that date in an old church that was being excavated on Rhodes during the pontificate of Neilos II (1355–1369), metropolitan of the island. It bears St. Fanourios's name and depicts him as a young soldier holding in his right hand a cross, with a lighted

candle (probably an allusion to his name) on top of it.

29. The Eastern designation for SS. Cosmas and Damian. They are called the *anargyroi*, or "penniless ones," because of the tradition that they accepted no fees for their practice of the art of healing.

30. This writer acknowledges gratefully the efforts of the Reverend John Fibelkorn, pastor of the Church of the Redeemer, Newark, New Jersey, to interview Archbishop Joachim on this writer's behalf.

31. *The Nature and Purpose of the Shrine and So On* (4-page undated pamphlet), p. [2].

33. The leaven in the bread "is the Spirit dwelling in the flesh" (*Meaning of the Universal Faith, and So On* [6-page undated pamphlet], p. 6).

33. *Meaning of the Universal Faith, and So On*, pp. 2-6.

34. Letter from the Most Reverend Mark Athanasios Constantine Karras, Archbishop of Byzantium.

35. *American Orthodox Catholic Church: Ecclesiastical Proclamation 1967* (pamphlet), p. [3].

36. Walter M. Propheta, *Divine Liturgy for 20th Century Christians 1967* (New York: The American Orthodox Catholic Church, 1966).

37. Ibid., p. iii (Constitution, Article 3).

38. The late Metropolitan of Louisville (Kentucky) and the Southern States was the Most Reverend Christopher J. Stanley, D.D., 4018 Vermont Avenue, Louisville. At one time he reportedly was the ecumenical patriarch of the United Old Catholic Patriarchate of the World (Peter F. Anson, *Bishops at Large* [New York: October House, 1964], p. 433, n. 3). According to Anson, Stanley derived his orders from Grant Timothy Billett, primate of the Old Catholic Church in North America, (ibid., p. 433).

39. Letter from the Very Reverend Milton A. Pritts, prime bishop of the Grand Synod of the American Orthodox Catholic Church and president of the corporation in the State of Colorado.

40. Information supplied by the most Reverend Colin James Guthrie.

41. Batchynskiy (Eugène de Batchinsky) is a Russian emigré count who fled his native land in 1905 and now resides in Rougemont, Canton Vaud, Switzerland. In the early 1920s he was in contact with the Kiev autocephaly under Archbishop Lipkivskiy and reportedly declared that he had received some sort of official mandate from the latter. In 1955 Batchynskiy was consecrated at Florence, Italy, by Nikolai Urbanovich of Winnipeg, Canada, assisted by Efrem Maria Mauro Fusi, the Mariavite bishop for Italy. Urbanovich, who came to Canada in 1929, was consecrated in 1949 for work in Canada by Anthony Aneed, who in turn claimed consecration in 1911 by the Roman Catholic Melkite Archbishop Athanasius Sawaya of Beirut, Lebanon. Fusi derives his episcopal orders from the Old Catholic Church of Utrecht via Jean Marie (Michael) Kowalski, founder of the Polish Mariavite Church, Marc Marie Paul Fatome, regionary bishop of the Mariavite Church for France, and Paul Maria Helmut Naberto Maas, Mariavite bishop of Germany. Batchynskiy claims the titles of titular bishop of Berne and Geneva and primate of the Sainte Église Orthodoxe Ukrainienne Conciliaire Autocéphale en Exil. In the "Table des différents branches de successions apostoliques de l'Église Catholique Gallicane de Normandie," an eight-page typewritten document that details the fourteen channels of apostolic succession that Irénée d'Eschevannes (Charles Marie Joseph Poncelin d'Eschevannes, also called Charles-Borromée d'Eschevannes), archbishop of Arles in the Église Gallicane Autocéphale, conferred upon "Ignatius III" when he consecrated him to the episcopate in 1966, Batchynskiy is called "Orthodox Bishop of the Apostolic Succession of Kiev (Ukraine)" (op. cit., p. 2). ("Ignatius III" is Lutheran Professor Helmut Echternach [b. 1907] of the University of Hamburg.) This writer's repeated requests to Batchynskiy for information about his North American affiliate went unacknowledged.

42. The present writer's repeated requests to Sawyna for information about the history, canonical connections, and size of his jurisdiction went unacknowledged. The efforts of the Reverend John Daniel, M.A., D.D., pastor of St. John's Church, Allentown, to secure a personal interview were likewise unavailing.

BIBLIOGRAPHY

Anson, Peter F. *Bishops at Large*. New York: October House, 1964. The author is a highly knowledgeable Roman Catholic layman.

Brandreth, Henry R. T. *Episcopi Vagantes and the Anglican Church*. 2nd edition. London: SPCK, 1961. The author is an Anglican Oratorian priest.

Terry-Thompson, Arthur Cornelius. *The History of the African Orthodox Church*. New York; African Orthodox Church, 1956. This source is of interest primarily for the documents that it reproduces.

6. The Russian Old Believers

A tragic schism split the Russian Orthodox Church in the seventeenth century. Nikon (1605–1681), the brilliant, ambitious, imperious, and severe metropolitan of Novgorod, became patriarch of Moscow in 1652 by order of Tsar Alexis. Between 1653 and his deposition in 1658 Nikon introduced into the rite and ceremonial of the established church a number of changes designed to make the Russian Church more like the contemporary Greek Church. The result was that increasing numbers of the Russian faithful withdrew from the established church in order to retain the practices that had become for them a hallowed tradition. They insisted on making the sign of the holy cross with two fingers, not three, as the reforms directed. They sang Alleluia only twice, not three times, at the end of psalms. They insisted on the cross with three bars, the bottom one aslant, as the symbol of the true Eastern Orthodox faith. They used a minimum of seven loaves at the Eucharist, not five. They refused to venerate any icons except those that antedated the Niconian reforms or that at least were painted in strict adherence to the old prescriptions. They rejected the textual modernizations of the Niconian reforms and insisted, for instance, that the holy name of Jesus must be pronounced and written *Isus* and not *Iisus*. They insisted on confessing the creed in the old Russian way, "I believe in the Holy Spirit, the Lord, true and life-giving, who proceeds from the Father."[1]

The representatives of what the Old Believers called the "dominant church" (*gospodstvuyushchaya tserkov*) persecuted the proponents of the old ways with great severity. Many of the Old Believer leaders were burned alive. Among them was one of the great examples of Russian spirituality, Archpriest (Protopope) Avvakum (Habakkuk) (1620?–1682) of Yurievets.[2] The latter met martyrdom with three companions, Theodore, Lazarus, and Epiphanius, all of whom had previously suffered having their tongues cut out.[3] Deportation was the lot of thousands of other Old Believers; but instead of annihilating dissent this merely spread it. At first the Old Believers regarded Nikon as the Antichrirst. Then, when after Nikon's deposition the Old Believers saw the tsar supporting the Niconian reforms, they were ready to believe that the government was the embodiment of Antichrist.[4]

The "lesser church" that came into being in 1667, when a council in Moscow deposed Nikon, on the one hand, and excommunicated the Old Believers as heretics, on the other, received various names. The established church called them the Schismatics (*Raskolniki*), a stigma from which Nicholas II freed them in 1905, although the term has lived on. They themselves gloried in the names Old Believers (*Starovertsy*) and Old Ritualists (*Staroobriadtsy*), although some of them were reluctant to describe themselves by the latter term.

The defenders of the old tradition divided into two groups, the Priestists[5] (*Popovtsy*) and the Priestless (*Bezpopovtsy*). The Priestists insisted upon an episcopally ordained priesthood to conduct their ancient services. No bishops, except Paul of Kolomna, who died in 1656, joined the Old Believers, and the priests ordained prior to the Niconian reforms all finally died. For that reason the Priestists had to depend for nearly two centuries almost exclusively on the services of priests who for one reason or another left the established church, although there were differences in the way in which they received these converted priests as Old Believer officiants.[6]

After more than a century of fruitless effort, some wealthy Priestist Old Believers prevailed on the Austro-Hungarian government in 1844 to establish an episcopal see at Bela Krynica (Belokrinitsa) for Priestists residing in the Austro-Hungarian Empire. In 1846 they procured to fill this vacancy the former metropolitan of Sarajevo, Ambrose, whom the Turks had deposed and who was living in retirement in Istanbul. Before the tsar was able to induce the Austro-Hungarian government to depose Ambrose once more, the latter consecrated a number of other bishops both for Russia and for the diaspora. This "Belokrinitskaya" line of succession has continued down to the present in two branches. One hierarchy exists in the Union of Soviet Socialist Republics, with an archbishop in Moscow at its head. Since the Soviet takeover of Belokrinitsa after World War II, the primate of the diaspora hierarchy has resided in Galati, Romania.[7]

In the meantime, another group of Priestist Old Believers had received from the established church the assurance that their parishes could continue in the undisturbed practice of their ancient customs and that the Russian hierarchy would ordain priests for them with permission to use the Old Rite. In 1800/1801 these "Yedinovertsy"[8] parishes were reconciled to the established church. Since 1905 they have gone by the designation Pravoslavniye Staroobriadtsy (Old Rite Orthodox). In 1918 Patriarch Tikhon consecrated a bishop for them in the person of Archpriest Semyon Shleyov. As bishop of Ufa he suffered martyrdom at the hands of the communists in 1921. The fate of his successor, Andrey (Prince Ukhtomsky), is not wholly certain. Reportedly he too died a martyr.

A third Priestist group bears the name Beglopopovtsy (Wandering Priestists). After World War II a Beglopopovtsy hierarchy came into being for them in the Soviet Union; the archbishop-primate resides in Kuibyshev (Samara). There are no organized Beglopopovtsy communities in North America.[9]

When some of the Old Believers found it impossible, or at least inconvenient, to obtain ordained Russian priests after the death of the first-generation clergy, they made a virtue of necessity. They rejected in principle the idea of an episcopally ordained priesthood and became Priestless. They argued that by accepting the anti-Christian Niconian reforms and by anathematizing the Old Believers, the established church had forfeited its Christian character and its status as a community of divine grace. Even if episcopally consecrated priests were available, said the Bezpopovtsy, they could not transmit grace through their sacramental ministrations. Some of the Bezpopovtsy defended their position by arguing that every Christian is a priest and that no priestly office is necessary. Others granted that their clergy did not have an episcopal succession, but that they had a presbyteral succession.

For the most part, the Bezpopovtsy claimed for themselves only the sacraments that laypeople can administer according to their teaching, that is, baptism and absolution. In some emergencies their teachers or seniors dispensed Communion with elements allegedly consecrated in the days of the "pious priests," and some also solemnized marriages. At the other extreme were Bezpopovtsy who held that every meal reverently received with thanksgiving is a communion with Christ, and that the sacrament of the altar is unnecessary.

Marriage in particular presented a grave problem, since in Eastern Orthodoxy it is a sacrament that only an ordained priest can validly administer. Some of the Bezpopovtsy proposed to resolve the difficulty by requiring rigid celibacy, a program that inevitably failed. Others regarded the union of the sexes as a purely secular matter, a concession to the flesh, and ultimately mere concubinage. Since this too was an unsatisfactory solution of the problem, a variety of intermediate positions developed, including stable monogamous marriage protected by the sanction of community opinion and entered into with a simple blessing by the senior or teacher.

With no hierarchy and with no central organization, the number of Bezpopovtsy divisions and subdivisions multiplied beyond the possibility even of cataloguing. While many of these groups were short-lived, a considerable number have survived and at least two Bezpopovtsy groups exist in organized form in North America.[10]

Priestist Old Ritualists

As far back as 1755 the first Old Ritualist pioneers established colonies in Eastern Siberia. After the Revolution of 1917 many of them fled to Haerhpin (Harbin), Manchuria, where the Old Ritualist Bishop Joseph of the Far East organized them into a community. It ultimately grew to six parishes and managed to maintain itself until the Chinese Communists destroyed it in 1961. About sixty families, with a priest of their own, emigrated to Canada in 1923/1924; the bulk of this group settled at Hines Creek, Alberta, where they have built a permanent Old Ritualist church of wood. In 1960 the Canadian government admitted ten more families. Subsequently another eleven families came to Canada by way of Brazil, and a small trickle of immigrants continues. Old Ritualists are scattered throughout Canada. There are also small groups in the United States; Joann Emelianovich Starosadchev of Hines Creek visited adherents in the United States from time to time.[11] Both the Old Ritualist hierarchy in the Union of the Soviet Socialist Republics and the Old Ritualist primate in Galati, Romania, authorized him to minister to Old Ritualists in the American diaspora. But the communist rulers of both the Soviet Union and Romania have refused to concur in arrangements for the ordination of priests who might continue Father Starosadchev's ministry.[12]

In the eighteenth century some of the Priestist Old Ritualists from the Kuban River valley settled at Koca Göl (Eski Kazaklar) on Lake Manyas (Maynos) near the Sea of Marmora (Marmara Denizi) in Turkey. In the middle of the nineteenth century these "Nekrasovtsy" divided into two parishes; one drew its clergy from the Yedinovertsy, the other from the diaspora hierarchy at Bela Krynitsa. After World War I the Russian Orthodox Church Outside of Russia ordained priests for the first group and after World War II the Ecumenical Patriarchate in Istanbul provided this service for both groups. Around 1960 the bulk of this colony, numbering about a thousand, returned to the Soviet Union. In 1963 about twenty-five of the remainder found their way through the sponsorship of the Tolstoy Foundation to the United States. Some have scattered, others live in Paterson, New Jersey, and on the Tolstoy Farm at Valley Cottage, New York. They receive priestly ministrations from a Russian Orthodox priest of the Old Rite in Southbury, Connecticut, and from other Eastern Orthodox priests.[13]

The Old Orthodox Church (Russian Old Believers, Pomortsi)

Adherents of this church call themselves Pomortsi, because the largest group of opponents of the Niconian reforms settled in the north of Russia, along the shore (*pomorye*) of the White Sea. In the early persecutions some 4,000 colonists and their monastic leaders allegedly perished in the flames. Then the fugitives established a new settlement on the Vyg River in the province of Olonets, on the border of Swedish Finland. It centered around the Danilovsky Monastery of the Theophany, formed in 1695 by Daniel Vykulin and led by the two princely Denisov brothers, Andrew and Simeon. Originally Andrew Denisov sought to impose compulsory celibacy on all who joined the colony. This proved impossible, so he divided his followers into professed monks and nuns in their respective monasteries and secular villagers who were allowed to marry. By 1800 there were over 2,000 monks and over 1,000 nuns in the Vyg River monasteries, with special schools for the education of the movement's missionaries. In 1855 Nicholas I closed the monasteries, whereupon the colonies became simple villages and rapidly declined.

The movement published a statement of its faith in 1723 under the title *The Shore Dwellers' Answers.* In it the Pomortsi affirm their unqualified profession of the Orthodox faith as the pre-Niconian church understood it. They advocated the sign of the cross with two fingers, the double Alleluia, and the use of icons only of the ancient type. They affirmed that the church could exist without an episcopally ordained priesthood, and that in such a case there could be only the two sacraments that laymen could impart, baptism and absolution. In the absence of the Eucharist they regarded the fervent desire to receive the sacrament of the altar as sufficient. Characteristic was their doctrine of the "internal temple in the soul":

> All assemblies and services, feasts, communions and sacrifices were established to purify man of his sins in order that God may come in. The soul which bears God does not attach itself to the visible churches and sacrifices, to the numerous congregations and human feasts. It does not worship God on this mountain or in Jerusalem. The soul has God within itself, true spirit, interior altar-pure conscience, nonmaterial purifying tears, interior Jerusalem, joy of the spirit. The soul, being spiritual, brings forth spiritual sacrifices.[14]

The Pomortsi movement in Russia reached its peak around 1863, when an official estimate put their number at 2 million.

The Old Orthodox came to this country in moderate numbers in the late nineteenth century. The established their first parish at Marianna, Pennsylvania, in 1901, followed by three more at Erie, Pennsylvania (1916), Detroit, Michigan (1935), and Millville, New Jersey (1940).

The North American Old Orthodox hold that Greek Orthodoxy lost the "purity and original holiness of Christ's Orthodox faith" as a result of its reunion with the Roman see in the fifteenth century, and that the "dominant church" in Russia lost its character as a church and community of divine grace through its acceptance of the Niconian reforms and of the rule of the tzarist government. They reject the Beglopopovtsy, the Yedinovertsy, and the supporters of the Belokrinitskaya succession inside and outside of the Soviet Union because of the dubious "validity of the priestly grace of men that formerly belonged to the church which strayed from the right faith itself" and "put anathemas on" the Old Believers. They are content to believe that there is "no true apostolic succession left in the world," that "the holy fire on the altar was extinguished and there was nobody left capable of rekindling it."

They distinguish between the four "necessary" sacraments (Communion, episcopally ordained priesthood, chrismation, and the unction of the sick) and the three "life-necessary" or "utmost necessary" sacraments (baptism, absolution, and marriage). The former were once necessary to believers, but are no longer available. Without the latter it is impossible to become a member of the church, establish a legal family life, or obtain salvation. Presbyterally ordained priests may administer these sacraments and even laymen may administer baptism and absolution.

Their priests or "preceptors" are ordained through a "consecutive" blessing by an already ordained incumbent.

They accept the Bible, holy tradition, and the decrees of the seven universal councils; the deity of Christ, the head of the Church; and the perpetual virginity of the Theotokos. They venerate the cross, icons, and relics of the saints, but do not allow carved images. They reject the dogma of the immaculate conception of the Blessed Virgin Mary, indulgences, purgatory, and the infallibility of the bishop of Rome. They hold that justification comes by faith and works.[15] They endorse the ceremonial provisions of the One Hundred Articles Council (Stoglaviy Sobor) of 1551.

A typical parish constitution provides that "the priest is to be elected at a general assembly [of full male and female members over twenty-one years of age] by a two-thirds majority vote of full members then present."[16] Thereupon he makes his confession to his spiritual father, another priest, and the latter, with the assistance of another priest or priests (if available), ordains the candidate.[17] The priest "has the right to veto any decision of the church council if he feels that such a decision is against the church rules or customs," and the General Assembly must reconsider the vetoed decision before it can be executed.[18]

The priest is addressed as "Father."

The total membership of the four parishes is about 3,000. The parish at Erie is the largest and exerts a measure of leadership among the others.[19]

Other Bezpopovtsy

Around the turn of the century a group of Old Ritualists living in Brăila (Brailov) on the Danube,[20] in a part of Romania that had at one time been under Turkish rule, moved to Kazak Köyü, near Akşehir, in the Asia Minor heartland. In 1962 a few of them elected repatriation to the Soviet Union, but the remainder, about 175, came to the United States under Tolstoy Foundation sponsorship and settled in Freewood Acres and Millville, New Jersey. In 1964 about thirty-three families crossed the continent to Woodburn and Gervais, Oregon.

Although they are in fact priestless at the present time, their worship indicates that they were originally Beglopovotsy Priestists. When at some point in their history they were not able to obtain priestly services from converted Eastern Orthodox priests, they abandoned their Priestist position. Later, even when they might have regularized their status by accepting the ministrations of Yedinovertsy or Belokrinitskaya succession priests, they refused to do so. A lay reader (*dyak*), usually elected for one year at a time, conducts the services. In emergencies he administers Holy Communion from reserved elements allegedly consecrated by a "pious priest" of the past. While they do not have sacramental marriage, they bless the bride and groom with a simple form and do not depreciate matrimony. They still observe very strictly some traditional Old Believer rules, such as refusing to eat and to drink with outsiders, but they have relaxed others, such as the prohibition of being photographed. The men wear beards and the women dress traditionally. When a Priestist Old Ritualist joins their community, they baptize him anew.[21] They have diligently preserved the liturgical usages of the sixteenth and seventeenth centuries as far as the lack of priests permits, and they sing the chants from memory. They follow the Julian calendar.[22]

In the communities at Woodburn and Gervais, Oregon, there were at the beginning of 1967 more than a hundred families, totaling more than 500 persons, who call themselves Chapel Union (Chasovennoye Soglasiye) Old Ritualists. An additional hundred families arrived during 1967. Originally some of these people came from Siberia and Manchuria and others from the Chinese province of Sinkiang. They emigrated to Brazil with the aid of the Ford Foundation in 1958 and began to come to Oregon in 1964.

As their name suggests, they too were apparently at one time Beglopopovtsy. They intercommunicate (that is, eat, drink, and pray together) with the Priestless Old Believers from Turkey and intermarry with them freely.

They use Old Slavonic in their services, and keep Sunday and all the traditional holy days of the Orthodox calendar. The officiants (*nastavniki*) are elected to their office. The books used in the service are the personal property of the worshipers. Of the traditional mysteries they observe baptism, the Eucharist, absolution, and marriage.[23]

NOTES

1. The Old Russian version of the creed translated the Greek word *kyrion* twice, as "Lord" and as "true," corresponding to two possible meanings of the Greek vocable. In support of the Old Russian rendering, the Old Believers cite the Old Slavonic translation of St. John 15:26: "When the Counselor comes, whom I shall send you from the Father, even the true Spirit, who proceeds from the Father. . . ."

2. See his illuminating autobiography, "The Life of Archpriest Avvakum by Himself," in G. P. Fedotov, ed., *A*

Treasury of Russian Spirituality (New York: Sheed and Ward, 1948) pp. 134-181.

3. According to the "Autobiography of the Hieromonk Epiphanius," his tongue had been cut out for resistance to the Niconian reforms but had miraculously grown back. At his second trial the government officials allegedly asked him two questions: "Do you believe in God the Spirit not true [sic]? Will you bless yourself with a three-finger cross instead of a two-finger cross?" He reportedly replied that he could not believe in a not true Spirit,

and that he would not change his way of crossing himself, which was the All-Russian way. Thereupon his judges had his tongue cut out a second time and the four fingers of his right hand chopped off.

4. The year 1666 was regarded as especially ominous because the number of the Beast of Revelation is 666 and the year in question was the 666th of the second millennium of the Christian era. After the Old Believers began to identify the czar as the Antichrist, their conviction on this point grew stronger when Peter the Great attempted to Europeanize Russia in the eighteenth century. His use of the style Peter I, instead of the conventional Peter Alexeyevich, confirmed for the Old Believers the suspicion that he was not really the son of Alexis but of Satan.

5. The English term is Serge Bolshakoff's.

6. Some Old Believers merely chrismated priests of the "dominant church" when they joined Old Believer ranks. Other Old Believers went to the length of rebaptizing these converted priests by immersing them in their sacredotal vestments.

7. The Roman Catholic Church has de facto acknowledged the validity of the orders and sacraments of the Belokrinitskaya hierarchy, but the Russian Orthodox Church has not done so on the ground that canon law requires three bishops for a valid episcopal consecration, while Ambrose was the only consecrator of the prelates' that perpetuated the Belokrinitskaya hierarchy. The Old Believer movement was intimately linked to the nationalist feelings of the Great Russians, which felt itself threatened by the alien Niconian reforms. The Old Believer movement accordingly never achieved much success outside of Great Russia. Priests in Great Russia who might have joined the Old Believer movement out of conviction were safer outside of Russia. For that reason the lack of priests became an acute problem inside Russia before it did in the diaspora.

8. The word means "those of one and the same [faith]." The translation "uniat[e]," which Conybeare uses, is not wholly inappropriate, but it is confusing because it has become a technical term to describe a union of an altogether different type, the union that has produced Oriental Rite Roman Catholics.

9. Prior to the introduction of the Yedinoveriye and the establishment of the Belokrinitskaya hierarchy, the Russian authorities forbade Priestist Old Believers to call their places of worship churches, since only a bishop may consecrate a church, either personally or by sending an *antiminsion* for the altar. In Russia such an Old Believer chapel (*chasovn'a,* a place where the daily office [*chasy*] could be said, but not the divine liturgy) could have no sanctuary and no altar. The iconostasis was "blind," that is, it had no doors and rested directly against the liturgical east wall of the building. Outside of Russia the Priestists could build structures with sanctuaries and altars and call them churches.

10. This writer gratefully acknowledges the assistance of the Reverend Dimitri Alexandrow, Southbury, Connecticut, in the preparation of this section.

11. There has been a considerable immigration of Old Ritualists from Manchuria to Australia. The first wave, after World War II, settled in Melbourne and on Tasmania. The second wave, after the Chinese Communist penetration of Manchuria in 1961, went chiefly to Sidney.

12. Letter from the Reverend Joann Emelianovich Starosadchev, Hines Creek, Alberta, Canada.

13. Letters from the Reverend Dimitri Alexandrow, Southbury, Connecticut. Metropolitan Philaret of the Russian Orthodox Church Outside of Russia ordained Father Dimitri in 1965 to minister to Old Rite adherents who accept the Russian Orthodox priesthood.

14. Vladimir Anderson, *Staroobriadchestvo i sektanskvo* (St. Petersburg: V. Gubinsky, 1909), p. 144, quoting *The Shore Dwellers' Handbook*; the present translation is by Serge Bolshakoff, *Russian Nonconformity: The Story of "Unofficial Religion" in Russia* (Philadelphia: The Westminster Press, 1950), p. 73. To designate their chapels, the Pomortsi (as well as other Bezpopovtsy) preferred the term *molennaya,* that is, "[house of] worship or prayer."

15. "The Priestless Old Orthodoxians," in

Vladimir Smolakov, ed., *Church Calendar 1957* (Erie, Penna.: Old Orthodox Church of the Nativity, 1956), pp. 19-36.

16. Section a, Article XIX, *By-Laws of the Old-Orthodox Parish of the St. Nicholas Church of Millville, New Jersey, 1961*, p. 9.

17. Letter of the Reverend Vladimir Smolakov, pastor of the Old Orthodox Church of the Nativity, Erie, Pennsylvania.

18. Sections h and i, Article XIX, *By-Laws,* loc. cit.

19. Letters of the Reverend Vladimir Smolakov and of Mr. Theodore Daniloff, secretary of the Old Orthodox Church of St. Nicholas, Millville, New Jersey.—On the Old Orthodox Church, see Vladimir Smolakov, "The Old Orthodoxy," in *Church Calendar 1967*, Vladimir Smolakov, ed. (Erie, Penna.: Old Orthodox Church of the Nativity, 1966), pp. 21-30.

20. Russian, *Dunay*, hence the nickname for this group, "Dunaki."

21. So do the Priestist Old Believers when a Priestless Old Believer joins them.

22. Letter from the Reverend Dimitri Alexandrow, Southbury, Connecticut.

23. Letters from Mr. Efim Podgornoff, Gervais, Oregon, and Mr. Prohor Martushev, secretary of the Old Ritualist Society in Oregon, Gervais, Oregon; the cited letter of the Reverend Dimitri Alexandrow; Robert Olmos, "Russian Immigrants Arrive in Portland," *Portland Oregonian,* December 4, 1964.

BIBLIOGRAPHY

GENERAL

Bolshakoff, Serge. *Russian Nonconformity: The Story of "Unofficial" Religion in Russia.* Philadelphia: The Westminster Press, 1950. Chaps. 4-6, pp. 46-82.

Cherniavsky, Michael. "The Old Believers and the New Religion," in *Slavic Review* 25 (1966): 1-39.

Conybeare, Frederick Cornwalls. *Russian Dissenters.* New York: Russell and Russell, 1962. An unaltered reissue of the 1921 Harvard University Press edition. Part I (pp. 1-258) deals with "The Old Believers of Great Russia."

PART III

THE CHURCH IN THE WEST: THE FIRST FIFTEEN CENTURIES

Even before Latin replaced Greek as the language of the city of Rome, a Western type of Christianity was already in existence. It culminated in the Western Christianity of the fourteenth and fifteenth centuries. By then the process of dissolution that climaxed in the sixteenth century had already begun in earnest. This late medieval Western Christianity continues to affect for good or for ill not only the Western churches who cherish the historical links that bind them to their past, but even—although often unwittingly—branches of the church that affirm no love for Christendom in its historical aspect.

The agencies that molded this Western type of Christianity were many—individual theologians; councils ranging from local assemblies to the pan-Western conclaves of the late Middle Ages; the developing self-consciousness of both the church and the bishops of Rome, before as well as after the conversion of Constantine; the pagan or at best imperfectly Christianized nations on their marches across Europe and western Africa; the developing patterns of liturgical worship; the rivalry and the collaboration of Roman popes and Holy Roman emperors from the ninth century onward; the slow melding of surviving elements of the classical heritage with the novelties that were the contribution of the barbarians; the genius of philosophers, the insights of mystics, and the contradictions of heretics; and the always imponderable and unpredictable hand of God in history.

Part III, it should be noted, is not intended to be even a summary history of the Western church, or of Christian thought. It merely proposes to sketch in broad outlines and at the risk of oversimplification the development of the issues that the Christian community in the West from the sixteenth century onward deemed theologically important.

7. Theological and Ecclesiastical Leadership

Theologians

Among the theologians St. Irenaeus of Lyons (130?–200?), probably a native of Smyrna, is both an early and an important link between the Church of the East and the Church of the West. In a sense he is the founder of Christian theology in the West, even though he wrote in Greek. He was an articulate adversary of Gnostic dualism and docetism, an observant critic of heresy, and an energetic apologist. He stressed the already existing theological tradition; he operated with a New Testament canon that included the Revelation of St. John and the Shepherd of Hermas but lacked the Letter to the Hebrews; he insisted on the importance of the Incarnation and of Christ's complete humanity for the Christian faith. At the center of his theology was his doctrine of *anakephalaiosis* (literally "recapitulation"), a basically Pauline idea that St. Irenaeus developed into the taking up into Christ of everything since creation. That is, in Christ mankind has been recreated, renewed, restored, and revitalized; in Christ God has killed sin, taken away from death its power, conquered the demonic adversary, and saved all human beings. For St. Irenaeus the sacrament of the altar is the body and blood of Christ; it confers on the bodies of the communicants the hope of their own resurrection.

Another eminent early Western theologian, whose work earned him the title "Father of Latin theology," was the Carthaginian layman-lawyer Tertullian (Quintus Septimius Florens Tertullianus, 160?–220?). Almost intuitively his legal mind developed the formulas for the Trinity—indeed, he is the first to use the term—and the Incarnation of Christ on the usefulness of which the whole Catholic Church ultimately came to agree. God, he said, is "three 'persons' in one 'essence' " and Jesus Christ is God and a human being in "one 'person.' " He also spoke of the "vice of origin," the evil desire that has penetrated human nature as a consequence of the sin of Adam.

St. Cyprian (Thascus Caecilius Cyprianus) (200?–259), bishop of Carthage and martyr, helped greatly to determine the direction that the evolving office of bishop would take and to fix the way in which the church would reflect on her oneness and on her essentiality.

St. Jerome (Eusebius Hieronymus) (347?–420?) gave the Latin-speaking West its most authentic vernacular Bible, the Vulgate,[1] and revealed his own theological competence in his influential commentaries.

Through St. Ambrose (339?–397) of Milan many accents of Eastern Christian theology found their way into Western Christian thought. Among them were the trinitarian theology of St. Basil the Great and the allegorizing exegetical method of Origen. From him too came a strong insistence upon the actual presence of the body and blood of Christ in the sacrament of the altar.

St. Augustine (Aurelius Augustinus) (354–430), bishop of Hippo Regius in Africa, stands unequaled in stature as a theologian during the twelve hundred years between St. Paul and St. Thomas Aquinas, even though his influence was not altogether an unmixed blessing.

The Manichean solution to the problem of evil was assertion of a radical dualism, with a good divine principle and an evil divine principle engaged in endless conflict. Over against this view St. Augustine taught the essential goodness of creation. God, he asserted, is the creator of all things and he alone sustains their being. Evil in his view is the lack of some good that ought to be present. Physical evil results from creaturely imperfection. Moral evil is the result of the misuse of free choice by human and angelic beings.

His doctrine of the sacraments helped to distinguish "validity" and "regularity" in their administration. The definition of a sacrament as an outward and visible sign of an invisible, interior, and spiritual grace has an Augustinian origin. His contention that "the word comes to the element and a sacrament happens" provides an explanation that has been quoted ever since. There is a kind of bifurcation of his eucharistic thought that he himself seems to have been able to maintain in fruitful tension; sometimes he seems to have inclined toward a spiritualizing understanding of the sacraments; sometimes his view seems to have been more realistic. Thus he provided later generations with documentation that enabled them to claim him for both approaches. The idea of a "spiritual communion" when a literal reception of eucharistic elements is not possible or feasible goes back to his epigram: "Believe and you have eaten" (*Crede et manducasti*).

On the issue of the relation between government, with its coercive authority, and the church, St. Augustine affirmed that government was good only to the extent that it was founded on justice, which for him included worship of the true God. For that reason, while he refused to approve the imposition of the death penalty on heretics, he saw the coercive punishment and suppression of heresy and schism within the church as a legitimate office of the government.

St. Augustine's understanding of the fall of Adam as implying the loss of certain supernatural gifts with which God has endowed human beings at creation has continued to inform the thinking of many Western Christians.

Augustine staked out the theological boundaries of the sovereignty of God. Under the head of "original sin" he affirmed that human beings suffer from a hereditary moral disease from which only God can save them; that human beings are utterly incapable of any spiritual good through their native powers; and that each human being has an inherited legal liability for Adam's trespass.

In other contexts St. Augustine insisted on the divine initiative in the salvation of human beings (grace). His symbolical understanding of the millennium marked a break with the more literal chiliasm of many of the early Fathers. He defined for centuries to come one of the major Christian attitudes toward war by differentiating just from unjust wars, by condemning aggressive wars for territorial expansion, and by insisting that war is morally defensible only when it is waged for the common good of society and to achieve peace.

Without using the terms, he adumbrated a later distinction between the "visible church" and the "invisible church." The former is a mixed body in which there are believers whom their faith is gradually transforming morally as well as sanctimonious pretenders without faith. By contrast the "invisible church" is composed exclusively of good people.

Along with all this, he baptized Neoplatonism for the West and introduced a spiritualizing and antimaterial skew into Christian thinking about God's creation. His teaching about predestination developed strongly deterministic overtones, particularly in his later works. His views on grace give some readers the impression that it is irresistible. His reflections on the last things laid the foundation for the medieval idea of purgatory.[2]

There are other Western theologians of influence and distinction beside and after St. Augustine. There is St. Celestine of Rome (d. 432), whose forthright condemnation of Nestorius played a significant role at the Council of Ephesus (431). There are the "Semiaugustinians" like Blessed John Cassian (360?–435) and St. Vincent of Lerins (d. before 450). There is St. Leo the Great (d. 461) of Rome, whose *Tome* provided the Council of Chalcedon (451) with fundamental direction. There are St. Caesarius of Arles (470?–542), St. Gregory the Great (540?–604) of Rome, Blessed Alcuin (730?–804), and the "solitary luminary" John Scotus Erigena (810?–877?).[3] But until we come to St. Anselm of Canterbury (1033?–1109) there is none that even approaches Augustinian dimensions.

Scholasticism—the application of the dialectical treatment inherited from classic antiquity to the traditional materials of medieval theology and philosophy—begins with St. Anselm. He preferred to defend the Christian faith less with appeals to the Scripture and to theological and philosophical authorities than with intellectual reasoning. Against the assertions of atheism, he sought to establish the being of God entirely on the basis of reason. In the process he equated God with the Platonic "idea of the good." With St. Augustine he saw faith as the prerequisite for the right use of reason, but he insisted on the duty of the Christian to exercise his intellect in apprehending the truth that God has revealed.

One of the views that St. Anselm opposed was an early form of "nominalism"—the philosophical doctrine that the words that human beings use for universals are only names and do not correspond to actually existing entities. Against this teaching he affirmed that "universals are real things," even though as realities comprehensible to reason they were realities of a higher order. His opposition had more than a philosophical concern behind it. Nominalism, as he saw it, was incompatible with the church's teaching about the Trinity and about Christ's Incarnation. In the teaching about God it must lead either to tritheism or to a monotheism that erased the differences between the Father and the Son and the Holy Spirit. Since the heart of the Incarnation is that Christ assumed our humanity, or, to use the traditional term, our human nature, to say that Christ took on himself a human person would seem to prevent him from being the Savior of all human beings.

One of the theologically most influential of St. Anselm's treatises was the dialogue with his pupil Boso that in its title posed the question, "Why did God become a human being?" (*Cur Deus homo?*). In it St. Anselm argues that at the beginning God determined to establish a realm of rational beings that would obey his will and live under his lordship. The fall of some of the angelic beings resulted in the creation of human beings as replacements for the fallen angels. The subsequent fall of Adam again imperiled the divine plan and violated God's honor. This insult God could not endure. Justice demanded that the honor taken away be restored. The alternative was punishment: "It is necessary that satisfaction or punishment follow every sin." But to punish human beings would involve their destruction and would thus frustrate God's plan; the only other option was compensation or satisfaction. This lay beyond human ability, since perfect obedience was already the minimum that God's plan demanded. Thus only God could make the satisfaction that God's honor demanded. The instrument of God's satisfaction was Christ, who is both God and man. As a human being he owed God perfect obedience; for that reason it is by his death rather than by his life that Christ redeemed human beings. He himself did not have to die, but by voluntarily undergoing death he acquired the superabundant merit that God by a divine decree could apply to human beings and thus reconcile them to himself. It is through St. Anselm that the medieval West came to stress the forensic metaphor of the atonement and to think of Christ's redemptive work predominantly as a vicarious satisfaction. St. Anselm's teaching, which reflected and in turn helped to inform the medieval practice of penance, with its careful matching of guilt and satisfaction, helped to make the Middle Ages increasingly merit-conscious.[4] In its efforts to explain how Christ's merits are applied to the individual, medieval theology often tended to evoke the impression that salvation is something that human beings must earn themselves rather than a gratuitous gift of God.

A contemporary of St. Anselm's, Peter Abelard (1079–1142), took a different tack. For him Christ's death has saving power because the love for us which he there exhibits elicits our love in return and thus destroys our sins. Another major contribution of Abelard was his *Sic et non* ("So and not [so]"). In this book he quoted in opposition to one another apparently contradictory affirmations of Christian theologians. To show how such seeming inconsistencies should be approached, he then proceeded to remove the apparent contradictions. In some cases a critical historical review indicated that the apparent contradictions were speaking to quite diverse issues. In other cases, Abelard resolved the difficulty by affirming a graduated authority, with an infallible divine revelation at the top standing in contrast to fallible human constructions. Others he resolved by applying the principles of reason; reason, he felt, derives from divine truth as much as faith does, and so they cannot contradict one another.

What St. Anselm began, Hugh (1096?–1141) and Richard (d. 1173) of St. Victor—the Parisian abbey school where both of them flourished—carried farther. In their treatment of the tradition they combined rational speculation with a mystical reflection that led from natural thinking (*cogitatio*) by way of an intuitive meditation on the divine thoughts hidden in both creatures and the Scriptures to purity of life and loving contemplation. Hugh's *De sacramentis Christianae fidei* ("On the sacred things of the Christian faith") is the first scholastic systematic treatment of the Christian religion. Richard's *De trinitate* ("On the Trinity") stresses the importance of demonstration and argument in theological reflection, as opposed to an appeal to an array of authorities. It goes even to the point of affirming that speculative reasoning could bring a person to the essentials of the Christian doctrine of the Trinity.

Peter Lombard (1100?–1160) is the synthesist who combines the methodologies of St. Anselm, Hugh, Richard, and Abelard. His *Sententiarum libri quattuor* ("Four books of opinions") provided a favorite matrix of systematic reflection for the next five centuries. The four books cover the mystery of the Trinity, creation and sin, the Incarnation of the divine word and the virtues, and the "signs" (that is, the sacraments) and the last things. He sees philosophy as of some help in providing solutions to theological problems, but he attaches great importance to authorities, with the sacred Scriptures in a preeminent place. Among his patristic authorities are not only the Fathers of the Western tradition, but also Eastern theologians, notably St. John of Damascus. Peter Lombard is among the first to insist on seven sacraments and to distinguish these from the "sacramentals" that the church has instituted.

Among the scholastics from St. Anselm to Peter Lombard, the Augustinian tradition is prominent in its doctrine of grace. At creation, it holds, the first human beings possessed righteousness (*justitia*) and a right attitude of the will as gifts of divine grace. The "fall" deprived human beings of this right attitude of the will; because the will is now curved in on itself, human beings are not able to be righteous by their own power. No creature—including the individual himself—can restore the right attitude of the will; it can be restored only if divine grace takes the initiative (*gratia praeveniens*) and it can be preserved only when grace continues to support it (*gratia consequens*). The human counterpart and product of grace is living faith. Faith and righteousness imply each other; to will what is right demands faith, while to have faith demands a right will. The schematic structure of the process is this: God pours his grace into a human being; this gives the latter's will a new direction; as a result he deplores his sin; and in this way he receives forgiveness.

The rise of "high scholasticism" with its impressive synthesis of faith and reason is marked by a number of developments that contributed to it. One was the commitment of the new begging orders—the Franciscans and the Dominicans—to the theological enterprise. A second was the movement of learning out of the cloister into the university. A third was the fuller recovery by the Western world of the works of Aristotle, of his Arabic commentators, and of the Neoplatonists; this made possible a new view of the world—both a new natural science and a new metaphysics—into which the old biblical-Augustinian tradition could be inserted.

The Franciscan line begins with Alexander of Hales (1170?–1245), whose *Summa universae theologiae* ("The sum of all theology") was formally a commentary on Peter Lombard's *Sentences* but actually was a comprehensive systematics in its own right.

The Franciscan tradition continues with St. Bonaventure (John di Fidanza) (1221–1274), an able administrator and an eminent mystic. Like Alexander, St. Bonaventure was more of an Augustinian than an Aristotelian. His reflections on the nature of created things as shadows, vestiges, and images of that which is divine—neither wholly distinct from nor wholly identical with it—is a counterpart to the doctrine of the "analogy of being" (*analogia entis*).

Before proceeding with the Franciscan tradition, we need to consider the parallel Dominican tradition. The first great name of the latter is St. Albert the Great (1200?–1280), an eclectic and somewhat unsystematic universal genius who made important contributions to natural science as well as to theology. In the latter area he succeeded in reshaping Aristotelian philosophy so that it harmonized with the teaching of the church.

Not the least of St. Albert's contributions to the history of ideas was his influence upon St. Thomas Aquinas (1225?–1274), the greatest of the medieval theologians. The latter's *Summa theologiae* ("Compendium of theology") has exerted a profound influence on Western theological thought for 700 years. The first part deals with the being of God and with creation. The second part deals with God as the goal of human activity. The third part treats Christ the Savior and the sacraments as the way to that goal;

the original plan called for the *Summa* to have concluded with a discussion of everlasting life.[5] In the decade following 1277, propositions drawn from St. Thomas's works were condemned as heretical and for a time the Franciscan authorities forbade Friars Minor to study St. Thomas. His rehabilitation came about with his canonization in 1323.

St. Thomas differentiated sharply between reason and faith. Many of the basic tenets of the Christian faith are not accessible to reason, even though they are not against reason. These tenets include the Trinity, the creation of the universe by God in time, the native sinfulness of human beings, Christ's becoming a human being, and the resurrection of the body at the end of the age. These tenets and their like belong in the realm of faith, where the will rather than the intellect dominates, and the believers accept these tenets as a matter of moral decision.

Metaphysical underpinnings—both Aristotelian and Platonic—play an important role in St. Thomas's theology. Among these metaphysical underpinnings are the pairings of act and potency, matter and form, substance and accidents, and being and existence.

When human beings use human language to talk about God, St. Thomas says, they speak analogically, not univocally or equivocally. That is, their use of human language to talk about God does not understand the human terms in precisely the same sense that these terms have when human beings talk about other human beings. But these terms do not have an utterly different sense. What they have is a sense that is related to the ordinary meanings that the terms in question possess because of a degree of similarity between God and human beings.

St. Thomas holds that anything that is good is so not because God arbitrarily wants it to be good, but because it is good in itself. He stresses the priority of grace in relation to the free will of human beings. Human beings are not able by their own powers to prepare themselves to receive the grace of God. Gradually St. Thomas came to the insight that whatever preparation for grace in which a human being engages is itself the result of grace and is not meritorious and it does not by itself bring about the salvation of the individual. The beginning of faith takes place simultaneously with the coming of grace. While St. Thomas does not stress faith as extensively as the reformers of the sixteenth century did, he gives it a decisive role, even to the point of affirming that St. Paul teaches that "there is no hope of justification in [the] commandments [of the decalogue], but in faith alone" (*sed in sola fide*). Justification in turn is a supernatural work of God, which takes place in a moment when God pours in his grace.

St. Thomas teaches that Christ would not have become a human being unless the first human beings had fallen into sin. He rejected the teaching that the Blessed Virgin Mary was immaculately conceived.

He affirms that Christ acquired an infinite amount of merit by his life and death, much more than enough to outweigh all the sins of all human beings of all times. God communicates grace—on the divine side the ever-lasting loving will of God toward human beings, on the human side a supernatural and graciously imparted subjective disposition (*habitus*) in a person's soul—to human beings through the sacraments. The sacraments are not only symbols of the grace that God confers invisibly; they are the actual instruments through which God imparts grace to the recipients.

Of the sacraments themselves the sacrament of the altar is the "sacrament of sacraments." Further, since the highest purpose of the sacrament of order is the consecration of the bread and wine of the Eucharist to be the body and blood of Christ, priesthood is the highest of the seven orders; from this St. Thomas concluded that the episcopal office was not a separate order.

In explicating the teaching of transubstantiation St. Thomas made effective use of the Aristotelian substance-accidents vocabulary. From the teaching that the body and blood of Christ are present under the appearance both of the consecrated bread and of the consecrated wine ("concomitance"), he argued for the adequacy of Holy Communion under one appearance only.

In John Duns Scotus (1264?–1308), the Franciscan tradition reacts against the Dominican tradition and reaches a kind of climactic phase. Duns accords first place in his system to love and to will instead of to knowledge and to reason. He divides scientific knowledge, which deals with universal laws and principles, from theological truth, to which the sacred Scriptures and the Christian tradition bear the ultimately authoritative witness. The divine will is sovereign and to it the freedom of human choice must be subordinated and accommodated. Scotus differentiates the absolute and the covenanted (*ordinata*) power of God. God is completely sovereign; while he normally acts in a way that is consistent with the orders of creation and salvation and saves men through the work of Christ and the church's sacraments, he could operate independently of all of the rules that he has made.

Scotus's doctrine of Christ tended to stress his humanity, rather than the taking up of Christ's humanity into the Godhead. Again, Scotus related the salvation of human beings to Christ's suffering and death, but affirmed that this relationship exists only because God has freely willed to regard Christ's sacrifice as the substitute for human satisfaction.

In his treatment of the sacraments Scotus revives the Augustinian understanding of them as the symbols of God's gracious activity: God's communication of grace is a direct effect that accompanies—but is not caused by—the use of the sacraments.

In the case of the sacrament of the altar specifically, Scotus holds that the substance of the bread remains after consecration; through the consecration the substance of Christ's glorified body comes down into the bread and exists without quantity in every part of the bread. (This theory—adopted by some of the later nominalists—is variously called "consubstantiation" or "impanation.") As an alternative, Scotus suggested that in the consecration the substance of the bread is destroyed and replaced by the body of Christ.

The classic example of Scotus's opposition to the Dominicans is his defense of the immaculate conception of the Blessed Virgin Mary. He holds that while Christ's redemption freed other human beings from original sin, his mother remained free of its contagion from her conception.

The period following high scholasticism is usually regarded as one of decline. Nevertheless it is not without eminent and influential theological thinkers. Among the most distinguished names are those of William of Occam (1300?–1349), Gregory of Rimini (d. 1358), Peter d'Ailly (1350–1420), John le Charlier de Gerson (1363–1429), Nicholas of Cusa (1400–1464), and Gabriel Biel (1420?–1495).

William of Occam is the initiator of late medieval nominalism. The task of philosophy and of science, William said, is to investigate concepts and the words that convey them. While this might have led to empiricism, William actually took refuge in intuition as the ordinary means of acquiring knowledge. The next step was a kind of philosophical agnosticism. Applied to theology, this meant that there was no logical way of proving the tenets of Christianity. William did not reject the doctrines of Christianity; he felt that articles of faith have no other support than the divine revelation. (At the same time he insisted that theological propositions can appropriately be subjected to logical and dialectical treatment; the result was that Occamist theology received a highly philosophic flavor.)

Nominalism devised its own theory of the immediate inspiration of the sacred Scriptures and laid the foundation for the conviction that the canonical authority of the Scriptures results from the divine inspiration of the words of the Bible.

Nominalism saw faith as explicit, involving a knowledge of each article of the faith, and implicit, involving commitment to the Christian faith only in a general way. The teachers of the church had to have explicit faith, it held, while the layfolk needed only implicit faith.

Original sin to Occam was God's verdict on human beings, each one of whom shared in the guilt of Adam, but he did not regard original sin as actually existing in the nature of human beings. So he concluded that human beings are able, by their own powers, even to love God above everything else. In his view sins are only individual volitional acts. Grace became mere acquittal or forgiveness. William revived the principle that St. Thomas had rejected, namely, that when a person does all that he can (*quod in se est*) God rewards these actions with grace. Since God is pure will (a Scotist idea), the salvation of every individual depends entirely on God's decree; so does the meritorious character of every human action.

William's involvement on the side of the Franciscan Spirituals against John XXII led him to flee from the papal court at Avignon (to which he had been cited for an inquiry into his theology) to the protection of Emperor Louis of Bavaria. His position in this controversy undoubtedly colored his attitude toward the papacy.

It was William's conviction that Christ did not found the papacy, but that it is the result of a historical process. He insisted that popes can err and fall into heresy and that they are subject to the authority of a general council. He further held that a general council, which represents the whole church, should have women as well as males in its membership. Of interest likewise is his distinction between the church as a genus and the Roman Church as a species.

Gregory of Rimini, general of the Hermits of St. Augustine at the time of his death in 1358, combined Augustinian views with Pauline theology, nominalism, and biblicism. He professed to reject metaphysics and philosophy in general; he insisted that God's predestination is sovereign, gratuitous, and eternal; he stressed the native egoism of the will of unreborn human beings; he declared that good works require special grace in addition to general and sacramental grace and that works without divine grace are sinful. For reviving the teaching of St. Augustine that unbaptized infants are forever damned, he acquired the title of "tormentor of babies (*tortor infantium*)."

Peter d'Ailly, made a cardinal by the antipope John XXIII, was one of the most influential disciples of William of Occam. At the Council of Constance (1414–1418) Peter supported the theory of the supremacy of a general council over the pope. His *Treatise on the Reformation of the Church* exerted extensive influence in England and in the Holy Roman Empire and even helped to determine some of the reforms of Trent. Theologically he stood squarely in the Occamist tradition: the existence of God is not rationally demonstrable; sin is not intrinsically evil but is evil only because God declares it to be so; bishops and priests receive their authority from Christ directly and not through the pope; popes and councils alike can err.

Nicholas of Cusa was a conciliarist turned papalist, an eclectic philosopher, and a mystic in the Neoplatonist tradition. "Learned ignorance" (*docta ignorantia*) and the "convergence of opposites" (*coincidentia oppositorum*) are the two basic concepts in his thought. Truth, in its absoluteness, unity, and simplicity, lies beyond the scope of man's knowledge. All that human beings can know is relative, complex, plural, and approximate. God they can know only by intuition. In him all opposites converge. He is infinitely huge and infinitely tiny, the greatest and the least, the center and the circumference, everywhere and nowhere, not one nor three, but triune.

John le Charlier de Gerson, chancellor of the University of Paris and one of the accusers of John Hus at the Council of Constance, was a friend of d'Ailly and like him a nominalist. Gerson taught the superiority of a general council over the pope (but without rejecting his primacy), and demanded that doctors of theology be given voice and vote in general councils along with the bishops. The sinfulness or goodness of an act depends, he said, entirely on God's will. He was an advocate of frequent communion and an eclectic mystic whose affinities were strongly with the tradition that runs from St. Augustine via St. Bernard, the Victorines, and St. Bonaventure; his influence touched such varied people and movements as Nicholas of Cusa, the Brethren of the Common Life, St. Ignatius Loyola, and Martin Luther.

Gabriel Biel combined a consistent commitment to nominalism with tolerance for other philosophical systems. The existing order of salvation was rooted for him in God's absolutely free will; it has validity in fact but not of necessity. He stressed the individual's contribution to his salvation by virtue of the merit that it pleases God to assign to the individual's works. Biel emphasized both the analogy between the will of human beings and the will of God and the positive achievements of which the human will is capable. His Christology saw God becoming a human being and sacrificing his glory to take on himself the miseries of our human plight; but Biel also insisted that this entailed no diminution or loss of any of Christ's divine attributes.

Biel's complex doctrine of the sacrifice of the Mass combined Ambrosian realism and Augustinian symbolism. He affirmed the importance of receiving the Holy Communion. He saw the Mass as the making present again (*re-praesentatio*) of the sacrifice on the cross. Nevertheless the Mass ultimately remained for Biel a second sacrifice. Biel is the last of the great scholastic thinkers.

Councils

During the first eight centuries the great councils of the church met in the East. Nevertheless, some Western councils exerted great influence on the developing doctrine and organization of the Western church.

The Council of Serdica (or Sardica), the modern Sofia, Bulgaria, was Eastern in geography (at least from our point of view) but, because the Eastern bishops refused to meet with their Western counterparts, Western in composition. Although the emperors Constans and Constantius called it in 343(?) to settle the orthodoxy of St. Athanasius, its chief claim to fame consists in its disciplinary canons, including one which constituted the bishop of Rome as a court of appeal for bishops in certain circumstances.

The tiny, fifteen-bishop Second Council of Orange (Arausio), at the encouragement of St. Caesarius of Arles, in 529 approved twenty-five dogmatic chapters—drawn chiefly from the writings of St. Augustine and of his lay disciple, St. Prosper Tiro of Aquitaine (390?–463?). It added a "conclusion" of its own that St. Caesarius edited. This "conclusion" pronounced on grace, human cooperation with the Holy Spirit, and predestination. The council affirms the completely gratuitous nature of divine grace; it rejects divine predestination to evil; and it asserts that saving faith is not something that human beings can natively produce, but is itself a generously conferred gift of grace.[6]

The Third Council of Toledo in 589 affirmed the procession of the Holy Spirit from the Son as well as from the Father. Under pressure from the

Western emperor, Charlemagne, the Council of Aix-la-Chapelle did likewise in 809.

The Imperial Council of Frankfurt-am-Main in 794 condemned both iconoclasm and the veneration of images. A misunderstanding of the distinction that the Second Council of Nicaea (787) had made between *latreia* ("adoring worship") and *proskynesis* ("reverence, veneration") may have underlain the condemnation of iconoclasm. The Council of Paris in 825 approved the veneration of images for the Western church.

Another significant synod of this period was the Council of Friuli (Forum Julii, Friaul) in 796 under St. Paulinus of Aquileia (726?–802). It is remembered chiefly for its rejection of Adoptianism, a Spanish heresy that regarded Christ in his humanity not as the true and proper Son of God but only as God's "putative" and "adoptive" Son.[7]

What the Latin West came to count as the Eighth Ecumenical Council,[8] that of 869–870, was actually held in the imperial palace in Constantinople, with the Eastern emperor, Basil I, presiding. The supporters of St. Photius, whom the emperor had deposed as patriarch of Constantinople, boycotted it; as a result the attendance ranged from a mere twelve bishops at the beginning to 103—the maximum—at the end. Very reluctantly, the bishops (who at one point were almost ready to declare the five ancient patriarchs equal) responded to imperial pressure. They condemned St. Photius and his absent supporters, signed a profession of faith that expressed unqualified submission to the authority of the Roman pope, condemned interference by the state in episcopal elections, and declared that no one can be permitted to condemn the pope, as St. Photius had done. But Ignatius, whom Basil had installed as patriarch of Constantinople in the place of St. Photius, refused to concede Rome's claim to Bulgaria. For this reason Adrian II (d. 872) refused to approve the council's decrees. A decade later, when Basil had restored St. Photius to the patriarchal dignity, the emperor asked John VIII (d. 882) to recognize the appointment. To secure the emperor's assistance against the Saracens, John agreed.

As late as the mid-eleventh century the Roman see acknowledged only seven ecumenical councils. It was not until the close of that century that canonists who were striving to maintain the authority of the church against the civil government in the investiture controversy discovered anew the disciplinary canons of the Fourth Council of Constantinople that forbade lay interference with episcopal elections. It was thus that the Fourth Council of Constantinople achieved ecumenical status in the eyes of the Latin West.

A new series of councils of the Western Church begins in 1123 with the First Lateran Council, so called from the fact that it met in the Lateran Palace at Rome. Convoked by Callistus II (d. 1124), it solemnly approved the Concordat of Worms (1122) that had ended the investiture controversy.[9] It reaffirmed past condemnations of simony[10] and on marriage and concubinage in major orders. It granted Crusaders a plenary indulgence, "remission of sins," and threatened excommunication to all those who broke the "truce of God," the church's device for reducing the persistent private warfare between petty lords.

In 1139 the Second Lateran Council followed. In 1130 the election of Innocent II had provoked a schism. St. Bernard of Clairvaux, acting on "the intuition of his own conscience," declared in favor of Innocent and succeeded, with the help of St. Norbert (1080?–1134), in winning over France and Germany to Innocent's side. The council confirmed the election of Innocent and condemned his opponents with such vindictiveness that even St. Bernard protested. All but seven of its thirty canons repeated previous legislation. It forbade the use of catapults and arrows in warfare as too lethal and threatened excommunication to those who disobeyed. Contrary to the accepted doctrine of the medieval Church of the West, it pronounced null ordinations conferred by the antipope Anacletus and other schismatics. It also condemned the followers of Peter de Bruys (d. 1140?), a deprived priest who rejected infant baptism, the Mass, church buildings, prayers for the dead, the veneration of the cross, significant sections of the Scriptures, and the authority of the church. Similarly condemned were the followers of Arnold of Brescia (d. 1155), a medieval reformer who attacked the worldiness of the church, rejected the confession of sins before priests, held that the immorality of a priest invalidated the sacraments that he administered, and taught that committed Christians ought not possess temporal goods or exercise secular authority.

The Third Lateran Council in 1179 was occasioned by a schism which attended the election of Alexander III (d. 1181) in 1159. Frederick I, called Barbarossa because of his red beard, had decided in favor of Alexander's rival, Victor IV (d. 1164),[11] who was to be succeeded by Pascal III (d. 1168) and Callistus III before the latter would submit to Alexander in 1178. With the schism healed and peace between emperor and pope restored, the council was convoked to remove the vestiges of the schism. It passed twenty-seven disciplinary decrees. These included denunciation of excommunication on all who assisted the Saracens in their warfare with Christians and the prohibition of the common practice of Christian governments to confiscate the possessions of Jewish converts to the faith. Likewise condemned were the Cathars[12] of southwestern France; in contrast the followers of Peter Waldo, whom the church still hoped to reconcile, received only a mild rebuke.

Most important of the Lateran councils was the Fourth, convoked in 1215 by Innocent III (1160–1216). It defined the faith of the church against the Cathars and the Albigenses.[13] In the process it used the term "transubstantiated" of the elements in the sacrament of the altar for the first time in a conciliar document. It similarly rejected certain errors of the late Franciscan Spiritual Joachim of Fiore (1132?–1202). It condemned the Waldensians because they had no "canonical mission" for their preaching;

criticized the "pride" and "contempt" that Eastern Orthodoxy exhibited for the rites of the Latin West; reaffirmed the primacy of Rome and the subordinate position of the other four ancient patriarchates; and forbade physicians to direct their patients to perform immoral acts in order to recover their health. It declared clandestine marriages illicit; condemned abuses in connection with relics and the granting of indulgences; forbade establishment of new religious orders; and enjoined priests against wearing secular garb (especially red and green). Altogether the council passed some seventy decrees. Particularly noteworthy is *Omnis utriusque sexus* ("Everyone regardless of sex"), which required all Christians above the age of discretion annually to make a private confession to their respective parish priests and to receive the Holy Communion at Easter.

The series of Lateran councils was broken by the First Council of Lyons in 1245. It met in France because the power of Frederick II made Italy unsafe. Innocent IV (d. 1254) announced the themes of the council in his opening sermon; he was oppressed by the behavior of the prelates and of the people, by the advance of the Saracens, by the Greek schism, by the Tatar invasion, and by the enmity of Frederick. It passed no dogmatic decrees, but contented itself with excommunicating Frederick, devising additional means of providing financial support for the Latin empire of Constantinople and the Christian kingdom in Palestine, and promised privileges and a plenary indulgence, "the forgiveness of their sins," to participants in the crusade in which the council's host, St. Louis IX of France, would be captured.

Gregory X (1210–1276) designed the Second Council of Lyons in 1274 to bring about a union with Eastern Orthodoxy, to liberate the Holy Land, and to reform the morals of Christians. The times favored his first objective. The Byzantine emperor Michael VIII Palaeologus felt himself threatened by the Muslims, by rival Greek princes, and most of all by the possibility of a revived Latin empire of Constantinople under Charles of Anjou. He determined to strengthen his position by submitting to the pope. The patriarch of Constantinople, John XI Veccos (d. 1297), approved. Among those present at the council were St. Albert the Great and St. Bonaventure. The council affirmed the procession of the Holy Spirit from the Father and the Son, "not as from two sources, but as from one source, not by two spirations, but by one spiration." When the Greeks finally arrived, they affirmed "total obedience to the Holy Roman Church" and acknowledged its faith and its primacy. At the singing of the creed in the solemn Mass of thanksgiving on June 29, the Feast of SS. Peter and Paul, the Greeks three times confessed their faith in the Holy Spirit "that proceeds from the Father and the Son" and chanted the solemn liturgical acclamations of the pope. On July 6 the representative of the Greek emperor affirmed in his sovereign's name the confession of faith that the council had drafted, including the procession of the Holy Spirit from the Father and the Son; the single divine authorship of both testaments; penance as the remedy for sin after baptism; purgatory; hell for those who die in mortal sin or in original sin alone (that is, who die unbaptized); a universal judgment of all human beings; the seven Western sacraments; unleavened bread and the transubstantiation of the bread into the body and blood of Christ in the sacrament of the altar; and the primacy and principality of the Roman pope over all of Christendom.

Disciplinary canons called for the election of a new pope within eight days, demanded reverence in liturgical worship, and required bowing of the head at the mention of the holy name of Jesus.

The Byzantine emperor's capitulation to Rome was met with endless resistance on the part of the Orthodox clergy and laity, and the last vestiges of the artificial union were gone by 1281.

Clement V (1264–1314), the first of the Avignonese popes, convoked the Council of Vienne (1311–1312) to deal with the question of the Knights Templars. The order had been founded as the Poor Knights of Christ in 1118. They did not remain poor long, and in the thirteenth century their wealth tempted Philip the Fair of France to seek their suppression. He lodged charges of superstition, immorality, and heresy against them. A committee of the council recommended that the Templars be heard in their own defense, then reversed itself and recommended the suppression of the order. Clement V on his own authority decreed the suppression and prohibited debate in the council on his action. Philip seized most of the Templars' properties in France; the rest were transferred to the Knights Hospitalers.

The council also passed some minor doctrinal decrees on the "state of perfection." These pertained to errors entertained by some of the more enthusiastic Beguines and their male counterparts, the Beghards. The Beguines and the Beghards were independent communities of men and women given to charitable works among the sick and the poor; the members lived under a fairly austere rule, but did not bind themselves by vows.

Other decrees of the council condemned views ascribed to Peter John Olieu (Olivi) (1248?–1298), a Franciscan rigorist, among them the thesis that "the rational or intellective soul is not in itself and essentially the form of the human body." The council likewise declared that it was heretical to defend usury, that is, the taking of interest.

To heal the great Western schism that had begun in 1378 a number of cardinals summoned a general council at Pisa in 1409. The well-attended and initially successful council deposed and excommunicated Gregory XII (d. 1417) and Benedict XIII (d. 1423) as heretics and perjurers and elected Alexander V (d. 1410). On the latter's death the antipope John XXIII (d. 1419) succeeded him. The status of the council has been debated.[14]

Under attack by Ladislas of Naples, John appealed to Emperor Sigismund for help. The latter made convocation of a general council the price of his assistance. It convened at Constance from 1414 to 1418. As a means to end the schism, a majority of the participants favored the abdication of all three rivals for the papal throne. John promised to abdicate, but instead fled. At this point the council passed the Articles of Constance. These declared the Council of Constance to be a general council, deriving its authority directly from Christ, and declared that every Christian, including the pope, was bound to obey its decisions.

After John had returned to Constance under arrest, the council found him guilty of fifty-four charges covering the whole gamut of infamy and deposed him. A little later it deposed Benedict XIII. Gregory XII resigned. During the interregnum of over two years, the council ruled the church. Finally it elected a new pope, Martin V (1368–1431).[15] The council also condemned forty-five articles from the writings of John Wyclif as heretical, and directed the exhumation and burning of his corpse. It also ordered the administration of the Holy Communion under the appearance of the bread alone on the ground that the entire body and blood of Christ is present under either appearance. It judged thirty articles of John Hus to be heretical, and, in spite of the imperial safe conduct under which he had agreed to come to Constance, the council delivered him to the judgment of the secular government, "since the church of God has nothing more that it can do," to be burned at the stake. His companion and friend, Jerome of Prague, met the same fate.[16]

Martin V himself convoked the Council of Basel, but he died before it convened in 1431. Because of its antipapalist attitude and because both he and the Eastern Orthodox envoys to the proposed council (at which the East and the West were to be reunited) wanted it to meet in Italy, Eugene IV (1383–1447) dissolved it at the end of the year and tried to reconvene it at Bologna. The council ignored the pope's bull, and in 1433 he again recognized it. But the council continued on its antipapal course, and in 1436 the pope bitterly denounced it in a memorandum to all the princes. In 1437 the council granted the Bohemian Utraquists the privilege of Holy Communion under both appearances in exchange for their return to the church.

Eugene IV transferred the council to Ferrara that same year, but few of the participants obeyed the papal bull. Instead the council of Basel deposed Eugene and elected Felix V (d. 1461), the last antipope. (It also anticipated the papal action of 1854 by defining the dogma of the immaculate conception of the Blessed Virgin Mary.) In 1448 the council moved to Lausanne and on the abdication of Felix the next year (to become cardinal bishop of Sabina) it formally elected Nicholas V (1397–1455), Eugene's successor, as pope and dissolved itself.[17]

Like Lyons II, the Council of Ferrara was to be a union council. The situation of the Byzantine Empire had become even more grim than it had been in the late thirteenth century. Constantinople was on the brink of capture. John VIII Palaeologus was determined on reunion, apparently for religious as well as political motives. In 1437 he, Ecumenical Patriarch Joseph II (d. 1439), and some twenty members of the Greek hierarchy set sail in a papal convoy sent to bring the eastern participants to Ferrara. The Armenian Church was represented by two patriarchs. The council began in 1438 and occupied itself with fruitless discussions about purgatory and the procession of the Holy Spirit from the Son. For reasons of greater security and health, Eugene wanted to transfer the council to Florence; he finally succeeded, although the Greek reluctance was great.

The council began its Florentine phase in 1439. The same year saw the publication of two decrees, one for the Greeks, one for the Armenians. The former affirmed the procession of the Holy Spirit from the Father and the Son; permitted either leavened or unleavened bread in the Eucharist; asserted that the words of institution in the sacrament of the altar possess consecratory power; stated that there is a purgatory (without identifying fire as its punishment); declared that even before the last day souls enter the state of perfect bliss, or suffering and that the blessed behold the triune God himself (and not merely an "energy" or a light separate from God's being); and asserted papal supremacy.

The decree for the Armenians is important because it represents the climax of the medieval doctrine of the seven sacraments. The matter of baptism is water, the temperature of which is unimportant. The form of baptism is "I baptize you in the name of the Father and of the Son and of the Holy Spirit," although it is conceded that the verb may be in the passive. The minister is a priest, but in a case of emergency anyone—a layman, a woman, a pagan, a heretic—may baptize as long as the person preserves the church's procedure and intends to do what the church does. Baptism's effect is the forgiveness of all original and actual sin.

The matter of confirmation is chrism made of olive oil and balsam, blessed by the bishop. The form is: "I sign you with the sign of the cross and I confirm you with the chrism of salvation in the name of the Father and of the Son and of the Holy Spirit." The ordinary minister is the bishop; by dispensation a simple priest may administer the sacrament. The effect of confirmation is the gift of the Holy Spirit for strengthening the recipient to confess Christ's name courageously.

The matter of the Eucharist is wheat bread and wine from the vine, mixed with a little water. The form consists of the words with which Christ instituted the sacrament and which the priest speaks in Christ's name. Through these words the substance of the bread is converted into Christ's body, and the substance of the wine is converted into Christ's blood, in such a way that the whole Christ is contained in every part of the consecrated bread and the consecrated wine. The effect is the union of the human being with Christ, through grace, an increase of grace in those receiving worthily, and a spiritual effect upon the soul parallel to that which material food and drink have on bodily life.[18]

The material in a manner of speaking (*quasi materia*) of repentance are the three acts of the penitent: heartfelt contrition (accompanied by sorrow for sin and the purpose not to sin again); oral confession of all remembered [mortal] sins to the confessor; and satisfaction (especially prayer, fasting, and almsgiving) as the confessor judges proper. The form is "I absolve you." The minister is a priest with authority to absolve. The effect is absolution from sin.

The matter of the last anointing is olive oil, blessed by the bishop, and administered only to a dying person on his eyes, ears, nostrils, mouth, hands, and feet, and over his kidneys. The form is "By this holy anointing and his most merciful kindness may the Lord forgive you the sins you have committed through seeing (and so on)." The minister is a priest. The effect is healing of the mind and, to the degree that it benefits the soul, of the body also.

The matter of the sacrament of order is the giving to the recipient of the instrument(s) of his grade; in the case of the presbyterate it is the giving of the chalice with wine and of the paten with bread. The form in the case of the presbyterate is "Receive authority to offer sacrifice in the church for the living and the dead, in the name of the Father and of the Son and of the Holy Spirit." The ordinary minister is a bishop.[19] The effect is an increase of the grace appropriate to a servant of Christ.

The sacrament of marriage is a sign of the joining together of Christ and the church. The efficient cause is regularly the mutual consent of the bride and groom expressed in words that pertain to the present (de praesenti). The good of marriage is threefold: obtaining offspring and rearing them to worship God; mutual faithfulness; indivisibility. Immorality may justify a separation, but the bond of a legitimately contracted marriage is perpetual.

In 1442 a bull for the reunion of the Copts (and of the Ethiopians) was published. It asserts that the biblical canon includes Tobit, Judith, the Wisdom of Solomon, Ecclesiasticus, Baruch, and First and Second Maccabees. It declares that no one has ever been saved from the devil's dominion except by the faith[20] of our Lord Jesus Christ, the mediator between God and man. Baptism is to be administered as soon as possible after birth and is not to be postponed forty or eighty days. No one outside the Catholic Church—including not only pagans, but also Jews, heretics, and schismatics—can be saved; unless they are joined to the church before they die they will go into everlasting fire. A person may contract not only up to three, but four or more otherwise licit marriages.

In 1443 Eugene moved the council again, this time to the Lateran Palace. In 1444 a union was effected with the Non-Chalcedonian Syrian Orthodox, and in 1445 with the Chaldaeans (that is, members of the present-day Church of the East and of the Assyrians) and the Maronites on the island of Cyprus.

Except for the union with the Maronites, these unifications were all short-lived.[21] The council came to an unchronicled end some time before the death of Eugene in 1447.

Four French cardinals convoked a second council of Pisa late in 1511. It officially condemned the soldier-pope Julius II (1443–1513). The pope responded by summoning the last of the medieval general councils of the

West, the Fifth Lateran Council of 1512–1517. The most important doctrinal decision to come out of the council was not really a conciliar pronouncement at all, but a papal decree set forth in the name of Leo X (1475–1521), a humanist and a member of the Medici family. The great Renaissance philosopher Peter Pomponazzi (1464–1525)[22] had taught that natural reason could neither affirm nor deny the mortality (or immortality) of the human rational soul. The immortality of the human soul, he said, is an article of faith. The papal decree condemned all those that assert that the rational soul of a human being is mortal and labeled as heretics and infidels those who assert any opinion that contradicts the faith.

The council came to an end in March of the fateful year 1517.

The Bishops of Rome

It is exceedingly difficult to write a succinct chronicle of the role of the bishops of Rome in the Church of the West during the first 1,500 years without seeming to take sides or to engage in polemics. For one thing, the issue is highly charged emotionally. For another the 220 (or 216) bishops of Rome on the official roster through Leo X—to say nothing of the thirty-six or so rivals from St. Hippolytus to Felix V—were men of widely diverse character, gifts, and competence. On balance they were good men; through St. Celestine V (d. 1294), the last medieval bishop of Rome to be canonized, seventy-nine have been given the title of "saint." Officially—and in the vast majority of cases personally as well—they put the very considerable power of their office on the side both of sanctity and of orthodoxy. Their contributions to the well-being of the Church in the West were undeniably great. The tenacity with which they defended the indissolubility of Christian marriage is one of many cases in point. Thus the section that follows is not a polemic attempt to find fault with the incumbents of the see of Rome or to record primarily those events that may seem to bring discredit on them: It does try to account in the fifteen centuries of history under survey for the mighty controversy about the role of the bishop of Rome in the necessary structure of the church that agitated Western Christendom in the sixteenth century.

Traditions going back to the first century count both St. Paul and St. Peter as the martyred joint founders of the church in the city of Rome. St. Paul's name often precedes that of St. Peter in the first two centuries. By the middle of the third century bishops of Rome count their succession from St. Peter alone. From the fourth century on St. Paul was all but completely forgotten, until from the time of St. Nicholas I (d. 867), the bishops of Rome began the custom of issuing decrees in the joint names of the two apostolic princes.

In 253 Valerian succeeded Gallus as Roman emperor; he decided that the empire was too big for one man to rule and appointed his son Gallienus to rule the West while he attempted to stabilize the tottering

East. From the time of Diocletian, who became emperor in 285, and Maximian, whom Diocletian named Augustus in 286 to rule the West, the two-emperor arrangement became permanent and lasted until the invaders from the north deposed the last Western emperor, the usurper Romulus Augustulus, in 476. Thereafter the Christian clergy and the lay aristocracy ruled the declining city of Rome in an uneasy partnership until Charlemagne's coronation in 800.

It is not until well after St. Celement of Rome (flourished 96) that one can speak of a "bishop of Rome." Around 300 the incumbent of the Roman see acquired the title of metropolitan or archbishop. Pope, at first the title of the primatial sees of Carthage and Alexandria, comes into general use for bishops of important centers in the fourth century; it seems first to have been applied officially to the bishop of Rome by the Council of Arles in 314.[23] Around 450 St. Leo I (d. 461) was the first bishop of Rome to be called patriarch; he also adopted the title "servant of the servants of God." St. Damasus (d. 384) was the first bishop of Rome to claim for his diocese the title "apostolic see," and St. Hormisdas (d. 523) the first to claim it as a peculiar title of the Roman see.

Some have understood the praise that St. Ignatius of Antioch around 110 conferred on the church "that presides in the country of the region of the Romans"—a presidency "in love," he hastens to add—as a sign of the preeminence of the chief pastor at Rome, but it is the church and its members that St. Ignatius explicitly refers to. St. Irenaeus of Lyons (130?–200?) states that around 155 St. Polycarp (69?–155?), on a visit to Rome, and St. Anicetus (d. 166?), the bishop of the imperial capital, were unable to persuade one another about the rightness of their respective dates for keeping Easter.

After the destruction of Jerusalem in 135, the church at Rome has the most distinguished reputation of any church in Christendom. But down to 200 at least there is no evidence that the church at Rome derived its authority from its bishop as the successor of St. Peter.

The early greatness of the church in Rome is attested by the very ancient (late second century) epitaph of Abercius, who refers to "queen with the golden robe and golden slippers in royal Rome."

Again, the church at Rome had a distinguished reputation throughout the primitive Christian world for its virtues, especially the open-handed liberality that St. Dionysius of Cornith (flourished around 170) praises.

The city of Rome attracted both great Christian teachers and great heretics in the second century. Among the former were St. Hegesippus, St. Justin Martyr (100?–165?), St. Irenaeus of Lyons, and Hermas the author of *The Shepherd*. Among the heretics were Marcion (d. 160?), whose own bishop-father had allegedly excommunicated him for immorality, and the Gnostic leaders Cerdo (flourished around 140), Marcellina, Tatian (flourished around 160), and Valentine.

In a passage that bristles with difficulties, and that survives only in a Latin translation of the original Greek, a minority of scholars see St. Irenaeus of Lyons in his *Against Heresies* (around 185) affirming the sovereign importance of the church at Rome and that church's preeminence over all Christendom. But most scholars reject this interpretation.

In 195, St. Victor I (d. 198) of Rome, Eusebius asserts in his *Ecclesiastical History*, attempted to cut off the bishops of Asia from communion with Rome because they kept Easter on a different day from the one that Rome had traditionally observed, an action for which other bishops, like St. Irenaeus of Lyons, strongly criticized the bishop of Rome.

St. Cyprian—who, interestingly, bore the title "pope" at Carthage before the same title was used for the bishop of Rome—wrote a book, *The Unity of the Church*, of which chapter 4 exists in two recensions. One version sees Christ building his church on Peter and entrusting his sheep to Peter to be fed, refers to Peter's primacy to demonstrate the unity of the church, and asks rhetorically if a person who "deserts the chair of Peter on which the church is founded" can continue to think of himself as still in the church. The other recension omits these references. But whatever the solution to the problem of these two recensions may be, St. Cyprian finds it possible to speak of the "arrogant, extraneous, or self-contradictory" statements and the "blindness of mind, perverseness, and obstinacy" of St. Stephen I (d. 257) of Rome.[24] At the Council of Carthage in 256 St. Cyprian, supported by all of the other eighty-seven bishops present, condemned St. Stephen for setting himself up as "bishop of bishops" and "by tyrannical terror coercing his colleagues into the necessity of obeying."[25]

In a similar vein, St. Firmilian of Cappadocia (d. 268) warns the same St. Stephen that if by virtue of sitting on the "chair of Peter" he undertakes to excommunicate St. Firmilian and his Cilician and Cappadocian associates, "you have merely excommunicated yourself from all."[26]

With the conversion of Constantine and the political establishment of the church, the church's organization was consciously conformed to the imperial pattern. One of the consequences was a wider jurisdiction and a great measure of authority for the bishops of Old Rome.[27]

By the end of the fourth century the claims of the bishops of Rome were becoming more and more widely accepted in principle, at least in the West. The federally organized Church in the East continued to go its own way to a considerable extent and, being out of communion with Rome, was not a source of acute distress. The mid-fifth century saw the claims of the bishop of Rome put to the test when St. Leo the Great refused to approve Canon 28 of the Council of Chalcedon (451), which, following Constantinople I (381), gave the bishop of New Rome, that is, Constantinople, first rank after the bishop of Old Rome and ahead of the patriarchs of Alexandria and Antioch on explicitly political grounds. St Leo's protest was in vain; the prerogatives and the status of bishop of New Rome became more and more those accorded to the bishop of Old Rome, and from the sixth century on the bishops of Constantinople were styled ecumenical patriarchs.

In spite of the great prestige that St. Leo had added to the See of Rome, the situation had changed there by the end of the fifth century. Apart from the alienation of the Christian East, the last legitimate emperor of the West, Nepos, had been driven into exile and murdered. The usurper, Romulus Augustulus, seems to have been deposed and pensioned by Odoacer. The kings of Rome were now Arians and their bishops were Arians.

Within the Catholic community at Rome seven years of intermittent schism followed the death of Anastasius II in 498, with two rival claimants to the Catholic see of Rome.

In the mid-sixth century Vigilius (d. 555) displayed a dismaying vacillation. At first he refused to sign the imperial decree condemning the "Three Chapters." Then he anathematized them, and a council in Carthage severed communion with him. Then he withdrew his anathema. Then he anathematized anew, with careful qualifications, everything that smelled of Nestorianism. Finally he revoked this anathema and subscribed to the decision of the Fifth Ecumenical Council (Constantinople II, 553). That same year the metropolitan of Milan severed communion with Rome for the next eighteen years, the metropolitan of Aquileia for the next 147 years.

Under St. Gregory the Great (d. 604), an incontestably great and good bishop of Rome, the church in the capital recovered much of its influence. Some of his followers were less happy choices. The great controversy of the seventh century was over the Monothelite ("one-will") doctrine, which ascribed a single will to the incarnate Christ. The first Roman interventions were a fiasco. Honorius (d. 639) not only used the term "one will" in a letter to Sergius of Constantinople, but in a subsequent letter he explicitly rejected the "two-wills" formula that was the badge of orthodoxy. St. Martin I (d. 655) and the Lateran Council of 649 condemned the one-will teaching unequivocally as heresy, even though some Eastern prelates still professed it. After St. Martin, St. Agatho (d. 681), imitating St. Leo (whose *Tome* had instructed the Council of Chalcedon), but apparently forgetful of St. Martin's determination of the Monthelite issue, sent a letter to the Sixth Ecumenical Council (Constantinople III, 680) in which he too condemned the one-will doctrine. The council gratefully declared that "Peter was speaking through Agatho" and anathematized Honorius.[28]

As early as the end of the fourth century the wealth of the church in Rome had become very great. During the next four centuries it continued to become even greater. In the middle of the eight century, Stephen III (d. 757) of Rome secured the signature of Pepin, whom Stephen crowned as king of the Franks, on a Franco-Roman treaty and on a no longer extant document called the Donation of Pepin. It gave the bishop of Rome title to a large part of northern Italy and represents the historical beginning of the States of the Church. Two decades later Charlemagne confirmed the grant of Pepin and expanded it to include almost two-thirds of Italy. These grants helped to usher in the "millennium of mammon," when the bishops of Rome were secular rulers.

Around this time the pseudonymous Donation of Constantine was fabricated. It purported to give to St. Silvester of Rome (d. 335) and to his successors supremacy over all the ancient patriarchates and over all churches of God in the entire world. It undertook to grant to the bishop of Rome for the time being the city of Rome, all the provinces of and all the regions of the West. The Donation of Constantine found its way into the great collections of medieval canon law; no one appears to have doubted its authenticity until the 1400s.

In the middle of the ninth century a collection of forged epistles of early bishops of Rome from St. Clement to St. Gregory the Great appeared in France under the name of Isidore Mercator ("the Merchant"), apparently to suggest at least a connection with St. Isidore of Seville (d. 636). These letters present ninth-century teaching about the authority of the bishops of Rome as apostolic doctrine that came directly from Christ's own mouth.[29]

The revival of the empire in the West under Charlemagne introduced a new situation. Some of the authority that the bishop of Rome had enjoyed as long as there was no Western emperor was no longer his. Charlemagne, it was true, was meticulously careful to accord the bishop of Rome the highest respect. But in his day-by-day administration he appeared to see in the bishop of Rome merely the most eminent bishop in the empire, and the emperor had no compunction about interfering even in questions of doctrine.

Under the generally weak successors of Charlemagne, the bishops of Rome gradually increased first their independence and then their own authority. The right of the bishop of Rome to crown the emperor soon acquired the status of a reverend tradition. At the same time it came to be understood as implying that the right to reign was in the gift of the bishop of Rome. Ultimately this led to the idea—increasingly popular in the Middle Ages—that the pope had transferred the imperial authority from the Greeks to the Franks (*translatio imperii*).

The growing political weakness of the emperors was reflected in the increasing role of the Roman nobility in determining who the bishop of the capital was to be. As a result, from the last decade of the ninth century through 1046 the bishops of Rome for the most part were either vicious rascals[30] or impotent figureheads.[31]

Meanwhile the power of the Ottonian emperors north of the Alps had been growing. Beginning with the brief episcopate of Clement II (d. 1047)— chosen to end the unseemly rivalry of three claimants to the papal dignity, one of them a fifteen-year-old count of Tusculum—the emperor and the bishop of Rome worked together for the reform of the church. The pontificate of St. Leo IX (1002–1054), a determined reformer marked as much by his personal humility as by his pastoral zeal, did much to create a new image of the papacy. It was overshadowed, however, by the widening breach between Rome and Constantinople that led to a complete break on July 16, 1054, three months after St. Leo's death. Concord between pope and emperor quickly changed to confrontation when Henry IV and St. Gregory VII began to oppose one another. The bitter conflict between the bishop of Rome and the various temporal authorities in the West was marked by such events as the emperor's barefoot penance at Canossa in 1077 and the concordat of Worms, of 1122, which put an end to the investiture controversy.

Not the least significant development of this period was the *Dictatus papae* ("Declaration of the pope"). It described the bishop of Rome as "priest of the world"; claimed for him exclusive power to appoint, translate, depose, and reconcile bishops; gave his legate precedence in councils over all prelates; demanded that all princes kiss his feet; asserted his control over the insignia of the empire; made his order authorization an essential requirement for any synod to be called a general synod; denied that anybody can reverse a decision that he makes; exalted him above all courts of law; and asserted that his canonical election makes him holy. It concluded triumphantly: "The Roman church has never erred and will never err to all eternity, as the scripture testifies."

The twelfth and thirteenth centuries were marked by the long-drawn-out contest for supremacy between Frederick I Barbarossa and Frederick II, on the one hand, and the popes, on the other.

At the beginning of the thirteenth century, Innocent III (1160–1216)—the first pope apparently to claim the title of "vicar of Christ" for himself alone—demonstrated unique determination and probably enjoyed the greatest actual success in defining, extending, and enforcing the "fullness of authority" of the Roman see.

A kind of climax was reached with the publication of the bull *Unam sanctam* (1302) by Boniface VIII (1234?–1303). In it he affirmed that "Christ and his vicar constitute only one head," and in the closing words of the bull, he declared, stated, and defined "that for every human being it is absolutely necessary for salvation to be under the bishop of Rome."[32] The bull was part of the pope's struggle with Philip the Fair of France. Philip countered by bringing Boniface to trial. While the pope was readying a bull excommunicating the French king, the latter sent a band of mercenaries to take Boniface prisoner at Anagni. Although his release came after only three days, the pope died broken in health a month later. His next successor but one, the French archbishop Bertrand de Got (1264–1314) who ruled as Clement V transferred the seat of the popes to Avignon in French territory. This "Babylonian captivity" paved the way for the great Western schism of 1378–1415, during which ultimately each of three rival popes claimed to be the successor of Peter. The final solution—deposition of all three and the election of a fourth—created formidable theological problems.

The healing of the schism appeared to the Renaissance popes and their supporters as a validation of the papal claim to both the spiritual and the temporal swords. As a result, by the end of the pontificate of Julius II (1443–1513) the historical stage had been set for a widespread rejection of the papacy.

NOTES

1. The Vulgate was not the first Latin version of the Scriptures. The earliest African Latin translations go back to the second century, the earliest European ones are somewhat younger. The interrelation of these translations is still uncertain. The reason why St. Jerome undertook the preparation of a new translation directly from the Greek, Hebrew, and Aramaic originals was the chaotic variation that the existing Old Latin manuscripts exhibited.

2. A number of Christian writers before St. Augustine—among them St. Clement of Alexandria (150?–215?), Origen, the author of the early third-century *Passion of St. Perpetua,* and St. Ambrose—had tentatively explored the possibility of some kind of purification after death.

3. Erigena is important both as an original theologian in his own right and as a translator. In particular, the influence of Erigena's translation of the works of Pseudo-Dionysius the Areopagite (flourished around 500) on subsequent Western theology has been incalculable.

4. Originally, the verb *mereri,* from which we have the Latin *meritum* and the English "merit," meant merely "to account worthy" or "to regard as worthy." It still has this meaning, for instance, in the ancient collects for the first and second Sundays in Advent, for the first Sunday after Christmas, for Palm Sunday (the Sunday before Easter), and for the Tuesday in Holy Week, for example, with their otherwise strong anti-Pelagian theological thrust.

5. St. Thomas never completed the *Summa theologiae.* A profound mystical experience on the Feast of St. Nicholas (December 6), 1273, led him to regard everything that he had written as straw in comparison to the overwhelming knowledge of God that

had been given to him. He died on his way to the Council of Lyons. He had laid the *Summa* aside in the middle of the treatment of the sacrament of repentance; on the basis of St. Thomas's commentary on the fourth book of the *Sententiae* of Peter Lombard, a later compiler, usually now identified as St. Thomas's confessor, friend, and amanuensis, Reginald of Piperno (1230?–1290?), drafted the *Supplement* that completes the *Summa* in the printed editions. See "On Thomas Aquinas," in Josef Pieper, *The Silence of St. Thomas: Three Essays,* trans. John Murray and Daniel O'Connor (New York: Pantheon Books, 1957), pp. 3-41.

6. The Council of Quiercy-sur-Oise (Carsiaca) in 853 condemned Gottschalk's doctrine of a double predestination and followed Orange II in setting forth the orthodox position on divine grace, predestination, the loss of human freedom of choice through Adam's fall and the believers' recovery of it in Christ, the gift-character of salvation, the universal scope of God's saving will and the universal effect of Christ's suffering, and the cause of the condemnation of those who are lost. The Council of Valence-sur-Rhône in 855 in turn affirmed a double predestination and denied the universality of Christ's atonement. The canons of the latter council were subsequently revised to remove the offensive passages, and the Council of Toul in 860 affirmed both the canons of Quiercy and the revised canons of Valence. Subsequently Orange II was almost totally forgotten, until its canons were rediscovered during the debates at the Council of Trent.

7. Also noteworthy is the concern of this council for the protection of the ideal of Christian marriage as the lifelong union of one man and one woman, for the moral behavior and the fidelity

to duty of the priests, and for the proper administration of private confession and absolution. These concerns are not untypical, as a comparison of the canons of both earlier and later councils demonstrates. Concrete examples are the Council of Soissons in 744, the Council of Aix-la-Chapelle in 802, and the reforming Councils of Arles, Rheims, Mayence, Tours, and Châlon-sur-Saône in 813 and of Mayence and Paris in 829.

8. On the origins of the different attitudes toward the number of ecumenical councils between the Eastern Orthodox churches and the Roman Catholic Church, see Francis Dvornik, "Which Councils Are Ecumenical?" *Journal of Ecumenical Studies*, 3 (1966): 314-328.

9. The dispute that went on from 1059 to 1122 between the popes, on the one hand, and the Holy Roman emperors and other lay princes, on the other, over the right of the secular authorities to invest bishops-elect (and abbots-elect) with ring and staff and to receive homage from them prior to their consecration.

10. The purchase and/or sale of spiritual things, such as ordinations and positions in the church.

11. To be distinguished from an earlier antipope Victor IV, Cardinal Gregory Conti, who succeeded antipope Anacletus II on the latter's death in 1138 and who made his submission to St. Bernard of Clairvaux before the year was out.

12. A sect that had emerged in the early eleventh century. The Cathars are not always carefully differentiated from the Albigenses.

13. A dualistic and rigoristic sect that interpreted the New Testament allegorically and apparently rejected many of the key teachings of Christianity.

14. The Roman Catholic Church does not count it as a general council on the ground that it was not convoked by a pope, although conciliarists like Gerson, d'Ailly, William of Occam, and the leaders of the Gallican movement regarded it as a general council.

15. After John submitted to the new pope, he was reinstated as a cardinal and became dean of the Sacred College. Gregory became the cardinal bishop of Porto and papal legate. Benedict remained irreconcilable; after Spain and Portugal withdrew their support, he withdrew to the Templar fort at Peñiscola. Here he died.

16. Roman Catholics debate how much of the Council of Constance was ecumenical. Some limit its ecumenicity to the decisions reached after Martin's election. Others see it as ecumenical from the time that Cardinal John of Ragusa convoked it in the name of Gregory XII to receive the latter's resignation and authorized and confirmed whatever it might do for the reformation of the church and the extirpation of heresy. Martin V himself, like some contemporary Roman Catholics, regarded the decisions reached in all the plenary sessions of the whole council as ecumenical.

17. The leaders of the Gallican movement regarded the Council of Basel as ecumenical. The modern Roman Catholics who accord the council any degree of ecumenicity limit this to the first twenty-five sessions at most.

18. The minister is not named, but it is taken for granted that he will be one ordained to the priesthood.

19. It is noteworthy that in this century three popes published four documents referring to the power of simple priests, when authorized by the pope, to ordain.

20. A variant reads "merit."

21. The Greek Church formally repudiated the Council of Florence in 1484; although the decree of union had finally been proclaimed in Constantinople in December 1452, it was never really accepted by the Eastern Orthodox.

22. See the introduction of John Herman Randall, Jr., to the section on Pietro Pomponazzi in Ernst Cassirer, Paul Oskar Kristeller, and John Herman Randall, Jr., *The Renaissance Philosophy of Man*, 4th impression (Chicago: University of Chicago Press, 1959), pp. 257-269.

23. St. Gregory VII (1073–1085) seems to have been the first to make a serious attempt to have the title limited to the Roman metropolitan; he was successful only in the West. (The Council of Pavia in 998 before him had criticized the archbishop of Milan for calling himself "pope.")

24. *Letter 74.*—St. Stephen I was "the first

bishop of Rome to recognize the potential of Matthew 16:18-20 as an exclusive charter" (Edward George Weltin, *The Ancient Popes* [Westminster, Md.: The Newman Press, 1964], p. 130, citing Cyprian, *Letter 75*, 17). It has been suggested that Tertullian, *On Modesty*, 1, 6, in referring to the "peremptory edict" of "the *pontifex maximus,* the bishop of bishops," has St. Callistus of Rome (d. 223?) in mind and that he implies that in issuing this edict St. Callistus claimed as the basis for doing so the grant of authority by Jesus to Peter and to his successors in St. Matthew 16:18-19. But many scholars reject the identification with St. Callistus: for a summary of the discussion see Johannes Quasten, *Patrology* 2 (Westminster, Md.: The Newman Press, 1953): 204-206, 234-235, 312-315.

25. *Letter 73.*

26. St. Cyprian's correspondence, *Letter 75.*

27. Milan provides an instructive parallel case history. The church there came into being only at the end of the second century. By the mid-fourth century it was a metropolitical see. At the end of that century the bishops of Gaul, Spain, and Africa, were turning to the bishop of Milan and the bishop of Rome jointly for the settlement of controversies. The reason was that Milan in the late third century had become the capital of the imperial *dioecesis* of [northern] Italy, as well as the secular capital of the West and the seat of the imperial court. It lost its prestige in 404 when the emperor Honorius moved the imperial capital to Ravenna, but it remained outside the Roman patriarchate until 1059.

28. The Seventh Ecumenical Council (Nicaea II, 787) repeated the condemnation of Honorius. So did the Fourth Council of Constantinople (869–870), which the West later came to count as the Eighth Ecumenical Council. Down to the eleventh century, according to the *Liber diurnus,* every bishop of Rome, in the solemn confession of faith that he had to make at his election, reaffirmed the Sixth Ecumenical Council and specifically its anathematization of Honorius. The famous canon *Si papa* in Part One of the *Decretum* (distinctio 40, caput 6), which provided that the pope

"was to be judged by no one," made an exception in the case of a heretical pope (*nisi deprehendatur a fide devius,* "unless he be caught wandering away from the faith"). Besides Honorius the Middle Ages often cited as examples St. Marcellinus (295–304), who was charged with having sacrificed to the pagan gods under Diocletian; St. Liberius (352–366), who was charged with having purchased release from exile through his willingness to renounce the Nicene faith, with having concurred in the excommunication of St. Athanasius, and with having subscribed to the creed of the Council of Sirmium of 358 (although with qualifications); and St. Anastasius II (496–498), because of what was regarded as an excessively conciliatory attitude in connection with the "Acacian Schism."

29. Papalist apologists continued to use them into the mid-sixteenth century until the Lutheran *Magdeburg Centuries* left no doubt about the spurious nature of the decretals.

30. For example, Stephen VII (d. 897), who at the "Cadaver Council" of 897, had the body of his predecessor, Formosus (d. 896), nine months in his grave, exhumed, dressed in his pontifical garb, tried by the pope and the council, condemned, mutilated, and dumped into the Tiber. (A few months later Stephen himself was strangled in a dungeon cell.)

31. The brief and unhappy pontificate of John XI (d. 936?) is fairly typical. A common rumor on the truth of which modern historians are divided made him out to be the illegitimate son of Sergius III (d. 911), although he has the reputation of having been morally upright himself. His mother was the de facto ruler of the city of Rome, Marozia, countess of Spoleto and Tuscany. She put him on the papal throne at twenty-five, in March 931. His personally pious but politically ambitious half-brother Alberic II imprisoned both Marozia and John XI in June 932 as an incident of his rivalry with his newest stepfather, King Hugh of Italy, for whose coronation as Holy Roman emperor the pope was making preparations. John XI was deposed in December 935 and died in prison—apparently poisoned.

32. Henry Denzinger, *Enchiridion symbolorum definitionum et declarationum de rebus fidei et morum,* 32nd edition by Adolf Schönmetzer (Barcelona: Herder, 1963), no. 875. It is not without its interest that on December 19, 1516, the Fifth Lateran Council reasserted his thesis (Josephus Alberigus and others, eds. *Conciliorum oecumenicorum decreta* [Basel: Herder, 1962], pp. 619, 38-620, 6).

BIBLIOGRAPHY

THE BISHOPS OF ROME

Barraclough, Geoffrey. *The Medieval Papacy.* New York: Harcourt, Brace, and World, 1968.

Burn-murdoch, H. *The Development of the Papacy.* London: Faber and Faber, n.d. [not before 1953].

Giles, E., ed. *Documents Illustrating Papal Authority (A.D. 96–454).* London: SPCK, 1952.

Gontard, Friedrich. *The Chair of Peter: A History of the Papacy.* Trans. A. J. and E. F. Peeler. New York: Holt, Rinehart and Winston, 1964.

Marot, Hilaire. "The Primacy and the Decentralization of the Early Church," in Roger Aubert, ed., *Historical Problems of Church Renewal. Concilium: Theology in the Age of Renewal,* vol. 7. Glen Rock, N.J.: Paulist Press, 1965. Pp. 15-28.

Runciman, Steven. *The Eastern Schism: A Study of the Papacy and the Eastern Churches During the XIth and XIIth Centuries.* London: Oxford University Press, 1956.

Ullmann, Walter. *A Short History of the Papacy in the Middle Ages.* London: Methuen, 1974.

Weltin, Edward George. *The Ancient Popes.* Westminster, Md.: The Newman Press, 1964.

COUNCILS

Andresen, Carl. "History of the Medival Councils in the West," in Hans J. Margull, ed., *The Councils of the Church: History and Analysis.* Philadelphia: Fortress Press, 1966. Pp. 82-240.

Conway, J. D. *Times of Decision: Story of the Councils.* Notre Dame, Ind.: University of Notre Dame Press, 1962.

Dvornik, Francis. *The Ecumenical Councils.* New York: Hawthorn Books, 1961.

Franzen, August. "The Council of Constance: Present State of the Problem," in Roger Aubert, ed., *Historical Problems of Church Renewal. Concilium: Theology in the Age of Renewal,* Vol. 7 (Glen Rock, N.J.: Paulist Press, 1965): 29-68.

Gill, Joseph. *The Council of Florence.* Cambridge, England: University Press, 1959.

———. *Eugenius IV: Pope of Christian Union.* Westminster, Md.: The Newman Press, 1961.

———. *Personalities of the Council of Florence.* New York: Barnes and Noble, 1964.

Hess, H. *The Canons of the Council of Sardica, A.D. 343.* New York.: Oxford University Press, 1958.

Oberman, Heiko A.; Zerfoss, Daniel E.; and Courtenay, William J.; ed. and trans. *Defensorium Obedientiae Apostolicae et Alia Documenta.* Cambridge, Mass.: The Belknap Press of Harvard University Press, 1968. Sections 1 through 5 of the introduction, "The Twilight of the Conciliar Era," pp. 3-55.

Watkin, Edward Ingram. *The Church in Council.* New York: Sheed and Ward, 1960.

THEOLOGIANS

Bettoni, Efrem. *Duns Scouts: The Basic Principles of His Philosophy.* Trans. and ed. Bernardine Bonansea. Washington, D.C.: The Catholic University of America Press, 1961.

Bougerol, J. Guy. *Introduction to the*

Works of Bonaventure. Trans. José de Vinck. Paterson, N.J.: St. Anthony Guild Press, 1964.

Brehier, Emile. *The Middle Ages and the Renaissance*. Trans. Wade Baskin. Chicago: University of Chicago Press, 1965.

Brown, Peter. *Augustine of Hippo: A Biography*. Berkeley: University of California Press, 1969.

Chenu, M. D. *Toward Understanding St. Thomas*. Trans. Albert M. Landry and Dominic Hughes. Chicago: Henry Regnery Company, 1964.

Congar, Yves M.-J. *A History of Theology*. Trans. and ed. Hunter Guthrie. Garden City, N.Y.: Doubleday & Company, 1968.

Dolan, John Patrick, ed. *Unity and Reform: Selected Writings of Nicholas de Cusa*. Notre Dame, Ind: University of Notre Dame Press, 1962.

Fortman, Edmund J. *The Theology of Man and Grace: Commentary*. Milwaukee, Wis.: Bruce Publishing Company, 1966. Chaps. 6 through 8 (pp. 106-201).

Gilby, Thomas, and T. C. O'Brien, general eds. *St. Thomas Aquinas: Summa Theologiae*. New York: McGraw-Hill Book Company, 1965—. A new, annotated sixty-volume edition of the *Summa* with a "sound working" resultant Latin text and an English translation on facing pages.

Gilson, Etienne. *The Philosophy of St. Bonaventure*. Trans. Illtyd Trethowan and Frank J. Sheed. Paterson, N.J.: St. Anthony Guild Press, 1965.

González, Justo L. *A History of Christian Thought*. Vol. 1: *From the Beginnings to the Council of Chalcedon*. Nashville: Abingdon Press, 1970.

Hägglund, Bengt. *History of Theology*. Trans. Gene J. Lund. St. Louis, Mo.: Concordia Publishing House, 1968.

Lohse, Bernhard. *A Short History of Christian Doctrine*. Trans. F. Ernest Stoeffler. Philadelphia: Fortress Press, 1966.

Oberman, Heiko Augustinus. *Forerunners of the Reformation: The Shape of Late Medieval Thought*. New York: Holt, Rinehart and Winston, 1966.

———. *The Harvest of Medieval Theology: Gabriel Biel and Late Medieval Nominalism*. Cambridge: Harvard University Press, 1963.

Pelikan, Jaroslav. *The Christian Tradition: A History of the Development of Doctrine*. Vol. 1: *The Emergence of the Catholic Tradition (100–600)*. Chicago: University of Chicago Press, 1971.

Petitot, L. H. *The Life and Spirit of Thomas Aquinas*. Trans. Cyprian Burke. Chicago: The Priory Press, 1966.

Pieper, Josef. *Scholasticism: Personalities and Problems of Medieval Philosophy*. Trans. Richard and Clara Winston. New York: Pantheon Books, 1960.

Ratzinger, Joseph. *The Theology of History in St. Bonaventure*. Chicago: Franciscan Herald Press, 1971.

Scharlemann, Robert P. *Thomas Aquinas and John Gerhard*. New Haven, Conn.: Yale University Press, 1964.

Weinberg, Julius R. *A Short History of Medieval Philosophy*. Princeton, N.J.: Princeton University Press, 1964.

8. Dogma and Doctrine

Creeds

A development of exceptional importance between the third and the seventh centuries was the creation of three Western statements of faith that, once admitted to the church's public worship, exerted increasing influence on the formation of the faith of Western Christians. These were not the only confessions of faith to be produced. Indeed, down to the very threshold of the sixteenth century scores of creedal statements were composed by individuals (many of them anonymous), by communities, and by synods or councils, both for pedagogical and for liturgical use. But these three exhibited a particularly great hardihood and still exert vast influence.

1. *Te Deum laudamus*

The oldest of these creedal statements to come down to us in substantially its present form is the anonymous hymn *Te Deum laudamus* ("You We Praise as God"), which seems to have been sung in the monastery on the island of St.-Honorat (Lérins, the ancient Lerinum, off the French coast at Cannes) at least as far back as the time when St. Caesarius of Arles joined the community in 498.[1] In a literal translation it reads:

> You we praise as God;
> You we confess as Lord;
> You the whole universe venerates as the eternal Father.
> To you all the angels—
> To you the heavens and all the powers [above]—
> To you the cherubs and the seraphs call out with never-ending voice:
> Holy, holy, holy Lord God of Sabaoth.[2]
> The heavens and the earth are full of the majesty of your glory.
> You the apostles' glorious troop—
> You the [Christian] prophets' praiseworthy company—
> You the white-robed army of martyrs—
> You the holy church throughout all the world confesses:
> The Father of infinite[3] majesty;

Your venerable, true and only Son;

The Holy Spirit, the Paraclete,[4] as well.

You are the King of Glory, Christ,

You are the Father's everlasting Son,

You did not shrink from the womb of the virgin when you took humanity on yourself to set humanity free.

You vanquished death's sharp sting and opened the realms of heaven to the believers.

You sit at God's right hand in the Father's glory.

It is an article of our faith that you are coming as the Judge.

You we now beg to help your servants whom you bought back with precious blood.

Give[5] them unending glory with your holy ones.

Save your people, Lord, and bless your heritage.

Rule over them and exalt them for ever.

Day after day we bless you

And we praise your name for ever and ever and into the ages of ages.

Deign, Lord, to preserve us from sin this day.

Be merciful to us, Lord, be merciful to us.

Let your mercy, Lord, be over us

As we hope in you.

In you, Lord, I have hoped; let me never be put to shame.

2. *Whoever Wishes to Be Saved (the Athanasian Creed)*

The second creed in terms of age was the Symbol Whoever Wishes to Be Saved (*Symbolum Quicunque vult*), commonly and quite incorrectly known as the Athanasian Creed.[6] It comes from the age, although probably not from the pen, of St. Caesarius of Arles. From the ninth century it has been a part of the office of monastic prime,[7] that is, the service at the first hour of the day.

A literal rendering reads:

Whoever desires to be saved must before everything hold fast to the Catholic faith. Unless a person preserves it whole and inviolate he will without doubt perish for ever.[8]

Now this is the Catholic faith, that we venerate one God in the Trinity and the Trinity in the unity,

Neither mixing the hypostases[9] together nor breaking up the [divine] substance.

The hypostasis of the Father is one hypostasis, that of the Son another one, and that of the Holy Spirit still a different one.

But there is a single Godhead of the Father and of the Son and of the Holy Spirit, an equal glory, a coeternal majesty.

Whatever the Father is, the Son is, and the Holy Spirit is too.

The Father is uncreated, the Son is uncreated, the Holy Spirit is uncreated.

The Father is infinite,[10] the Son is infinite, the Holy Spirit is infinite.

The Father is eternal, the Son is eternal, the Holy Spirit is eternal.

Nevertheless there are not three eternal ones, but a single eternal one.

Just as there are not three uncreated ones or three infinite ones, but a single uncreated one and a single infinite one.

Similarly, the Father is almighty, the Son is almighty, and the Holy Spirit is almighty.

Nevertheless there are not three almighty ones but a single almighty one.

In the same way the Father is God, the Son is God, the Holy Spirit is God.

Nevertheless there are not three gods, but a single God.

In the same way the Father is the Lord, and the Son is the Lord, and the Holy Spirit is the Lord.

Nevertheless there are not three lords, but a single Lord.

Because just as the Christian truth compels us to confess each individual hypostasis singly to be both God and the Lord,

Just so the Catholic religion forbids us to talk about three gods or lords.

The Father has been made out of no one else,[11] nor has he been created or sired.

The Son is out of the Father alone; he has not been made or created, but he has been sired.

The Holy Spirit is out of the Father and the Son;[12] he has not been made or created or sired, but he issues forth.[13]

So there is a single Father, not three fathers; a single Son, not three sons; a single Holy Spirit, not three holy spirits.

And in this Trinity, nothing[14] is earlier or later, nothing is greater or less,

But all three hypostases are coeternal and coequal with one another

In such a way that throughout, as it has already been said, both the Trinity in the Unity and the Unity in the Trinity is to be venerated.

As a result, let whoever desires to be saved think in this way of the Trinity.

But it is necessary for everlasting salvation that he also faithfully believe the Incarnation of our Lord Jesus Christ.

This is the correct faith, that we believe and confess that our Lord Jesus Christ, God's Son, is equally God and a human being.

He is God sired out of His Father's substance before the ages, and he is a human being born in time out of his mother's substance.

He is completely God and completely a human being that consists of a rational soul and of human flesh.

He is equal to the Father with respect to his Godhead, less than the Father with respect to his humanity.

Even though Christ is God and a human being, he is not two but one.

Yet he is not one through the transformation of his Godhead into flesh, but by the taking up of his humanity into God.

He is one, admittedly not by a mixing together of substances but through a oneness of his hypostasis.

For just as the rational soul and flesh are a single human being, so [here] God and a human being are a single Christ.

He suffered for our salvation, went down to the netherworld, rose from the dead, ascended into the heavens, sat down at the Father's right hand, will come from there to pronounce judgment on the living and the dead.

At his coming all human beings will have to rise with their bodies

And are going to give an account of their own deeds.

Those who acted well will go into everlasting life, those who acted badly into everlasting fire.

This is the Catholic faith. Unless a person believes it faithfully and firmly he will not be able to be saved.[15]

3. *The Apostles' Creed*

Toward the end of the fourth century the apostolic origin of the various baptismal creeds current in the West began to become widely affirmed. Not much later the legend turns up that before dispersing for their mission of evangelizing the world the apostles agreed on a single simple formula of faith. The number of these "apostles' creeds" in the West is quite large; the differences among them range from relatively unimportant to relatively significant.

The age of origin of many of these symbols is arguable. There are creed-like formulas in the writings of many of the primitive Fathers; indeed, creedlike formulas appear in the New Testament itself.

Baptismal creeds in the form of questions and answers ("interrogatory creeds") that go back into the third century have survived at least in part.

Scholars have attempted to reconstruct local confessions of faith ("declaratory creeds") from sermons and other writings of individual writers. The best known case is the Old Roman Creed, purporting to represent the earliest recoverable declaratory creed in the capital of the West.

In spite of all this scholarly probing, the fact remains that prior to about 340, when Marcellus of Ankara (Ancyra) communicated his personal confession of faith in Greek[16] to St. Julius I of Rome (d. 352), we do not have a declaratory creed that does not have to be abstracted and reconstructed from another document. Scholars commonly hold that by rehearsing as his own the baptismal creed of Rome, Marcellus hoped to demonstrate beyond doubt his own orthodoxy to St. Julius. If this conjecture is true, the mid-fourth-century creed of the Church at Rome read like this:

> I believe in God the All-ruler; and in Christ Jesus his only son, our Lord, born out of the Holy Spirit and Mary the virgin, crucified under Pontius Pilate and buried and risen from the dead on the third day, gone up into the heavens and seated at the Father's right hand, from where he will come to pronounce judgment on the living and the dead; and in the Holy Spirit, a holy church, a forgiveness of sins, a resurrection of the flesh, a life everlasting.

A little over half a century later we have two commentaries on the so-called Apostles' Creed. One of them, written by St. Niceta[s] of Remesiana (335?–414), bishop of the modern Bela Palanka, Yugoslavia, in the closing decades of the fourth century, takes as its basis the Latin text that the Apostles' Creed had achieved in this Christian community on the very border between the East and West:

> I believe in God the almighty Father,[17] and in his son, Jesus Christ,[18] born out of the Holy Spirit and out of the virgin Mary, suffered under Pontius Pilate, crucified, dead. On the third day he rose alive from the dead. He ascended into the heavens. He sits at the Father's right hand, from where he is coming to pronounce judgment on the living and the dead. And in the Holy Spirit, the holy catholic church, participation in the holy things,[19] forgiveness of sins, resurrection of the flesh, and life everlasting.

The second commentary, by the presbyter Tyrannius Rufinus (345?–410), is dated between 401 and 404, and uses the text of the church of Aquileia at the head of the Adriatic:

> I believe in God the almighty Father, invisible, and impassible,[20] and in Christ Jesus, his only Son, our Lord, who was born from the Holy Spirit out of Mary the virgin, crucified under Pontius Pilate and buried. He went down to the netherworld.[21] On the third day he rose from the dead. He ascended into the heavens. He sits at the Father's right hand, from where he is coming to pronounce judgment on the living and the dead. And in the Holy Spirit, the holy church, the forgiveness of sins, the resurrection of this flesh.[22]

By the end of the seventh century a conflated version—possibly of French origin—of some of these local creeds had begun to replace them. It appears to have established itself in the city of Rome in the mid-ninth-century. At an early date it began to acquire liturgical currency in the daily prayers of the monastic communities. This received text since shortly after 1000 has become known in the West[23] as *the* Apostles' Creed in the strict sense:

> I believe in God the almighty Father, creator of heaven and earth; And in Jesus Christ, his only Son, our Lord, who was conceived from the Holy Spirit, born out of Mary the virgin, suffered under Pontius Pilate, crucified, dead, and buried; he went down to the netherworld. On the third day he rose from the dead. He ascended into the heavens. He sits at the right hand of God the almighty Father, from where he is coming to pronounce judgment on the living and the dead. I believe in the Holy Spirit, the holy Catholic church, participation in the holy things, the forgiveness of sins, the resurrection of the flesh, and life everlasting. Amen.[24]

4. *Western Changes in the Nicene Creed*

The Creed of the 150 Fathers of Constantinople (Nicene Creed) underwent minor modifications in the West after it began to be used increasingly at celebrations of the sacrament of the altar after the Third Council of Toledo in 589. The plural "We believe" became "I believe." "God out of

God" was added before: "Light out of light." "Of the same being as the Father" was rendered as "consubstantial with the Father." "Out of" now preceded "Mary the virgin." "In" dropped out before "a single holy Catholic and apostolic church," but with no intention of effecting a theological change.

The most significant change came some time prior to the last third of the eighth century. It was the introduction of the words "and the Son"[25] after "who proceeds from the Father," first in the western and northern provinces of the Western Empire and finally in the city of Rome itself.[26]

Specific Doctrines

1. *The Sacrament of the Altar*

The sacrament of the altar became the subject of serious theological study (and controversy) in 831 with the publication of a treatise on *The Body and Blood of Christ* by the Benedictine theologian St. Paschasius Radbertus (785?–860?). After the consecration, he held, the body and blood of Christ are present—really but spiritually—under the form of bread and wine. The body imparted in the sacrament is the same body that was born of the Blessed Virgin Mary, that hung on the cross, and that rose again on Easter. The symbolic aspect of the sacramental event is limited to the elements and their reception. Because Christ himself declares—through the words of the celebrant—"This is my body," that which the communicant perceives inwardly is a veritable reality and no figure.

Ratramnus (d. 868), another Benedictine, replied to St. Paschasius with a second treatise with the same title. He rejected the realism of St. Paschasius and maintained that the consecrated elements were the body and blood of Christ only in a figurative sense: "Christ's body must be understood not physically but spiritually." St. Rhabanus Maurus (776?–856) shared Ratramnus's position (which the Synod of Vercelli formally condemned in 1050).

In the late eleventh century Berengar of Tours (999?–1088), following Ratramnus, rejected the idea that the consecration effects the presence of the body and blood of Christ in the sacrament of the altar. Christ's body is in heaven, he argued, and he cannot be brought down to earth before the Last Judgment. In the meantime his body is effective for humanity through its sacramental counterpart, the eucharistic elements. These are signs and pledges that the communicant is spiritually receiving the body and blood of the heavenly Christ. One opponent of Berengar was Lanfranc (d. 1089), archbishop of Canterbury, who went so far as to affirm explicitly that unbelieving communicants receive the body and blood of Christ. Berengar was compelled to recant. He did so several times. The most famous formulas are the profession of faith that Cardinal Humbert of Silva Candida drafted and that Nicholas II prescribed for Berengar in 1059 and the oath that St. Gregory VII demanded of him twenty years later.

The relationship between the consecrated elements in the sacrament of the altar and the body and blood of Christ continued to engage the attention of theologians. They put forth many theories, among them consubstantiation (the idea that the "substance" of Christ's body and blood coexists with the "substance" of the consecrated bread and wine under the latter's "appearances" or "species"), and annihilation (the idea that the "substance" of the bread and the wine is annihilated at the consecration and replaced by the "substance" of Christ's body and blood under the "appearance" of the bread and wine). What became the official terminology seems first to have been set forth by Orlando (Roland) Bandinelli, later Alexander III (d. 1181), who taught the total conversion of the "substance" of the bread and wine into the "substance" of Christ's body and blood while the "appearance" of the bread and wine remained. This is the terminology that the Fourth Lateran Council adopted in 1215.

The primary concern was to ensure that the faith in the actual presence of the body and blood of Christ would be preserved against the view that the bread and wine merely signified Christ's body and blood.[27]

From a very early date the church had come to speak of the sacrament of the altar as a sacrifice of praise and thanksgiving and a sacramental making present again (*repraesentatio*) of the sacrifice of Christ on the cross as the climactic act of his life, death, and rising to life again. During the period here surveyed the sacrament of the altar came increasingly to be regarded—especially at the popular level—as a sacrificial act with independent expiatory and propitiatory value that could be applied on behalf of the living on earth and the souls of the departed in purgatory. This view reinforced, and was in turn reinforced by, the shift in the common understanding of the term *opus operatum* ("the work performed"), or, in a slightly fuller formula, *ex opere operato* ("through the performance of the work"). Originally the term was intended to safeguard the objectivity of the sacraments and to assert that they produce their proper effect not on account of the virtue or the personal merits of the officiant or the recipient (that is, not *ex opere operantis*, "through the work of the one engaged in its performance"). By the sixteenth century people came to understand the term *ex opere operato* as implying that the sacraments produced their effect in an automatic and mechanical kind of way, "without any good interior movement [that is, faith] in the user" (*sine bono motu utentis*), as the phrase ran. In the case of the sacrament of the altar, many Western Christians believed that the Mass needed merely to be said in order to accomplish the intention for which it was offered, whether this intention contemplated the needs of living persons or, more frequently, the needs of the departed in purgatory.[28]

The exaggerated awe with which the consecrated elements of the sacrament of the altar were regarded and the fear of spilling the eucharistic blood of Christ led to communion "under one kind" (that is, in the form of the bread only). Intinction (dipping the consecrated bread in the consecrated wine before it was administered to the communicant) was formally forbidden by a number of councils between the eighth and twelfth centuries. Increasingly, and with only rare exceptions, lay awe and clerical concern combined to make reception of the eucharistic blood of Christ less and less frequent by anyone except the celebrant. Periodically the practice of communion "under one kind" was criticized by some element in the church. The most effective protest came from the Bohemian Calixtines (from *calix*, "chalice"). The Council of Constance condemned them in 1415, but the Council of Basel acceded to their demand in 1437. The privilege was again withdrawn twenty-five years later, but it remained a burning issue.

The frequency with which Christians received the Holy Communion declined more or less consistently throughout the medieval period. In the latter half of the first millennium valiant efforts were made to have each Christian receive the sacrament of the altar a minimum of four times annually, but the decline could not be stemmed. Finally in 1215 an annual Communion during Eastertide provided a canonical minimum that a communicant could not evade without loss of status in the church.

As the annual number of times of reception of the sacrament of the altar went down, the value that had been attributed to the oral reception of the sacrament transferred itself to the Christian's "assisting" (from *adsistere*, literally "standing at") at the celebration of the Holy Eucharist. Particular importance came to be attached to the "elevation" of the bread and the chalice so that the worshipers could see them.

Concomitantly the cultus of the "reserved" sacrament gained increasing popularity. Initially the consecrated sacramental elements had been "reserved" (that is, a portion of them had been set aside at the celebration) in the church for the communion of the sick without any special veneration being paid to them. The growing awe in which the reserved elements were held invited cultic veneration. At first this was notably true in the northern parts of Europe. The practice spread, and in the thirteenth century the Feast of Corpus Christi ("the body of Christ") in honor of the Holy Eucharist was instituted. It became a feast of universal obligation in the next century.

Admittedly the popular understanding of the reserved sacrament frequently had its superstitious aspects. At the same time the devotion to the reserved sacrament had also undeniably positive effects upon the church's spirituality. In their veneration of "God's flesh and blood" in the sacrament, the worshipers intended to address Christ himself. In the words of the thirteenth-century Anglo-Saxon *Ancren Riwle* ("Anchoresses' Rule"), they were hailing him as "the ground of our creation, the price of our redemption, the supply of our pilgrimage, the reward of our expectation."

2. Excommunication and Reconciliation

From the beginning the church found it necessary to exclude from its fellowship those who committed scandalous sins, like murder, apostasy, and grave sexual derelictions. Gradually a system was codified for readmitting to the communion of the church those who desired such reconciliation. In its developed form, this discipline required the person concerned to be enrolled in a separate order of penitents, normally for a period of seven years. Initially, at least, it could be undergone only once in a person's lifetime. Finally, it carried with it certain lifelong restrictions; a penitent could not, for instance, serve as a soldier and he was committed to total continence. Such rigor turned out to be self-defeating; offenders, barring occasional exceptions, tended simply to postpone their repentance to the threshold of death. Indeed, many adult converts, uncertain of their own capacity for fidelity, prudently postponed baptism for the same reason.

In place of public penance a new procedure arose, in large part the result of experiments devised by the missionaries that came to continental Europe from Britain. At least at the beginning, the new system was still extremely rigorous by modern standards. But it had certain features that made it more attractive than the older procedure. For one thing, the details of the sin in question were confessed privately. Furthermore, the formal forgiveness (or absolution) was gradually moved back from the point in time where the penitent had completed his penance to the time when he made his confession and before he began his penance; his restoration to the communion of the church thus took place immediately upon confession. The replacement of the old system by the new did not proceed everywhere in Western Christendom at the same pace, but by the end of the first millennium the process was substantially complete almost everywhere. (Yet as late as the twelfth century theologians were hard put to supply a rationale for private confession.[29])

Out of this altered approach to repentance grew the medieval triad— "contrition in the heart, confession in the mouth, and satisfaction in deed." This form of repentance received its authoritative charter in 1215 with the prescription of an annual Communion at Eastertide by each Christian, preceded by priestly confession and absolution. When the contrition of the penitent was imperfect, the act of confession before a priest supplied what was missing. The proper "matter" of confession was seen as limited to mortal sins, that is, sins that killed and deprived the soul of supernatural life. Where the penitent remembered no mortal sins that he had committed since his last confession, he might confess a venial sin, even though such a sin, as the very word venial (from *venia*, that is, "pardon" or "forgiveness"), was by definition already forgiven. Or the penitent might confess a mortal sin forgiven in an earlier confession. The difficulty of defining a mortal sin tended to make confession a painful experience for scrupulous penitents, especially when the confessor tended in the direction of rigorism.

The common theory regarded the consequences of sin as twofold—temporal and eternal. The eternal consequences were blotted out by perfect contrition or by the forgiveness, because of the merits of Christ, either of God (in the case of venial sins) or of the confessor acting in God's name (in the case of mortal sins). The temporal consequences remained. For these the penitent had to satisfy by patiently accepting suffering that overtook him in this life or by special acts of piety. If at the end of the penitent's life these satisfactions outweighed the temporal punishments that he had incurred by his sin, he entered upon the beatific vision of God. If the temporal punishments exceeded his satisfactions, he could expect to suffer in purgatory until he had expiated these remaining temporal punishments, whereupon he would be admitted to the beatific vision. To reduce the demand for these satisfactions in life and satispassions in purgatory, indulgences, in virtue of the merits of Christ and of the saints, became available in the eleventh century. After that date they became increasingly common. A limited indulgence offered the penitent as much benefit as he could have acquired by performing public penance for a specified period (forty days, or a "quarantine," for instance) in the days when the primitive penitential discipline was in effect. (Such indulgences did not pretend to shorten the sufferings of purgatory by as many days or years.) A plenary indulgence remitted—under the prescribed conditions—the whole of the temporal punishment due to an individual's sins. It could be applied by the individual either to himself or to a deceased Christian in purgatory.

The fifteenth and early sixteenth centuries witnessed the increase of abuses in this area, particularly in cases where doctrinally unsound and morally irresponsible professional "pardoners" were engaged to "preach" indulgences in order to raise funds for one or the other ecclesiastical project through the contributions that the recipients of the letters of indulgence were expected to make.[30]

3. The Sacrament of Order

The differentiation of the bishop from the presbyter was substantially completed in the West by the end of the second century, but even in the fifth century St. Jerome could recall that the differentiation was a matter of practical convenience and not of divine right. With the geographic expansion of the dioceses, the bishop became more and more the administrator of the entire diocese, while the pastoral care of the emerging parishes (in the modern sense of the term) rested with presbyters. As the supervisor of the diocese, the bishop was vested with the "ordinary" authority to ordain; but there is a significant body of evidence that ordinations by presbyters were not regarded as necessarily defective, far less invalid.[31]

The deacon's primitive responsibility for the material side of the church's work was initially reflected in his status, which was more lay than clerical. This situation changed as the deacons' responsibilities for more and more aspects of the public worship of the community increased and their place among the major orders of the church became secure. At the same time, it became necessary in the seventh century to stress their inferiority to the priesthood.

The demand for a celibate clergy in the West goes back to the fourth century. The original purpose was to exemplify totally in the priest the undivided concern for "the affairs of the Lord" (1 Corinthians 7:32) that the sacred Scriptures commend to all Christians. Clerical celibacy also reflected the high value that the sacred Scriptures attached to virginity, in the sense of the desire to anticipate the resurrection state where "they neither marry nor are given in marriage" (Mark 12:25), and the willingness to give up all forms of secular security for the sake of the kingdom of heaven.

From the sixth century forward the canons compelled ordained persons to separate from their spouses. The continuing necessity for intervention by synods and councils indicates the resistance this prescription encountered. One concern that lay behind this development was to prevent the alienation of church property to the families of married clerics. In the Holy Roman Empire imperial law reinforced the ecclesastical canons that made ordination to major orders a diriment impediment to marriage. With marriage thus foreclosed as an option, clerics engaged increasingly in more or less open concubinage.

4. The Cultus of the Saints

Western Christendom in the period under review exhibits distinctive traits in connection with the veneration of the great heros of the Christian faith, although developments in the West and in the East follow parallel lines.

First to receive veneration—as far back as the second century—were the martyrs. They were remembered with celebrations of the sacrament of the altar on the anniversary, and where possible at the site, of their death. In the course of time churches were often at the place where a distinguished martyr had given his life for the faith. Relics that could be related to him or her were treated with great respect.

Next to join the martyrs as recipients of this veneration were the confessors, Christians whose testimony had jeopardized their lives but who had not actually been killed.

Distinguished bishops followed the confessors. St. Paulinus of Trier (d. 358), St. Denys of Milan (d. 359), St. Martin of Tours (d. 397), and St. Ambrose were among the first. In the fifth century the Blessed Virgin Mary began to receive public veneration. As time went on the calendar began to include ascetics and virgins, royal and noble patrons and patronesses of the church, and widows.[32]

St. Leo affirmed that the intercession of the saints secured the divine mercy for their clients, and St. Gregory the Great urged the faithful to place themselves under the protection of the saints. In the fifth century the names of the saints began to be mentioned in the celebrations of the sacrament of the altar in various parts of the West. From the eight century onward readings from the lives of the saints became a part of monastic matins.[33]

While the Christian East tended to stress the veneration of the icons of the saints, the Christian West tended to stress the veneration of their relics.

The positive benefits of the veneration of the saints were undeniably great, even though the sacred Scriptures offered little explicit guidance in this area. Here were human beings who had exemplified the willingness to put loyalty to the Christian faith ahead of every human value, even life itself. Here were human models who had actually realized in a heroic degree the dynamic holiness and the specific virtues that being a Christian called for. The gifts that they had received from the Holy Spirit had been imparted for the benefit of their fellow Christians as well as of themselves. The sense of solidarity with the saints in the common salvation that baptism had mediated to all was a powerful stimulus to imitate the faith and the virtues of the saints and in this way to share in their victory.This was so throughout the period under consideration. But while the official theology of the church set the saints before the Christians who were still in this present life as examples of faith and good works that the latter were to follow during their pilgrimage, a good deal of superstition actually developed. Increasingly the invocation of the saints moved from pleas for their intercessions ("pray for us") to petitions for their help. The catastrophes that periodically spread over Europe in the shape of war, famine, and pestilence turned human beings who were despairing in their helplessness to superhuman helpers; God and even his Son had become so remote for many medieval Christians that the saints became welcome intermediaries.

The roles of individual saints became specialized. St. Anne, "God's grandmother," as she was often called affectionately, was the patroness of the poor. St. Sebastian, who had been shot to death with arrows, protected his clients from the metaphorical arrows of pestilence. St. Valentine was invoked against epilepsy and gout. St. George the soldier was the patron of knights. St. Barbara, whose father had been struck by lightning for ordering her execution, ensured that those who sought her aid did not suffer sudden death (especially by lightning) without priest and sacrament. St. Christopher who in his lifetime had according to tradition carried travelers across the ford of a river, defended those who invoked him from the perils of travel.

Access to any saint was believed to be easier in a church or shrine dedicated to him or her. Popular saints, with a reputation for helping their clients, acquired great prestige. Their shrines attracted pilgrims from all over Europe.

Relics of the saints were in great demand, especially after indulgences began to be attached to their veneration, and a lively traffic in real and counterfeit relics developed.[34]

Some of the saints that were venerated were at best legendary.[35] From 993 on, when a bishop of Rome for the first time formally canonized a saint —St. Ulric of Augsburg (890?–973)—the Roman see sought valiantly but vainly to limit the cult of new saints to persons whose veneration it had officially approved.

Both the proponents and the opponents of the veneration of the saints were guilty of excess. Among those in favor one must list here St. Peter Damien (1007–1072), St. Anselm, and St. Bernard of Clairvaux. Among those who opposed the practice in its beginnings one thinks of the eccentric contemporary and adversary of St. Jerome, Vigilantius. Later there was Claudius of Turin (d. 827), whose opposition to pilgrimages and to the veneration of images, relics, and Christ's cross and whose cavalier disrespect for the authority of the Roman see have led both Waldensians and Baptists to count him among their spiritual forebears. Around the turn of the millennium Guibert of Nogent (d. 1024), best known for his rapt devotion to the Blessed Virgin Mary, insisted that piety was better than the veneration of relics.

The great scholastics were also among those who raised voices pleading for a moderation of the excesses to which folk piety was going.

But the thrust was too strong to be held back, and the abuses in connection with the veneration of the saints provided the sixteenth-century reform movements with some of the most popular weapons in their arsenal.

5. The Blessed Virgin Mary

The veneration of the Blessed Virgin Mary in the West has its own history.

From the time of St. Augustine it was generally held that she had taken a vow of virginity.

St. Hippolytus of Rome is often credited with having been the first to coin the term that was officially sanctioned at the Council of Ephesus (431), theotokos ("the woman who brought forth God") or, in Latin, Deipara. (But some scholars regard the reference as a later interpolation into the text.)

Although there were eminent early Latin fathers like Tertullian and St. Jerome who taught that she did not remain a virgin after the birth of Christ, the opinion that she did became increasingly the standard Western view from the time of SS. Augustine and Ambrose. The belief that she gave birth to Christ without pain and without the loss of her physiological virginity is documentable as far back as the early second- or the late first-century Ascension of Isaiah, but it does not become dominant until the seventh, when the Lateran Council of 649 formally confirmed the formula that describes her as "a virgin before giving birth (ante partum) [to Christ], while giving birth (in partu), and after giving birth (post partum)."

St. Augustine taught that the Blessed Virgin Mary is the spiritual mother of those who are the members of Christ's body. He thus anticipated such titles as "Mother of Christians" and "Mother of the Church." Some of the earliest Western invocations of the Blessed Virgin appear in his writings.

He also taught that she was sinless, but not in the sense of the later immaculate conception (the teaching that the Blessed Virgin Mary was preserved from the contagion of original sinfulness from the first movement of her conception).

The Blessed Virgin was named in the eucharistic prayer of consecration at Rome as early as the sixth century.

From the seventh century on the number of Marian feasts increased greatly.

As early as the ninth century the title of "Redeemer" (*redemptrix*) was applied to her.

In the ninth century the Eastern feast of "the child-conception of St. Anne, the mother of the Mother of God" entered the West as the Feast of the Conception (but not of the immaculate conception) of the Blessed Virgin Mary. St. Bernard of Clairvaux rejected the idea of her immaculate conception. But Eadmer of Canterbury (1055?–1124?), the most famous English disciple of St. Anselm, provided the first theological exposition of the doctrine. He invoked the principle *potuit, voluit, fecit*, that is, "[God] was able to [have the Blessed Virgin Mary immaculately conceived; it is obvious that] he willed [it; consequently] he did it!" While St. Thomas Aquinas continued to reject the immaculate conception, William of Ware (flourished before 1300) and Duns Scotus came out explicitly for it and it rapidly became part of the Franciscan and Carmelite tradition. The breakthrough was facilitated by the distinction that William made between Christ's "preventative redemption" with reference to his mother and his "liberative redemption" with reference to all other human beings.

From the twelfth century onward the role of the Blessed Virgin Mary in worship increased significantly. Some of the most familiar "Marian antiphons," like the *Salve regina* ("Hail, Queen") and the *Alma redemptoris mater* ("Kind Mother of the Redeemer"), come from this period. The Little Office of Our Lady began as a private devotion in the tenth century and had become universally authorized by the end of the next. The *Ave Maria* ("Hail, Mary")—in its short biblical form, without the subsequently added plea to the Blessed Virgin to pray for her clients "now and in the hour of our death"—came in at the same time.

The use of beads to keep count of one's prayers while meditating turned up in the first half of the twelfth century, but the rosary evolved slowly and it was just emerging at the end of the fifteenth century in the form under which it was to become generally known. (The ascription of the rosary to St. Dominic, though widely affirmed, is a legend.)

In general, early and medieval Western liturgical texts affirm or assume that she died. The earliest writer that discusses her bodily assumption (that is, her "being taken up") into heaven is St. Gregory of Tours (540?–594). The contrary skeptical voices were loud and emphatic. One of these was the letter called *Cogitis me*; the middle ages ascribed it incorrectly to St. Jerome, but it is today commonly regarded as the work of St. Paschasius

Radbertus. Around the twelfth century it began to yield some of its influence to an eloquent sermon, falsely ascribed to St. Augustine, which affirmed her bodily assumption.

Popular devotion to the Blessed Virgin Mary continued to increase in the waning Middle Ages. There is hardly an imaginable title or honor that is not bestowed upon her by some devotee. (Typical are the sermons of the persuasive Franciscan preacher St. Bernardine Albizzeschi of Siena [1380–1444] and the formidable *Mariale* of Bernardine of Busti [d. 1515].) The peasant girl of Nazareth whom God chose to become the mother of the Son of God had become the queen of heaven.

NOTES

1. The reference to "the [Christian] prophets' praiseworthy company" indicates a very early date for at least this part of the *Te Deum*. In form the hymn is a reworking of a primitive Easter eve baptismal liturgy that cannot be later than the first half of the fourth century.

2. "Sabaoth" is the transliteration of the Hebrew ṣᵉva'oth, "the [angelic] armies."

3. Latin, *immensae*.

4. Latin, *paraclitum* ("counselor"), transliterating the Greek *paraklêtos*.

5. Latin, *munerari*. The classic translation, "Make them to be numbered," is based on a variant reading, *numerari*.

6. The ascription to St. Athanasius is at least as old as the Second Council of Autun (Augustodunum) around 670, and may go back to St. Caesarius of Arles himself.

7. In 1955 the Roman Catholic Church reduced its use to Trinity Sunday. The creed continues in use in the Lutheran Church and in the Church of England.

8. The stress is on the conservation of the faith from one generation to another. The creed is not identifying saving faith with ability to articulate intellectual propositions.

9. "Hypostasis" is used to translate the Latin *persona* wherever it occurs to avoid the misleading modern implications of the term "person."

10. Latin, *immensus* ("unmeasured, unmeasurable").

11. The Middle Ages coined the word *aseity* ("the quality of being from oneself [alone]") for this.

12. This phrase betrays the Western origin of this creed.

13. Latin, *procedens*. The differences in causation are the only way in which the hypostases can be differentiated from each other within the Godhead.

14. The gender of "nothing" and of the comparative adjectives is deliberately neuter.

15. The most modern treatment of the Symbol Whoever Wishes to be Saved is J. N. D. Kelly, *The Athanasian Creed* (New York: Harper & Row, 1964).

16. The transition from Greek to Latin in the Christian community of Rome seems to have taken place during the third and fourth centuries. St. Cornelius (d. 253) is the first bishop of Rome whose grave has a Latin epitaph, but there may have been congregations using Latin before then. By around 370 the transition to Latin as a liturgical language seems to have been all but complete.

17. The words "creator of heaven and earth" may have followed.

18. The words "our Lord" may have followed.

19. It is clear that *sanctorum communionem* (which occurs for the first time in a creed in this creed of Remesiana) and its Greek equivalent, *koinônia tôn hagiôn,* meant "participation in the holy things," that is, the eucharistic body and blood of Christ. Although it acquired other meanings very early, the original understanding is documentable in France as late as 1325, in England as late as 1575, and in the Holy Roman Empire until the last decade of the sixteenth century.

20. That is, incapable of suffering and hence of change.

21. This phrase occurs in any creed for the first time in the "dated" creed of Sirmium (359). It occurs in a Western —and an incontestably Catholic— creed for the first time in Aquileia.

22. For a scholarly English translation of the *Commentary* of Rufinus, see J. N. D. Kelly, trans.-ed., *Rufinus: A Commentary on the Apostles' Creed* (Westminster, Md.: The Newman Press, 1955).

23. The Apostles' Creed was never formally adopted by or widely used (or even widely known) among Eastern Christians.

24. On the history of the Apostles' Creed, see J. N. D. Kelly, *Early Christian Creeds* (London: Longmans, Green and Company, 1952), chaps. 4-6, 12-13 (pp. 100-204, 363-434).

25. Latin, *filioque,* hence the common name for this addition, "the Filioque."

26. Tradition has this happen in 1014 when Benedict VIII reportedly succumbed to the pressure of Emperor Henry II and consented to have the Creed of Constantinople sung at the Eucharist.

27. James F. McCue, "The Doctrine of Transubstantiation from Berengar through the Council of Trent," part I, in *Lutherans and Catholics in Dialoque*, III (*The Eucharist as Sacrifice* (Washington, D.C.: United States Catholic Conference, 1967): 89-108.

28. A concrete example was the plenary indulgence for the relief of a soul in purgatory gained by the celebration of a Mass at St. Gregory's altar in the Church of St. Gregory the Great on the Caelian Hill in Rome, without other conditions. The same privilege was conferred on many other altars ("Gregorian altars *ad instar* ['equivalent']") throughout Western Christendom. Such a Mass, from the standpoint of the Church's intention and of the church's exercise of the office of the keys, as the Middle Ages understood it, was regarded as having the effect of immediately delivering the soul for whom it was offered from the pains of purgatory.

29. In a personal communication Professor McCue makes the point "that with confession at least the rite evolved first and the theory followed after, often rather breathlessly."

30. A famous project in the early sixteenth century was the building of St. Peter's basilica in Rome. It was the preaching of this indulgence by the Dominican monk John Tetzel (1465?-1519) across the upper Saxon border from Wittenberg that precipitated Martin Luther's famous Ninety-five Theses against indulgences in 1517. In this particular case part of the contributions of the faithful went to reduce the indebtedness of Cardinal Albert of Brandenburg (1490-1545), archbishop-elector of Mainz and archbishop of Magdeburg, to the international banking house of Fugger.

31. See for documentation Kilian McDonnell, "Ways of Validating Ministry," *Journal of Ecumenical Studies* 7 (1970): 209-265, and Arthur Carl Piepkorn, "A Lutheran View of the Validity of Lutheran Orders," in *Lutherans and Catholics in Dialog* 4 (*Eucharist and Ministry*) (Washington, D.C.: United States Catholic Conference, 1970): 209-226 (especially pp. 216-225).

32. It is an indication of the way in which virginity was valued above marriage that after the era of the martyrs no married woman who predeceased her husband was declared a saint.

33. These readings (*legenda*, literally "things to be read") sometimes rested on very slender historical foundations and tended to be concentrated on marvels connected with the holy person in question. While they tended to foster credulity among the simple, they led to a corrosive skepticism among the thoughtful. "He lies like the second nocturn at matins," one proverbial observation went, referring to the fact that the readings of the saints occurred in the second of the three divisions of the monastic night office.

34. Thus, to cite a single instance, the parish church of St. Mary the Virgin in Wittenberg, Saxony, had 5,005 relics in 1509, with indulgences totaling 1,443 years attached to them. They included what purported to be a tooth of St. Jerome, three hairs of the Blessed Virgin Mary, one of the nails that pinned Christ to the cross, and a twig from the burning bush that Moses had seen on Mount Sinai. The indefatigable energy of Elector Frederick the Wise, Martin Luther's protector, in gathering relics had increased this collection by 1520 to

19,013 relics with indulgences totaling 1,902,202 years and 270 days (Roland H. Bainton, *Here I Stand: A Life of Martin Luther* [Nashville: Abingdon-Cokesbury Press, 1950], pp. 69-71).

35. Among them St. Alexis, the St. Anastasia commemorated on December 25, St. Apuleius, St. Bacchus, St. Barbara, St. Bibiana (Vivian), St. Bonaface of Tarsus, St. Catharine of Alexandria, St. Christopher, St. Chrysogonus, the St. Crescentia commemorated on June 15, the SS. Cyprian and Justina commemorated on September 26, St. Domitilla, St. Eusebius of Rome, the St. Eustace commemorated on September 20, St. Felix of Valois, St. George the Martyr, the St. Hippolytus commemorated on August 22, the SS. John and Paul commemorated on June 26, the St. Margaret commemorated on July 20, St. Martina, St. Maur the Abbot, St. Nympha, St. Paul the Hermit, St. Philomena, St. Placid the Martyr, St. Praxedes, the St. Prisca (Priscilla) commemorated on January 18, St. Pudentiana, St. Respicius, St. Sabina of Rome, St. Susanna, St. Symphorosa, St. Thecla of Iconium, the Twelve Holy Brothers commemorated on September 1, St. Ursula, and St. Venantius of Camerino. (The Roman Catholic Church dropped all of these from its calendar in 1969.) A popular treatment of the whole issue is Lancelot Sheppard, *Saints Who Never Were* (Dayton, Ohio: Pflaum Press, 1969). In a similar category is St. Wilgefortis (Uncumber, Kümmernis, Livrade), patroness of unhappily married wives. Iconographically she is a hypostatization of one of the robed and bearded crucifixes that received widespread veneration from the twelfth century on, possibly that of Lucca (Herbert Thurston and Donald Attwater, eds., *Butler's Lives of the Saints* 3 [New York: P. J. Kenedy and Sons, 1962]: 151-152). Even the historical saints present problems to the hagiographer. A case in point is the well-named St. Christina the Astonishing (1150–1224) (ibid., pp. 176-178).

BIBLIOGRAPHY

Bainton, Roland H. *Early and Medieval Christianity: The Collected Papers in Church History, Series One.* Boston: Beacon Press, 1962. Chap. 4, "The Ministry in the Middle Ages," pp. 45-81.

Congar, Yves. "The Historical Development of Authority in the Church: Points for Reflection," in John M. Todd, ed., *Problems of Authority: An Anglo-French Symposium.* Baltimore: The Helicon Press, 1962. Pp. 119-155.

Graef, Hilda. *Mary: A History of Doctrine and Devotion.* Vol. 1: *From the Beginnings to the Eve of the Reformation.* New York: Sheed and Ward, 1963.

Guzie, Tad W. *Jesus and the Eucharist.* New Jersey, Paulist Press, 1974.

Haran, John P. *Mary, Mother of God.* Indiana: Our Sunday Visitor, 1973.

Kelly, J. N. D. *The Athanasian Creed.* New York: Harper & Row, 1964.

———. *Early Christian Creeds.* London: Longmans, Green and Company, 1952.

King, Archdale A. *Eucharistic Reservation in the Western Church.* New York: Sheed and Ward, 1965.

Marthaler, Berard L. "The Eucharist, Bond of Unity—Before the Council of Trent," in Berard L. Marthaler, ed., *The Holy Eucharist and Christian Unity: Report of the Forty-Third Annual Meeting of the Franciscan Educational Conference, August 6-8, 1962.* Louisville, Ky.: The Franciscan Educational Conference (Bellarmine College), 1963. Pp. 241-254.

Neuner, Joseph, and Dupuis, James, eds. *The Christian Faith in the Doctrinal Documents of the Catholic Church.* Maryland: Christian Classics, 1975.

Rahner, Karl. *Encyclopedia of Theology: The Concise Sacramentum Mundi.* New York: Seabury Press, 1975.

9. Worship and Church Life

Liturgy and Worship

The basic structure of the eucharistic liturgy was the same in the East and the West. But in its separate development the Western rites exhibited some characteristic peculiarities, particularly brevity, a sobriety of expression that reflects the cast of the Western mind, and the presence of many more elements in the rite that changed from week to week ("propers").

Within the West itself there was a considerable diversity of rites. There was a Latin Rite in Africa that antedated the Latin Rite of Rome, but we know very little about it. The Roman Rite was initially the use of the city of Rome and of the parts of Italy that came directly under its influence. The Gallican tradition, a little more flamboyant than the Roman, was fostered in France, Germany, and parts of Italy. Related to the Gallican Rite were the Celtic Rite of Celtic Britain and the Mozarabic[1] Rite of Spain. The English Rite differed only in minor details from the Roman Rite. Milan had a rite of its own (Ambrosian Rite), with both Roman and Gallican features. These rites were of course not as completely homogeneous and as comprehensively detailed as rites are today. There was a considerable amount of variation within any given rite from province to province, from diocese to diocese, and even from parish to parish.

Ultimately the Roman use superseded its rivals; these survived only in a small number of churches in Milan and Toledo and in local vestiges elsewhere. In the process the Roman Rite underwent considerable modification and elaboration through the absorption of features from the rites that it superseded. The evolution of the Roman Rite was still going on—somewhat sluggishly—in the sixteenth century.

An important consequence of this relative uniformity was the general acceptance throughout the West of certain liturgical forms with great theological significance.

One set of such forms was the collection of Sunday and festival "collects,"[2] the first variable prayers in the celebration of the sacrament of the altar.[3] These prayers were also used in the daily prayers of the monastic communities. Theologically these prayers are deliberately and demonstrably "anti-Pelagian," that is, they emphasize the spiritual helplessness of human beings without the grace of God and underline the total dependence of the church and of Christians upon the Holy Spirit.

Another commonly accepted prayer was the prayer of consecration ("[greater] canon") at celebrations of the Holy Eucharist. It consisted of a rather haphazardly composed and imperfectly integrated collection of prayers out of the fourth to the sixth centuries. It achieved substantially its present form prior to St. Gregory the Great, who had some reservations about it. Its general use helped to underline a sacrificial interpretation of the sacrament of the altar, although without specifying the kind of sacrifice involved.

During the later Middle Ages a considerable number of theologically fateful liturgical developments took place. We have already adverted to the decline in the frequency of receiving the Holy Communion, the rise of the cult of the reserved sacrament, and the increase in devotion to the Blessed Virgin Mary and the saints. But there were other parallel developments, of which the following are typical.

While the old tradition called for the Mass to be sung, growing numbers of Masses were spoken. Ostensibly in the interest of heightened reverence, many portions of the Mass were said in a whisper; this limited congregational participation severely. In the case of sung Masses, the music became increasingly complicated until only choirs of specially trained singers could execute it. Latin, the only liturgical language in use in the European West once it had replaced Greek, had the advantage of being *the* international language. But with the conversion of the Germanic peoples and the rise of Romance vernaculars, Latin became more and more unintelligible.

Initially the weekly celebration of the Holy Communion was thought of as a representation of the entire Easter mystery, with special stress on Christ's victory over death. Increasingly, the scope of the meaning of the Mass came to be restricted to a reenactment of Christ's suffering, as the various parts and ceremonies of the Mass were related, as realistically as possible, to the events that climaxed in his crucifixion and death. The coming in of the crucifix (that is, a cross with a corpus ["body"] on it), sometimes intensely realistic in conception and execution, was a related development. So was the predilection of artists for producing crucifixion scenes. The development of the church year and the multiplication of intrusive feasts of saints also tended to obscure the ancient Paschal understanding of the mystery.

In addition, the increase in the number of festivals on which people were obligated to go to church, to a point where there were an average of one a week in addition to Sunday, had obvious social and economic as well as religious consequences.

The demand for votive Masses grew. These were said for the repose of the testator's or someone else's soul or for protection against such mundane perils as various diseases, threats to the peaceful possession of one's property, and the alarums and incursions of war. The frequently rehearsed assurances that seemed to guarantee certain results were part of a vicious circle. This was part of a general shift of emphasis in the purpose of the Eucharist away from the glorification of God and the occasion for the reception of his Son's body and blood to a calculated means for achieving a desired good for oneself or for someone else. These vast numbers of Masses required not only extensive architectural changes in cathedral and parish churches to provide additional chapels, chantries, and altars, but they also demanded huge additional numbers of clerics. In some towns the Mass-saying clergy totaled 20 percent of the population. The cathedral of Strasbourg at one point had on its staff 120 clerics whose only employment was to say a votive Mass once daily and to recite the divine office. The number of pious foundations increased to where one-third of the land of the Holy Roman Empire belonged to the church. Here too the effects were social and economic as well as religious.

While at first the celebrant at the sacrament of the altar had normally stood facing the congregation across the altar, the growing veneration of the saints and their relics resulted in architectural changes about the altar that made it increasingly necessary for him to stand between the altar and the congregation with his back to the congregation. This helped to widen the gap between clergy and layfolk.

Indeed, it is not inappropriate to speak of a general privatization and subjectivization of worship in the Middle Ages. With the people unable to understand the rite (except for the sermon), unable to join in the service except for a few ritual acclamations, an occasional vernacular hymn, and the recitation of fixed formulas of prayer (such as the Hail Mary and the Our Father) on command, and with the decline in the number of communions annually, it was almost inevitable that the devout would have recourse to paraliturgical devotions to occupy their attention while they were in church. Related to this was the de facto rejection of the institutional church by some of the most spiritually oriented persons in Europe, notably many of the mystics of the last three centuries before the sixteenth.

Finally, not least important for its erosive effect on the liturgical piety of the West and its sense of Christian community was the final general ratification by Leo X—in 1517—of a privilege that had been building up over several centuries. This privilege dispensed every Christian from the traditional obligation of attending the Sunday community Mass in his parish church and allowed him to perform his Sunday duty by attending any Mass at any time anywhere.

Religious Life

In the history of the Western church during the period under consideration, monasticism—understood in its broadest sense to include men and women, solitaries ("hermits") and cenobites (that is, those who live in communities)—possesses an importance that almost defies exaggeration. From the monastic ranks came a disproportionate number of the missionaries, the saints, the mystics, the ascetics, the teachers, the theologians, the prelates, the artists, the scholars, and the scienists of Western Christendom. From the same source the civil authorities drew some of their most competent administrators. Indeed, medieval civilization and medieval Christianity at their best are quite unthinkable without monasticism.

Gradually monastic self-understanding crystalized around the conviction that there are two kinds of Christians—the run-of-the-mill believers whose commitment and practice are minimal and marginal, and the genuinely committed elite seeking to achieve the Christian ideal to the fullest. The former, it was felt and taught, are bound only by the explicit precepts of the sacred Scriptures and of the church. The latter are obligated to implement in their lives every counsel of perfection in the gospel. The monastic ideal stressed continual reflection on the divine world in order to achieve, if possible, a mystical vision of God even in this life. It called for the giving up of possessions, of the practice of a "worldly" vocation, and of sexual relations. It demanded an austere lifestyle and an unremitting striving for moral perfection through the practice of humility, continence, and self-denial.

At Marseilles and at Lérins Blessed John Cassian (350?–435) and St. Caesarius of Arles (470?–542) mediated the Eastern monastic traditions of SS. Pachomius, Anthony of Egypt, and Basil the Great to the West without making substantial alterations. St. Patrick (389?–461?) carried the Lérins tradition of St. Caesarius to Ireland.

More typically Western was the monasticism of the north Italian ascetics like St. Eusebius of Vercelli (d. 371). They provided the basis for the North African monasticism of St. Augustine of Hippo and the pastoral-missionary monasticism of St. Martin of Tours (d. 399) that radiated from Marmoutier. In the fifth century St. Ninian (360?–462?) took the tradition of Marmoutier to Scotland. From the Candida Casa (White House) at Whithorn in Wigtownshire it spread to Ireland and absorbed the Lérins tradition planted there by St. Patrick. St. Columba (550?–615) in turn brought the Celtic tradition back to the continent and established it at Luxeuil (the Luxovium of the Romans) in Burgundy around 590.

The rule ascribed to St. Benedict of Nursia (480–543) marks a new direction. It displaced all the older rules in the West, so that from the eighth to the twelfth centuries the Benedictine ideal, with its concern for the tradition of worship, extensively informed monastic life in the West. "Canons regular" came into existence in the early ninth century as a clerical parallel and counterpart to monasticism. In reaction to the growing laxity of the Benedictines a number of reforms were undertaken in the tenth century. Best known is the monastery at Cluny, founded in 910. From it the famous Cluniac reforms emanated.

The eleventh century saw the formation of the Knights Hospitalers, the organization of the Canons Regular of St. Augustine, the establishment of the Camaldolese and Vallumbrosan orders, and the initiation of the Hirsau reform (1075). At the end of the century the Carthusians and the Cistercians came into existence. The last-named order owed much of its subsequent influence to its most famous son, the evangelical mystic and theologian St. Bernard of Clairvaux (1090–1153).

The creation of new orders continued at an impressive pace in the next two centuries. Among those founded in the twelfth century were the Order of Fontevrault, the Premonstratensians, the Order of Grandmont, the Gilbertines, and the Trinitarians.

The twelfth was also the century of the establishment of the great military orders, the Templars, the Nova Milicia—subsequently renamed the Order of Evora and the Order of Aviz—in Portugal, the orders of Alcantara, Calatrava, and Santiago di Compostela in Spain, and the Teutonic Knights.

The thirteenth century was noteworthy for the founding of the four great mendicant (or begging) orders—the Franciscan Order of Friars Minor, the Dominican Order of Preachers, the Carmelites, and the Hermits of St. Augustine. It also saw the establishment of the Humiliati, the short-lived Fratres Militiae Christi (Brothers of the Sword) and the Militia Christi de Prussia, as well as the Order of the Holy Cross, the Paulites (named after St. Paul of Thebes), the Mercedarians (the Order of Our Lady of Ransom), the Sylvestrines, the Servites (Servants of Mary), the tiny order of Crucifers of the Red Star, founded by Agnes of Bohemia, and the Celestines, and the rise of the Magdalenes (White Ladies) and the Beguines.

Official restrictions on the proliferation of new orders ultimately had their effect. Nevertheless, the fourteenth century witnessed the founding of the Order of Montesa, the Brigittines in Sweden, the Jesuates (Apostolic Clerks of St. Jerome), and the Hermits of St. Jerome, as well as two important reform movements among the Benedicts, the Olivetans and the austere and perpetually enclosed congregation of Valladolid.

During the fifteenth century the establishment of the Cassinese and Bursfeld congregations continued the tradition of Benedictine reform, while Windesheim forms a parallel thrust among the Canons Regular of St. Augustine. Among the independent foundations of the century the Minims, with their fourth vow of perpetual abstinence from eggs and dairy products as well as from meat and fish, represent the trend toward rigor.

The lofty spirituality of the *devotio moderna* ("modern piety"), with its emphasis on methodical mediation and the development of the inner life of its adherents, found expression in the Brethren of the Common Life. The members took no vows and continued in their ordinary vocations; their emphasis was upon the establishment of free schools that imparted quality education.

By the beginning of the sixteenth century the monastic communities of Europe, male and female, exhibited every degree of laxity and rigor and every degree of spirituality from profound devotion to cynical skepticism.

Possibly the most regrettable development was the widespread popular conviction that monastic life provided more than merely an opportunity to achieve greater holiness and that it was a state of perfection itself. This distortion found expression in the belief that taking the vows of a religious was in effect a new baptism, and that the religious life was a source of merit that could be applied on behalf of others, living and dead.

Missions

Christianity began in the West as an urban religion and only gradually established itself in the countryside.[4]

The New Testament provides the evidence that there were Christian communities in Rome and elsewhere in Italy during the lifetime of the apostles. Tradition has Spain evangelized in the first century. We know that the Christian communities of Lyons and Vienne in France underwent persecution in 177, and that the churches of North Africa were similarly persecuted in 202 and 203. About this time St. Irenaeus of Lyons attests the existence of Christians in the provinces of Upper and Lower Germany, and by 300 Christianity had secured a solid base in Roman England. Ireland was evangelized from England and Scotland from France in the fourth century.

From the reign of Emperor Constantine on, the Christian community spread rapidly throughout the western part of the empire. The invasion of the Arian Vandals from 429 resulted in the repression of Catholic Christianity in North Africa. After the reconquest of Africa and the reestablishment of Catholic orthodoxy, the Christianization of the Berbers began, only to be halted by the Muslim conquest.

In the sixth and seventh centuries missionaries from Ireland carried their evangelistic efforts to the territories of the German tribes. In the eighth and succeeding centuries English missionaries, among them SS. Willibrord and Boniface, also began to penetrate the pagan areas of Germany. The conversion of the Slavs of the Lower Danube in the ninth century was sufficiently a joint effort to cause both the Eastern and the Western churches to claim an interest in the territory.

In the ninth century St. Ansgar made his first missionary journey to Scandinavia, and Hamburg-Bremen was established as a missionary see. Missionaries from England ultimately played a decisive role in the propagation of the gospel in Denmark, which became a Christian state under St. Canute (d. 1035); in Norway, which became nominally Christian under St. Olaf Haraldsson (d. 1030); and in Sweden, where Christianity became dominant in the early twelfth century. Norse colonies in Iceland were evangelized from Norway in the late 10th century. Under Leif Ericson Christianity penetrated Greenland; but there is no evidence of an effective Christian presence in North America prior to the fifteenth-century voyages of discovery.

Hungary, Bohemia, and Poland became Christian, chiefly as the result of evangelization from the West, between 950 and 1050. Except for the Lithuanians (who were forced to accept Christianity in 1386) and the Finns (the Christianization of whom continued into the sixteenth century), Western and Central Europe had been converted by 1350.

The Franciscans and the Dominicans began to penetrate North Africa, the Muslim Near East, and the Mongol Empire (including China, India, Central Asia, and Iran) from the fourteenth century on, but with only limited and transient success in the conversion of non-Christians.

Canon Law

Every institution with permanent existence requires some kind of codified rules in the interest of just administration. This is true not only of secular societies, but also of church organizations. This is part of the origin of canon law. Other factors also played a role. Thus, for instance, when Christians before the peace of the church were unable to turn to the imperial Roman courts to settle their differences, they argued their cases before religious authorities. Again, in the era of the Barbarian invasions, Christian bishops often had to assume judicial functions. In the troubled ninth and tenth centuries, clerics were often the only persons with enough prestige and learning to enable the judicial system to function. The scope of canon law was at an early date broadly enough conceived to include ethics and liturgical practices as well as ecclesiastical jurisprudence in the strict sense.

Compilations of conciliar canons appeared as far back as the fourth century. Many—even among the early collections—exhibited a tendency on the part of the legists of the bishop of Rome to edit the texts in the interest of the supremacy of the Roman see and its incumbent. This tendency reached its peak in the very competent forgeries of the ninth century.

Notable for their extent and influence among the collections out of the early period are those of Dionysius Exiguus (flourished around 550), a Scythian monk who lived in Rome, and the Hispana Collection (fifth/sixth century) of the canons and decretals of the Roman bishops.

The encyclopedic interests and the practical experience that St. Isidore of Seville (560?–636) gained as the president of a series of Spanish councils make his name important in the history of canon law.

Under Charlemagne the science of canon law made great progress in the direction of standardization.

A pastoral concern characterized the collection of Regino of Prüm (d. 915), *De synodalibus causis* ("On synodical matters") and the *Decree* of Burchard of Worms (965–1025).

Canonists played an important role in the reform movements of the eleventh century—among them Cardinal Humbert of Sylva Candida, St. Gregory VII, Anselm the Younger of Lucca (d. 1086), Cardinal Deusdedit (d. 1097?), and St. Yves (Ivo) of Chartres (1040?–1116). Irnerius of

Bologna (1055?–1139?) tried to revive the *corpus juris civilis* (the body of civil law) in the twelfth century and gave law its charter of independence from theology as a separate discipline.

From the eleventh century onward the scope of canon law gradually widened to include all "clerics" (except bigamists, forgers, and inveterate heretics), widows, orphans, students, crusaders, and pilgrims; all cases where the church's interest was involved, such as tithes, benefices, and wills; "religious" crimes like sacrilege, blasphemy, and witchcraft; and all matters pertaining to vows, ecclesiastical discipline, and sacraments.

The *Concordantia discordantium canonum* ("Harmony of diverging canons") (1152), sometimes simply called the *Decree* (*Decretum*), of the Camaldolese monk Gratian, teacher of canon law at Bologna in the latter half of the twelfth century, is a watershed document. Its author is variously looked on as the last theological canonist and as the first juridical canonist. This gigantic harmonistic effort proposed to parallel the revived concern of the secular legists of Bologna for Roman law[5] with an equally comprehensive reconstruction of the law of the church. Although a private effort, Gratian's *Decree* recommended itself to the next five centuries as an indispensable resource. During the first 200 years after its publication it precipitated an impressive array of glosses and summas. The last distinguished name in this phase is John Andreae (1272–1348).

The canonists that followed Andreae have their monument in what in 1580 became officially known as the *Corpus juris canonici* ("Body of canon law"). It combined into a single document Gratian's *Decree*; the five books supplementary of the *Liber extra* ("The book beyond"), compiled by St. Raymond of Peñaforte (1185?–1275) in 1234; *Liber sextus* ("Sixth book"); which carried the collection down to 1298; the Clementine Constitutions (1317); the Extravagants (that is, the canons that were "wandering around outside" the previous collections) of John XXII (compiled in 1325); and the Common Extravagants, drawn from the legislation of various popes from 1281 to 1484.

The virtues of canon law were many. Canon law was generally prompter, more liberal, more humane, and—granting its assumptions— more equitable than civil law. It limited the horrors of war and the abuse of power by parents over children and by husbands over wives. It guaranteed the rights of widows and orphans and of the weak generally. By establishing the privilege of asylum it made the judicial process not quite so implacable.

The vices of canon law have been variously catalogued. It operated coercively, and in this way helped to make of the church less the community of charity than it ought ideally to have been. It is of course true that law by its nature tends to be coercive, but the resurrection of Roman ideals of jurisprudence in canon law unduly emphasized this characteristic, as abstract principles tended to become more important than the human beings who were the subjects of the legislation. More serious was the thrust of canon law to put the decrees of the bishops of Rome on a par with—and on occasion even over—what seemed to be the divine requirements and precepts in certain cases. No less serious was its tendentious (and to that extent unjust) character; it was the law of the popes and of the bishops, devised and administered in such a way as to aggrandize the church and to give the officials of the church an advantage over their often helplessly frustrated secular contemporaries.

It was not therefore accidental that at a famous demonstration sponsored on December 10, 1520, by faculty members and students of the university at the site just outside Wittenberg in Saxony where the clothing of those infected with pestilence was ordinarily burned, the two books that were most deliberately consigned to the flames were the *Corpus juris canonici* and the casuistic *Summa* of Angelo de Chiavasso.

Advocates of Reform

It is not always easy to differentiate dissidents from advocates of reform. Dissenters harassed the Church of the West from the beginning. Some perished in the course of time—among them the Montanists, the Novatianists, the Donatists, the Manichaeans, the Catharists, the Albigenses, and others.

With the gradual breaking up of the West after the thirteenth century, a number of advocates of reform arose who made contributions that persisted into the era of reconstruction that followed.

One was Marsilius of Padua (1275?–1342).[6] His *Defensor pacis* ("Defender of the peace") (1324), probably written jointly with John Jandun (d. 1328), taught that the church is subject to the state, which derives its authority from the people. The church has no jurisdiction, temporal or spiritual, and it may own no property. Its hierarchy is of purely human institution. St. Peter never received the primacy. The principal authority in the church is a general council, which should be composed of priests and laymen.

The Dominican John of Paris (d. 1304) denied that the pope had a right to define dogmas and insisted that the pope could be deposed for cause.

The canonist Conrad of Gelnhausen (1320?–1390), one of the earliest proponents of conciliarism, urged that the circumstances of the great Western schism justified the convocation of a general council even without the pope. He frankly granted that his arguments reflected the necessity of dealing with an emergency situation by extraordinary means. He appeals to the concept of reasonable forbearance (*epieikeia*), urging that necessity transcends positive law. The papacy, he stresses, exists for the sake of the church, not vice versa, and the good of the whole is more important than the good of a part. His documentation of the ideas that he had drawn from Marsilius of Padua and from William of Occam was liberally levied on by d'Ailly, Gerson, Henry Heimbuche of Langenstein (1324–1397), and Theodoric (Dietrich) of Nieheim (Niem) (1340–1418).

Henry of Langenstein held a general council to be infallible, but insisted that it represented the whole church and not merely the pope and the hierarchy. To elect delegates to a general council, he proposed that national councils be convoked.

Theodoric of Nieheim differentiated between the universal church, with Christ as its head, and the Roman Church, "whose head is believed to be the pope," which is only a part of the universal church. The Roman Church may go astray, it may suffer schism and heresy, and it may even fail. A general council is superior to the pope; the pope himself is obliged to obey a general council; a general council can elect, deprive, and depose the pope; from its judgment there is no appeal.

John Ruch[e]rat of Wesel (1400?–1481) rejected indulgences, original sin, transubstantiation, compulsory fasting, and extreme unction, and held that the sacred Scriptures are the final authority for faith.

Wessel Gansfort (1420?–1489) was a nominalist theologian and a proponent of the "modern piety" (devotio moderna). He was quite critical about papal and conciliar claims to infallibility; and he voiced frank doubts about the scope of the church's jurisdiction, about indulgences, and about purgatory.

In addition, there were individual reformers like the persuasive preacher of repentance Jerome Savonarola (1452–1498), excommunicated and finally executed in Florence for his attacks on the Roman Curia and the person of Alexander VI.

Other dissenters gathered about them—even though that was not their intention—self-perpetuating blocks of followers.

Thus the Waldensians, excommunicated by the Council of Verona in 1184, looked back on Peter Waldo (d. 1217) of Lyons as their founder.

The Lollards, their doctrines propagated by the Poor Preachers, were a powerful dissident force in England during the first half of the fifteenth century. They took their inspiration from John Wyclif (1329?–1384). Their stress was on personal faith, on the sole authority of the sacred Scriptures and the right of every Christian to read them for himself, and on divine election. They held that the validity of a cleric's ministry depended on his personal moral character, and they rejected clerical celibacy, transubstantiation, indulgences, pilgrimages, the pope, the hierarchy, and ecclesiastical endowments. Wyclif, a strong opponent of Scotist and Occamist nominalism, had argued for many of these positions, and the Poor Preachers had popularized them. On the principle that lordship depended on grace, Wyclif had called for the confiscation of ecclesiastical property. He attacked the veneration of the saints, identified the papacy with the Antichrist of the last days, denounced the morals of the monks, and criticized the nonresident clergy who regarded their benefices merely as sources of income.

Wyclif exerted considerable influence not only in his native England but also in Bohemia, where his views were introduced largely as a result of the marriage in 1298 of Anne of Bohemia to Richard II of England. Wyclif's teachings provided powerful corroboration to the parallel views that the leaders of the native Bohemian reform movement of the fourteenth century had been asserting.

The leadership of the Bohemian reform rovement devolved on John Hus (1369?–1415). His criticism of the morals of the clergy opened the way for a continuing attack on his theology as a whole that finally led to his execution and that of Jerome of Prague (1370?–1416) at the Council of Constance.

The Bohemian reform movement survived their deaths and eventuated in the establishment of a separate communion, the Unity of the Brethren— sometimes called Calixtines (from the Latin *calix*, "chalice") and Utraquists from their demand that the Holy Communion be administered under the species of the wine as well as under the species of bread (*sub utraque specie*). The Unity maintained its distinctive character until its all but total destruction in 1620.

The disintegration of Western Europe and the rise of Renaissance humanism created a climate of vigorous dissent. By the early sixteenth century the demands for reform of the Western church in doctrine and morals, "in head and members," had become widespread, involving such disparate proponents as Desiderius Erasmus (1466?–1536), John Colet (1466?–1519), John Major (1470–1550), Gaspar Contarini (1483–1542), and Reginald Pole (1500–1588).

NOTES

1. From the Spanish *mozarabe,* usually derived from the Arabic *musta'rib* ("a would-be Arab").

2. Probably so called because after inviting the people to pray in silence for the needs they most keenly felt the celebrant would "collect" these individual intercessions in a brief general petition through which the whole congregation made the prayers of each worshiper its own.

3. Various names were used to reflect different aspects of this service, among them Mass (from the Latin *missa,* "dismissal"), Eucharist, the Lord's Supper, the Holy Communion, and the Holy Sacrifice.

4. Hence the name "pagan" (that is, someone from a *pagus,* a village or country district) to describe persons not yet converted to Christianity.

5. From Bologna the study of Roman law spread rapidly. England and France were among the first to be penetrated, but Roman law met with considerable resistance in both countries. The reason for this was that the Roman law was at bottom imperial law and the kings of Europe regarded it as potentially more dangerous to their status than customary law. But by the beginning of the fourteenth cenutry they had discovered that they needed only to replace "emperor" with "king" in Roman law to make it a very efficient adjunct of royal despotism.

6. Some of Marsilius's critics insist that he was not an impartial and objective scholar but a venal propagandist ready to put his pen in the service of the highest bidder. In 1326, when his part in the production of the *Defensor pacis* became public knowledge, he fled to the court of the newly excommunicated Emperor Louis of Bavaria. In 1327 John XXII condemned five propositions of the *Defensor pacis*

and excommunicated Marsilius. From 1327 to 1329 Marsilius was in Rome with Louis as the latter's imperial vicar. After Louis's policy failed, Marsilius returned to Munich, where he remained at the imperial court until his death.

BIBLIOGRAPHY

Bouyer, Louis. *Eucharist: Theology and Spirituality of the Eucharistic Prayer.* Trans. Charles Underhill Quinn. Notre Dame, Ind.: University of Notre Dame Press, 1968.

Eisenhofer, Ludwig, and Lechner, Joseph. *The Liturgy of the Roman Rite.* Trans. A. J. and E. F. Peeler, ed. H. E. Winstone. New York: Herder and Herder, 1961.

Jungmann, Josef Andreas. *The Early Liturgy: To the Time of Gregory the Great.* Trans. Francis A. Brunner. Notre Dame, Ind.: University of Notre Dame Press, 1959.

Knox, Ronald A. *Enthusiasm: A Chapter in the History of Religion—With Special Reference to the XVII and XVIII Centuries.* New York: Oxford University Press, 1961. Chaps. 5 and 6 (pp. 71-116).

Oakley, Francis. *Council Over Pope? Towards a Provisional Ecclesiology.* New York: Herder and Herder, 1969. Chaps. 1-4 (pp. 33-131).

Oberman, Heiko. "From Occam to Luther," in Roger Aubert, ed., *Historical Investigations. Concilium: Theology in the Age of Renewal* 17 (New York: Paulist Press, 1966): 122-132.

Parker, G. H. W. *The Morning Star: Wycliffe and the Dawn of the Reformation.* Grand Rapids, Mich.: Wm. B. Eerdmans Publishing Company, 1965.

Runciman, Steven. *The Medieval Manichee: A Study of the Christian Dualist Heresy.* New York: The Viking Press, 1961.

Roguet, A. M. *Holy Mass: Approaches to the Mystery.* Collegeville, Minn.: The Liturgical Press, 1975.

Russell, Jeffrey Burton. *Dissent and Reform in the Early Middle Ages.* Berkeley, Calif.: University of California Press, 1965.

Sigmund, Paul E. *Nicholas of Cusa and Medieval Political Thought.* Cambridge, Mass.: Harvard University Press, 1963. Chap. 4 (pp. 67-118).

Spinka, Matthew, ed. *Advocates of Reform from Wyclif to Erasmus.* Philadelphia: The Westminster Press, 1953. Representative works of John Wyclif, some of the major conciliarists (Henry of Langenstein, John Gerson, Theodoric [Dietrich] of Niem, John Major), John Hus, and Desiderius Erasmus.

———. *John Hus' Concept of the Church.* Princeton, N.J.: Princeton University Press, 1966.

Stacey, John. *John Wyclif and Reform.* Philadelphia: The Westminster Press, 1964.

Strauss, Gerald, ed. and trans. *Manifestations of Discontent in Germany on the Eve of the Reformation.* Bloomington: Indiana University Press, 1971. Documents of protest out of the century that followed the influential (and anonymous) *The Reformation of [Emperor] Sigismund* (around 1437).

Waley, Daniel. *Later Medieval Europe: From St. Louis to Luther.* London: Longmans, Green and Co., 1964.

Weinstein, Donald. *Savonarola and Florence: Prophecy and Patriotism in the Renaissance.* Princeton, N.J.: Princeton University Press, 1970.

PART IV

THE ROMAN CATHOLIC CHURCH

10. From the Council of Trent to Vatican II

The Council of Trent

Modern Roman Catholicism[1] can in a sense be said to have been born at the Council of Trent (1545–1547; 1551–1552; 1562–1563).

By the mid-1530s the failure of the initial efforts of the Roman see to contain the Reformation had become apparent. More, rather than fewer, princes, magnates, and cities were reforming their churches according to the conservative principles of the Saxon reformers or the more radical principles of the Swiss reformers. At this point the Roman see determined to use a general council in order to try to bring the lost provinces back to the papal obedience. Appearing to accede to the demands of both the emperor and the reformers, Paul III (1468–1549) in 1536 convoked a general council to meet at Mantua in the spring of 1537. During the next three years he postponed the actual opening date four times for a variety of reasons (chiefly political), changed the meeting-site from Mantua to Vicenza, and finally suspended the proposed council altogether.

In 1542 he fixed All Saints' Day (November 1) of that year as the new date and Trent as the place, but very few bishops accepted his invitation. Political considerations dictated another suspension. A handful of bishops finally came together at Trent in May 1545. But it was not until December 13 that the three papal legates formally opened the council in the presence of a mere thirty-one officially accredited voting members beside themselves. The council determined to engage simultaneously in the task of doctrinal definition and of practical reform.

Work on this program began in earnest in April 1546. The first phase continued until September 1547.

The first subject of discussion was the sacred Scriptures and tradition. The equal validity and the supreme doctrinal authority of both was affirmed. The church, the council determined, has the sole right to interpret sacred Scripture. The canon that the Council of Florence had prescribed—including the so-called Old Testament apocrypha—was reasserted. The Latin translation of St. Jerome—the Vulgate—was declared to be the authentic and authoritative version of the sacred Scriptures.

Original sin, understood as the native alienation from God that marks all human beings, was the next subject to receive consideration. All of Adam's posterity have incurred it, the council affirmed, and only baptism in fact or in desire can take original sin away. The council condemned the doctrine that concupiscence—the desire to do something wrong—is itself sin. It also left open the question if the Blessed Virgin Mary had been conceived without original sin.

The third subject was justification, understood not as the forgiveness of sins but as the entire process of sanctification and renewal of the Christian. The council Fathers seemed determined to take a position opposite to that which they believed that the reformers were taking. Thus while the council's doctrine laid great stress on divine grace, the council condemned the proposition—along with thirty-two others—that a human being is justified by faith alone, since, the council insisted, he must freely accept and cooperate with the grace that justifies him.

The fourth subject to be taken up was the doctrine of the sacraments. The number was fixed at seven—"no more and no less." Christ instituted all seven, said the council; they are necessary to salvation; and they are effective by the performance of the rite (*ex opere operato*).

Baptism and confirmation were next taken up in detail.

At this juncture (March 1547) Paul transferred the council to Bologna, partly because the plague had descended upon Trent and partly to escape the political pressure that Charles V was exerting on the bishops subject to him. Charles countered by forbidding his bishops to leave Trent; thereby he effectively paralyzed the prelates who met in Bologna.

On September 13 Paul suspended the council indefinitely. In November 1549 he died.

Julius III (1487–1555), one of the cardinal-legates during the first phase of the council, called the council together again in 1551, with only fifteen voting members present. One reason for the poor attendance was the refusal of Henry II of France to send bishops.

By October the number of voting members had climbed to fifty-two. The council took up the sacrament of the altar. It affirmed the real presence of Christ in the sacrament and the doctrine of transubstantiation.

Then it took up penance and extreme unction.

In January 1552 a number of Lutheran participants began to arrive. Of the Lutheran princes represented, only the somewhat ambivalent Elector Joachim II of Brandenburg was ready to accept the decisions that the council had previously reached. The representatives of the elector of Saxony, of the duke of Württemberg, and of the now Lutheran imperial free city of Strasbourg demanded the reopening of the discussion of the previously published decrees, the release of the council Fathers from their oath of loyalty to the pope, and the subordination of the pope to the council. Julius forbade the council to discuss any of these demads. The defeat of Charles V at the hands of Elector Maurice of Saxony and his Lutheran allies alarmed the pope's supporters and he suspended the council again in April 1552.

Julius died in 1555. His successors were Marcellus II (1501–1555), who reigned for only twenty-two days, and Paul IV (1476–1559), who had no stomach for reconvoking the council.

Paul's successor, Pius IV (1499–1565)—who actually approved Communion under both kinds for the Holy Roman Empire and who was ready to authorize a married clergy—summoned the council to reassemble in April 1561, but so few bishops responded that he had to delay the formal opening until January 1562.[2] This time there were 113 voting members; for the first time the French hierarchy was well represented, but the bishops of the Holy Roman Empire and the Lutherans were conspicuous by their absence. The Society of Jesus exerted a great deal of influence during this session.

With the prelates arrayed against the pope on issue after issue, the council almost broke up. A plan for reform prepared by Ferdinand II and strongly urged by Charles of Lorraine (1525–1574) went down to defeat. Finally, in mid-1562, the discussion of the Eucharist was once more taken up after a ten-year lapse. Communion under one kind was decreed, the sacrifice of the Mass affirmed, and the prayers and ceremonies of the liturgy and private Masses regulated.

Once more the quarrels of the participants threatened to destroy the council. But by July 1563 the number of voting participants finally achieved the relatively respectable number of 235. The council addressed itself to the sacrament of order, then to the sacrament of marriage, and finally, in a two-day session in December 1563, to purgatory, the veneration of images, and the efficacy and value of indulgences.

In the course of the twenty-five sessions the practical reforming activities of the council had included the prescription of censorship over religious books, the establishment of theological seminaries and the suppression of ignorant and unauthorized preaching. The council insisted that bishops must reside in their dioceses, priests in their parishes, and religious in their houses. It discountenanced the holding of more than one benefice by clerics; it regulated the procedure of the episcopal courts; and it settled various issues of clerical discipline.

Early in 1564 Pius approved the council's decrees, appointed a commission of cardinals to interpret them, published the first edition of the index of prohibited books, and drafted the Tridentine profession of faith.

The great intrinsic importance of Trent was heightened by the way in which popes like St. Pius (1504–1572), Gregory XIII (1502–1585), and Sixtus V (1521–1590) made the causes of the council their own concerns.

The doctrinal decrees and canons of Trent bear the hallmarks of their authors—largely Iberian and Italian theologians and prelates schooled in the scholasticism of the late Middle Ages. To a noteworthy extent, Trent is the canonization of the late medieval scholastic position on most issues.

But this is not the whole story.

Non-Roman-Catholics have tended to read the Tridentine canons and decrees through the eyes of relatively unfriendly commentators. The most distinguished of these was the brilliant Lutheran theologian Martin Chemnitz (1522–1586). His immensely influential *Weighing of the Council of Trent* (*Examen Concilii Tridentini*) drew heavily on the interpretation that the Portuguese theologian James Payva de Andrada (1528–1576?), himself a participant at Trent, gave to the council's canons and decrees. *The Weighing of the Council of Trent* has been reissued in the Latin original and in various vernaculars from century to century down to the twentieth.[3]

Helping to inform the non-Roman-Catholic view of Trent was the instructive but prejudiced *History of the Council of Trent* (*Istoria del Concilio Tridentino*) of the Servite procurator-general Paul Sarpi (1552–1623), writing under the pseudonym Peter Soave Polan. It likewise enjoyed a very great circulation through the years in the original and in translations.

Within the Roman Catholic Church, the official "school theology" has until quite recently tended to interpret Trent in terms of the rigorist views of the Counter-Reformation.

Really to understand Trent, however, calls for an appreciation of the historical situation. The defenders of the authority of the Roman see sensed that the tide was running against them; indeed, things tended to grow worse for the Roman Catholic Church, at least superficially, for almost a decade after Trent.

Under these circumstances the supporters of the apostolic see were concerned about achieving maximum agreement within their own ranks. They had no hesitancy about attacking the positions of the reformers as they understood them. But they had great reluctance to start any new controversies among those that were loyal to the Roman see. For that reason the final texts of Trent often represent a consensus based upon careful compromises in formulation, made with the deliberate intent of enlisting maximum support for the final product. In many instances it has remained for contemporary scholarship, both Roman Catholic and non-Roman-Catholic, to discover these nuances and to appreciate the very considerable latitude of interpretation that the fathers of Trent deliberately put into these texts in order themselves to be able to subscribe them with good conscience.[4]

The Counter-Reformation

The reaction of the Roman see to the Reformation that since the mid-nineteenth century has widely received the designation Counter-reformation[5] was actually under way by the time of the Council of Trent.

In one sense the founding in 1524 of the Theatines (officially the Clerks Regular of the Divine Providence) was a step in the direction of needed reform of the parish clergy.[6] The chief organizers were St. Thomas de Vio (1480–1547), called Gaetano (in Latin, Cajetanus) and John-Peter Caraffa (1476–1559), the bishop of Chieti (the ancient T[h]eate) and later Pope Paul IV. Both of them were members of the Oratory of Divine Love in Rome.

Parallel monastic foundations were the Capuchins, founded as an offshoot of the Franciscans by Matteo di Bassi (d. 1552), with a rule that goes back to 1529, and the Clerks Regular of St. Paul (Barnabites), founded in 1530 by Anthony Mary Zaccaria (d. 1539).

Even before Paul III convoked the Council of Trent, he deliberately raised proponents of reform to the cardinalate—among them Caraffa, Gaspar Contarini, James Sadoleto, and Reginald Pole—and in 1536 he put them on a commission whose report was an unsparing affirmation of the need for immediate reform of intolerable abuses.

In the meantime Ignatius of Loyola (1491?–1556) had founded the Society of Jesus, destined to become probably the single most effective instrument of the Counter-Reformation.

The bull *Licet initio* of Paul III in 1542 established the papal inquisition and gave it authority, expanded by Pius IV and St. Pius V, to supervise the whole church.

The Counter-Reformation moved forward on a tide of authentic sanctity and devotion, exemplified by such individuals as St. Charles Borromeo (1538–1584), St. Philip Neri (1515–1595), St. Francis of Sales (1567–1622), St. Theresa of Ávila (1515–1582), St. John of the Cross (1542–1591), and St. Vincent de Paul (1580?–1660).

By 1534 St. Francis Xavier (1506–1552) had established a Jesuit mission in Goa (now part of India) under the patronage of King John III of Portugal. From Goa Francis moved on to Malacca, Amboina, the Molucca Islands, Ceylon, and Japan; death overtook him on the way to China. Simultaneously Alphonse Salmeron (1515–1585), another early Jesuit, went to Ireland. The Jesuits came to Germany in 1542, to Poland in 1570, to England in 1580, to Switzerland in 1586, to Paraguay (where they established the "Jesuit Republic") in 1608/1609, and to Canada in 1611. The Jesuit missionary efforts were paralleled by the revived evangelistic outreach of the Dominicans, the Franciscans, and the Augustinians. In 1622 Gregory XV (1554–1623) created the Congregation for the Propagation of the Faith to supervise Roman Catholic missionary efforts.

From the time of the Counter-Reformation to the mid-twentieth century, Roman Catholic theology stressed the continuity that the Roman Catholic Church claimed to have with the apostolic church, as distinguished from other denominations, which were allowed much briefer spans of historical existence. In the teaching about the church, the emphasis fell on the total identification of the Roman Catholic Church with the one holy catholic and apostolic church of the Creed of the 150 Fathers (the Nicene Creed) and with the mystical body of Christ. Similar emphasis fell on the sacraments and sacramentals with a correspondingly minor emphasis on the word of God written and proclaimed, and on the authority of the Roman Catholic hierarchy in both teaching and morals. In analytical terms, the objective tended to receive greater emphasis than the subjective, the ontological tended to receive greater stress than the functional, and the organizational aspects of the Roman Catholic Church's life tended to receive greater stress than the "charismatic" aspects.

The Seventeenth and Eighteenth Centuries

The wave of expansion that marked the early years of the Reformation spent itself during the third quarter of the sixteenth century. In turn, the Roman see bent every effort and resource—political, educational, diplomatic, financial, and propagandistic—to reassert its authority over the territories that it had lost to the Reformation.

In this effort it was highly successful in many places. Political historians tend to think of the Counter-Reformation as coming to an end with the treaties of Münster and Osnabrück in 1648. But theologically the Counter-Reformation can be said to have continued into the mid-twentieth century and to have been brought to an end only by Vatican Council II.

By the mid-seventeenth century the ecclesiastical boundaries of the world had become relatively fixed. The Roman Catholic Church had solidly in its grasp Latin Europe and Latin America, France and French Canada, Ireland, the southeastern part of the Holy Roman Empire and a few principalities and imperial cities elsewhere (especially along the Rhine), parts of the Low Countries and Switzerland, that part of the upper Danube valley that was not under the domination of the Ottoman sultan in Istanbul, the islands of the western Mediterranean, Poland-Lithuania, and the Middle Eastern and Far Eastern colonies of the Roman Catholic powers in Europe.

The victory of the Roman see in France had come hard and involved the military destruction of the Huguenots and their flight from their homeland.

The ambivalence of the Roman Catholic Church of the sixteenth and seventeenth centuries toward natural science is exemplified by the skillful reform of the calendar by Gregory XIII in 1582, on the one hand. On the other hand, it comes out in the execution by burning of the Copernican astronomer Giordano Bruno (1548–1600) and in the trial of Galileo Galilei (1564–1642) in 1633 for "holding and teaching" the Copernican theory.[7]

In 1588 the Spanish Jesuit theologian Luis de Molina (1535–1600) triggered the Molinist controversy with his *Concordia liberi arbitrii cum gratiae donis* ("A Harmony of Free Will with the Gifts of Grace"). He and many of his fellow Jesuits, along with others who took the same stand, held that the ultimate basis for the efficacy of grace is not to be found in the divine gift itself but in the human cooperation with this gift that God has foreseen. This required the assumption that God has a unique conditioned (*conditionata*) knowledge of all possible future contingents. The more conservative theologians, like Dominic Bañez (1528–1604) and other Dominican Thomists, condemned Molina. The pope appointed a special congregation in Rome to decide the escalating controversy. The congregation worked for almost a decade (1598–1607). It allayed, but did not settle, the controversy and Molinism continued to be an influential system in Roman Catholic theology.

The first half of the seventeenth century was marked by the beginnings of what became known as Jansenism, after Cornelius Otto Jansen (Jansenius) (1585–1638), bishop of Ypres. Jansen had written a book entitled *Augustinus seu doctrina S. Augustini de humanae naturae sanitate, aegritudine, medicina adversus Pelagianos et Massilienses* ("Augustine, or the Teaching of St. Augustine on the Health, Sickness, [and] Remedy of Human Nature, against Pelagians and Followers of John Cassian").[8] It was published in 1640, two years after Jansen's death. In 1649 the Sorbonne condemned as heretical five propositions that it professed to have extracted from the work and in 1653 Innocent X (1574–1655) added his own anathema in the bull *Cum occasione*. The rejected propositions in effect taught that fallen human beings cannot without a special grace from God keep his commandments. They further taught that God's saving will and the redemptive value of Christ's death are limited to those whom God arbitrarily predestined to salvation and that grace is irresistible. The papal anathema evoked a flood of controversial literature. The controversy continued through most of the eighteenth century. On the Jansenist side in the course of the controversy were John-Ambrose Duvergier de Hauranne (d. 1643), abbot of Saint-Cyran; the Cistercian nun Angelica Arnauld (d. 1661), abbess of Port-Royal; Blaise Pascal (1623–1662); Anthony Arnauld (d. 1694); Pasquier Quesnel (1634–1719), whose doctrines Clement XI (1649–1721) condemned in 1708 in the bull *Unigenitus*; the founders of the Old Catholic Church of Utrecht (1724); and the Tuscan Synod of Pistoia in 1786.[9] The opponents of Jansenism were for the most part the Jesuits, who would naturally be prejudiced against Jansenism by their advocacy of de Molina's views on free will, by their strong commitment to papal authority, and by their tolerant "probabilism"[10] that was the opposite of the rigorism in morals that marked the Jansenists.[11]

Another seventeenth-century religious movement that agitated the Roman Catholic Church was Quietism, linked particularly with the name of Miguel de Molinos (1640?–1697). His *Guida spirituale* ("Spiritual Guide"), published at Rome in 1675, was his most famous work, but it is his letters that most fully set forth his doctrine that the state of perfection is to be found in perpetual union with God and a total transformation into him. External observances (like almsgiving and going to confession), ascetic disciplines, and even resistance of temptation are at best superfluous, at worst hindrances. He urged a form of mental prayer in which the soul avoids any distinct act, even that of loving Christ or adoring the Trinity, and rests in pure faith in the presence of God. Rising from devotion first to the church, then to Jesus, and finally to God alone, the soul in his system achieves the state of perfection when the will of the human being is totally annihilated. From this point on, the human being can no longer commit sin, because everything that he does or thinks is the work of God in him, even though the devil may coerce him into actions that in others would be sin.[12] Less extreme in their advocacy of Quietism were Jeanne Marie Bouvier de la Mothe Guyon (Madame Guyon) (1648–1717) and, for a time, François de Salignac de la Mothe Fénelon (1651–1715), the archbishop of Cambrai, In 1687 Innocent XI[13] (1611–1689) condemned Quietism in the bull *Coelestis pastor*.

Before the end of the seventeenth century Gallicanism arose to disturb the Roman Catholic Church. It began with the "Four Principles" of James Benignus Bossuet (1627–1704), bishop of Meaux. These asserted the administrative freedom of the French Roman Catholic Church from the authority of the Roman see. In the form of Febronianism[14] and Josephinism (from Joseph II, Holy Roman emperor from 1765 on) the doctrines of Gallicanism spread into Germany[15] and Austria, and found echoes in Spain, Naples, and Tuscany.[16] In the eighteenth century Jansenists generally made common cause with the Gallicans and their allies. The suppression of the Society of Jesus by Clement XIV in 1763 was in part the result of the Roman see's efforts to moderate the tide of nationalism within the Roman Catholic Church by removing from the scene one of the major targets of the proponents of total decentralization.

The Nineteenth Century

The irreversible changes brought on by the French Revolution and the Napoleonic wars terminated much of this intramural quarreling. The Treaty of Tolentino in 1797 marked the beginning of the partition of the States of the Church among Italy's secular rulers; the process ended in 1809 with the annexation of what was left to the French Empire and the incarceration of the captured Pius VII (1740–1823) at Fontainebleau.

A new era began in 1814. The Society of Jesus, the Inquisition, and the Congregation of the Index (responsible for the censorship of religious books) were reestablished. With the reestablishment of the Society of Jesus the way was paved for the revival of Ultramontanism,[17] which reached its climax half a century later with the publication of the *Syllabus of Errors* in 1864 and the definition of papal supremacy and primacy at Vatican Council I in 1870.

A decade before the publication of the *Syllabus of Errors* another significant theological event took place, the dogmatic definition of the immaculate conception of the Blessed Virgin Mary.

Since 1708 Roman Catholics had been required to observe the Feast of the Immaculate Conception as a holy day of obligation.[18] In 1854 the bull *Ineffabilis Deus* of Pius IX (1792–1878) required them to believe as a divinely revealed article of faith the mystery that they had been celebrating at the altar, namely, that "by a unique grace and privilege of Almighty God and in view of the merits of Jesus Christ, the Blessed Virgin Mary was kept free from every stain of original sin from the first moment of her conception." In a sense at least, the definition is as significant a clue to the Roman Catholic theological climate of the middle nineteenth century as the publication of the *Syllabus of Errors*.[19]

The *Syllabus of Errors* rehearsed eighty previously condemned theses and positions. In four chapters it denounced pantheism, naturalism, and absolute rationalism; moderate rationalism; indifferentism and latitudinarianism; and socialism, communism, secret societies, Bible societies,[20] and liberal-clerical societies. Five further chapters denounced what Pius IX regarded as errors with reference to the rights of the Roman Catholic Church, the relation of civil society to the church, natural and Christian ethics, marriage, and the temporal power of the pope. The tenth and final chapter censured modern liberalism and ended with a condemnation of the thesis that "the Roman Pontiff can and ought to reconcile and accommodate himself to progress, liberalism, and modern civilization."

Six years later the decrees of Vatican Council I incorporated many of the teachings of the *Syllabus*. Pius IX announced the council, the first since Trent, in 1868. It was to consider a wide range of subjects—dogmas, discipline, canon law, religious orders, the Eastern churches, foreign missions, and the relations between civil powers and the Roman Catholic Church. It was clear that the council would involve a contest between an Ultramontane majority and a liberal minority. The latter included John Henry Cardinal Newman (1801–1890), John Joseph Ignatius von Döllinger (1799–1890), Bishop Felix Anthony Philibert Dupanloup (1802–1878) of Orléans, most of the German bishops, and many American and Austrian bishops.

Almost 700 bishops were present for the opening session in December 1869. The acceleration of the leisurely pace at which the council proceeded initially probably aided the majority. The constitution *Dei Filius*, promulgated in April 1870, began with an introduction that lamented the pantheism, materialism, and atheism of the period, and reaffirmed Roman Catholic teaching on God the creator of everything, on revelation, on faith, and on the relation between the spheres of faith and of reason.

In the meantime, the pope had announced that the council would take up the infallibility and primacy of the pope. After some debate the council decided to give these issues priority over the other subjects in the draft *schema* on the church. The debate on the question if a definition on these issues was opportune consumed over two weeks. In the question of the pope's primacy the minority without success took exception to the proposal to define the pope's jurisdiction as "ordinary, immediate, and truly episcopal." In the debate on papal infallibility the minority tried vainly to have some qualification introduced along the lines of the fifteenth-century formula which declared that the pope could not err when he "availed himself of the advice and sought the assistance of the universal church."

When the issue came to a vote, 451 bishops voted in favor of the definition as proposed, sixty-two voted for it with reservations, and eighty-eight voted against it. When the final vote was taken on the constitution *Pastor aeternus*, which solemnly promulgated the definition, many of the minority had left Rome to escape the embarrassment of casting negative votes and others simply refused to vote. The document was approved 533 to 2—one of the negative votes being cast by the bishop of Little Rock, Arkansas.

Pastor aeternus asserts that Christ himself conferred the primacy on Peter "as the chief of all apostles and the visible head of the entire church militant." This primacy, the document says, is perpetuated in the bishops of Rome and is ordinary, truly episcopal, and immediate. Finally, *Pastor aeternus* declares that it is a divinely revealed dogma "when the Roman pontiff speaks *ex cathedra* [literally, "from his chair," hence, "officially"], that is, when he carries out the office of the pastor and teacher of all Christians in accord with his supreme apostolic authority and explains a doctrine of faith or morals to be held by the universal church, through the divine assistance promised him in blessed Peter, he operates with that infallibility with which the divine Redeemer willed that his church be instructed in defining doctrine in the area of faith and morals, and so such definitions of the Roman pontiff are unalterable, not as a result of the agreement of the church but from his own self (*ex sese*)."

On July 19, the day after the constitution was promulgated, France and Prussia went to war. The French troops evacuated Rome, the Italians marched in, and the council came to an abrupt stop. The Roman Catholic Church accepted the definitions of the council generally, if unenthusiastically; serious opposition emerged only in Germany and Austria. Von Döllinger was excommunicated; others withdrew and organized the Old Catholic Church, which united with the Church of Utrecht.

The papal states were absorbed into the new Italy, and in the moment of its theological triumph Ultramontanism became an ideological rather than a territorial reality.[21]

During the nineteenth century, the continuing influence of David Hume (1711–1776), Immanuel Kant (1724–1804), Arthur Schopenhauer (1788–1860), August Comte Louis (1798–1857), Andrew Feuerbach (1804–1872), Charles Darwin (1809–1882), Joseph Ernest Renan (1823–1892), Frederick William Nietzsche (1844–1900), and others in the intellectual arena helped to erode the foundations of the faith for some Roman Catholics. Nevertheless, on the political side the Roman Catholic Church was able to record some victories.

One such advance took place in England in 1829 when the Test Act of 1673 was abolished. This had the net effect of opening political offices under the British crown to Roman Catholics. The Roman see also successfully negotiated concordats with Bavaria, Spain, and Austria. But on balance the politically negative forces of this period were more powerful—the increasing alienation of the urban proletariat from the church, the growth of revolutionary sentiment in Europe that climaxed in the publication of the Communist Manifesto in 1847 and the revolutions of 1848, the *Kulturkampf* ("culture conflict") that the German imperial government under Prince von Bismarck waged chiefly against the Roman Catholic Church between 1872/1873 and 1886, and the *Los-von-Rom* ("Away from Rome") movements in Austria and other countries that began just before the turn of the twentieth century.

On the other hand, Leo XIII's epochal encyclical of 1891 on the condition of the laboring class, *Rerum novarum*, exhibited a creative capacity for taking the initiative in the new situation that the industrial revolution had created. The conservatives promptly denounced it as a revolutionary subversion of the established order. But it has come to be regarded—in spite of some attitudes that now seem archaic—as one of the most influential religious pronouncements on social justice to come out of the nineteenth century.

Two further significant developments in Roman Catholic theology during the nineteenth century were the theological revival that is usually connected most prominently with the Roman Catholic faculty at the University of Tübingen and with the name of Johann Adam Möhler.[22] Möhler's *Symbolik, oder Darstellung der dogmatischen Gegensätze der Katholiken und Protestanten nach ihren öffentlichen Bekenntnisschriften* ("Symbolics, or, an Exposition of the Dogmatic Antitheses of Roman Catholics and Protestants on the Basis of Their Public Confessional Writings") first came out in 1832. It was unabashedly polemical, but it was also a serious and honest effort to outline objectively the theological differences between Roman Catholics and non-Roman-Catholics. It gave evidence that a new understanding of the church was arising in Roman Catholicism. Although the full impact began to become apparent only a century and a quarter later, perceptive readers sensed the difference and many conservative Roman Catholics took offense at the work.

The other noteworthy development was the revival of neoscholasticism that began during the last third of the century. Thomism—the philosophy and theology of St. Thomas Aquinas—in particular received new eminence through the bull of Leo XIII *Aeterni Patris* (1870), which directed the study of Thomism in all Roman Catholic theological seminaries. The next year Leo proclaimed St. Thomas the patron of all Roman Catholic universities.[23]

Into the Twenieth Century

The twentieth century began with the Vatican and the Spanish government embroiled in controversy over the application of the Law of Associations to the mushrooming religious orders and societies in Spain. In France anticlericalism culminated in the separation of the state from the Roman Catholic Church in 1905. In 1911 Portugal disestablished the Roman Catholic Church. Religious strife occupied the first two decades of the century in Ireland; it came to an indecisive and uneasy end in 1921 with the separate establishment of the state of Eire (90 percent Roman Catholic) and Northern Ireland (preponderantly non-Roman-Catholic).

In 1917, under Benedict XV (1854–1922), the thirteen-year process of codification of Roman Catholic law for Latin Rite[24] Roman Catholics came to an end with the publication of the *Codex juris canonici*.

The period between the two world wars was punctuated by the papal condemnation of the *Action française* movement in France in 1926 on the ground that it made religion a tool of politics and by the concordats that the Roman see negotiated with the fascist government of Italy in 1929,[25] with the national socialists in Germany (1933),[26] and with Antonio de Oliveira Salazar's corporative state of Portugal (1940).

World War II brought the Roman Catholic Church into new collisions with communism in Eastern Europe. In the Union of Soviet Socialist Republics the Oriental rites of the Roman Catholic Church were suppressed. Members of these rites had the option of becoming Latin Rite Roman Catholics or Eastern Orthodox. In Romania and Bulgaria Oriental Rite Roman Catholics were compelled to join the Eastern Orthodox community. Relations between the Vatican and the other countries of Eastern Europe were frequently tense, and in Hungary, Yugoslavia, Czechoslovakia, and Poland, Roman Catholic leaders were imprisoned on a variety of charges.

In France the priest-worker movement was discontinued in the 1950s, to be resumed on a limited basis under the control of the French hierarchy in 1965. In Italy the size of the communist minority made for certain tensions and frictions within the population of this Roman Catholic nation. A new concordat with Spain, negotiated in 1953, gave the pope slightly greater influence in the choice of bishops; the Spanish government justified the continuing restrictions imposed on the non-Roman-Catholic minority in the exercise of their religion, in spite of the constitutional guarantee of freedom of worship, on the ground of public order. The international Roman Catholic secular institute[27] called Opus Dei (the Work of God) became an increasingly important influence in Spanish public life from the 1950s on and claimed many governmental officials as members. Simultaneously an increasing number of priests quite untraditionally associated themselves with dissident elements in the Spanish (and Portuguese) national cultures.

Latin America, where the priest-faithful ratio is roughly 1 to 5,000 and where barely one out of eight nominal Roman Catholics practices his religion,[28] continued to depend on the Iberian peninsula for over 10 percent of its priests and religious. Coordinated North American efforts to provide extensive personnel support to the Roman Catholic Church in Latin America began to get under way only in the 1960s. Especially since the second Latin American Episcopal Conference at Medellin, Colombia, in 1968, an increasing number of bishops, priests, and religious in Latin America have openly taken up the cause of the disfranchised and exploited segments of the population, sometimes to the great embarrassment of their politically more conservative co-religionists.[29]

In the developing countries, notably of Africa and Asia, stress in the twentieth century has been increasingly laid upon the Roman Catholic Church's supranationality to minimize the taint of association with Western political power structures; upon the development of an indigenous clergy and, especially after World War II, of an indigenous episcopate; and upon adaptation to traditional local cultures, especially in music, ceremonial, liturgy, and catechetical instruction.

The first instance when a pope formally availed himself of the privilege of infallible utterance took place eighty years after the definition of papal infallibility. In 1950, in the bull *Munificentissimus Deus*, Pius XII (1876–1958) defined as a divinely revealed dogma a tradition that went back to the fifth/sixth century, "namely that the Virgin Mary, the immaculate Mother of God, when the course of her life was finished, was taken up, body and soul, into heaven."[30] In so doing, he observed, he was confirming "the unanimous doctrine of the ordinary teaching office of the church and the unanimous belief of Christian people." His action responded to an almost unanimously affirmed conviction of the worldwide Roman Catholic episcopate, whom the pope had polled in 1946, that such a definition was both possible and desirable. At the same time he left open the question whether or not the Blessed Virgin Mary had undergone physical death, something that Marian maximalists in the Roman Catholic Church have energetically denied.[31]

Vatican Council II

The definition of the bodily assumption of the Blessed Virgin Mary into heaven confirmed the widespread conviction of many persons inside and outside the Roman Catholic Church that the promulgation of the dogma of the infallibility of the pope in 1870 had made any further general councils of the Roman Catholic Church unnecessary. During the pontificate of Piux XI, the proposal was made that a council be convened to deal with the modernist issue, but nothing came of it. It remained for John XXIII (1881–1963), addressing seventeen cardinals in the Church of St. Paul Outside the

Walls in Rome in 1959, to announce his decision to convene a diocesan synod for the church in Rome and a general council for the entire Roman Catholic Church. In his mind the council was to be a "new Pentecost" that would provide an occasion for renewal and updating (*aggiornamento*) as well as for inviting the separated Christians of East and West to join in a new search for the unity of believers.

He solicited the worldwide episcopate, the Roman congregations, and the Roman Catholic universities to suggest items to go on the agenda. In 1960 he appointed ten commissions, corresponding to the parallel Roman curial congregations, and two special secretariats (for mass media and for the promotion of the unity of Christians[32]) to prepare the drafts (*schemata*) that the council Fathers were to consider.

The first session (1962) was attended by over 2,500 of the more than 2,900 prelates and religious superiors who were entitled to a seat. Thereafter the normal attendance ranged between 2,000 and 2,200, rising again to just under 2,400 at the last voting session. Some of the absences resulted from the reluctance of communist governments to allow bishops from their countries to attend the council. A novel feature was the presence of from thirty-five to ninety-three observers invited by the Secretariat for the Promotion of the Unity of Christians or delegated by their respective denominations at the pope's invitation. A number of Roman Catholic religious and laypeople, both men and women, and a few priests, attended as official auditors. The bishops had a staff of experts (*periti*) who counseled their patrons on matters of canon law and theology.

The first session opened on the Feast of the Maternity of the Blessed Virgin Mary (October 11) 1962. Early in the session the council rose up in arms against the highly conventional, traditional, and conservative (on occasion reactionary) schemata that the commissions had drafted. These drafts were committed for reconsideration to new commissions, of which the council selected sixteen members, the pope nine. The council attacked the mountain of work before it in somewhat leisurely fashion and by the end of the first session on the Feast of the Immaculate Conception of the Blessed Virgin Mary (December 8) it had failed to complete action on any of the five documents that it had taken up.

The universally lamented death of John XXIII on June 3, 1963, between the first and the second session, automatically suspended the council, but the new pope, Paul VI (b. 1897), promised to continue the conclave. The second session, begun on Michaelmas (September 29) 1963, completed work on the vitally important constitution on the liturgy (*Sacrosanctum concilium*) and a somewhat blander decree on the instruments of social communication (*Inter mirifica*).[33]

It was hoped that the third session, begun on the Feast of the Exaltation of the Holy Cross (September 14) 1964, would be the last. To accelerate action, the commissions had recast some of their drafts in the form of basic propositions to which, it was hoped, the council Fathers would readily agree. Instead, the bishops continued to debate the new drafts with vigor and at length and recommitted them to the commissions for further elaboration. The council majority, by a vote of over 3 to 1, referred a draft on marriage to the pope for decision. By the end of the session on the Feast of the Presentation of the Blessed Virgin Mary (November 21), three more documents were ready for promulgation—the epochal dogmatic constitution on the church (*Lumen gentium*), the hardly less important decree on ecumenism (*Unitatis redintegratio*), and the decree on the "Eastern churches," that is, the Eastern rites of the Roman Catholic Church (*Orientalium ecclesiarum*).

The day after the opening of the fourth session on Holy Cross Day (September 14) 1965, Paul on his own initiative (*motu proprio*) announced the creation of an "apostolic synod" of bishops that would meet from time to time after the council. The bishops of the Roman Catholic Church would select at least 85 percent of the synod's members. At the discretion of the pope, who would convoke the synod and provide it with its agenda, this synod of bishops could have not merely consultative, but also deliberative powers.

The session produced eleven additional documents, a noncommittal dogmatic constitution on divine revelation (*Dei verbum*), which left open the question of the relation of sacred Scripture and tradition, a long and optimistic pastoral constitution on the Roman Catholic Church in the modern world (*Gaudium et spes*),[34] a decree on the pastoral office of the bishops in the Roman Catholic Church (*Christus Dominus*), a decree on priestly formation (*Optatam totius*), a decree on the proper renewal of the religious life (*Perfectae caritatis*), a decree on the apostolate of the laity (*Apostolicam actuositatem*), a decree on the ministry and life of priests (*Presbyterorum ordinis*), a decree on the Roman Catholic Church's missionary activity (*Ad gentes*), a declaration on Christian education (*Gravissimum educationis*), a controversial declaration of the relationship of the Roman Catholic Church to non-Christian religions (*Nostra aetate*), and a long-awaited and epoch-making declaration on religious freedom (*Dignitatis humanae*).[35] The council closed solemnly on the Feast of the Immaculate Conception of the Blessed Virgin Mary (December 8) 1965.[36]

The council defined no new dogmas, but the accumulated impact of the theological development of the century and a quarter that preceded it is extensively evident. At the same time, the tension between the more liberal "pastoral" element among council Fathers and the more conservative traditionalists is also apparent.[37] The documents exhibit throughout a palpable desire not to alienate either party. As a result, the documents admit both a "liberal" and a "conservative" interpretation. Both thrusts have revealed themselves in the way in which subsequent theological developments have sought to justify themselves on the basis of the council documents. During the first decade after the council the "liberal" thrust appears to have been slightly more potent. Yet the conservative element in the Roman Catholic Church has not been idle. It will probably take several decades and a number of pontificates before a final balancing of the council's theological account can take place.

Developments since Vatican Council II

In 1966 the pope reformed the procedures of the Holy Office and changed its name to the Congregation for the Doctrine of the Faith. He hoped thereby to remove the image of inquisitorial proceedings from doctrinal discipline.[38] He also made minor concessions to non-Roman-Catholics entering marriages with Roman Catholics, and received the titular head of the Anglican communion, the archbishop of Canterbury, with the kiss of peace in Rome.

The Dutch hierarchy's new catechism, which departed radically from traditional models, came in for widespread criticism in 1967. During the same year the pope set up a Council of the Laity and a Commission for Studies on Justice and Peace (in the tradition of his predecessor's memorable 1963 encyclical *Pacem in terris*) and gave them both a charter in an urgent and unusually concrete encyclical *Populorum progressio*. Notable ecumenical contacts included the reception of the Armenian catholicos of Cilicia-Kis, Khoren I, and an exchange of visits with the ecumenical patriarch. Approximately 200 prelates gathered for the first synod of bishops. Although the pope accorded the assembly no deliberative authority, the participants on their own initiative provided him with extensive recommendations on doctrine, the reform of canon law, worship, mixed marriages, and training for the priesthood.[39] For areas that had an acute shortage of priests the pope authorized restoration of the permanent diaconate and provided that some of the incumbents of the office might be married.

The long-awaited papal decision on birth control—a subject which the pope had withdrawn from consideration at Vatican II—came in the summer of 1968. The encyclical *Humanae vitae* repeated the prohibition of artificial contraceptives. Except for conservatives within the church and churchpeople in developing countries which regard programs of contraception as inspired by Western colonialism, the document was received with consternation.

For the first time Roman Catholics participated as full members of the Commission on Faith and Order at the 1968 Uppsala meeting of the World Council of Churches. Just before the Uppsala meeting the pope issued a new *Credo* in which he strongly emphasized the traditional Roman Catholic positions with reference to clerical celibacy, papal infallibility, and the Marian dogmas. Continuing the tradition of worldwide travel that has already taken him to the Holy Land, India, and the United States (to address the United Nations General Assembly in 1965), Paul VI flew to Bogotá, Colombia, in 1968.

Papal pronouncements during 1969 reflected the tensions within the

Roman Catholic Church, which had increased to the point where the pope himself suggested that a schism might be in the offing. The problems facing the church were underlined by an international conclave of theologians in Brussels; its members declared that the freedom which Vatican II secured for theologians and theology must not be allowed to be lost.[40] Partly in apparent response to this assembly, the pope implemented a proposal of the 1967 synod and established an international theological commission. Its initial membership included a broad spectrum of theological opinion, but it soon became clear that its scope and its ultimate effectiveness would depend altogether on the papal pleasure. Through a papal *motu proprio* the Roman Catholic liturgical calendar underwent extensive changes, including a reduction in the number of saints commemorated. Paul VI convened an extraordinary synod of bishops at Rome to discuss episcopal collegiality with the pope; the schema initially proposed for discussion evoked strong protests because it seemed to many of the bishops to make of them less fraternal co-workers of the pope than his assistants. The schema was withdrawn and a less intransigent draft replaced it. Subsequent debate indicated the need for additional theological reflection on the limits of primacy and collegiality. The publication of *Co-responsibility in the Church* by the cardinal-archbishop of Brussels-Malines, Leon Joseph Suenens, one of the "pastoral" party's leaders at Vatican II, became the focus of much of the discontent in the church.

The pope's visits to Australia and to the Republic of the Philippines in 1970 were seen as symbols of the growing independence of national Roman Catholic churches. A variety of events underlined the growing restiveness and polarization within the Roman Catholic Church in Latin America. Disaffection with many of the structures of the church were widely and increasingly voiced, notably by dissident priests. A significant ecumenical step was the trip of Paul VI to Geneva, Switzerland, where his address to the International Labour Organisation provided him with an opportunity to visit the headquarters of the World Council of Churches. He described the council as "a marvelous movement of Christians, 'of children of God scattered abroad.' " But he reminded the council's staff: "Our name is Peter. Scripture tells us which means Christ has willed to attribute to this name, what duties he lays upon us, the responsibilities of the apostle [that is, St. Peter] and his successors."[41] In Holland the Dutch Pastoral Council voted for the abolition of compulsory celibacy for priests.[42]

The publication of the procedure that the Congregation for the Doctrine of the Faith was to follow, five years in the making, was published early in 1971. It met a critical reception. While it reemphasized the need for giving the accused author an opportunity to be heard on his own behalf and for providing him with a defense counsel, it failed to incorporate many of the proposals that a committee of thirty-eight theologians had made in 1968 in connection with their review of the Roman Catholic procedures for censuring theological views.

A Roman commission had been working for a number of years on successive drafts of a basic charter (*lex fundamentalis*) for the Roman Catholic Church. It was to serve as the basis for the forthcoming revision of the church's canon law. The final draft was to be discussed at the 1971 synod of bishops in Rome. When confidential copies of the draft became public, a storm of protest rose. The basic criticism was that the document expressed neither the spirit nor the documents of Vatican II and that adoption of the charter would cancel out much of the progress that the Roman Catholic had made since the council. As a result the document was withdrawn for further study.

The apostolic letter *Octogesima adveniens* commemorated the eightieth anniversary of *Rerum novarum*. Written in the spirit of Paul's encyclical of 1967, *Populorum progressio*, it received wide approbation for its absence of theological apparatus, its intelligibility, and the high degree of contemporary social awareness that it revealed in its discussion or urbanization, the status of young people and women, the problems of labor and poverty, discrimination, the right to emigrate, communications media, and the environment.

The international episcopal synod of 1971 addressed itself to only two issues, the ministerial priesthood and social justice in the world. It responded to the call of Paul VI at the opening session to resist pressures to alter traditional Roman Catholic convictions and practices. The synod recommended no changes in the requirement that Western Rite Roman Catholic priests be celibates or in the official attitude toward artificial means of birth control.

NOTES

1. "Catholic" as a predicate of the church goes back to St. Ignatius of Antioch (35?–107?) (*To the Smyrnaeans,* 8). Since the era of the Enlightenment, "Catholic" has has come to be a very common popular designation in European vernaculars, including English, for that part of Christendom that accepts the authority of the Roman see. At the same time, many denominations besides the Roman Cathoilc Church profess to be Catholic. Furthermore, the terms "Roman" and "Roman Catholic" have the sanction of long and official usage, even in the Roman Catholic Church, although some Roman Catholics profess to be offended by a failure to refer to them simply as "Catholics." This volume uses the term "Roman Catholic" as a denominational and confessional designation and the term "Catholic" to describe the traditional faith and practice of historic Christianity generally.

2. In 1562 James Laynez (1512–1565), second general of the Society of Jesus, wrote to Huguenot Prince Louis Condé de Bourbon and urged him to discuss with King Philip II of Spain and Holy Roman Emperor Ferdinand the new situation resulting from the papal convocation of the council. Laynez felt that "the heads of the new churches in France and Germany should go to the council, so that, besides helping with their experience of reform, they might discuss their controversial teachings, and the Holy Spirit, author of true peace and union (just as in other councils he was present in the midst of those gathered in his name and brought about harmony in great controversial matters regarding the faith),

might be hoped to be present in this council and harmonize the differences that exist." He proposed the fifteenth century Council of Ferrara-Florence as a model of procedure. "There what was treated was concluded without a formal vote. Some were deputed on one side and others on the other to study in common passages of Holy Scripture and the Fathers. . . . Let those of the new churches be assured that they will be very well treated and cherished before and after reunion, which [may] God allow us to see." See C. J. McNaspy, "An Ecumenical 'If,'" *America*, (1971): 655-656.

3. The most recent English version is a translation of part I by Fred Kramer under the title *Examination of the Council of Trent* (St. Louis: Concordia Publishing House, 1971). See also Arthur Carl Piepkorn, "Martin Chemnitz' Views on Trent: The Genesis and the Genius of the *Examen Concilii Tridentini*," *Concordia Theological Monthly* 37 (1966): 5-37.

4. See Giuseppe Alberigo, "The Council of Trent: New Views on the Occasion of Its Fourth Centenary," in *Historical Problems of Church Renewal (Concilium: Theology in the Age of Renewal,* vol. 7) (Glen Rock, New Jersey: Paulist Press, 1965), pp. 69-87, and Robert E. McNally, *Reform of the Church: Crisis and Criticism in Historical Perspective* (New York: Herder and Herder, 1963), chap. 6.

5. The term owes its currency to Leopold von Ranke (1795–1886), who described the period of Roman Catholic reaction to the Reformation as the "era of the Counter-Reformation." The first to use the term to describe the program of bringing individual territories back to the Roman obedience seems to have been John Stephen Pütter (1725–1807) of Göttingen. Some Roman Catholic historians prefer to use the term "the Catholic Reformation" for the period. They deny that the reforming activities of the era were a response to the challenge that the Reformation represented. Instead, they see them as a continuation of the efforts at reform that marked the entire Middle Ages and that were renewed in the sixteenth century in Italy during the pontificate of Leo X.

6. Two years earlier, in his instructions to Francis Chieregati (1478–1539), the legate that he sent to the diet of the Holy Roman Empire at Nuremberg in 1522, Adrian VI (1459–1523) eloquently conceded the need for comprehensive reforms in the church.

7. Under threat of torture Galileo recanted and was sentenced to life imprisonment. Paul V (1552–1621) commuted this sentence to house arrest. In 1965 Paul VI by implication repudiated the censures of the Roman Catholic Church against Galileo when at Pisa the pope formally hailed Galileo—along with Dante and Michelangelo Buonarroti—as "great spirits [of] immortal memory."

8. Blessed John Cassian, also known as John of Marseilles, was a leading exponent of what came to be called Semipelagianism.

9. See Mario Rosa, "Italian Jansenism and the Synod of Pistoia," in Roger Aubert, ed., *Historical Investigations (Concilium: Theology in the Age of Renewal,* vol. 17) (New York: Paulist Press, 1966).

10. Probabilism is the system of moral theology which holds that when there is doubt about the permissibility of an action one may take a clearly probable course that favors liberty even though the opposite view that favors the law may be more probable.

11. In connection with Jansenism, see Henri de Lubac, *Augustinianism and Modern Theology*, trans. from the French by Lancelot Sheppard (New York: Herder and Herder, 1969).

12. The teaching of de Molinos influenced some German Pietists like August Herman Francke (1663–1727) and Godfrey Arnold (1666–1714), both of whom defended it.

13. Innocent XI was the inveterate opponent of the French king Louis XIV, who had prevented Innocent's election to the papacy in 1669 but was unable to do so in 1676. The pope opposed Gallicanism; he disapproved of the revocation of the Edict of Nantes by Louis in 1685 (even though it reportedly had resulted in 400,000 "conversions" to Roman Catholicism in two months); and he opposed the measures which the English king James II took to restore Roman Catholicism in England, especially his

Declaration of Indulgence of 1687, which (after the pattern of the short-lived Declaration of Indulgence for Tender Consciences of Charles II in 1672) proclaimed full liberty of worship for all, including both Roman Catholics and Nonconformists. For his opposition to Louis XIV, Innocent is regarded by some Roman Catholics as the "patron saint of religious freedom." The opponents of Jansenism regarded Innocent as having shown too much favor to the Jansenists; they blocked the process of his beatification, which Clement XI (1649–1721) initiated. It ground to a halt under Benedict XIV (1675–1758), and Innocent was not beatified until 1956, under Pius XII (1876–1958).

14. Justinus Febronius was the pseudonym under which John Nicholas von Hontheim (1701–1790), the suffragan bishop of Trier, in 1763 published his *De statu ecclesiae et legitima potestate Romani pontificis* ("On the State of the Church and the Lawful Authority of the Roman Pontiff").

15. An incident of the parallel development in Germany was the "Emser Punktation" ("Bad Ems Draft") at the Bad Ems Congress of 1786, which in effect called for creation of a German National Roman Catholic Church.

16. All of these movements can be seen as a revival of medieval "episcopalism." This view of church polity locates authority in the bishop locally and in a general council on a church-wide basis and accords to the pope only a primacy of honor.

17. Ultramontanism, from *ultra montes*, "beyond the mountains," that is, the Alps seen from north of Italy, describes the thrust in Roman Catholicism toward centralization of power and authority in the Curia ('Court') of the Roman see and a corresponding restriction of episcopal-diocesan and national freedom. The word goes back to the eleventh century, but it clearly acquired its technical meaning in the seventeenth with the rise of Gallicanism.

18. A day of obligation is one on which lay Roman Catholics must attend Mass and must abstain from "servile" work, that is, as generally interpreted, work in which the body plays a greater part than the mind.

19. The basic idea of the Syllabus has been traced to Leo XIII (1810–1903), the successor of Pius IX. As bishop of Perugia he had suggested such a comprehensive frontal attack on the heresies of the nineteenth century at the Council of Spoleto in 1849.

20. As early as 1816, Pius VII (1740–1823) in the letter *Magno et acerbo* voiced his "great and bitter sorrow" at learning of "a pernicious plan, by no means the first, whereby the most sacred books of the Bible are being spread everywhere in every vernacular tongue, with new interpretations which are contrary to the wholesome rules of the church." He cited the constitutions of Innocent III (1199), Pius IV (1564), Clement VIII (1595), and Benedict XIV (1753) on behalf of the precaution that "if Scripture should be easily open to all, it would perhaps become cheapened and be exposed to contempt" (trans. Roy J. Deferrari, [*Denzinger:*] *The Sources of Catholic Dogma* [St. Louis: B. Herder Book Company, 1957], pp. 399–400). The successor of Pius VII, Leo XII (1760–1829), in the encyclical *Ubi primum* warned against "a certain 'Society,' commonly called 'Biblical,'" which was "boldly spreading through the whole world" and "which, spurning the traditions of the holy fathers and against the well-known decree of the Council of Trent [1546], is aiming with all its strength and means toward this, to translate—or rather mistranslate—the sacred books into the vulgar tongue of every nation." He called on the bishops to "avert this plague" by taking zealous care "to remove [their] flock away from these poisonous pastures" (ibid., p. 401).

21. Geddes MacGregor, *The Vatican Revolution* (London: Macmillan and Company, 1958), is an objective account of Vatican I in its context by a Scottish Presbyterian historian.

22. See Herve Savon, *Johann Adam Möhler: The Father of Modern Theology*, trans. Charles McGrath (Glen Rock, N.J.: Paulist Press, 1966).

23. In 1923, on the sixth centenary of the canonization of St. Thomas, Pius XI in *Studiorum ducem* again asserted

the authority of St. Thomas as the teacher of the Roman Catholic Church.

24. "Latin Rite" or "Western Rite" Roman Catholics constitute the overwhelming majority of Roman Catholic Christians who until recently worshiped at services conducted chiefly in Latin. "Eastern Rite" or "Oriental Rite" Roman Catholics accept the authority of the bishop of Rome in the same way that their Western Rite co-religionists do, but they customarily worship in a variety of vernaculars and according to a number of rites deriving from Greek, Russian, Syrian, Coptic, Ethiopic, and other originals.

25. The concordat with Mussolini marked the formal recognition of the pope as temporal sovereign over the 108.7-acre state of Vatican City.

26. In 1937 a disillusioned Pius XI recorded the breaches of the agreement by the nazis in his encyclical *Mit brennender Sorge* ("With burning concern").

27. Secular institutes first received papal approval in 1947 in a series of directives (*Provida mater ecclesia, Primo feliciter,* and *Cum sanctissimus Dominus*). The term describes a society whose members profess the evangelical counsels (such as poverty, celibacy, and obedience) in order to gain Christian perfection and to achieve the full exercise of the apostolate. They do not take public vows, they need not and normally do not live in communities, and they wear no distinctive garb. They are thus different from orders and congregations, on the one hand, and from societies of common life, on the other.

28. The estimated number of non-Roman-Catholic Christians in Latin America increased from 123,000 in 1916 to 1,300,000 in 1937 and to 10 million before the end of the 1960s. The denominations involved range from Lutherans (largely of immigrant origin) and Methodists to Baptists and Pentecostals. Some of this growth reflects the inability of the Roman Catholic Church to provide adequate religious coverage.

29. Camilo Torres Restrepo (1929–1966), a Colombian Roman Catholic priest killed in a skirmish by government forces after becoming a revolutionary, is held in high veneration by many young Latin American Roman Catholics. In Brazil the archbishop of Recife, Helder Camara (b. 1908), is internationally the best known of a number of prelates who have deliberately identified themselves with the poor of their country. On Torres, see John Alvarez García and Christian Restrepo Calle, eds., *Camilo Torres: His Life and His Message,* trans. Virginia M. O'Grady (Springfield, Ill.: Templegate Publishers, 1968). On Camara, see José de Broucker, *Dom Helder Camara: The Violence of a Peacemaker,* trans. by Herma Briffault (Maryknoll, N.Y.: Orbis Books, 1970).

30. The feast had been in the calendar for centuries. In 1568 the lessons of the breviary of the feast which left the question open were replaced by lessons which advocated the bodily assumption of the Mother of God. In the mid-eighteenth century Benedict XIV had declared the bodily assumption of the Blessed Virgin Mary a probable opinion which it would be blasphemous and impious to deny. The first petitions that the dogma be defined had gone to the Roman see in 1849, and at Vatican I almost 200 bishops signed a similar petition.

31. The primitive church has commonly believed that the Blessed Virgin Mary had undergone physical death, but differed on whether she had died at Ephesus or at Jerusalem.

32. The Secretariat for the Promotion of the Unity of Christians was later raised to parity with the ten commissions.

33. This decree evoked the largest negative final vote, under 8 per cent, of any of the sixteen council documents.

34. The sixteen council documents totaled over 100,000 words. *Gaudium et spes,* with 23,335 words, was the longest. It was also the only one to be initiated in response to a demand from the council itself.

35. On the declaration on religious freedom, see Neophytos Edelby and Teodoro Jimenez-Urresti, eds., *Religious Freedom (Concilium: Theology in the Age of Renewal,* vol. 18) (New York: Paulist Press, 1966).

36. Other incidents of the fourth session included a ceremony in which Paul and the representative of the ecumeni-

cal patriarch "committed to oblivion" the mutual anathemas of 1054; the first visit of a reigning pope to North America, when Paul addressed the General Assembly of the United Nations; the announcement of the initiation of the reform of the Roman Curia and of the process that would hopefully lead to the elevation of Pius XII and John XXIII to the rank of "blessed"; and a "sacred celebration" for promoting Christian unity at St. Paul's Outside the Walls, where John had first announced the council, with the pope, the Fathers of the council, and the observers and delegated guests taking part.

37. The determination of Paul VI to assert his authority was repeatedly demonstrated at the council. Among the notable instances was his action in making nineteen changes in the decree on ecumenism after the council had voted on it chapter by chapter and had accepted it. Another was his proclamation of the Blessed Virgin Mary as "Mother of the Church," a title that the bishops had deliberately omitted from the chapter on the Blessed Virgin Mary in the constitution on the church. A third was his

decision to side with a minority of about 120 bishops and to overrule the wishes of the other 1,830 in postponing action on the declaration on religious liberty from the third to the fourth session, an action that was widely understood as a denial of the principle of collegiality.

38. Among the theologians that the reorganized congregation subsequently investigated were Hans Küng, Edward Schillebeeckx, John McKenzie, Herbert Haag, and Ivan Illich.

39. A good account of the assembly is Peter Hebblethwaite, *"Inside" the Synod, Rome, 1967* (New York: Paulist Press, 1968).

40. For digests of the congress papers and a discussion of the resolutions that it passed, see *The Catholic Mind*, vol. 68, no. 1248 (December 1970), pp. 1-51.

41. *Time*, June 20, 1969, p. 70.

42. A dramatice interview that Cardinal Suenens gave to the French newspaper *Le Monde* in this connection attracted world wide attention and precipitated the "Suenens affair." See José de Broucker, ed., *The Suenens Dossier: The Case for Collegiality* (Notre Dame, Ind.: Fides Publishers, 1970).

BIBLIOGRAPHY

THE COUNCIL OF TRENT

Jedin, Hubert. *Crisis and Closure of the Council of Trent: A Retrospective View from the Second Vatican Council.* Trans. by N. D. Smith. London: Sheed and Ward, 1967.

——. *A History of the Council of Trent.* Trans. Ernest Graf. St. Louis: B.

Herder and Company, 1957—. Two volumes have appeared to date.

Schroeder, H. J. *Canons and Decrees of the Council of Trent: Original Text with English Translation.* St. Louis: B. Herder Book Co., 1941. Still a standard resource.

THE COUNTER REFORMATION

Daniel-Rops, Henri, [pseudonym]. *The Catholic Reformation.* Trans. John Warrington. Garden City, N. Y.: Doubleday & Company, 1962. 2 vols.

Dawson, Christopher. *The Dividing of Christendom.* New York: Sheed and Ward, 1965. A Roman Catholic lay

historian's exposition of his conviction "that the main sources of Christian division and the chief obstacle to Christian unity have been and are cultural rather than theological" (p. 17).

De Guibert, Joseph. *The Jesuits: Their Spiritual Doctrine and Practice—A His-*

torical Study. Trans. William J. Young. Ed. George E. Ganss. Chicago: The Institute of Jesuit Sources and Loyola University Press, 1964.

Hollis, Christopher. *The Jesuits: A History.* New York: The Macmillan Company, 1968.

VATICAN COUNCIL II

Abbott, Walter M., and Gallagher, Joseph, eds. *The Documents of Vatican II.* New York: Guild Press, 1966. The handiest edition of the texts of Vatican II in English.

Barth, Karl. *Ad Limina Apostolorum: An Appraisal of Vatican II.* Trans. Keith R. Crim. Richmond, Va.: John Knox Press, 1968. An evaluation of the council by Europe's most influential non-Roman-Catholic theologian.

Baum, Gregory, and Campion, Donald R. *The Pastoral Constitution on the Church in the Modern World.* New York: Paulist Press, 1967. A commentary by two distinguished Roman Catholic theologians.

Bea, Augustin. *The Church and the Jewish People: A Commentary on the Second Vatican Council's Declaration on the Relation of the Church to Non-Christian Religions.* Trans. Philip Loretz. New York: Harper & Row, 1966.

Berkouwer, Gerrit C. *The Second Vatican Council and the New Catholicism.* Trans. Lewis B. Amedes. Grand Rapids, Mich.: W. B. Eerdmans Publishing Company, 1965. A well-known conservative Dutch Reformed theologian appraises the council.

Brown, Robert McAfee. *Observer in Rome: A Protestant Report on the Vatican Council.* Garden City, N. Y.: Doubleday & Company, 1964. The author is a member of the United Presbyterian Church in the United States of America.

Caird, George B. *Our Dialogue with Rome: The Second Vatican Council and After (The Congregational Lectures, 1966).* London: Oxford University Press, 1967.

Deretz, J., and Nocent, A., eds. *Dictionary of the Council.* Washington, D.C.: Corpus Books, 1968.

Flannery Austin, ed. *Vatican Council II: The Conciliar and Post Conciliar Documents.* Delaware: Scholarly Resources, Inc., 1976.

Gilbert, Arthur. *The Vatican Council and the Jews.* New York: The World Publishing Company, 1968. An analysis by an American Jewish leader.

Gremillion, Joseph, ed. *The Gospel of Peace and Justice: Catholic Social Teaching since Pope John.* New York: Orbis Books, 1976.

Lee, Anthony D., ed. *Vatican II: The Theological Dimension.* Washington, D.C.: The Thomist Press, 1963.

Lindbeck, George A. *The Future of Roman Catholic Theology: Vatican II—Catalyst for Change.* Philadelphia: Fortress Press, 1970.

———, ed. *Dialogue on the Way: Protestants Report from Rome on the Vatican Council.* Minneapolis, Minn.: Augsburg Publishing House, 1965. A review of the first three sessions.

MacEoin, Gary. *What Happened at Rome? The Council and Its Implications for the Modern World.* New York: Holt, Rinehart and Winston, 1966.

Miller, John H., ed. *Vatican II: An Interfaith Appraisal—International Theological Conference, University of Notre Dame, March 20–26, 1966.* Notre Dame, Ind.: University of Notre Dame Press, 1966. The Notre Dame conference was an important international assembly that brought together leading theologians who had played significant roles in the council as advisers and observers.

Murray, John Courtney, ed. *Religious Liberty: An End and a Beginning—The Declaration on Religious Freedom: An Ecumenical Discussion.* New York: The Macmillan Company, 1966.

Outler, Albert C. *Methodist Observer at Vatican II.* Westminister, Md.: The Newman Press, 1967.

Pawley, Bernard C., ed. *The Second Vatican Council: Studies by Eight Anglican Observers.* London: Oxford University Press, 1967.

Pierini, Francis. *Catechism of Vatican II.* Staten Island, N.Y.: Alba House, 1968.

Quanbeck, Warren A.; Kantzenbach, Friedrich Wilhelm; and Vatja, Vilmos; eds.

Challenge . . . and Response: A Protestant Perspective of the Vatican Council: Minneapolis, Minn.: Augsburg Publishing House, 1966.

Ratzinger, Joseph. *Theological Highlights of Vatican II*. New York: Paulist Press, 1966.

Tracy, Robert E. *American Bishop at the Vatican Council*. New York: McGraw-Hill Book Company, 1966.

Vorgrimler, Herbert, ed. *Commentary on the Documents of Vatican II*. New York: Herder and Herder, 1967–1969. An authoritative five-volume work by a panel of internationally known experts.

11. Movements within Roman Catholicism

Roman Catholic Modernism

The theological revival that had begun somewhat precariously in the Roman Catholic Church during the nineteenth century continued in the twentieth and ramified in a number of directions.

One development was Roman Catholic modernism. The movement arose more or less independently in several countries and without a common program. It was at least in part a reaction to the rigorous orthodoxy that the *Syllabus of Errors* and Vatican I represented.

In Italy the movement is associated with the names of the liberal poet-novelist Antonio Fogazzaro (1842–1911) the priest-leader of Democrazia Christiana (Christian Democracy), Romolo Murri (1870–1944), and the church-historian Ernesto Buonaiuti (1881–1946).

In France it was represented by the archbishop of Albi, Eudoxe Irenée Mignot (1842–1918), the biblical scholar Alfred Firmin Loisy (1857–1940), the Oratorian theologian Lucien Laberthonniere (1860–1932), the philosopher Maurice Blondel (1861–1941),[1] the biblical scholar Albert Houtin (1867–1926), and the mathematician-philosopher Edouard LeRoy (1870–1954).

In England the modernist movement was led by the ex-Anglo-Catholic Jesuit theologian and author George Tyrrell (1861–1909), excommunicated in 1907, and the lay theologian, mystic, and biblical scholar Friedrich Baron von Hügel (1852–1925), the Italian-born son of an Austrian diplomat and his Scots wife.[2]

When Leo XIII (1810–1903), ascended the papal throne, the liberals took hope from his positive attitude toward learning and from his intention, announced in his initial encyclical *Inscrutabili Deo consilio* (1878), to build bridges between the church and the modern world. But with the passage of time he became more and more unenthusiastic about the movement.

His successor, St. Pius X (1835–1914), was hostile to the modernists from the very beginning of his reign and in 1907 he approved the decree of the Holy Office *Lamentabili* which condemned sixty-five propositions that it attributed to the modernists in the areas of biblical interpretation, the inspiration and inerrancy of the sacred Scriptures, revelation and dogma, Christ, the sacraments, the structure of the church, and the immutability of religious truths. Later in the same year Pius published a systematic condemnation of modernism in the encyclical *Pascendi dominici gregis*. In 1910 he imposed upon all clergy engaged in pastoral and teaching activities the stringent "Antimodernist Oath" (*Sacrum antistitum*).

Until Vatican II (1962–1965), the repressive antimodernist measures of the Roman Catholic integralists hung like a dark shadow over Roman Catholic theological inquiry.[3]

The consequences of the modernist crisis for Roman Catholic theology were catastrophic. A kind of paralysis set in that immobilized all but the most courageous and venturesome theologians and scholars. Many of these were silenced by deprivation of the offices where they might have exercised influence;[4] their works were placed on the index of prohibited books,[5] or they were simply forbidden to publish.[6]

The Biblical Movement

A second theological movement of great significance was the biblical revival. Actually it operated at two levels. One was at the level of the people. The proponents of the biblical movement were concerned about implementing practically the role that the sacred Scriptures had always played theoretically in the life of the church. They encouraged the laypeople to have Bibles and New Testaments of their own in their homes and to use them for spiritual reading and for the enrichment and confirmation of their faith. Efforts were made to increase the people's awareness of the role of the sacred Scriptures in the worship of the church. Encouragement was given to holding nonliturgical services in which the Bible was explained. For all of this the production of fluent modern translations of the Bible into various vernaculars was a prerequisite and in due course these translations—some of them of very great merit—began to appear. It cannot be denied that to some extent this was a deliberate attempt by the leaders of the biblical movement to recover for the Roman Catholic Church some of the familiarity with the sacred Scriptures that they observed in the communities that had achieved autonomy in the sixteenth century.

The other level at which the biblical movement operated was the scholarly level. The encyclical of Leo XIII *Providentissimus Deus* in 1893 had sought to erect barriers to the invasion of the Roman Catholic Church by the "liberal school." But in many circles the awareness grew that there must be a tenable middle position between the integralist[7] position that ignored the human aspects of the sacred Scriptures and the radical position that saw the Bible merely as another book. The first step toward the recovery of this position was the establishment of the Biblical Commission in 1902 with a view to restraining intemperate higher criticism.[8] The second step was the creation of the Pontifical Biblical Institute in Rome, under direct and immediate papal jurisdiction, in 1909.[9] Over the years the two grew apart. The Biblical Commission's "responses" to controversial questions tended to be on the conservative side,[10] while the Biblical Institute was more open to the findings of biblical scholarship.

A milestone in the movement was the encyclical *Divino afflante Spiritu* in 1943. It redefined the status of the Vulgate, differentiated the literal and the spiritual sense of sacred Scripture, recognized the existence of literary genres in the Bible, and approved a responsible freedom for scientific investigation in biblical matters. In this encyclical Pius XII paralleled the incarnate word of God and the written word of God; heresy, he said, emerged both when the divine and human elements in either case were too radically separated and when they were too intimately confused.

The next generation saw a massive and determined entry into the field of biblical scholarship by Roman Catholic exegetes.[11]

The Liturgical Movement

Linked to the biblical movement at many points was the liturgical movement. In many ways it was a reaction against the freezing of liturgical forms in the period immediately after the Council of Trent.

Like the biblical movement it operated at both a popular and a scholarly level. At the popular level it involved such concerns (expressed at the highest level by St. Pius X himself) as the active participation of the people in the singing of the Gregorian chant (plain chant) and in the ritual worship activities of the church, first Holy Communion for children at the age of discretion (that is, about seven years), and frequent—ideally daily—reception of Holy Communion by the faithful. After World War I it increasingly addressed itself to the problem of the local vernacular in the liturgy in place of the Latin universally used in Latin Rite Roman Catholic churches.

As in the case of the biblical movement, the stimulation provided by sacramentally oriented non-Roman-Catholic denominations, such as the Lutherans in Europe and the Anglicans in English-speaking communities, was a significant factor.

The beginning of the "scholarly" liturgical movement has been variously dated. A considerable amount of research and publication in liturgics had taken place from the seventeenth century on, and thus had prepared the way for what came later.

One commonly identified starting point for the twentieth-century liturgical movement is the first Liturgical Week that was held at the Benedictine Abbey of Maria Laach in Germany in 1914.[12] Under the initial leadership of Ildefons Herwegen (1874–1946), Odo Casel (1886–1948), Cambert Beauduin (1873–1960) Pius Parsch (1884–1954), and others, the movement spread at a somewhat uneven pace throughout the church during the period between the two world wars.

In the United States it was sedulously fostered by the Benedictines of St. John's Abbey at Collegeville, Minnesota, in particular. Their periodical *Orate Fratres* (later *Worship*) became the organ of the movement in North America.

In the process of spreading, the liturgical movement evoked considerable opposition. The conservatives objected to it in part because they resented what they regarded as unsettling changes in the inherited worship habits of the faithful. In part, however, they also saw in the liturgical movement a revival of "heresies" that had been urged by the sixteenth-century reformers, by the later eighteenth-century Jansenists (like Jube d'Asnieres), by theologians of the Roman Catholic enlightenment like John Michael Sailer (1751–1832), and by the recently condemned modernists.

In connection with its attempt to renew the interior spiritual life of the priests and the people through an intelligent participation in the mysteries of the church, the liturgical movement provided a stimulus to deeper theological knowledge overall, to an appreciation of long-obscured dimensions in the person and work of Christ, and a maturing doctrine of the church.

The leaders of the movement combined patient research and exact scholarship with a profound pastoral sense. The movement's impact upon the art and architecture of the Roman Catholic Church was of major proportions. As a consequence it prepared the ground for the liturgical reforms of Vatican II in much the same way that the biblical movement had prepared the ground for a new awareness of the significance of the sacred Scriptures.[13]

Changing Roman Catholic Attitudes toward the Ecumenical Movement

A fourth phenomenon was the changing relation of the Roman Catholic Church to the ecumenical movement.

Initially the official Roman Catholic reaction to the organized ecumenical movement was thoroughly hostile. This is understandable. A major and perduring root of the ecumenical movement as far back as the sixteenth century lay in the efforts particularly of the Reformed churches to create through a union, or at least a federation, of denominations a political-theological counterweight to Roman Catholicism. Coupled with this was a tendency in the same circles to depreciate Eastern Orthodoxy as a theologically stagnant relic of the past, to characterize nineteenth-century Anglicanism—especially its Anglo-Catholic form—as a compromise with "popery," and to regard the Lutheran community as suffering chronically from a case of arrested reformation. It was not until 1920 that the organized ecumenical movement had finally transcended these attitudes and had become, at least at the official level, as genuinely ecumenical in its intention as the word "ecumenical" intended to imply. This development was in considerable part the result of the insistence of the Scandinavian Lutheran and Anglican hierarchies on this point.

The official early twentieth-century Roman Catholic attitude toward the ecumenical movement found expression in the thoroughly critical and condemnatory encyclical of 1928 *Mortalium animos*.

At the same time the seeds of the maturer doctrine of the church that Möhler and others had planted in the nineteenth century did not remain without fruit. Individual Roman Catholics participated, often without, but sometimes with, official approval, in interdenominational efforts. Even the official language of papal documents from time to time showed signs of a less negative attitude toward Christians of other communities.

Into the 1950s the thaw seemed hardly perceptible, but once more the patience, the scholarly theological reflection, and the prayers of ecumenically interested Roman Catholics—lay and clerical—paved the way for the breakthroughs that came at Vatican Council II and afterward.[14]

The Lay Movement

A fifth development was the lay movement. The eighteenth and nineteenth centuries were eras of growing secularism and anticlericalism. In this situation the Roman Catholic Church in Europe recognized that its lay members had special competence in defending the church and its privileges against the revolutionary, free-thinking, and absolutist trends, and in helping to solve the pressing social questions that confronted the church. Some of the lay movemnts organized under the aegis of the church sought frankly political ends. All of them functioned under rigid ecclesiastical and hierarchical control.

Around the beginning of the twentieth century Roman Catholic leaders came increasingly to recognize the independence of the temporal realm. As a result two trends became identifiable in Roman Catholic lay movements.

One group of Roman Catholic lay movements and organizations embodied a thrust in the secular and temporal direction; it found expression in political and socioeconomic activities. The other thrust embraced more spiritual and more strictly ecclesiastical concerns. At first both thrusts were lumped together under the designation Catholic Action. Gradually, and especially between 1915[15] and Vatican II, Catholic Action came to be applied more and more to the movements and associations of the second type.

During this period certain insights gradually emerged and received formal sanction at Vatican II. One is that the laity have a special role in the church's task of evangelizing and sanctifying human beings and in the development of the kind of conscience that enables laymen to live responsible Christian lives and to apply Christian principles in their daily activities. Another insight is that laypeople must enjoy the confidence and trust of the church's leadership as they make their specifically lay contribution to the church's life. The older view, which defined laypeople as an extension of the bishops in such a way that they became the collaborators, the instruments, and the execctive arms of the hierarchy, became outmoded. The church's leadership came to realize that while the laypeople act under the ultimate guidance of the members of the hierarchy, who have final responsibility in the church, the laypeople are themselves responsible in part for the mission of the whole church. This lay mission is different from the mission of the hierarchy; if it were not, the laity would not be able to make a specifically lay contribution to the church. In this sense, Catholic Action has come to be described as "the official participation of the laity in the apostolate of the church."[16]

NOTES

1. See Maurice Blondel, *The Letter on Apologetics* and *History and Dogma*, trans. and ed. Alexander Dru and Illtyd Trethowan (New York: Holt, Rinehart and Winston, 1964).
2. Franz-Xaver Kraus (1840–1901) and Hermann Scheel (1850–1906), both proponents of German "Reform Catholicism," are sometimes counted among the modernists. So is the American Paulist, William L. Sullivan (1872–1935), who ultimately became a Unitarian.
3. See Roger Aubert, "Recent Literature on the Modernist Movement," in Roger Aubert, ed., *Historical Investigations (Concilium: Theology in the Age of Renewal*, vol. 17) (New York: Paulist Press, 1966), pp. 91–108.
4. The Dominican biblical scholar Marie-Joseph (Albert) Lagrange (1855–1938), for example, was for a time forced out of the directorship of the presitigious Ecole Biblique in Jerusalem that he had founded.
5. For example, *L'eucharistie*, by the anti-modernist historian of dogma Pierre Batiffol in 1907. The indexing of this work led to its author's deposition from the rectorship of the Institut Catholique at Toulouse.
6. Pierre Teilhard de Chardin (1881–1955), the Jesuit anthropologist and philosopher, is an example. Others who were considered suspect at Rome were Henri de Lubac, Karl Rahner, Yves M.-J. Congar, Jean Danielou, Marie Dominique Chenu, and John Courtney Murray.
7. Integralism is the view that the church

is entirely self-sufficient as far as faith and morals are concerned and that the faith that the church proposes is the only norm for both.
8. It is debatable if the establishment of the Biblical Commission at an earlier date, given the mentality of the period, could have forestalled the modernist crisis.
9. The Pontifical Biblical Institute was staffed from the start by Jesuits; since 1928 it has been a part of the Jesuit Gregorian University for administrative purposes.
10. The Biblical Commission, for example, ruled in 1909 that the first three chapters of Genesis contain accounts of real events, no myths, no mere allegories, no legends.
11. Excellent illustrations are the one-volume commentary on the sacred Scriptures edited by Raymond E. Brown, Joseph A. Fitzmyer, and Roland E. Murphy, *The Jerome Biblical Commentary* (Englewood Cliffs, N. J.: Prentice-Hall, 1968), and John L. McKenzie, *Dictionary of the Bible* (Milwaukee: The Bruce Publishing Company, 1965).
12. Others would trace the modern liturgical movement back into the nineteenth century. They suggest 1833 as the benchmark year, when Prosper Gueranger, later the author of *L'Année liturgique* (published in English as *The Liturgical Year*), and five other priests settled in the ancient Benedictine Monastery of St. Peter at Solesmes (Sarthe), France, Another more recent date sometimes given is 1903,

when St. Pius X published his church music manifesto *Tra le sollecitudine (Inter sollicitudines)*. Yet another is the Catholic Congress at Mechelen (Malines), Belgium, in 1909, where Lambert Beauduin proposed a program that included the use of the vernacular, consciously liturgical expressions of piety, the fostering of plain chant, and annual retreats for choir members.

13. The encyclical *Mediator Dei* of Pius XII in 1947 was both a sympathetic papal recognition of the aspirations of the liturgical movement and a warning against unauthorized views and experiments.

14. See Gregory Baum, "The Ecclesial Reality of Other Churches," in Hans Küng, ed., *The Church and Ecumenism (Concilium: Theology in the Age of Renewal*, vol. 4) (New York: Paulist Press, 1965), pp. 62–86; the contributions of Baum, Yves M.-J.

Congar, George H. Tavard, Gustave Thils, and Maurice Villain in Luis V. Romeu, ed., *Ecumenical Experiences* (Westminister, Md.: The Newman Press, 1965); and the 1963 Charles Chauncey Stillman Lectures on the Unity of Christians delivered at Harvard University by Augustin Cardinal Bea in Samuel H. Miller and G. Ernest Wright, eds., *Ecumenical Dialogue at Harvard: The Roman Catholic-Protestant Colloquium* (Cambridge, Mass.: The Belknap Press of Harvard University Press, 1964).

15. The year in which Benedict XV set up "a directing committee of Catholic Action" for Italian Roman Catholic laypersons under the Unione Popolare.

16. Quoted in Ferdinand Klostermann, "Laity," in Karl Rahner and others, eds., *Sacramentum Mundi: An Encyclopedia of Theology* 3 (New York: Herder and Herder, 1969): 267.

BIBLIOGRAPHY

CHANGING ROMAN CATHOLIC ATTITUDES TOWARD THE ECUMENICAL MOVEMENT

Bea, Augustin. *The Unity of Christians.* Ed. Bernard Leeming. New York: Herder and Herder, 1963.

Baum, Gregory. *Progress and Perspectives: The Catholic Quest for Christian Unity.* New York: Sheed and Ward, 1962.

———. *That They May Be One: A Study of Papal Doctrine.* London: Bloomsbury Publishing Co., 1958.

Brown, Robert McAfee. *The Ecumenical Revolution: An Interpretation of the Catholic-Protestant Dialogue—Based on the William Belden Noble Lectures, 1964–65.* Garden City, N.Y.: Doubleday & Company, 1967.

Congar, Yves M.-J. *Dialogue between Christians: Catholic Contributions to Ecumenism.* Trans. Philip Loretz. Westminister, Md.: The Newman Press, 1966.

Curtis, Geoffrey. *Paul Couturier and Unity in Christ.* Westminster, Md.: J. William Eckenrode, 1964.

Leeming, Bernard. *The Churches and the Church: A Study of Ecumenism.* London: Darton, Longman & Todd, 1960.

O'Brien, John A., ed. *Steps to Christian Unity.* Garden City, N.Y.: Doubleday & Company, 1964.

Sartory, Thomas. *The Oecumenical Movement and the Unity of the Church.* Trans. Hilda Graef. Westminster, Md.: The Newman Press, 1963.

Swidler, Leonard J. *The Ecumenical Vanguard: The History of the Una Sancta Movement.* Pittsburgh, Pa.: Duquesne University Press, 1966.

Tavard, George H. *Two Centuries of Ecumenism.* Trans. Royce W. Hughes. Notre Dame, Ind.: Fides Publishers, 1960.

Ward, Hiley. *Documents of Dialogue.* Englewood Cliffs, N.J.: Prentice-Hall, 1966.

Willebrands, Jan G. M., and others. *Problems before Unity.* Baltimore: Helicon Press, 1962.

THE LITURGICAL MOVEMENT

De Marco, Angelus A. *Rome and the Vernacular.* Westminster, Md.: The Newman Press, 1961.

Devine, George. *Liturgical Renewal.* New York: Alba House, 1974.

Koenker, Ernest Benjamin. *The Liturgical*

Renaissance in the Roman Catholic Church. St. Louis: Concordia Publishing House, 1966. An objective appraisal by a Lutheran theologian.

Sheppard, Lancelot. *The Mass in the West.* New York: Hawthorn Books, 1962.

ROMAN CATHOLIC MODERNISM

Heaney, John J. *The Modernist Crisis: von Hügel.* Washington, D.C.: Corpus Books, 1968.

Ratte, John. *Three Modernists: Alfred Loisy, George Tyrrell, and William L. Sullivan.* New York: Sheed and Ward, 1968.

Reardon, Bernard M. G. *Roman Catholic Modernism.* Stanford, Calif.: Stanford University Press, 1970.

Vidler, Alec R. *A Variety of Catholic Modernists.* London: Cambridge University Press, 1970.

12. Theology and Doctrine

Roman Catholic Theology Today

In spite of the charges of adversaries and the assertions of some defenders of the Roman Catholic Church, Roman Catholic theology has never been a totally monolithic system.

There have always been schools of theological thought within the Roman Catholic Church. Even the preeminence that Leo XIII and his successors gave to Thomism did not mean either that Thomism was uniformly interpreted or that other systems of Roman Catholic theology were suppressed. Again, there have always been national and regional differences in Roman Catholic theology. Sometimes basically secular political forces have zealously exaggerated such differences; sometimes they represented nothing more than different national or regional histories.

The church-political rivalries that have always existed in the Roman Catholic Church have had their bases of power within the church's structure up to the very highest levels of administration. It was inevitable that rival theologies would thus reflect in their waxing or waning influence the fortunes of their proponents. But while the party in power for the time being could exert great influence, it was never able to enjoy undisputed sway. Changes were always under way, but sometimes they took place with glacial slowness.

The updating of the Roman Catholic Church since the pontificate of John XXIII and particularly through Vatican Council II has greatly accelerated the process of change and broadened the base of dissent. The views of the architects of the altered theology that achieved recognition at Vatican II—men like Karl Rahner, Yves M.-J. Congar, Edward Schillebeeckx, Piet Fransen, Heinrich Schlier, Louis Bouyer, Bernard Lonergan, Michael Schmaus, Walter Burghardt, John Courtney Murray, Marie Dominique Chenu, Pierre Teilhard de Chardin, Henri de Lubac, Jean Danielou, and many others almost equally eminent—are in turn gradually giving way to a new generation of theologians bent on exploiting aggressively the advantage that their seniors were finally and painfully able to carve out.

As a result, Roman Catholic theologians argue if the distinctive features of Roman Catholicism are confessionally divisive marks or if they are merely characteristic emphases within the underlying Christian unity.

Confronted with the rapid changes of the last third of the twentieth century, the pluralism of dogmatic interpretation among Roman Catholic theologians, the diversities in lifestyle found within Roman Catholicism, the openness of Roman Catholic theologians to other Christian traditions, the disputes going on within Roman Catholicism about certain doctrines and about the nature and limits of doctrinal authority, some Roman Catholic theologians profess to find it difficult to identify even characteristic Roman Catholic emphases.

Increasingly they are admitting to a greater awareness of the historical dimension in doctrines, structures, and practices. They are recognizing the phenomenon of growing cultural secularity. A majority of them seem to be accepting some kind of personalism. A stress on differences between Roman Catholicism and other Christian traditions is giving way to a concern for complementarity and a sense for unity-in-diversity and subsidiarity.

All this makes the task of describing the range of theological positions in the Roman Catholic Church more difficult than would have been the case, say, in the early 1950s.

Theological Degrees of Certainty

There are various degrees of certainty in Roman Catholic theology. Truths of the highest order of certainty are said to be *de fide* (having to do with the faith). These include immediately revealed truths, which are to be believed "on the authority of God revealing." In the case of certain teachings, part of the task of the teaching office of the Roman Catholic Church is to establish that the teaching in question is indeed contained in revelation; this is what Pius XII did in 1950 in the case of the dogma of the bodily taking up of the Blessed Virgin Mary into heaven. Less certainty attaches to a "teaching proximate to the faith," that is, a doctrine that theologians generally regard as a truth of revelation, even before the teaching office of the Roman Catholic Church finally so defines it. At a still lower level are "theologically certain teachings" or "teachings pertaining to the faith"; the intrinsic connection of the teaching in question (that the church is indefectible, for example) with the teaching of the divine revelation is seen as guaranteeing the truth of the former. There are also "more common opinions," that is, views held by a majority of theologians, such as the view that the Blessed Virgin Mary actually died. "Common opinions" are held generally by theologians; an example would be the view that in the sacrament of penance imperfect contrition is sufficient for the forgiveness of the penitent's sins. "More probable opinions," like the view that individual bishops receive ther pastoral power directly from the pope," and "probable opinions," like the view that the "poor souls" in purgatory can intercede for one another and for the faithful on earth, are seen as having some solid reasons in their favor and are taught by some respectable theologians. "Pious opinions" are views that are regarded as in harmony with the Roman Catholic understanding of the faith. "Tolerated opinions" have only a very weak theological basis and the Roman Catholic Church—as the designation indicates—merely tolerates them. There is a comparable scale of "theological censures." These range from a "badly expressed proposition" on up to a "heretical proposition," which stands in opposition to a formal dogma of the Roman Catholic Church.[1]

Books that have received official review bear the notation *nihil obstat* ("nothing stands in the way") by the diocesan censor. Either the bishop or his vicar general (if he agrees with the censor), adds the notation *imprimatur* ("let it be printed"). In the case of a work by a religious there may also be a notation by the authorities of the author's order, *imprimi potest* ("it is printable"). Some small documents, like leaflets and pamphlets, may have the notation *cum permissu superiorum* ("with the concurrence of the authorities") or a similar notation.

These notations do not make the document "official." Nor do they imply that those who have made the notations agree with the contents, opinions, or statements expressed in the book. These notations are merely declarations that the reviewers who granted them regarded the document as free from doctrinal or moral error.

Many books by Roman Catholics are now published without undergoing review by the authorities. In other cases, where the notations are considered to be possible liabilities, they may be printed on a separate piece of paper and inserted in the book for the reassurance of Roman Catholic purchasers and users.

God and the Universe

Through the natural light of reason, Roman Catholic theology has held, it is possible even for fallen human beings to know with certainty the one true personal God, the creator of the universe. It has laid particular stress on the possibility of proving God's existence with absolute validity from the principle of causality. St. Thomas Aquinas formulated this principle in these terms: "Whatever is moved [referring to the transition to act from potency] must . . . be moved by something else."[2] In this connection Roman Catholic theology is sensitive not only to atheism and to what it regards as the agnosticism of the Roman Catholic modernists, but especially to Immanuel Kant and in particular to his *The Critique of Pure Reason*. Kant saw the phenomenal world as the only object of pure reason and denied that human reason had access to anything that lay beyond the senses.

This natural knowledge of God is founded on the "analogy of being" (*analogia entis*) that the inevitable similarity of a creature to its creator implies. At the same time, the "analogical" knowledge that human beings can have of God, although true, is always limited by the greater dissimilarity between the finite creature and the infinite creator, so that ultimately the real nature of God is incomprehensible to human beings in this life.

Nevertheless, Roman Catholic theology declares that God's existence is for human beings in this life an object of supernatural faith as well as of rational knowledge. Faith is here (and commonly in Roman Catholic theology) thought of as an act of assent of the intellect to those things that God has revealed. This supernatural faith corresponds in the order of grace in this life to the immediate beatific vision of God in heaven, thought of as the state and place of eternal happiness. Faith is thus a kind of anticipation of the immediate vision of God.

Roman Catholic theology has historically laid great stress on the name "I am that I am" (Exodus 3:14) as indicating the real nature of the divine being. Because of God's absolute simplicity, Roman Catholic theology sees God's attributes—such as his infinite perfection, uniqueness, truthfulness, faithfulness, justice, goodness, mercy, holiness, changelessness, omniscience, omnipresence, omnipotence, providence, love, and infinity—as identical with each other and with his being.

God does not desire physical evil—such as suffering, illness, or death—in itself, but he may will natural evil and punitive evil in order to achieve some higher end in either the natural or the moral order. But he never wills moral evil (that is, sin), either as an end or as a means to an end.

The Roman Catholic Church stands committed to the Apostles' Creed, the Creed of the 150 Fathers (Nicene Creed), and the Symbol Whoever Will Be Saved (Athanasian Creed). Accordingly, it affirms that there are in the one God three persons or hypostases—the Father, the Son, and the Holy Spirit—each of whom possesses the unique divine being. The Son proceeds from the Father by generation and is related to him as a son is to a father. The Holy Spirit proceeds from the Father and from the Son by spiration; to safeguard itself against misunderstanding by Eastern Christians, Roman Catholic theology stresses that there is only one spiration and that the Holy Spirit proceeds from the other two hypostases as from a single principle.

In its view of the Trinity, Roman Catholic theology has been profoundly influenced by St. Augustine. He viewed the Trinity as "immanent," that is, he saw God as existing in himself. He also insisted that the actions of the Trinity *ad extra* ("toward the outside," that is, toward the created universe) are indivisibly the work of all three hypostases. As a result, Roman Catholic theology in the past has given little attention to the Godhead as an "economic" Trinity, that is, as a Triune God who deals with human beings in order to bring about their salvation.

But significant changes are happening. At Vatican II a concern for relating the Trinity more closely to the "economy" (or plan) of salvation manifested itself. In addition, some contemporary Roman Catholic theologians stress the historically conditioned character of the classic creedal and theological formulations of the doctrine of the Trinity. Indeed, in some quarters there is a deliberate effort to do without a special discussion of the Trinity as such. The *New Catechism* of the Dutch hierarchy is a case in point.

At the same time the terms and the perspectives of the passages that refer to the Trinity in the confession of faith set forth by Paul VI in 1968 are quite traditional.

Creation

The Holy Trinity created the entire universe—in the sense of everything that exists outside of God—out of nothing. In this the Trinity acted without exterior compulsion and without an interior necessity. Accordingly, the universe had a beginning in time.

In the past, Roman Catholic theology has inclined to a literal interpretation of the creation account in Genesis, and for a long time it was hostile to every kind of evolution. This was true particularly in contexts where evolution was seen as necessitating a materialistic view of the universe. More recently Roman Catholic biblical theologians have thought of the opening chapters of Genesis as a kind of past-oriented "etiological prophecy." That is, the compilers of the book undertook to trace God's activity back to creation, to give theological information about the beginning of the universe, and in their account of the universally significant decisions of the first human beings to provide a kind of foreword to the history of God's saving acts in the patriarchal period. The garden of Eden existed only in the mind of God; the account of Eve's creation is intended to assert dramatically the similarity of the sexes.

A very great age for the universe is commonly conceded, and the concept of biological evolution is generally regarded as scientifically justified.[3] The emergence of human beings, seen as a new type of organism with the gift of speech and a unique capacity for spiritual behavior, is commonly conceded to have taken place long ages ago. The encyclical of Pius XII *Humani generis* (1952) rejected the idea of polygenism, that is, the idea that the evolutionary transition from beast to human being took place in an unspecified number of cases. It affirmed monogenism, the teaching that all human beings, at least those who lived after the original sin, trace their origin biologically to a single pair of ancestors, whom the sacred Scriptures call Adam and Eve. Some Roman Catholic theologians now argue that Pius was rejecting polygenism only because it did not seem to be compatible with the church's teaching about original sin. But this incompatibility does not seem theologically irremediable, they believe, and so they regard it as possible for a Roman Catholic prudently to maintain some form of polygenism, particularly since anthropologists have generally settled the question of the origin of human beings in favor of polygenism.

God continues to keep the universe in existence, and to protect and guide everything that he has created. In so doing, according to the common opinion of Roman Catholic theologians, he cooperates immediately in all the acts of his creatures. Theologians differentiate three kinds of providence. One is a general providence, which includes all creatures, whether or not God has endowed them with reason. The second is a special providence, which embraces all rational creatures, including sinners. The third is a most special providence, which God exercises over the human beings that he has predestined to enjoy the beatific vision. Nothing in the universe happens without God's providence or independently of it, and his eternal plan is immutable. Since God has foreseen from eternity the prayers that would be offered in time, prayer is included as a secondary cause in his providence.

Angels and Demons

The created universe, Roman Catholic theology has traditionally held, includes the spiritual beings that the sacred Scriptures call angels. God created them out of nothing at the beginning. Their number is very great. They are naturally immortal. Their power and their understanding, although still finite, are vastly greater than the power and understanding of human beings.[4]

God destined the angels for the beatific vision of himself, but he subjected them first to a moral testing. In the process some of them became evil through their own fault.

The mission of the good angels, now established in a state of grace, is to glorify God and to protect his human creatures and promote their salvation. It is a certain opinion in Roman Catholic theology that every human being has a guardian angel of his own from birth. According to Roman Catholic teaching it is appropriate that angels receive the same invocation and veneration that is properly accorded to the saints.

The evil angels have as their leader Satan, or the devil,[5] whom the sacred Scriptures describe as the "prince" and "god" of this world. Evil angels try to injure human beings by tempting them, by inflicting physical harm on them, and by taking forcible possession of their bodies (demoniacal possession or obsession).[6]

Contemporary Roman Catholic theology is aware of the difficulty that twentieth-century human beings have with the idea of angels and devils. It stresses that past metaphysical speculation about angels belongs in the realm of free opinions. It asserts that angels exist, and it depicts their relation to the material universe in such a way that they are seen as genuinely cosmic "principalities and powers," rather than as beings that arbitrarily intervene in the world in ways contrary to their authentic nature. It emphasizes their creaturely character, and warns against letting them become all-but-divine beings on a par with God (particularly in the case of the devil and the evil angels).

Some theologians observe that human beings tend to profess belief in the existence of a devil that is purely and simply evil in order to be able to excuse themselves. They warn against overstressing such ideas as that of individual guardian angels and discourage the faithful from exaggerating the veneration that is given to the angels. They see the present theological situation as one which does not require preachers and catechists to give angelology primary attention.

Some presentations go even further. They say that the sacred writers describe the Deity in terms of an Oriental monarch. In an era without rapid means of communication, a monarch without a multitude of servants and messengers would be a sorry little ruler. So the sacred writers surrounded God with a vast corps of such messengers and servants who waited on him and relayed his messages to his people on earth. Whether the angels really exist or whether they are merely literary devices for describing God's communication with human beings is regarded as an unimportant open question on which biblical scholars are not agreed. When liturgical prayers mention angels, the worshiper should think of all the creatures that God created and should consider "that it may be even that the traditional angels really exist."[7]

Predestination

The traditional Roman Catholic doctrine of the predestination of certain rational beings to enjoy the beatific vision of God leaves a number of questions unresolved. Thus for the purpose of discussion, Roman Catholic theology differentiates between incomplete predestination, that is, a predestination either to grace in this world or to glory hereafter, and complete predestination, a predestination to grace in this world and to glory in the world to come.

Roman Catholic theology has also affirmed that in the eternal divine plan of his providence, God by an eternal and immutable resolution of his will predetermined certain human beings to eternal blessedness. Left open is the question whether or not God's resolution did or did not take into account the merits of the individual concerned (which, of course, the divine omniscience was able to foresee).

An individual can know that he is among the number that God has chosen only by divine revelation, but it is highly probable that an individual belongs to the number of the predestined if he perseveringly practices the virtues that the beatitudes recommend, if he receives Holy Communion frequently, if he actively loves Christ, the church, and his neighbor, and if he venerates the Mother of God.

The Roman Catholic Church has also taught that on account of the sins which God has foreseen that certain human beings will commit he has immutably predestined these human beings to eternal reprobation. Again the question is left open if this reprobation is merely not having been chosen, or if it is an actual or positive rejection. Who the rejected (or the unchosen) are is, of course, not known to human beings without a special divine revelation.

Relatively little change has taken place in recent Roman Catholic theology on the teaching about predestination. For the individual human being, his predestination still remains an unknown matter, to be approached in hope and prayer. It is part of the mystery of God's universal causality. It must not be understood in a "predestinarianistic" sense, that is, it must not be taught in such a way that it seems to rule out human freedom and responsibility in the achievement of salvation. Nor is there an active divine predestination to sin.

Recent Roman Catholic theology makes the point that many of the past controversies about predestination took place within too narrow an angle of view. God is not in time and he acts in an eternity that has neither past nor future. Stress is laid on the necessity of keeping in their proper tension and relationship the biblical affirmations about God's almighty power, his limitless mercy, the necessity of his grace if human beings are to do anything that is more-than-naturally good, and the individual's human freedom. The assertion of the immutability of predestination is regarded as nothing more than an affirmation that an omniscient God does not need to wait until the end of the age to know what the final destiny of each human being will be.

Revelation and Dogma

Historically the Roman Catholic Church has taken the position that dogmas do not change. For Roman Catholics a dogma is a truth that God has immediately (or formally) revealed by incorporating it explicitly or implicitly in the divine revelation; the magisterium ("teaching office") of the Roman Catholic Church in turn has proposed it for all members of the church to believe. This setting forth of a truth to be believed may take place solemnly and extraordinarily by a decision on a matter of faith that the pope makes on his own authority or that a general council decrees and the pope formally approves. But this setting forth of a truth to be believed may also take place through the ordinary and general magisterium of the church, say through the catechisms that the bishops authorize, through the sermons that parish priests preach by the authority that their bishops have delegated to them, and through the liturgy that is repeated week after week.

The divine revelation within which dogmas must be found either explicitly or implicitly has traditionally been described as sacred Scripture and tradition.

For Roman Catholics the Bible consists of seventy-three books—forty-six in the Old[8] and twenty-seven in the New Testament—which the teaching office of the Roman Catholic Church has declared to be the divinely inspired written word of God.

Until the twentieth century, Roman Catholics dated the biblical documents conservatively. Moses wrote the five books ascribed to him, Isaiah, Jonah, and Daniel the documents that bear their names. The three synoptic Gospels were written between A.D. 40 and 63. St. John, author of the latest documents in the New Testament, completed his work by the year 100.[9]

The Roman Catholic Church has fixed the canon of the Bible, according to Roman Catholic theology, and determines its proper interpretation. While tradition is the proximate rule of faith, the Bible is the remote rule. Although the Roman Catholic Church has never formally defined the inerrancy of the Bible, Roman Catholic theologians regard inerrancy as an article of faith.

Both inspiration and inerrancy were defined in a rather fundamentalistic fashion into the nineteenth century. After the collapse of the theory of inspiration as verbal dictation, the initial efforts at theological redefinition of the terms are not regarded as particularly happy.

More recently inspiration has been seen as a positive divine influence on the composition of the biblical documents that goes beyond later divine or ecclesiastical approbation and that is more than a negative assistance against error. As Roman Catholic theologians became aware of the complex literary processes that underlie the production of the biblical books, they realized that modern conceptions like "author" and "book" cannot be projected backward upon the biblical world.

One position sees inspiration as the divine illumination of the practical judgment of the inspired writer, compiler, or editor so that he is able to choose the form and style that will best suit his purpose. Other theologians see inspiration as a charismatic gift that the apostolic church possessed, but that it was not able to bequeath to later generations of Christians. There is a current tendency to emphasize the social character of inspiration as the necessary consequence of the social character of literary composition in the biblical period. The real human authors of the sacred Scriptures would thus be the community of Israel in the case of the Old Testament and the primitive church in the case of the New.

Inerrancy is no longer regarded as "a homogeneous oracular infallibility." On the contrary, the solution of each problem is to be looked for in its own context. Indeed, some Roman Catholic biblical scholars hold that the idea of the Bible's freedom from error as the Fathers of the church (like St. Augustine, for instance) formulated it is inconsistent with the biblical data, untenable, and confusing.

In general, inerrancy implies that the biblical words are to be regarded as true in the sense that the human writer conveys by them within the patterns and forms of his own speech. Erroneous beliefs of the biblical writers may appear in their work from time to time, but the biblical record does not affirm these mistaken notions. Inerrancy must be understood broadly enough to accommodate the linguistic usages that the biblical documents actually reveal, the personal styles of the writers, the literary forms that their cultures employed, the inability of the Semitic mind to voice abstract thought and subtle distinctions, and the biblical views of history and historiography.

Roman Catholic scientific biblical scholarship operates with all the tools of historical criticism, form history, and redaction history in the production of commentaries and translations. Both the commentaries and the translations make use of the original languages of the biblical documents rather than the Latin Vulgate to which the Council of Trent was understood as limiting older generations of biblical scholars.[10]

Tradition in the older view was historically thought of as the totality of revealed teaching that had come directly to the apostles from Christ's own lips, but that had not been committed to writing in the sacred Scriptures. Instead legitimate teachers of the church had handed it down from one generation to another. In the process parts of it were committed to writing in the works that the Fathers of the church produced.

The common view after the Council of Trent was that the divine revelation was to be found partly in the written documents of Holy Scripture and partly in the oral tradition of the church. In recent years, however, an increasing number of Roman Catholic theologians have argued that this was not the intention of the Council of Trent. They claim that Trent was unable to reach a final decision in the matter and that it had deliberately left the issue open. Even at Trent, research seemed to show, there were council Fathers who held that Scripture and tradition both witnessed to the same deposit of truth; the whole of the truth, they believed, was to be found explicitly or implicitly in the Scriptures and the whole of the truth was to be found in tradition.

At Vatican Council II the original draft of what became the dogmatic constitution on divine revelation clearly embodied the traditional view. It was even entitled *On the Two Sources of Revelation* and, if the council had adopted it, it would have canonized the understanding of revelation that its drafters brought to it. But many of the bishops proved to be opposed to this view. As a result the document was rewritten to take cognizance of the differences in viewpoint. As finally adopted, *Dei verbum* still leaves the issue open for new generations of theologians to debate until, it is hoped, the Roman Catholic Church achieves the necessary degree of clarity to promulgate a final decision.

Modern biblical studies have helped to give the entire Scripture-tradition problem a new dimension. It is seen with increasing clarity that the sacred Scriptures themselves are part of the process of tradition, and that hence the line of demarcation between written revelation (in the sacred Scriptures) and oral revelation (in ecclesiastical tradition) is no longer as sharp as it once was held to be.

An additional question that has arisen is if tradition is static or dynamic. Does it merely involve the transmission of a certain body of information, changed only by the necessity of making it intelligible to different people living in different periods, using different languages, and conditioned by different cultures? Or does it possess the possibility of synthesizing out of the inherited materials and out of the data and requirements of a novel situation something that is both linked to the past but also new? Roman Catholic theologians today would commonly affirm the later view.

Without conceding that the sacred Scriptures are the only source of faith and theology, Roman Catholics acknowledge the sacred Scriptures as the norm of their church's faith and practice. Many contemporary Roman Catholic theologians, however, reject as inadequate what they describe as a fundamentalist view of biblical authority that accepts the Bible as the sole norm of Christian faith uncritically and without qualification. They also repudiate the idea that the apostles handed down to their successors a body of unwritten traditions, outside of but equally normative with the sacred Scriptures. At the same time the opinions of Roman Catholic theologians about the way in which the sacred Scriptures are the norm of faith and practice are varied. Some hold that the divine revelation is available exclusively in the biblical account of God's saving acts in the midst of his ancient people of Israel and in Jesus Christ and that this revelation is offered to the church (and to all human beings) in the sacred Scriptures and nowhere else. In other words, although the Bible is a living and perennially new voice within the church, it always remains the unnormed norm of teaching and life which subjects to correction the church's most persuasive presentation of the gospel of divine grace and its implications for human living. Still other, even more liberal theologians see God present in the search of human beings for the truth even outside the community of Israel and Jesus Christ. Accordingly, although the sacred Scriptures are normative because of the finality of the uniquely privileged revelation that God gave of himself in Christ and that they attest, they are not the only place where the Logos and the Spirit have revealed God's grace. God, they hold, is present in the experiences of those who deeply wrestle in their search for truth both inside the Christian community and within the larger community of the Spirit-created brotherhood of all human beings. While God's external word in the sacred Scriptures is not able to define what Jesus will mean in the future, it will continue to call human beings away from those aspects of themselves that are shallow and inauthentic and will compel them to seek to discover what God's interior word has to tell them in the depths of their own lives and in the experience of the human community.[11]

The Roman Catholic Church has viewed defined dogmas as unchangeable, irreformable, and irreversible as far as their content is concerned. It has, however, had to face the problem of the development of dogma ever since John Henry Cardinal Newman's *An Essay on the Development of*

Christian Doctrine (1845). In reflecting on this issue, Roman Catholic theologians have granted that in the cumulative communication of the truths of revelation to human beings a great deal of growth took place through the centuries before the supreme, climactic revelation of God in Jesus Christ took place. With Christ and the apostles, the Roman Catholic Church held, general or public revelation—that is, revelations from God that all human beings must believe—ceased.[12]

Since then there has in this view been no expansion of the deposit of the faith. Admittedly, truths that the faithful once believed only implicitly were set forth to be explicitly believed; the dogma of the Trinity is a case in point. Similarly, ancient truths received new clarity by being given sharply defined form; an example is the dogma of the hypostatic or personal union of the divine and human natures in the single hypostasis or person of the Son of God in the flesh. Teachings that were at one time in dispute became clear and contradictory propositions, even though they had been tolerable in the absence of an authoritative definition, were condemned; Roman Catholics would cite the dogma of the immaculate conception of the Blessed Virgin Mary—once rejected even by such an authoritative doctor as St. Thomas Aquinas—as an instance.

In the process of clarification, theology may use new terms to reformulate dogmas that do not themselves change. There may be "deficiencies in the formulation of doctrine" arising out of "the influence of events or of the time"; these need to "be appropriately rectified at the proper moment."[13]

Some theologians make the point that binding formulations of church teaching are obligatory only when they have to do with teachings that God has revealed for the salvation of human beings. It is emphasized that the entire ministry of the word, including the church's teaching office, stands under the sacred Scriptures. Again, the Vatican II principle of the "hierarchy of truths" is invoked to imply that certain defined dogmas for some Christians are so far away from the central Christian message that these dogmas have no practical significance for the day-by-day religious life of these Chirstians.

In contrast to the scholastic-logical position, a different strain in Roman Catholic theology takes a "transformist" view. It refuses to concede that objective statements are part of the substance of revelation. Revelation itself is an experiential happening that takes place within the believer. Its unchanging character depends on a continuity of experience and inspiration. Because the experience has to be translated into some sort of human language if it is to be communicated, teachings are necessary, but they are always involved with the historical situation and for that reason they are inevitably changeable. This "transformist" view has not commended itself widely, because it is seen as leading step by step to an erosion of Christian faith and to a pervasive religious skepticism.

A third view synthesizes the scholastic-logical and the liberal-transformist views. It stresses that revelation is not primarily a set of commandments but a gospel, the good news of a loving heavenly Father's desire to make human beings his children in Christ. At the same time it operates with the thesis that revelation is less a communication of propositions about God and salvation than the actual self-impartation of the God who saves. The propositions in which the revelation is communicated are true expressions of the divine self-impartation but, because no theological system ever contains the entire truth that the grace of God presents to the mind of the believer, these doctrinal propositions and systematizations are inadequate. The theological enterprise in this view is charismatic, suprarational, and human (in that it is achieved by human thought guided by divine grace). The function of the church's teaching office is the public exposition of the church's self-awareness.[14]

Human Beings and Sin

Roman Catholic theology has classically taught that human beings consist of two essestial parts—a material body and a spiritual, intellective, or rational soul.[15] Each human being possesses an individual soul. In scholastic language, the rational soul is the essential form of the body. It is a certain opinion that God creates every individual soul at the moment of its union with the body.[16] (This doctrine, sometimes called creationism, implies the rejection of the teaching called generationism or traducianism, which holds that children receive their souls from their parents.)

Where biological evolution has been presumed, the special creation of the first human beings extended at least to the spiritual soul.

The various states of human beings that Roman Catholic theology has distinguished are the state of elevated nature or of original righteousness (*justitia*)[17] before their fall into sin. The first human beings occupied this state. The present state is that of fallen nature, in which human beings have lost their state of grace and the gifts of wholeness. The state of restored nature is the condition of those who have achieved their supernatural destiny, the beatific vision of God.[18]

Before the first human beings fell into sin, they were in a state of grace, they were free from concupiscence (or irregular desire), they possessed bodily immortality, they enjoyed the possibility of remaining free from suffering, and they had the needed degree of natural and supernatural knowledge.

The first human beings, Roman Catholic theology says, fell from their state of grace by disobeying an explicit divine commandment. This deprived them of their state of grace, called down on them God's answer and indignation, and made them subject to death and to the dominion of the devil. The initial sin of the first human beings has had as a universal consequence for all their posterity what theologians call original sin. The Council of Trent described original sin as the death of the soul (in the sense of the absence of the supernatural life of grace).

Original sin in this sense is transmitted to all human beings not by imitation, but by natural generation. All human beings are thus in the condition of the first human beings after their fall. Souls that depart this life in the state of original sin—including the souls of unbaptized children—are excluded from the beatific vision of God.[19]

In 1909 the Pontifical Biblical Commission ruled that certain elements in the Genesis account of the fall of the first human beings must be accepted as literal historical facts. Thus it was deemed necessary to hold that God gave the first human beings a commandment in order to test their obedience; that the first human beings violated the divine injunction through the temptation of the devil, who took the form of a serpent; and that as a consequence the first human beings lost their original condition of innocence.

More recent Roman Catholic theology sees the narrative in Genesis as an allegory in which Adam is Everyman or as an etiological account that provides the essential theological background for the existence of the mystery of evil and for the alienation of human beings from God.[20] It is this alienation from God that necessitated his intervention for the salvation, first of all, of those human beings whom he had chosen and, ultimately, of all human beings.

Contemporary Roman Catholic theology stresses the minimal role that the doctrine of original sin plays in the sacred Scriptures. To all intents and purposes this teaching is absent from the Old Testament and the Gospels, and finds explicit expression only in St. Paul. St. Paul's concern is to stress that original sin and being redeemed are two existential data of the human situation. God permitted sin only within the scope of his unconditional and stronger will to save human beings. Human beings lack the sanctifying Spirit of God precisely because they are human beings. This absence of the sanctifying Spirit of God is contrary to God's design and purpose, and for that reason it is, at least in an analogous sense, sin. As "children of Adam" human beings inherit this condition by the process of generation, although the mode of this linkage with the human past is irrelevant. In fact children are ordinarily produced by "libidinous generation," but their situation is not altered if they are produced by artificial insemination. Their evil desire (or concupiscence) is, like original sin, a contradiction of the condition that God has designed for human beings. They are wounded and weakened, unable to make a decision for salvation without the grace of God that comes from Christ. This grace is available to human beings, because they are as much redeemed through Christ as they are subject to original sin through their participation in humanity as "children of Adam."

Even those who have been received into grace through Christ are not exempt from original sin, from evil desire, and from death. This is so even though they are no longer in a state of guilt. Thus even for the baptized believers, original sin is a continuing problem. The presence of original sin demonstrates that salvation and grace are an unmerited gift of divine favor that God bestows on human beings because of Christ. Original sin has a further function for the baptized believer. It reminds him that although he is obligated to demonstrate the presence of grace by actively helping to plan and to realize a future that is marked by love and by justice, the task that confronts him is not one that he can complete in a world in which original sin is an inescapable datum.

Classically Roman Catholic theology has distinguished between original sin and personal (or actual) sins. The norm for the latter is the individual's conscience, understood as the verdict of his intellect on the morality of an action while he is debating whether or not to perform it. In concrete cases this verdict of the individual's intellect may be true or erroneous. If the conscience has been sincerely formed, however, it must be followed, because to act against conscience is itself a sinful act. (Mere temptation, however, is not sin.)

Personal sins may be material sins, if the action itself is objectively evil but the intention to do wrong is absent. When the intention to do wrong is present the sin is formal; it is a sin "from the heart."

Formal sins may be either mortal or venial (from the Latin *venia*, "forgiveness"). A mortal sin is a complete rejection of God that takes away from the soul the life-giving principle of grace and thus brings death to the soul. Mortal sins must meet three criteria. The matter must be serious; within the admitted difficulty of abstractly defining serious matter, a primary violation of the positive divine law, th enatural law, or a major law of the Roman Catholic Church would normally be so regarded. The offender must further have full knowledge of the seriousness of the action that he is performing. Third, he must give the action the full consent of his will. This full consent may be restricted by passion, external coercion or pressure, habit, or innocent or invincible ignorance of the wrongfulness of the action, with a corresponding reduction in the guilt attaching to the offender's action.

In the absence of any of these three requirements—even if the Roman Catholic Church had categorized a particular action as a mortal sin out of pastoral concern—a formal sin is venial. Venial sins do not deprive the offender of his status in grace nor do they merit eternal punishment, but they weaken the fervor of his service of God and merit temporal punishment; this must be satisfied in this life or it must be canceled by suffering in purgatory after death.

An offender can commit both mortal and venial sins by acting or by failing to act, that is, he can commit both sins of commission and sins of omission. He can likewise commit both mortal and venial sins by deeds, by words, and by thoughts.

More recent Roman Catholic discussions of sin have on occasion tended to call some of these traditional views into question. Theologians have urged that sin is not adequately described in terms of deliberate transgressions of the divine law. By this they have not intended to say that sin is not an of-fense to God, but that sin is primarily a disregard of God's call to us to love him and our fellow human beings. Because the love of God and the love of our fellow human beings is a unity, sin is an offense against both.

There has also been a tendency to emphasize that far from being a dichot-omy, material sin and formal sin are merely the limits of the continuum along which our concrete sinful actions fall.

The distinction between mortal and venial sins has also come in for reappraisal. Basically, a mortal sin is one that normally requires the sacra-ment of penance to be forgiven, while God can forgive a venial sin without the sacrament of penance. Actually, some theologians hold, the single real criterion that differentiates a mortal from a venial sin is the full knowledge and freedom of the offender. A mortal sin is a decision to break with divine grace that the offender makes at the core and center of his person and not merely on the periphery. Increasingly, the quality of sin is seen as exhibited less in an exceptional act and more in the whole style and direction of the individual's life.

Christ and Mary

The cardinal truth of the teaching about Christ in Roman Catholic theology is that he is true God and true man. In the Incarnation the second hypostasis of the Trinity assumed a real (as opposed to a merely apparent) human body and a rational human soul. He was conceived and brought forth by a human mother, the Blessed Virgin Mother, by the power of the Holy Spirit.

The hypostatic (or personal) union of his divine and human natures in a single person began at the moment of his conception. Although only the Son of God became a human being, the Incarnation is the cooperative work of the entire Trinity.

In the Incarnation, each of Christ's two natures continues unchanged and unmixed with the other nature, but they exist in the very closest kind of union with each other. Each nature has its own proper attributes and its own will, but the characteristics and the manner of operation of each nature can properly be affirmed of the whole person in whom the two natures are united. The hypostatic union was not interrupted by Christ's death and it will never end in the future.

Since Christ is God's Son not only as God but also as a human being, he is to be venerated with the same absolute adoration (*latria*)[21] that is due only to God.

From the first moment of its existence, Christ's human soul enjoyed the beatific vision of God, Roman Catholic theologians have held. His human knowledge was free from ignorance and from error. He was free from original sin through his conception by the Holy Spirit without the cooperation of a human male. In his life on earth he was not only free from actual sin, but he could not have sinned. As the instrument of the second hypostasis of the Trinity, his humanity was capable of performing miracles. At the same time his humanity was capable of suffering and his soul was capable of human emotions.

The purpose of Christ's incarnation was the redemption of human beings.[22] It is a central teaching of Roman Catholic theology that salvation from sin comes only through Jesus Christ. Historically Roman Catholic theology has tended to follow St. Anselm in explaining the manner of human salvation. Human beings cannot redeem themselves. Their guilt is infinitely great because their sin is an offense against an infinite God. While God was under no interior or exterior necessity to redeem mankind, the immutability of his decree of bliss for human beings constrained him to redeem them. Since only a divine person could provide the satisfaction for the infinite guilt of man, the incarnation of a divine person was necessary.

Christ fulfilled the work of redemption through the discharge of a three-fold office.[23] The first is his prophetic office; Christ is the great prophet foretold by Moses and the prophets of Israel and he is the supreme teacher of all human beings. The second is his office as king and shepherd; Christ is the lawgiver and judge—not merely the redeemer—of all human beings and as such he has legislative, judicial, and punitive authority. The third is Christ's priestly office. Christ is the eternal high priest of humanity, the mediator between God and man already by virtue of his hypostatic union. The distinctive function of a priest is to offer sacrifice, understood in the case of Christ as total self-surrender to God in obedience, climaxing in the reconciliation of God and human beings through an act of atonement and to the acknowledgment of Christ's majesty in adoration, praise, thanksgiving, and petition. Christ offered himself on the cross as a true sacrifice. By this act of vicarious atonement in suffering and dying he has offered to God an expiation greater in value than all the sins of all human beings required. In this way he has ransomed and redeemed all human beings from the dominion of the devil and reconciled them to God. Roman Catholic theology stresses that this vicarious atonement is not only for those whom God chose and predestined to salvation but that it is universal; there is no human being whom Christ's sacrifice has not redeemed.[24]

Christ's sacrificial death is both expiatory and meritorious. That is, Christ's suffering and death merited a reward from God. As far as Christ himself is concerned, he merited his exaltation, that is, his resurrection and ascension into heaven, there to take his place at the right hand of the Father. As far as human beings are concerned, Christ merited all the supernatural graces that any human being has ever received or will ever receive. Roman Catholic theology continues to reaffirm the statement of the Council of Ferrara-Florence that "nobody has ever been freed from the power of the devil except through the merits of Jesus Christ the mediator."

After Christ's death on the cross, his soul descended into the netherworld. Here he delivered the faithful of the Old Covenant from the limbo of the Fathers, which ever since has been empty. On this third day he rose again in a transformed body from the dead. Afterward he ascended into heaven, body and soul, and sat down at the right hand of God, that is, his human nature received its final elevation into the condition of divine glory. At God's right hand Christ intercedes for his own and sends them his gifts of grace, especially the Holy Spirit.

Contemporary Roman Catholic theology operates with the conviction that there is, in Karl Rahner's words, "a spontaneous, unanalyzed, 'inquiring Christology' in every human being," and urges Christians both in creed and in life to set forth Christ as calling all human beings to absolute love of their fellow men and neighbors, to the same readiness for death that he exhibited, and to hope in God's coming as the absolute future of the universe and of all history.

Contemporary Roman Catholic theology sees a need for reformulating the christological dogmas of the church in terms that will communicate with contemporary human beings better than the inherited formulas but without abandoning the formulas of the past. It calls for a doctrine of Christ that takes seriously the evolutionary view of the salvation history of the world. It demands a teaching about Christ that proceeds "from below," that is, from the human being Jesus, in contrast to (although joined with) a "transcendental" theology that proceeds "from above," that is, from the divine hypostasis that becomes incarnate. It regards as highly necessary a rethinking of a phrase like "Christ's preexistence" and of a term like "person" as conventionally used in discussions of Christ ("two natures in one person"). It calls for a reconsideration of the scope of Christ's human knowledge and his human freedom. It stresses that the death of Jesus must be seen as the death of God, not only in its redemptive outcome but in itself; that the hypostatic union has a history in Christ's life, his death, and his being raised to life from the dead; that the Incarnation and the hypostatic union themselves have saving significance; that the patristic conviction about the cosmic dimensions of Christ's presence and activity in the world has special relevance for Christians in the secularized present; and that there are people who authentically believe in Jesus Christ even though they may fail to use the right creedal formulas to express their faith in him.

Inseparably linked to the incarnate Son of God is the woman who gave him birth, the Blessed Virgin Mary. Her primary dignity and privilege is the fact that she is the God-bearer (*theotokos* in Greek, *Deipara* or *Dei genetrix* in Latin, commonly translated in English as "Mother of God").

While some Western Christians as far back as the twelfth cenutry had believed that the Blessed Virgin Mary was conceived without original sin, since 1854 Roman Catholics have been obliged to regard as divinely revealed the teaching "that at the first moment of her conception, by a singular gift of grace and privilege of Almighty God, in virtue of the merits of Jesus Christ, the Redeemer of mankind, the Blessed Virgin Mary was preserved unstained by original sin." That is, the victory over original sin that begins in other Christians at baptism and continues throughout their lives was accomplished in the case of the Blessed Virgin Mary in the first moment of her existence as a human being. From her immaculate conception, Roman Catholic theology argues that throughout her life she was free from every motion of inordinate desire or concupiscence and from every personal actual sin.

Before, during, and after the birth of Christ, his mother was a virgin, Roman Catholic theology has held, and she gave birth to Christ without any violation of her virginal integrity.

Roman Catholic theology commonly holds that the Mother of God died as other human beings do, but some theologians have denied this. The belief that she was taken up bodily into heaven at the end of her earthly career goes back as far as the sixth century, and since the thirteenth century it became more and more common among Western Christians. From 1950 on Roman Catholics were required to believe as an item of divine revelation that "the immaculate Mother of God, the ever Virgin Mary, having completed the course of her earthly life was assumed body and soul into heavenly glory," and that anyone who denied or doubted this "has fallen away completely from the divine and Catholic faith."

The Blessed Virgin Mary's being taken up into heaven is the basis of her queenship over heaven and earth in Roman Catholic eyes; her queenship in turn makes her supremely powerful as the maternal intercessor for her clients.

In addition to the poetic praise that popular piety and devotion accord to the Blessed Virgin Mary in a large number of hymns, litanies, antiphons, and prayers, Roman Catholic theology has reflected on the propriety of certain other titles. Thus it has held that since she gave to the world Christ the redeemer, who is the source of all graces, she is in this way the channel of all graces. Since her bodily assumption into heaven, some theologians have further held, no grace is conferred on human beings without her actual intercessory mediation.[25]

The title of *corredemptrix* ("Associate of the Redeemer") has been used in official church documents since the time of St. Pius X. It is not intended to imply that the Blessed Virgin Mary is directly and immediately involved in the objective redemption of human beings, since she herself as a human being needed to be redeemed by the merits of her Son. It is regarded as an appropriate title, however, because she willingly devoted her entire life to the service of the Savior and suffered under the cross with him. In addition, she constantly participates through her intercession—as all of God's people do in one degree or another by their prayers—in the subjective redemption of individuals.

Because of the graces and privileges that God has conferred on the Blessed Virgin Mary,[26] Roman Catholic theology holds that she is entitled to a higher degree of veneration (*hyperdulia*) than other saints, who are entitled merely to *dulia*.

As Mother of God, St. Mary in the eyes of the Roman Catholic Church possesses the fullness of grace.[27] Similarly, because she is the Mother of God, Paul VI at the end of the third session of Vatican II, of his own accord and not without some resistance on the part of the council fathers, conferred on her the metaphorical title "Mother of the Church," a term that goes back to a pseudo-Ambrosian work probably composed by Berengar of Tours (999?–1088).

There have long been diverse Mariological tendencies in the Roman Catholic Church. The "minimalists" tended to want to limit the veneration of the Mother of God to those aspects that could be clearly demonstrated from the sacred Scriptures or that the teaching office of the church had explicitly defined. The "maximalists" tended to want to expand the public and private devotion to the Mother of God to the limit of tolerability.[28]

Contemporary Roman Catholic theology tends away from a "maximalist" interest in Mariology. The relatively minor role of the Mother of God in the New Testament is conceded. The presence of obviously different traditions as well as of Old Testament and Jewish strains in the infancy narratives is recognized. Many no longer affirm the reverend tradition that the Blessed Virgin Mary had taken a vow of virginity prior to the annunciation. The virgin conception and birth of Christ is seen primarily as an occasion for letting God's creative might and his initiative in the work of redemption become manifest.[29] Contemporary Roman Catholic theologians stress that no title or prerogative of Christ's mother may be allowed to impair his sole mediatorship; her role in redemption is always within the perspective of Christ's saving activity, always derivative and subordinate.

Vatican II was a disappointment to some Marian devotees in the Roman Catholic Church. Among the original drafts was one that would have devoted an entire council document to her. What finally happened was the incorporation of a concluding eighth chapter on the Blessed Virgin Mary into the dogmatic constitution on the church, *Lumen gentium*. This section has the Blessed Virgin enter the salvation process through her own faith, by which she became the primary recipient of the salvation that is available in the church. Her major significance for her fellow members of the church is that she is the type and exemplar of every believing Christian and of the church itself.[30]

Pre-Vatican-II devotion to the Blessed Virgin Mary was many-faceted. It included the Hail Mary, the *Angelus* ("The angel [of the Lord announced to Mary]"), the *Regina caeli* ("Queen of heaven"), the *Salve regina* ("Hail, queen"), the *Memorare* ("Remember"), and the *Sub tuum praesidium* ("Under your protection"); the Litany of Loreto; at least twenty-five feasts and commemorations in the calendar; the Little Office of Our Lady; hymns like *Ave maris stella* ("Hail, star of the sea"); Marian devotions in May and October; novenas (originally cycles of nine services) in her honor; Lady chapels in every parish church; sodalities of Our Lady, the Legion of Mary, the International Pontifical Marian Academy, and Marian and Mariological societies and congresses at the national and international level; the publication of Mariological and Marian magazines, monographs, and encyclopedias; consecration of cities and nations to the Blessed Virgin under one of her many aspects; the invocation of her protection against the perils of the highway (as Santa Maria dell' Estrada) and of the airways (as Our Lady of Loreto);[31] pilgrimages to places where apparitions of the Blessed Virgin Mary had been reported (notably Lourdes and La Salette in France and Fatima in Portugal);[32] appeals to her "almighty intercession"; and the use of titles like Consoler of the Afflicted and Help of Sinners.

Since Vatican II many once very prominent aspects of Marian piety among the faithful have suffered deemphasis. In some cases this deemphasis has been incidental. The increasing use of the vernacular in the Mass is a case in point. As long as the Mass was said in Latin, it was normal for the worshiping faithful to occupy themselves during the service (except at a climactic point like the elevation of the host and chalice after the consecration) with meditating on the mysteries of the rosary. For the same reason, corporate Marian devotions—such as novenas honoring her in one of her many aspects, say as Our Sorrowful Mother, as Our Lady of Perpetual Help, or as Our Lady of the Miraculous Medal—afforded some of the most cherished opportunities for nonliturgical services in the vernacular. The introduction of the vernacular in the Mass and the general participation of the congregation in the rite has made recitation of the rosary during Mass all but impossible and it has taken away an important attraction of nonliturgical devotions in the vernacular.[33]

In some areas of the church the deemphasis of the rosary and of such things as Marian scapulars (like the small "brown scapular" promoted by the Carmelites) has been deliberate.

A considerable degree of nostalgia for the prominent veneration of the Mother of God continues, especially among some older Roman Catholics. The conservative movement in the Roman Catholic Church has tried to capitalize on this nostalgia and to rekindle some of the lost enthusiasm for Marian devotions in various ways. For example, where they have had the support of the bishop of the diocese they have promoted intricately scheduled "visits" to the parishes of the diocese of the "Pilgrim Virgin" statue that Paul VI blessed for the United States in 1967 on the fiftieth anniversary of the reported apparition of the Blessed Virgin Mary at Fatima.

Amid these divergent thrusts, contemporary Roman Catholic theology stresses that the *hyperdulia* accorded to the Mother of God relates to the *dulia* accorded to the saints and that it is altogether different in quality from the *latria* that God alone deserves. It calls for the frank recognition of the poetic hyperbole of some forms of Marian address. The Marian titles that in a strict sense apply primarily to Christ must be seen as applicable to the Blessed Virgin only in an analogous and derived sense. The faithful need assistance in properly interpreting to themselves their appeals to the Blessed Virgin for her intercession. To say that the invocation of the Blessed Virgin Mary is essential to salvation and that without it a Christian is deprived of salvaton would be a theologically unjustifiable assertion.

The tendency thus is to make the Blessed Virgin's divine motherhood—understood in the broadest sense—and her role as the archetype of the church the basic principle of postconcilar Roman Catholic Mariology. Theologians see this as adhering most closely to the realities of revelation and as emphasizing the Blessed Virgin's rightful place in salvation history. It also provides both the basis and the limits for a constructive veneration of the Mother of God.

NOTES

1. See Ludwig Ott, *Fundamentals of Catholic Dogma,* trans. Patrick Lynch, ed. James Bastible, 6th printing (St. Louis: B. Herder Book Co., 1964), pp. 9-10.

2. *Summa theologica,* pars prima, quaestio 2, articulus 3, in A. M. Fairweather, trans.-ed., *Nature and Grace: Selections from the* Summa theologica *of Thomas Aquinas* (Philadelphia: The Westminster Press, 1954), p. 54.

3. Even where contemporary Roman Catholic theologians are ready to see God as the ground of evolution, they stress that he himself does not evolve but is the basis that makes evolution possible.

4. From various biblical references theologians have concluded that there are nine "choirs" of angels. Six of these—seraphim, cherubim, thrones, dominations, virtues, and powers—stand around the throne of God. Three "choirs"—principalities, archangels, and angels—have as their chief work serving as God's messengers to his human creatures.

5. "Devil" comes from a Greek word meaning "adversary." It is a translation of the Hebrew word that is transliterated as Satan and that also has the meaning of "adversary."

6. Francis de Suarez (1548–1617), following some medieval and patristic teachers, held that every human being has an evil angel assigned to him from birth as well as a good angel. Few modern Roman Catholic theologians have concurred in this view.

7. John C. Kersten, *Bible Catechism* (New York: Catholic Book Publishing Company, 1967), p. 42.

8. Included are the "deuterocanonical" books of Maccabees, Tobit, Judith, Ecclesiasticus (Ben Sira, Sirach), the Wisdom of Solomon, and Baruch, as well as additions to the books of Daniel and Esther, all of which are to be received with a devotion and reverence equal to that accorded to the "protocanonical" books.

9. See Charles W. Paris, *The What and Why of Catholicism,* 3rd printing (New York: Joseph F. Wagner, 1965), p. 3.

10. Among the translations widely used in English-speaking Roman Catholic circles are *The Jerusalem Bible* (Garden City, N.Y.: Doubleday & Company, 1966), ed. Alexander Jones; Roman Catholic edition of the *Revised Standard Version* (identical with the regular edition except for a few minor changes in the text and notes); and *The New American Bible* (Paterson, N.J.: St.

Anthony Guild Press, 1970), trans. members of the Catholic Biblical Association of America and sponsored by the Bishops' Committtee of the Confraternity of Christian Doctrine.

11. See Gregory Baum, "Vatican II and the Reinterpretation of Doctrine," *The Ecumenist: A Journal for Promoting Christian Unity* 9 (1971): 1-4, and the same author's "The Bible as Norm," ibid., pp. 71-77.

12. The opposite of public or general revelation is a private revelation. Among these Roman Catholics would count Christ's reported revelation of his sacred heart to St. Margaret Mary Alacoque (1647–1690) at Paray-le-Monial in France and the reported apparitions of the Blessed Virgin Mary to Juan Diego at Guadelupe, Mexico, in 1531, to a peasant boy and girl at La Salette in the French Alps in 1846, to St. Bernadette Soubirous (1844–1879) at Lourdes in France in 1858, and to Lucia dos Santos (b. 1907) and two of her cousins at Fatima, Portugal, in 1917. (The authorities of the Roman Catholic Church have never revealed the whole "secret of Fatima.") The Roman Catholic Church may approve and even commemorate liturgically, such private revelations as containing nothing that contradicts its official doctrine, but it does not require belief in them as a condition of good standing in the Roman Catholic Church.

13. *Unitatis redintegratio*, 6, in Walter M. Abbott and Joseph Gallagher eds., *The Documents of Vatican II* (New York: Guild Press, 1966), p. 350. The editors observe: "It is remarkable, indeed, for an ecumenical council to admit the doctrinal deficiency of previous doctrinal formulations" (ibid., n. 33).

14. On the whole issue, see Herbert Hammans, "Recent Catholic Views on the Development of Dogma," in Edward Schillebeeckx and Boniface Willems, eds., *Man as Man and Believer (Concilium: Theology in the Age of Renewal,* vol. 21) (New York: Paulist Press, 1967), pp. 109-131.

15. In classic thought there are various kinds of soul (*anima*), the vegetative soul which is the life of the vegetable kingdom, the sensitive or animal (*animalis*) soul of animals, and the rational or spiritual soul of human beings. Sometimes the human soul is schematically thought of as three-tiered, with reason (*ratio*) as the "highest part" of the soul and the sensitive and vegetative components as the lower parts. These were seen as taking over successively in the development of fetal life.

16. The authorities that Roman Catholic theology has invoked have defined this moment variously. The medieval church held that the union of body and soul took place forty days after conception in the case of males, and eighty days after conception in the case of females. Prior to the union the fetus was regarded as unformed and purely animal; afterward it was regarded as formed and a human being. This had some relevance both to the question of abortion and to the question of the immaculate conception of the Blessed Virgin Mary. Modern Roman Catholic theology tends to hold that the union of soul and body takes place at the moment of conception.

17. "Righteousness," the Anglo-Saxon word, conveys the idea of "Moral uprightness" or "virtue" in a general sense. "Justice," the Latin word, conveys the more restricted idea of "concern for fairness and equity." Unlike most other European vernaculars, the English language normally differentiates between "righteousness" and "justice" as translations of the Latin *justitia*. Roman Catholic theological writers, desirous of reproducing the Latin concepts in which Roman Catholic theology has traditionally been formulated, routinely use "justice" to reproduce *justitia*.

18. Two other states—the state of pure nature and the state of unimpaired nature—are wholly theoretical. In a state of pure nature a human being would have everything that belongs to human nature, but nothing more, so that he could attain only the natural (but not the supernatural) end for which God created human beings. In the state of unimpaired nature a human being would have the preternatural gifts of wholeness, so that he could reach his natural final goal certainly and easily. The possibility of a state of pure nature played a considerable role in the controversies involving the Flemish theologian Michael

Baius (1513–1589), and Cornelius Otto Jansen(ius).

19. Roman Catholic theology traditionally saw the suffering that the lost undergo in hell as being, on the one hand, exclusion from the beatific vision of God and, on the other hand, actually felt pain. The trend among Roman Catholic theologians has been more and more to say that children who die unbaptized suffer only exclusion from the beatific vision, a condition that is not incompatible with natural bliss, and that they exist after death in a special borderland (*limbus*), the limbo of children. Indeed, some theologians have gone further and have speculated on the possibility that even unbaptized children may and do achieve the beatific vision of God.

20. In the chapter on "The Original Meaning of Original Sin" (pp. 50-56), Joseph Blenkinsopp, *A Sketchbook of Biblical Theology* (New York: Herder and Herder, 1968), declares that "to reduce the disobedience of the first man as presented in Genesis 3 to an original sin passed on by biological descent to all who came after would not only be far from the intention of the original writers but would also greatly impoverish the message which is here being conveyed to us."

21. Adoration or *latria* is to be distinguished from *dulia* (service), the veneration paid to creatures (like the angels and the saints in light), and *hyperdulia* (greater veneration), which the Mother of God receives. It is regarded as a certain opinion that the various parts of Christ's human nature (for example, his precious blood, his sacred heart, his holy face, and his bleeding head) and by analogy the mysterious events of his human existence (his conception, his nativity, his passion, his death, his resurrection) are entitled on a part-for-all basis to the same adoration that he himself rightfully receives.

22. Roman Catholic theology has been of two minds on the question if Christ would have become a human being if human beings had not sinned. Some follow St. Thomas Aquinas and teach a "conditioned predestination" of the Incarnation. Others follow the view of John Duns Scotus and teach that Christ would have become a human being (although in a body that would not have been capable of suffering) in order to crown the work of creation, even if human beings had not sinned.

23. The idea of a threefold office—rather than the twofold office set forth in the Middle Ages—has some ancient precedents, but it entered Roman Catholic theology from John Calvin and the Reformed community.

24. The fallen angels are not included in the scope of Christ's atoning sacrifice.

25. In 1854 Pius IX called her *mediatrix* ("go-between"); other popes since then have also done so. In 1921 the Feast of the Blessed Virgin Mary Mediatrix of All Graces was introduced into the calendar of the Roman Catholic Church.

26. The Holy Office explicitly ruled in 1916 and again in 1927 that the Blessed Virgin Mary is not entitled to the designation "priest" (*sacerdos*).

27. The Latin Vulgate translated the salutation of the angel at the time of the annunciation, "Hail, favored one," with *Ave, gratia plena* ("Hail, full of grace").

28. The increasing popularity of St. Joseph, Christ's foster-father, among Roman Catholics during the nineteenth and early twentieth centuries reflects two thrusts. One is the effort of the Roman Catholic Church to win back the European proletariat and provide a basis for Roman Catholic labor activities through designating St. Joseph, whom the sacred Scriptures represent as an artisan, as the patron of workers and adding the Feast of St. Joseph the Worker to the calendar of the Roman Catholic Church in 1955. The other thrust reflects an interest in him because of his association with the Blessed Virgin Mary and the child Jesus in the holy family of Nazareth. The Feast of St. Joseph goes back to Gregory XV in 1621. St. Joseph has become the patron of many countries, religious orders, fraternities, and other societies; in 1870 Pius IX named him the patron of the universal church. His name had been added to the litany of all saints in 1729. The month of March and the Wednesday of each week were consecrated to him. John XXIII put his name into the canon of the Mass in 1962. At the extreme edges of the Marian movement the

efforts to assimilate St. Joseph's life to that of the Blessed Virgin Mary have sometimes gone to extremes, with litanies inviting his intercessions and with assertions that, like the Blessed Virgin Mary, he had been immaculately conceived.

29. Some Roman Catholic theologians assert that the bodily virginity of the Blessed Virgin Mary and the virgin birth of Christ have never formally been made dogmas of the Roman Catholic Church and that they are thus open questions. They see the virgin birth as a poetic expression of the unique status of Jesus as God's son. See John C. Kersten, *Bible Catechism: A Meaning for Man's Existence* (New York: Catholic Book Publishing Company, 1967), pp. 63-64. It has also been suggested that in its definition *Munificentissimus Deus* (1950) "might even be said to suggest positively" that "the rest of mankind enjoys even now the same final state of glory in the same way that the Blessed Virgin does" (Donald Flanagan, "Eschatology and the Assumption," in Edward Schillebeeckx and Boniface Willems, eds., *The Problems of Eschatology [Concilium: Theo-*

logy in the Age of Renewal, vol. 41] [New York: Paulist Press, 1969], pp. 135-146; the quotation is from p. 146).

30. The omission of the recitation of the rosary among the helps to priestly spirituality in the Vatican II decree on the life and ministry of priests, *Presbyterorum ordinis,* appears to be significant.

31. Loreto is the Italian town to which the holy house of Nazareth was believed to have flown through the air in 1294.

32. A recent series of apparitions reportedly began to take place in the sky over the Coptic Orthodox Church of St. Mary in Zeitsun, Cairo, Egypt. Roman Catholic Cardinal Istaphanos I is quoted as declaring: "It is no doubt a real appearance confirmed by many Coptic (Roman) Catholic members."

33. After the *Novena Notes* of the Servite Fathers, published to promote novenas to Our Sorrowful Mother, declined from a peak circulation of 600,000 to 50,000, the magazine finally suspended publication. In the preceding five years the number of churches in which novenas to Our Sorrowful Mother were held dropped from 872 to 115.

BIBLIOGRAPHY

ANGELS AND DEMONS

Kelley, Henry A. *The Devil, Demonology and Witchcraft.* Rev. ed. New York: Doubleday, 1974.

Peterson, Erik. *The Angels and the Liturgy: The Status and Significance of the Holy Angels in Worship.* Trans. Ronald Wall. New York: Herder and Herder, 1964.

CHRIST AND MARY

Brown, Raymond E. *Jesus, God and Man: Modern Biblical Reflections.* Milwaukee, Wis.: Bruce Publishing Company, 1967.

Graef, Hilda. *Mary: A History of Doctrine and Devotion.* Vol. II: *From the Reformation to the Present Day.* New York: Sheed and Ward, 1965.

Laurentin, Rene. *The Question of Mary.* Trans. I. G. Pidoux. New York: Holt, Rinehart and Winston, 1965.

Llamera, Boniface. *Saint Joseph.* Trans. Sister Mary Elizabeth. St. Louis, Mo.: B. Herder Book Co., 1962.

Maloney, George A. *The Cosmic Christ from Paul to Teilhard.* New York: Sheed and Ward, 1968.

O'Donovan, Leo J. *Word and Mystery: Biblical Essays on the Person and Mission of Christ.* Glen Rock, N.J.: The Newman Press, 1968.

O'Meara, Thomas A. *Mary in Protestant and Catholic Theology.* New York: Sheed and Ward, 1966.

Schillebeeckx, Edward. *Christ the Sacrament of the Encounter with God.* New York: Sheed and Ward, 1963.

————. *Mary, Mother of the Redemption*. Trans. N. D. Smith. New York: Sheed and Ward, 1964.

Semmelroth, Otto. *Mary, Archetype of the Church*. Trans. Maria von Eroes and John Devlin. New York: Sheed and Ward, 1963.

Vollert, Cyril. *A Theology of Mary*. New York: Herder and Herder, 1965.

HUMAN BEINGS AND SIN

Alfaro, Juan, and others. *Man before God: Toward a Theology of Man—Readings in Theology Compiled at the Canisianum, Innsbruck*. New York: P. J. Kenedy and Son, 1966.

De Fraine, Jean. *The Bible and the Origin of Man*. New York: Desclee Company, 1962.

Dubarle, Andre-Marie. *The Biblical Doctrine of Original Sin*. Trans. E. M. Stewart: New York: Herder and Herder, 1964.

Gelin, Albert. *The Concept of Man in the Bible*. Trans. David M. Murphy. Staten Island, N.Y.: Alba House, 1968.

————. and Descamps, Albert. *Sin in the Bible*. Trans. Charles Schaldenbrand. New York: Desclee Company, 1965.

Haag, Herbert. *Is Original Sin in Scripture?* Trans. Dorothy Thompson. New York: Sheed and Ward, 1969.

Koszarek, (Sister) Clare. *The Catechesis of Original Sin*. Collegeville, Minn.: St. John's University Press, 1969.

Oraison, Marc, and others. *Sin*. Trans. Bernard Murchland and Raymond Meyerpeter. New York: The Macmillan Company, 1962. See especially Gustav Siewerth's chapter, "The Doctrine of Original Sin" (pp. 111-177).

Rahner, Karl. *Hominisation: The Evolutionary Origin of Man as a Theological Problem*. New York: Herder and Herder, 1965.

Ryan, Bernard. *The Evolution of Man: Some Theological, Philosophical, and Scientific Considerations*. Westminster, Md.: The Newman Press, 1965.

Schoonenberg, Piet. *Man and Sin: A Theological View*. Trans. Joseph Donceel. Notre Dame, Ind.: University of Notre Dame Press, 1965.

Trooster, Stephanus. *Evolution and the Doctrine of Original Sin*. Trans. John A. Ter Haar. Glen Rock, N.J.: The Newman Press, 1968.

Vandervelde, G. *Original Sin: Two Major Trends in Contemporary Roman Catholic Reinterpretation*. Amsterdam: Rodopi, 1975.

REVELATION AND DOGMA

Bauer, Johannes B., ed. *Sacramentum Verbi: An Encyclopedia of Biblical Theology*. 3 vols. New York: Herder and Herder, 1970.

Benoit, Pierre; Murphy, Roland E.; and van Iersel, Bastiaan; eds. *The Human Reality of Sacred Scripture (Concilium: Theology in the Age of Renewal*, vol. 10). New York: Paulist Press, 1965.

Bremer, Günter. *Newman on Tradition*. New York: Herder and Herder, 1967.

Burtchaell, James Tunstead. *Catholic Theories of Biblical Inspiration, 1810 to the Present: A Review-Critique*. New York: Cambridge University Press, 1969.

Chadwick, Owen. *From Bossuet to Newman: The Idea of Doctrinal Development*. New York: Cambridge University Press, 1957.

Congar, Yves M.-J. *Tradition and Traditions: An Historical and a Theological Essay*. Trans. Michael Naseby and Thomas Rainborough. New York: The Macmillan Company, 1967.

Evely, Louis. *The Gospels without Myth*. Garden City, N.Y.: Doubleday & Company, 1971.

Geiselmann, Josef Rupert. *The Meaning of Tradition*. New York: Herder and Herder, 1966.

Latourelle, René. *Theology of Revelation, Including a Commentary on the Constitution, Dei verbum of Vatican II*. Staten Island, N.Y.: Alba House, 1966.

Loretz, Oswald. *The Truth of the Bible*. New York: Herder and Herder, 1968.

Meredith, Anthony. *The Theology of Tradition*. Notre Dame, Ind.: Fides Publishers, 1970.

Monden, Louis. *Faith: Can Man Still Believe?* Trans. Joseph Donceel. New York: Sheed and Ward, 1970.

Moran, Gabriel. *Theology of Revelation*.

New York: Herder and Herder, 1966.

Rahner, Karl. *Inspiration in the Bible.* Trans. Charles H. Henkey. New York: Herder and Herder, 1961.

Schökel, Luis Alonso. *The Inspired Word: Scripture in the Light of Language and Literature.* Trans. Francis Martin. New York: Herder and Herder, 1966.

Scullion, John. *The Theology of Inspiration.* Notre Dame, Ind.: Fides Publishers, 1970.

Walgrave, Jan Hendrik. *Unfolding Revelation: The Nature of Doctrinal Development.* Washington, D.C.: Corpus Books, 1970.

ROMAN CATHOLIC THEOLOGY TODAY

Baum, Gregory. *Faith and Doctrine: A Contemporary View.* Paramus, N.J.: The Newman Press, 1969.

————. *Man Becoming: God in Secular Experience.* New York: Herder and Herder, 1970. See in connection with this work the exchange of views between William S. Morris and Baum, "Controversy on the God Problem," *The Ecumenist: A Source for Promoting Christian Unity* 9 (1971): 11-22.

————, ed. *The Future of Belief Debate.* New York: Herder and Herder, 1967. A reader's companion to the controversy evoked by Leslie Dewart's *The Future of Belief* (see below).

Bouyer, Louis. *Dictionary of Theology.* Trans. Charles Underhill Quinn. New York: Desclee Co., 1965.

Brown, Raymond E. *Biblical Reflections on Crises Facing the Church.* Glen Rock, N.J.: Paulist Press, 1975.

Burghardt, Walter J., and Lynch, William F., eds. *The Idea of Catholicism: An Introduction to the Thought and Worship of the Church.* New York: The World Publishing Company, 1964.

Campbell, Robert, ed. *Spectrum of Catholic Attitudes.* Milwaukee, Wis.: Bruce Publishing Company, 1969.

Concilium: Theology in an Age of Renewal. Glen Rock, N.J.: Paulist Press, 1965—This cross between a theological journal and a series of topical monographs was created to provide Roman Catholic priests after Vatican II with a convenient means of updating their theology. Publication continues with the release of about five volumes annually.

Connolly, James M. *The Voices of France: A Survey of Contemporary Theology in France.* New York: The Macmillan Company, 1961.

Cooney, Cyprian. *Understanding the New Theology.* Milwaukee, Wis.: The Bruce Publishing Company, 1969.

Dewan, Wilfrid F. *Catholic Belief and Practice in an Ecumenical Age.* Glen Rock, N.J.: Paulist Press, 1966.

Dewart, Leslie. *The Foundation of Belief.* New York: Herder and Herder, 1969.

————. *The Future of Belief: Theism in a World Come of Age.* New York: Herder and Herder, 1966.

————. *Religion, Language, and Belief.* New York: Herder and Herder, 1970.

Dolan, John P. *Catholicism: An Historical Survey.* Woodbury, N.Y.: Barron's Educational Series, 1968.

Domenach, Jean-Marie, and de Montvalon, Robert. *The Catholic Avant-Garde: French Catholicism since World War II.* Trans. Brigid Elson, Jacqueline Pace, Irene Uribe, and Frances Wilms. New York: Holt, Rinehart and Winston, 1967.

Dulles, Avery. *Revelation Theology: A History.* New York: Herder and Herder, 1969.

Gelpi, Donald L. *Life and Light: A Guide to the Theology of Karl Rahner.* New York: Sheed and Ward, 1966.

Hellwig, Monika. *What Are the Theologians Saying?* Dayton, Ohio: Pflaum Press, 1970. A theologian's capsuled restatement of the views of some of the most influential contemporary Roman Catholic theologians.

Jossua, Jean-Pierre. *Yves Congar: Theology in the Service of God's People.* Chicago: Priory Press, 1968.

Kersten, John C. *Bible Catechism: A Meaning for Man's Existence.* New York: Catholic Book Publishing Company, 1967. This catechism enjoys wide use as supplementary reading in connection with the instruction of adults.

Kessler, Marvin, and Brown, Bernard, eds. *Dimensions of the Future: The Spirituality of Teilhard de Chardin.* Washington, D.C.: Corpus Books, 1968.

Longergan, Bernard J. F. *Insight: A Study of Human Understanding.* New York: Philosophical Library, 1970.

Lubac, Henri de. *The Mystery of the Supernatural*. Trans. Rosemary Sheed. New York: Herder and Herder, 1967. Many observers regarded the first edition of this work as the target of Pius XII in his encyclical *Humani generis* (1952).

Maritain, Jacques. *The Peasant of the Garonne: A Catholic Philosopher Speaks His Mind on Present Dangers to the Church*. Trans. Michael Cuddihy and Elizabeth Hughes. New York: Holt, Rinehart, and Winston, 1968. A French Roman Catholic revered thinker speaks for thoughtful traditionalists as he sharply attacks the "new theology" that in his view is jeopardizing the inherited spirituality of the Roman Catholic Church.

McDermott, Timothy S. *Beyond Questions and Answers: The Creed for Today's Catholic*. New York: Herder and Herder, 1968.

McDonald, William J., ed. *The New Catholic Encyclopedia*. 15 vols. New York: McGraw-Hill Book Co., 1967. An indispensable resource for those seeking information about the contemporary Roman Catholic Church.

McKenzie, John L. *The Roman Catholic Church*. New York: Herder and Herder, 1969.

A New Catechism: Catholic Faith for Adults. Trans. Kevin Smyth. New York: Herder and Herder, 1967. The famed "Dutch Catechism."

O'Brien, Elmer, ed. *Theology in Transition: A Bibliographical Evaluation of the "Decisive Decade," 1954–1964*. New York: Herder and Herder, 1965.

Ott, Ludwig. *Fundamentals of Catholic Dogma*. Ed. James Bastible. Trans. Patrick Lynch. 6th edition. St. Louis: B. Herder Book Co., 1964. This work is an internationally respected compendium of Roman Catholic theology prior to Vatican II. The present writer has made extensive use of its formulations in his effort to present the theological views commonly held by Roman Catholics during the second quarter of this century.

Paris, Charles W. *The What and Why of Catholicism*. 3rd printing. New York: Joseph F. Wagner, 1965. A statement of the traditional Roman Catholic position designed for use in the instruction of adult candidates for Roman Catholic Church membership.

Rahner, Karl. *Theological Investigations*. Baltimore: The Helicon Press, 1961—. Five volumes have appeared to date.

———, and others, eds. *Sacramentum Mundi: An Encyclopedia of Theology*. 6 vols. New York: Herder and Herder, 1968–1970. The present writer has made wide use of this internationally influential reference work in outlining the post-Vatican-II position of the Roman Catholic Church on theological issues.

———, and Vorgrimler, Herbert. *Theological Dictionary*. Trans. Richard Strachan. Ed. Cornelius Ernst. New York: Herder and Herder, 1965.

Raven, Charles Erle. *Teilhard de Chardin, Scientist and Seer*. New York: Harper & Row, 1962.

Roberts, Louis. *The Achievement of Karl Rahner*. New York; Herder and Herder, 1967.

Schillebeeckx, Edward. *Revelation and Theology: Theological Soundings*. Trans. N. D. Smith. 2 vols. New York: Sheed and Ward, 1967–1968.

Schmaus, Michael. *Dogma*. New York: Sheed and Ward, 1968—. One of the "standard" dogmaticians of twentieth-century German-speaking Roman Catholicism undertook to prepare this dogmatics from scratch for English-speaking Roman Catholics. Three volumes have appeared to date, *God in Revelation; God in Creation;* and *God and His Christ*.

Schoof, T. Mark. *A Survey of Catholic Theology 1800–1970*. New York: The Newman Press, 1970.

Teilhard de Chardin, Pierre. *The Future of Man*. Trans. Norman Denny. New York: Harper & Row, 1964.

———. *The Phenomenon of Man*. Trans. Bernard Wall. New York: Harper & Brothers, 1959.

———. *Science and Christ*. New York: Harper & Row, 1968.

Tracy, David. *The Achievement of Bernard Lonergan*. New York: Herder and Herder, 1970.

Wilhelm, Anthony J. *Christ among Us: A Modern Presentation of the Catholic Faith*. New York: The Newman Press, 1967. A modern description of Roman Catholic theology for adult instruction.

13. Nature and Function of the Church

The Church

Traditionally, Roman Catholic theology has stressed the visibility of the church and has identified the Roman Catholic Church with the one holy catholic and apostolic church of the Creed of the 150 Fathers (Nicene Creed). The Roman Catholic Church, its theologians have declared, is the only community that possesses all four qualities, at least in the preeminent sense that the creed was seen as demanding.

In this view the church—to be understood as the Roman Catholic Church, built by Christ upon the rock that is Peter the Apostle—is unique and one, one in faith and one in communion. The primacy of the pope as the "center of unity" guarantees the unity of the church.

Similarly, the church is holy—in its sacraments, in its inviolate faith, in its holy laws, and in the celestial gifts that enable the church to bring forth so many authentically holy individuals. But this affirmation of the church's holiness is not intended to preclude the presence among its members of persons who are sinners in various degrees, even persons in mortal sin, as long as they are not schismatics, heretics, or apostates.

The church is also catholic. At any given moment in history the church's catholicity is "moral," that is, it extends simultaneously over the whole earth, but it has as its objective "physical" catholicity.

Finally, the church is apostolic—in its origin, in its teaching, and in the succession in office of its bishops and particularly of the occupants of the see of Rome.

In this understanding of the church, membership in the church is necessary for salvation. Such membership, normally at least, depends on being validly baptized, on professing the true faith, and on participating in the communion of the church. For that reason unbaptized persons, open apostates and heretics, schismatics, and those excommunicates that are classified as *vitandi* (that is, "persons to be shunned [even in nonreligious contexts]") are not to be regarded as members of the church.

Since the Council of Trent Roman Catholic theology has also affirmed that the church is both visible and invisible. Its visible side, as classically defined, embraces the priesthood (including those that possess the fullness of the priesthood, the bishops), the papacy, and the eucharistic sacrifice. Equally obvious to the senses are the sacramental means of grace, the common profession of the same faith, and the overt subordination to the same authority. But the church has an invisible side as well—the operations of the Holy Spirit, the gifts of salvation, and the truth and the grace that the church imparts.

Contemporary Roman Catholic thinking about the church does not contradict any of this. But it exhibits new emphases. It reveals a continuing concern for the dimension of community as a part of the life of Christians. It stresses the indefectibility of the Christian community in its decisive commitments. Its interest in churchly order focuses on specific offices within the church's structure—concretely, on the papacy, on the college of bishops, and on the priesthood.

Where the church was once seen as a limited and exclusive body, a battlemented fortress designed to enclose its members and to keep out the threatening world, modern Roman Catholic theologians see the church as a community that is to be found wherever the Holy Spirit is at work. This community is not of the world and dare not conform itself to the world, but it is willing to listen and to speak to the world and to show itself to the world as a, company of human beings who are seeking to be faithful to the gospel.

This shift in emphasis takes its starting point from the Vatican II constitution on the church (*Lumen gentium*). In a sense the constitution is an elaboration of the principle that God wills the salvation of all human beings and the restoration of everything in Christ. In giving graces to all human beings in a degree sufficient for their salvation, he actually brings about salvation among all human beings of all times.

"The divine design of salvation embraces all men," Paul VI declared in "The *Credo* of the People of God" in 1968. "Those who without fault on their part do not know the Gospel of Christ and his church, but seek God sincerely and under the influence of grace endeavor to do his will as recognized through the promptings of their conscience, [can,] in a number known only to God, . . . obtain salvation."[1]

While insisting that the church is necessary to salvation, contemporary Roman Catholic doctrine makes very clear that official Roman Catholic Church teaching does not assert that there is no salvation outside the Roman Catholic Church or that the salvation of non-Roman-Catholics is something unusual.

Viewed from another aspect, the church is the community of the redeemed. Christ founded it and it has its origin in his death and resurrection. It is his mystical body and bride.

On the first Pentecost, Christ sent the Holy Spirit to his disciples as he had promised. The Holy Spirit, or the Paraclete (from the Greek *paraklêtos*, "advocate, helper"), is present in a special way in the church, enlightens it, gives it life, protects it, guides it, and purifies its members by enabling them to respond to Christ's call to perfection. The Spirit empowers Christians to share the life of God himself, joins them to the Father and Christ in a union that death cannot destroy, gives them hope and courage, counteracts their spiritual weakness, and gives them the power to master their native passion and selfishness.

The church is also the institution that antedates every Christian and that God uses to bring Christians into existence. It is the sacrament (in the sense of sign and instrument) of intimate union with God and of the unity of the whole human race. It is the germ and the first fruits of the kingly rule of Christ, although that kingly rule is now present only in a mystery and must look for its fulfillment beyond the present age.

The church on earth is the new people of God of the present age, but filled with the blessings of the age to come. It is a visible and hierarchically organized society, but it is also a spiritual community, whose only life is the life of Christ and of grace.

It is consciously the heir of the divine promises that God gave to the patriarchs and the prophets of the Old Covenant. Assisted by the Holy Spirit, it has the responsibility of watching over, teaching, explaining, and spreading the truth that it has received from Christ and the apostles.

The variety of liturgical rites manifests rather than injures its unity. So does the legitimate diversity of theology, spirituality, and piety that exists within it. Because the church on earth is a society of sinful human beings, it is constantly in need of purification and renewal, but it looks with confidence to the Holy Spirit to purify and to renew both the church and its members.

Bishops, Cardinals, and Priests

The bishops of the Roman Catholic Church stand in the apostolic succession, that is, they profess to be able to trace their line of episcopal succession through an unbroken chain of episcopally consecrated bishops to the apostles themselves. Unlike the Eastern Orthodox Church (and most Eastern churches), which require at least three episcopal consecrators for a valid consecration, Roman Catholic canon law is content with a single episcopal consecrator.

By divine right, Roman Catholic theology teaches, a bishop possesses the power appropriate to the episcopal office ("ordinary power") in the government of his see or diocese.[2] This power includes the power to legislate within the scope of the bishop's authority, the power to judge, and the power to punish. Although the bishops are neither the delegated agents nor the vicars (that is, representatives) of the pope, each individual bishop receives his pastoral power immediately from the pope. A person in bishop's orders may be placed over some other comparable jurisdiction besides a diocese, such as a vicariate apostolic, as a kind of papal representative in a missionary territory.

In theory there is only one bishop in a diocese, on the principle that the bishop is analogously in Christ's stead the husband of the church, Christ's bride, in the diocese. When the duties of his office become too burdensome for a diocesan bishop, he may be given a bishop coadjutor or an auxiliary bishop. (The former has the right of succession when the see becomes vacant, the latter does not.) Such a bishop is consecrated as the titular bishop of a see that has been suppressed or abandoned because of the decline or extinction of its Christian (or Roman Catholic) population.[3]

A number of contiguous dioceses are normally combined into a province under a metropolitan who bears the title of archbishop. The see over which the archbishop presides is called an archdiocese. The bishops of the other sees in the province are called suffragans. The symbol of the archbishop's dignity is the pallium, a circular band of white wool two inches wide ornamented with crosses and with a pendant front and rear; the archbishop receives it directly from the pope. An archbishop does not have greater spiritual power than a simple bishop (except that he may grant an indulgence of 100 days, while a simple bishop is limited to fifty days), but canon law gives him certain limited juridical and administrative authority within his province.

According to current canon law, a cardinal is a priest or bishop whom the pope has named to the Sacred College of Cardinals. Theoretically they are the bishops, priests, and deacons of Rome, and as such they are the papal electors (unless they are disqualified by advanced age).[4] Each cardinal has a title, that is, he is assigned to one of the "suburbicarian" sees of Rome as a cardinal-bishop or to one of the Roman parish churches as a cardinal-priest or a cardinal-deacon. His title has nothing to do with his actual rank in the church; thus an archbishop in the United States could be a cardinal-priest of some Roman parish.

The cardinals are permanent advisers to the pope and are assigned to one or more Roman congregations. Unless they are foreign bishops, they are expected to reside in Rome. Their number is determined by the pope.

Cardinals have no spiritual powers beyond those of the order to which they have been ordained, but they have a great many other privileges. Thus they take precedence over all bishops, rank as "princes of the church" with princes of such reigning royal houses as still survive, and can be judged by no court except the pope. The red hat that was formerly given to them when they became cardinals as a badge of their office and their red robes are explained as reminders of the possibility of martyrdom. The cardinalatial dignity is associated by custom with certain important sees; but the pope may grant it to incumbents of other sees without obligating himself or his successors to confer the dignity on such incumbents' successors in office.

Domestic prelates of the papal household and prothonotaries apostolic are conventionally called "monsignors" in the United States. The titles are honorary distinctions borne by officials in the diocesan chancellery or by parish clergy who have distinguished themselves by their service. The status of domestic prelates is indicated by their right to use a bishop's purple on certain items of clothing. Prothonotaries apostolic[5] have the privilege of wearing certain episcopal vestments and ornaments in connection with liturgical functions.

Each diocese is divided into parishes, that is, defined territorial districts with a church and a congregation of which a priest is the pastor. While dioceses are seen as divisions that exist by divine right, parishes are administrative divisions that exist by human right only. The pastor functions in the parish as the bishop's delegate. If the parish is large, the pastor will have one or more assistant priests. Normally the parish clergy are secular priests, that is, they do not belong to a religious order or to some other religious institute. Nevertheless, parishes staffed—by the religious superior concerned at the pleasure of the bishop of the see—with religious priests are not uncommon in North America.

Strictly, a Roman Catholic is still bound to the parish in which he resides, but the once rigid rule has long since been extensively relaxed. It is regarded as desirable—although not obligatory—for a Roman Catholic to make at least his Easter Communion in his parish church. The permission of the parish priest or of the bishop must be secured if baptism is to be administered or a marriage is to be solemnized in another parish.[6]

A number of parishes may be combined into a (rural) deanery, presided over by a vicar forane, who has limited responsibilities of oversight over the discipline of the clergy in the deanery.[7]

Vatican Council II gave currency to the term "collegiality" to describe the relation of the bishops among themselves as the corporate successors of the apostles (minus Peter) and the relation between the bishop of Rome, seen as Peter's successor, and the college of bishops. Subsequently the term acquired an expanded significance. It designated the willingness of the pope to share some of his decision-making authority with his fellow bishops, and the willingness of bishops to share some of their decision-making authority with the priests and the laypeople of their dioceses. A practical result of the principle of collegiality was the establishment of regularly convened Synod of Bishops at Rome, with the members of the synod delegated by their respective national episcopal conferences. At the diocesan level priests' councils, lay councils, and other parallel organs resulted from the application of the collegial principle.

A highly sensitive area has been the procedure for appointing bishops (and of electing popes). Dissatisfaction voiced with past procedures led to the increasingly common demands for "co-responsibility,"[8] notably after the publication of the volume *Coresponsibility in the Church* by the primate of Belgium, Leon Joseph Cardinal Suenens. With reference to the selection of bishops, Roman Catholic historians and canonists observed that after the twelfth century bishops in the West were no longer chosen by a process that adequately reflected the old canonical rule "he who governs all should be chosen by all' or the will and the consent of the Christian people of the diocese. Typical was the assertion of the consensus statement drawn up at "A Symposium on Co-Responsibility in the Church" that the Canon Law Society and Fordham University sponsored at Cathedral College, New York, in the spring of 1970, that "co-responsibility in the church has a solid theological foundation in the call to all baptized persons to become not slaves or children but free men in Christ. . . . All who share the life of the Spirit through grace must necessarily have an active concern for the good of the church in which they live out their Christian existence."[9] The symposium further urged that "the principle of co-responsibility, the dignity and freedom of persons, the rights of Christians, and the long-standing tradition of church order all demand the meaningful participation of the whole community in the selection of its leaders and the formulation of laws affecting its life." It recommended "a return to the ecclesiastical practice of the election of bishops by the clergy and laity" and called for "future legislation in the church, universal and local, [to] be enacted only in synods and councils with the participation of clergy and laity."[10]

Roman Catholic theologians recognize that the New Testament does not provide a blueprint for the church's constitutional organization. The constants that were present in every period then and since, according to Roman Catholic theologians, were the people of God, the hierarchy, and Christ with his Spirit. The concrete structural forms that exist in time and in geography are inevitably related to the existing patterns of human culture; some theologians see this as an important aspect of the fundamental sacramentality of the church. In the process of taking over secular institutions as models for its own structure, the church always transformed them. Accordingly, no one pattern can claim to be the only one with which and within which the church can exist.

The Communion of Saints

The mystical body of Christ is the whole company of those whom divine grace has hallowed and redeemed—in heaven, on earth, and in the intermediate state, commonly called purgatory. Roman Catholics see the phrase "the communion of saints"[11] in the so-called Apostles' Creed as summarizing the truth that in this mystical body the saints in heaven, who are more closely united with God, intercede for his pilgrim people on earth and by the heroic example of their lives establish the faithful on earth more firmly in holiness. A similar concern on the part of the saints in heaven extends to the faithful departed in the intermediate estate.

In their turn the faithful on earth can pray for one another, obtain graces for one another, and by means of their good works render vicarious atonement for one another. They can profitably ask for the intercessions of the saints in heaven and venerate the relics and images of the saints as well as the saints themselves. The faithful on earth can also cultivate piously the memory of the faithful departed in the intermediate state, remember them in prayer "that they may be loosed from their sins,"[12] assist them by their good works and their Masses, and obtain indulgences on their behalf.

The designation "saints" in this context reproduces the Greek word *hagioi* ("holy persons"). The New Testament applies this adjective to living members of the Christian community generally. The Roman Catholic Church perpetuated the practice that had gradually grown up in the church of using the term "saint" to describe an individual who had given his life for the faith or who had exhibited Christian courage and constancy in an unusually heroic degree.

The necessity of securing papal approval for the public veneration of a saint was normally insisted upon. In 1558 Sixtus V made the Congregation of Rites responsible for preparing papal canonizations, that is, of enrolling persons in the official Roman Catholic list of saints. The present Roman Catholic process of canonization goes back to Urban VIII in 1642 and to Benedict XIV in the mid-eighteenth century.

There are two stages in this procedure. The first is the candidate's beatification, that is, the pope's declaration that the candidate is "blessed" (*beatus*). The bishop of the place where the candidate died or where he or she lived for a long time initiates the process with an examination into the life, the virtues, the writings, and the reputation for holiness—or the martyrdom—of the candidate. Normally this inquiry will have been preceded by a period in which the candidate received private veneration by individuals who believed in their own hearts that the candidate was already enjoying the beatific vision. If the candidate was not a martyr, the process of beatification requires evidence that God performed at least two incontestable miracles at the candidate's intercession.

If the local inquiry indicates that the candidate is indeed worthy of beatification, the Congregation for the Causes of the Saints[13] in Rome takes up the case and subjects the candidate's life, writings, and alleged miraculous intercession to careful examination. In the course of this "apostolic process" the pope may affirm in a solemn decree that the candidate is entitled to the designation "venerable," although this does not authorize the candidate's public veneration. Public veneration requires the pope's brief declaring the candidate "blessed." Normally the candidate may then be venerated only in a particular country, diocese, or order. If the Congregation for the Causes of the Saints is persuaded, after three discussions of the evidence, that the candidate's intercession brought about two additional miracles[14] after beatification, the pope decrees the candidate's canonization in a colorful public ceremony in St. Peter's Church, Rome. The new saint not only may but must thereafter receive public veneration. A day is appointed for the saint's feast. An office is composed for it. The relics are venerated publicly. Churches and altars may be dedicated in the saint's honor. Statues and pictures may be erected in churches. The saint may be publicly invoked.

It is commonly held that the pope is not infallible when he beatifies a candidate, but that he is infallible when he canonizes a saint.[15]

It is conceded that many saints have never been canonized. The uncanonized saints are remembered on All Saints' Day (November 1). If an individual Roman Catholic is persuaded in his own heart that a departed Christian has entered the enjoyment of the beatific vision he may with good conscience invoke that person. A case in point might be a child who is persuaded that his father or mother had died in a state of grace and had entered upon the beatific vision; he could with a good conscience, although obviously without the assurance that canonization provides, privately invoke the intercessions of the departed parent.

The careful study of the lives of the saints has engaged many generations of Roman Catholics, especially since the Bollandists—so named from John van Bolland (1596–1665), the founder and first editor of the *Acta sanctorum* ("Lives of the Saints")—began their work.[16] As a result, the lives of many saints have been placed on a sounder historical basis. At the same time, the acts attributed to some saints have come to appear historically dubious and the very historicity of some saints has been called into question. A number of these have been struck from the roster of saints in recent years.[17]

Vatican II discussed the veneration of the saints in chapter 7 of *Lumen gentium*, "The Eschatological Nature of the Pilgrim Church and its Unity with the Heavenly Church." In God's irrevocable act of conferring his salvation on the world, the council declared, the church on earth already experiences genuine eschatological sanctity; this is also true of the church expectant in purgatory and the church triumphant enjoying the beatific vision. Thus the church is acknowleging itself when it acknowledges the saints whom it is able to identify by name. By venerating the saints the church calls upon its living members to exhibit courage and constancy in the face of temptation, confusion, the ambiguities of life, sin, and the allurements of the world. In turn the saints have not lost their effectiveness in God's sight by dying; they are one in the communion of saints with the church that is still on the way.

At the same time Roman Catholic theologians recognize that this is not an age in which either saints or sainthood are as popular as they once were. The misgivings about the veneration of the saints that the reformers voiced in the sixteenth century have penetrated deep into the Roman Catholic community. A satisfactory contemporary answer to the question how a human being can attain to God himself through these created mediators, it is argued, demands the development of a deeper appreciation of the fact that the Christian's love of God is inseparable from his love of his fellow human beings. It likewise demands a fuller recognition of the permanent place that the humanity of Christ has in the order of salvation.

Religious Freedom

Classically Roman Catholic theology defined religious freedom as the inalienable right of all men to worship God according to the teaching of the Roman Catholic Church. It was held that no secular government could justifiably interfere with the exercise of this right. On the contrary every government has the duty to promote the true worship of God. God's sovereignty demands that human beings acknowledge it through worship. Christ established only one church, to which all human beings are obliged to subject themselves; thereby he established one single public worship. A secular government can tolerate false religions only to avoid a greater evil or to achieve a higher good, as long as these religions do not teach open immorality.[18]

For Gregory XVI, who condemned the freedom of conscience in 1832 in his encyclical *Mirari vos arbitramur*, and for Pius IX, who condemned the freedom of religion in the *Syllabus of Errors* in 1864, recognition of religious freedom seemed inseparable from indifferentism, naturalism, and "liberalism." As late as 1953, Pius XII in an allocution on tolerance condemned religious freedom on the grounds that truth had primacy over freedom and that truth possessed rights, but error did not.

The shift to the view that religious freedom is a fundamental right of human beings as persons and of religious groups as such came officially in 1965 at the end of the fourth session of Vatican II. Religious freedom is now seen as the right of every person to decide freely for or against religion, to voice his views on matters of religion without interference, and to make a public confession of his views by acts of worship, by mounting educational efforts, and by propagandizing on behalf of his convictions.

Although the Declaration on Religious Freedom (*Dignitatis humanae*) recognizes that objectively human beings have an obligation to try to find the true religion, it insists that human beings also have a right to "immunity from coercion in civil society." It grounds this right in the social nature of man. It warns that freedom and honesty are the criteria by which all efforts at spreading religion are to be judged. It affirms the rights of religious bodies to order their own inner structure, to select their own officials, to own property, to engage in public worship, and to carry on educational, cultural, and charitable activities. It asserts the right of parents to determine according to their own religious beliefs what kind of education their children are to receive.

At the same time the document is not an endorsement of a religiously pluralistic society as either an ideal or a goal. It does not imply a philosophy of religious indifferentism. It is a recognition that the indivdual human being's act of faith is the product of a free internal choice and cannot be coerced. It is a disavowal of the Roman Catholic Church's desire that anyone be brought against his will to embrace the Roman Catholic faith.

But there still remains a tension between the individual's conviction that freedom of conscience is good and his obligation to assent to revealed truth, between the duty of society to safeguard the rights of individual human beings and its obligation to honor God according to the dictates of revealed religion.

Religious Education and Catechetics

The Roman Catholic Church in the West since Trent has depended on religious education for transmitting its faith to the next generation. This education ideally takes place at all the available graduated levels from the home through the university. For four centuries schools and catechisms were its indispensable primary tools and instruments.

Since the beginning of Vatican II the changes in Roman Catholic theology, the increasing difficulty of maintaining separate Roman Catholic schools at each level, the decline in the number of religious available for the task of teaching and the need of training laypeople to replace them, the growing number of Roman Catholic children attending public and private schools beyond their church's effective reach, the mobility of the ever more mobile urbanized population, and the revolution in religious education have combined to produce an almost totally new situation.

This new situation has been marked by a wholesale abandonment of old techniques and tools. It has also seen the emergence of a doctrine of religious education that seeks the discovery of truth in human encounter and that tries to do more than inculcate academic knowledge about the Roman Catholic faith in prefabricated answers to prefabricated questions. Editors and publishers have incorporated these new insights with varying degrees of boldness and success into scores of series of catechetical and religious education programs and have drawn liberally on modern audio-visual technology in the hope of facilitating learning. In the necessary process of reeducating the teachers to perform successfully in their new role, the new catechetics has affected not only religious education, but also preaching, liturgics, and even the theological enterprise itself.[19]

The Religious

Distinct from other members of the Roman Catholic Church are the "religious."[20]

A religious is a person, lay or cleric, male or female, who is a member of a religious institute. A religious institute in turn is defined as a society of men or women approved by ecclesiastical authority. The members of such a society take public vows, according to the principles of their association, for the purpose of attaining the perfection to which Christ calls his followers in the gospel. The vows may be perpetual or temporary, but in the latter case they are to be renewed upon expiration. There are various kinds of religious institutes. Some are called orders, in which the members take solemn vows, that is, vows which make contrary acts not only illicit but invalid. Examples of orders are Canons Regular of St. Augustine, the Order of Friars Minor, the Order of Preachers, the Order of St. Benedict, and the Society of Jesus.[21] Other institutes are called congregations. In these the members take only simple vows, that is, vows which normally render a contrary act illicit but not invalid. Examples of congregations are the Congregation of Barefooted Clerks of the Most Holy Cross and Passion of Our Lord Jesus Christ (Passionists), the Society of Mary (Marists), and the Congregation of the Most Holy Redeemer (Redemptorists).[22] The vows of religion are obedience, chastity (celibacy), and poverty.[23] Some religious institutes add a fourth vow for some special purpose.

In 1947 Pius XII gave canonical recognition to a new type of religious life, the secular institute. The members of these societies are not strictly obligated to a form of common life, and the chief emphasis lies on the independent and in large part separated following of the evangelical counsels. In some cases they form small communities, in which each member has his or her own secular occupation. While the older religious institutes have suffered generally from a decline in vocations, the secular institutes with their relative freedom have succeeded in attracting increasing numbers of participants.

The number of religious institutes is very large and the variety of rules, purposes, and degrees of discipline is comparably great. Some religious institutes are primarily contemplative in character; the members occupy themselves primarily in prayer, adoration, and intercession. Others are primarily active and engage in such activities as operating schools of different kinds, engaging in domestic and foreign missons, caring for the sick and the handicapped, conducting parish missions, and publishing and disseminating literature.[24]

In the Decree on the Appropriate Renewal of the Religious Life (*Perfectae caritatis*), Vatican II called for a renewed commitment on the part of religious to the following of Christ and to the spirit of the founder as the rule and the mission of each order and congregation attests that spirit. This document must be read against the demand of *Lumen gentium* that everyone in the church is called to holiness in his respective state of life.

Contemporary Roman Catholic theology reflects the awareness that the religious is not automatically superior to the Christian in the world, but that the religious man or woman at his or her best is an eschatological sign inviting every Christian to the more dedicated discharge of the obligations of his own calling and state of life. The primary vocation of the religious is thus not to ensure his or her own salvation but by prayer and/or the particular apostolate of the religious order to serve the whole people of God in the fulfillment of its divinely given mission.

One of the most obvious recent changes in Roman Catholic religious life in North America has been the wholesale abandonment by religious women of the traditional garb that so long identified them. The changed appearance is simply an external sign of a widespread—sometimes sweeping and daring— accommodation to the spirit of the times on the part of religious themselves.

It has always been easier for nuns and sisters to be dispensed from their vows than for priests, and the recent past has seen within the Roman Catholic Church a relaxation of the pressures of society and family that tended to keep a female religious in her order or congregation, whether or not she found satisfaction in her religious state.

The 1960s saw both a sharp decline in the number of postulants and novices and a significant acceleration of the exodus of both lay brothers and female religious from their orders and congregations. The reasons given for these withdrawals are many. Some of the most often cited are: fearful superiors who are reluctant to make any real changes; a desire for deliverance from a style of life in which the religious of both sexes are treated as if they were immature children; the "infinite codification" that regulates almost every aspect of existence and all but eliminates individual spontaneity; changes in theological emphasis within the church that raise questions about the very reason for existence of some religious institutes;[25] impatience with the slow progress of renewal and the feeling that it often does not go beyond a superficial revision of outmoded forms that demand total abolition; and un- resolved basic questions about the purpose, size, and lifestyle of the commu- nity in the twentieth century. But withdrawal from a particular religious insti- tute has not invariably meant a renunciation of the religious ideal.[26]

The Priesthood of the Faithful

In the sixteenth century some of the reformers insisted upon the universal or common priesthood of the faithful in such a way that they seemed to deny the divine institution of what is called by contrast the "official priesthood" or the "ministerial priesthood." This led to a strong Roman Catholic reaction against the doctrine of the universal priesthood of the faithful that persisted for centuries. But in recent years—and especially since the publication of the encyclical *Mediator Dei* in 1947—the doctrine has succeeded in establishing itself as a legitimate biblical insight.

Vatican II repeated the view that the priesthood of the faithful and the official priesthood differ not only in degree but in essence. At the same time it acknowledged the interrelatedness of the two kinds of priesthood and declared that in its own way each is a participation in the single priesthood of Christ. All Christians, it said, are called to offer themselves as living sacrifices, to proclaim the power of God who has called them out of darkness into his marvelous light, to persevere in prayer and praise, to bear witness to Christ, to give an answer to those who seek an account of the hope of eternal life that Christians possess, to join the ministerial priests in offering the Eucharist, to receive the sacraments, and to live lives of holiness, self-denial, and active charity.

The Impact of the Ecumenical Movement on the Roman Catholic Doctrine of the Church

The impact of the ecumenical movement on the Roman Catholic Church has brought about a significant development of the Roman Catholic teaching about the church. Classically the Roman Catholic Church thought of those who were canonically members of its communion as constituting the body of the church, with individual well-intended but invincibly ignorant Christians who held membership in other denominatons as belonging to the soul of the Roman Catholic Church by an implicit desire.[27] It was regarded as theologically impossible to concede that such individuals were saved within and through the religious bodies to which they belonged and not merely in spite of their denominational affiliation. With the papal acknowledgment that the ecumenical movement was the result of the Holy Spirit's activity, the way was opened to regard other Christian bodies as organs of grace and salvation.

In a sense Vatican Council II represents a breakthrough. It refrained from asserting a one-for-one identification of the Roman Catholic and the "unique church of Christ which in the creed we avow as one, holy, catholic, and apostolic." Instead it contented itself with saying that "this church, constituted and organized in the world as a society, subsists in the [Roman] Catholic Church, which is governed by the successor of Peter and by the bishops in union with that successor."[28] It granted that many elements of sanctification and truth can be found outside the visible structure of Roman Catholicism. It saw these elements as gifts that strictly belong to Christ's church and that thus possess an inner dynamism toward unity with the Roman Catholic church.

The Decree on Ecumenism reasserted the doctrine that the Holy Spirit fosters the ecumenical movement among separated Christians who invoke the triune God and confess Jesus as Lord and Savior. They join in the ecumenical movement, it said, not only as individuals but also as members of the corporate groups in which they heard the gospel and which each of them regards as his church and God's church. The Roman Catholic Church accepts them as brothers and as being in a certain (but imperfect) communion with the Roman Catholic Church (even though not members of it). Through baptism they have been incorporated into Christ. They have a right to the name of Christian, and children of the Roman Catholic Church properly regard them as brothers in the Lord. They have the written word of God, the life of grace, the virtues of faith, hope, and charity, and other interior gifts of the Spirit and visible elements of the church. The sacred actions of the Christian religion that they carry out can truly engender a life of grace and can rightly be described as able to provide access to the community of salvation.[29]

A common current view among Roman Catholics recognizes the unique fulness of the Roman Catholic Church, sees it as the ordinary means of salvation, and affirms the obligation of Roman Catholics to share their church with all human beings. But this view includes the conviction that the genuine insights into the gospel to which other Christian traditions witness can enrich Roman Catholics also.

Vatican II did not hesitate to accord the designation "church" to the historic Eastern churches. Some Roman Catholic theologians assert that the council did not (and did not intend to) accord the name of church to the communions in the West which achieved autonomy in the sixteenth century and that it reserved for them the designation "ecclesial communities."[30] Other Roman Catholic theologians argue from the heading placed over section 19 of the Decree on Ecumenism and the first sentence of this section that the council did indeed intend to and did give the name of church to at least some of these communions.

The decree deplored the absence in these communities of the fullness of unity that should flow from baptism. It regretted their failure to preserve the genuine and total reality of the eucharistic mystery because of the lack of the sacrament of orders. But the document concedes that "when they commemorate the Lord's death and resurrection in the holy supper, they profess that it signifies life in communion with Christ and they await his coming in glory."[31]

Since Vatican II many responsible Roman Catholic theologians have not hesitated to call the Christian "ecclesial communities" of the West churches in contexts where it is clear that they are not using the term out of mere courtesy or that they are merely quoting the titles by which these religious bodies designate themselves.

An important ecumenical development was the issue in 1967 of the *Directory for the Application of the Decisions of the Second Ecumenical Council of the Vatican Concerning Ecumenical Matters* by the Vatican Secretariat for Promoting Christian Unity. It directed the establishment of diocesan and territorial ecumenical commissions, disapproved "indiscriminate conditional baptism" of those who desire to be received into the Roman Catholic Church; denied that those who have been validly baptized outside the Roman Catholic Church require absolution from excommunication; urged the fostering of "spiritual ecumenism" in the Roman Catholic Church; allowed a limited "communication in spiritual matters" between Roman Catholics and other Christians, provided that the dangers of indifferentism and proselytism were avoided; authorized a generous degree of sharing with separated Eastern Christians; forbade participation with other separated Christians in the sacraments of the Eucharist, penance, and anointing of the sick, or in the office of sponsor at baptism or confirmation; permitted mutual clergy participating in services which do not call for sacramental sharing; allowed the local bishop to authorize the use of Roman Catholic facilities by non-Roman-Catholics without places of their own to carry out their religious rites properly; and directed authorities of Roman Catholic schools, hospitals, and institutions "to offer to ministers of other communions every facility for giving spiritual and sacramental ministration to their own communicants" in such schools, hospitals, and institutions.[32]

Since Vatican II the Roman Catholic Church has engaged in extensive official bilateral conversations with various Christian denominations of the West. The most promising to date appear to have been those with representatives of the Anglican communion and of the Lutheran World Federation.[33]

The condemnation of Anglican orders by Leo XIII in the bull *Apostolicae curae* (1896) is a very sensitive point between the two denominations. A number of Roman Catholic works have come out criticizing the bull and calling for its revocation.[34] In the same vein the Anglican doctrine of eucharistic sacrifice has been declared by some Roman Catholic theologians to be no barrier to a reconciliation of the two communions.[35]

Both in North America and elsewhere impatient Roman Catholic priests, religious, and laypeople have on occasion and with varying degrees of publicity intercommunicated with other Christians. Roman Catholics have received the Holy Communion at non-Roman-Catholic altars and Roman Catholic priests have tacitly or by explicit invitation admitted non-Roman-Catholics to the Holy Communion. Except in the case of Eastern Rite Roman Catholics, who may receive the sacraments in Eastern Orthodox Churches under certain limited circumstances, such actions involving Roman Catholics are violations of their church's canon law.[36]

At the same time, many conservatives in the Roman Catholic Church are inclined to look with disfavor on the present ecumenical outreach of their church and to see in it a major cause of the decline in the number of individual adult conversions to the Roman Catholic Church.

One consequence of the increased openness of the Roman Catholic Church to other denominations has been a greater willingness on the part of Roman Catholics to accept a reinterpretation of the happenings of the sixteenth century. Roman Catholic historians, especially in Germany, have been setting forth such a reinterpretation since the 1930s. This reinterpretation revised the traditional Roman Catholic view that the reformers had been implacable, headstrong rebels who had tried to destroy the medieval Western church when they were not given their own way. On the contrary, according to the proponents of the new view, a large part of the fault lay with the leadership of the medieval Western church and at many points the criticisms of the reformers were justified. This new picture of the sixteenth century does not wholly exculpate the reformers, but it recognized that they acted in good faith and out of genuine concern for the religious and spiritual welfare of the church's members.

Martin Luther in particular has come in for a reappraisal.[37] In the process, the traditional picture of him as the archheretic that had been drawn by John Eck of Ingolstadt (1486–1543), Jerome Emser (1478–1527), and John Cochlaeus (1479–1552)[38] has been rejected in favor of one that tried seriously to do justice to Luther's critique of and contribution to the sixteenth-century church.[39]

Many Roman Catholic theologians over the past generation have exhibited a continuing interest in non-Roman-Catholic theologians that goes far beyond a desire to catalogue differences between these theologians and accepted Roman Catholic theology. This growing interest is accounted for in part by the growth in ecumenical concern. But in part it is evidence of a genuine respect for the theological competence of these theologians and of a desire to derive from their reflections insights that Roman Catholic theologians can use as they engage in the theological enterprise.[40]

The Pope

The visible head of the Roman Catholic Church—as distinguished from its invisible head, Jesus Christ—is the pope. Officially (since around 1200), he is the vicar (that is, representative) of Jesus Christ,[41] the bishop of Rome, the archbishop and metropolitan of the Italian ecclesiastical province, the primate of Italy, and the patriarch of the West. He is regarded as the personal successor of the apostle Peter, just as all the other Roman Catholic bishops of the world are corporately the successors of the other apostles. He is also the temporal sovereign of Vatican City.

Roman Catholic theology sees the papacy rooted in the mission of the apostle Peter, the first in rank of the apostolic company and the primary witness to Christ's resurrection. Christ intended Simon to be the rock on which the church was to be founded (Matthew 16:13–19), and Christ himself gave Simon the name of Peter ("rock-man," from the Greek *petra,* "rock"). It became Peter's responsibility to secure the stability, the permanence, and the oneness of the church. To Peter, Christ gave the special function of strengthening his brothers, understood as the whole community (Luke 22:33–34). Christ made Peter the shepherd of the Christian flock, that is, he appointed Peter as his representative to mediate the life of salvation (John 21:15–17). This threefold mission of Peter is seen as extending in the succession of popes to the corners of the earth and to the end of the age.

According to Roman Catholic theology the pope has by divine right a full and supreme primacy of jurisdiction and not merely of honor. All members of the Roman Catholic Church of every rite and of every rank are bound to respect this authority not only in matters of faith and morals but also in matters of discipline and church government. Although the jurisdiction of the pope is episcopal and direct throughout the Roman Catholic Church, this is seen as not impairing the ordinary and direct power of jurisdiction that the bishops have over their respective flocks.

The primacy of the pope makes him the supreme judge of Roman Catholics throughout the world. They have the right of appeal to him in any matter that may come under ecclesiastical examination. The pope's verdict is final and irreversible, and no one—and explicitly no general council—may pass judgment on any of his judgments. The pope succeeds to his primacy of jurisdiction as soon as he accepts election to the papal office.

It is conceded that not all popes in history have at all times been living in a union of heart with Christ, but the Roman Catholic Church feels that the primacy cannot be made dependent on an ultimately unascertainable interior disposition of an individual. Again, while it has always been felt that a pope who became a heretic would cease to be pope, no machinery exists for determining the possible fact of papal heresy.

As already stated Vatican II enunciated the doctrine of episcopal-papal collegiality. This implies that the pope always is and acts in essential union with the bishops of the Roman Catholic Church. While he can at any time exercise his full papal authority without the cooperation and consent of the bishops, he is like them bound to act in harmony with the divine revelation that the sacred Scriptures and tradition contain and that the Holy Spirit interprets within the church.

In addition to his primacy of jurisdiction, the pope, according to Roman Catholic teaching, also possesses under certain circumstances the charism of infallibility as part of the "assistance of the Holy Spirit" that is granted to the church. While the church as a whole, dispersed throughout the world, and the church representatively gathered in a general council of bishops possesses infallibility, the pope exercises this charism as the individual personal organ in which the whole church in a sense is concentrated and manifested. In order for him to exercise the charism of infallibility, the pope must be speaking *ex cathedra* (that is, "from the teacher's chair"), as the supreme pastor of the church, defining a matter of faith and morals for all his subjects to believe as a revealed truth. In such cases he has the supernatural help of the Holy Spirit, leading the supreme teacher of the church by external and internal grace to the correct knowledge and statement of the truth and keeping him from making a wrong decision.[42] An infallible papal statement is authoritative "of itself" (*ex sese*) and does not require any further validation. But this infallibilty does not attach to papal statements, public or private, that are not *ex cathedra*.[43]

The centennial of the definition of papal infallibility brought to a head a controversy that had begun within the Roman Catholic Church about the value of this teaching for the latter twentieth century. Contemporary Roman Catholic theology has come to stress the point—affirmed over a century ago by John Sebastian Drey (1777–1853) of the so-called Tübingen School—that the pope speaks representatively for the whole church. Therefore what is being asserted is not papal infallibility as much as it is the infallibility of the church.

Contemporary Roman Catholic theology likewise stresses that absolute infallibility belongs to God alone and that when it appears in the church it is always a gift from God; that the teaching office of the church is not over the word of God but exists to serve the word of God; that the individual conscience remains the norm of personal decision even in the case of infallible pronouncements on matters of faith and morals; that the vocabularly of infallible definitions is always conditioned by the times and that the existing world-picture may actually pollute such a definition; that infallible dogmatic definitions represent only extreme cases of the infallibility of the church; that in a pilgrim church that is "on the way" (*in via*) infallible dogmas are not the end but milestones along the way of doctrinal development; and that when Roman Catholics affirm the infallibility of the church as a whole they must keep in mind that there are separated Christian communities which Vatican II has also called churches and that this fact has implications for the doctrine of the church's infallibility.

Individual Roman Catholic theologians have attempted to resolve the problem of the infallibility of the pope and of the church in various ways. Some have stressed that Vatican I was intent on rejecting as strongly as it could the liberal thesis that there were in fact no supernatural truths for the church to proclaim and assert. Accordingly, they say, the assertion of papal infallibility is at bottom primarily a declaration that the church has an authentically supernatural faith to teach.

Other theologians stress that infallibility is a synonym for the indefectibility of the church, or, put positively, for the permanence of the church as church. Thus the infallibility of the church intends to say that the whole church will never move so far from divine truth that Christ's church will no longer exist upon earth. The infallibility of the pope, they say, is under the same limitation.

At a more basic level, some theologians are taking the position that the effort to formulate exhaustively the church's faith-commitment in propositional terms is in itself wrong. Accordingly, they assert, the definition of papal infallibility in 1870, at least as this definition has commonly been understood, was a mistake that the church needs to reinterpret radically—and possibly even to retract—if its proclamation is to remain credible.[44]

The Roman Catholic Church and Non-Christians

There have long been Roman Catholic theologians who have held to the possibility that human beings can be saved not only outside the Roman Catholic Church but even outside the Christian community. Redemption, they point out, is an objective fact. In Christ the Godhead took humanity upon itself, and these theologians appeal to the old axiom: "That which was assumed (namely, humanity) was redeemed (*quod assumptum est redemptum est*)." Again, the Incarnation of God in Christ achieved its full term, end, and scope only in his death and resurrection; by his death Christ has destroyed death for all human beings and by his rising to life again he has restored everlasting life to the world. It is obvious that not all human beings who have thus been saved through Christ are aware of the fact that they have been saved. If in his ignorance of God's act in Christ a human being responds to the divine call of grace that God causes to be heard even in the pagan world, his faith in God links him mysteriously with the church that Christ founded. The minimum content of this faith traditionally has been that God exists and that he rewards those who seek him.

Vatican II ratified a new direction in the official Roman Catholic attitude toward the Jews. Although the council's Declaration on the Relation of the Church to Non-Christian Religions (*Nostra aetate*) with reference to Jews was altogether not as forthright as either Jews or some Roman Catholics desired, it goes further than any document of comparable authority before it had gone.[45]

Contemporary Roman Catholic theology insists that the New Testament data are misused when the corporate guilt of the Jewish people is deduced from them. The writers of the New Testament, it is pointed out, saw the members of the Jewish high court as guilty of condemning an innocent prisoner to death and saw some of the residents of Jerusalem as implicated in Christ's crucifixion. But they also saw the responsibility for Christ's saving death as something that all human beings share and they regarded it, along with his resurrection, as effecting the salvation of Jews as well as of Gentiles.

The most common Roman Catholic view of the Jews today is that in the New Testament Christians replace the people of Israel as the people of God. Nevertheless his chosen people of the Old Covenant continue to be dear to God, because of what their forebears were in the past and because of the common future end-time salvation of both Jews and Christians. Other Roman Catholic theologians argue that since Christ's advent there is only one people of God. Because Christ's redemption is universal, it is possible within this single people of God for a person to belong to the Jewish religion because of his implicit faith in Christ. A third group of Roman Catholic theologians hazard—with various qualifications—the theory that until Christ is revealed at the end of the age there are two peoples of God. One of these is his ancient people, with whom his covenant is thought of as continuing. The other is the community of those who explicitly believe in Christ, toward whom both peoples of God are moving.[46]

Some Roman Catholic comparative religionists argue that all the great world religions—including not only Christianity and Judaism, but also Islam, Buddhism, and Hinduism—are in the process of achieving maturity simultaneously but separately. Each tradition, they say, is finally unique, but each must become a dimension of the others, complementing the others and giving them a new and previously unsuspected meaning together.[47] Others find a similar complementarity in the mystic and ascetic disciplines of Roman Catholic Christianity and those of Buddhism and Hinduism.[48]

More recently the phenomenon of contemporary atheism has raised the question whether or not God demands even the traditional minimum of faith that God exists and rewards those that seek him. Vatican II recognized that human beings who have not received the gospel can be related to the people of God, that is, to the church. After discussing this possibility with reference to Jews, Muslims, and pagan theists, *Lumen gentium*, the constitution on the church, categorically affirms that divine providence does not "deny the help necessary for salvation to those who, without blame on their part, have not yet arrived at an explicit knowledge of God but who strive to live a good life, thanks to his grace."[49]

One consequence of this position is the energetic dialogue with Marxists that some of the more "liberal" Roman Catholic theologians have opened up in many parts of the world,[50] notably in Germany, France, Italy, and South America, although not without strong criticism and resistance by conservative Roman Catholics.

The Roman Catholic Church and Secret Societies

Under canons 2335–2336 of the Roman Catholic code of canon law, Roman Catholics who become Freemasons or who join other societies that work against civil authority or the Roman Catholic Church incur automatic excommunication. Canon 683 prohibits, under pain of excommunication, membership in societies that are secret, condemned, seditious, or suspect, or that endeavor to withdraw themselves from the legitimate vigilance of the Roman Catholic Church. Only the Roman see can lift the excommunication of either class of persons.

The Roman Catholic Church's opposition to Freemasonry goes back to 1738, when Clement XII issued the constitution *In eminenti* against it. Later popes amplified this condemnation. In 1884 Leo XIII charged Freemasonry with aiming at "the overthrow of the entire religious, political, and social order based on Christian institutions" and with seeking to establish a state of things based on strictly naturalistic principles. Roman Catholic opposition to Freemasonry arose from the fact that European Freemasonry enrolled many anticlericalists among its members and that Freemasons supported many efforts at disestablishing the Roman Catholic Church and at bringing down the governments that had linked themselves with the Roman Catholic Church. But even in countries where Freemasonry is quite (or at least overtly) unpolitical and where the church is not established, as in the United States and Canada, the condemnation remains in force.

Roman Catholics have justified the condemnation on the ground that as a society committed to the mutual advancement of its members Freemasonry is against the common good and because as an unsupervised secret society it has a vast potentiality for evil.

The prohibition of membership extends to Masonic auxiliaries like the women's Order of the Eastern Star, the boys' Order of De Molay,[51] Job's Daughters, the Rainbow Girls, Acacia, and derivative associations.

Roman Catholics who join the Independent Order of Odd Fellows or the Knights of Pythias do not incur excommunication, but their church normally bars them from receiving the sacraments. Roman Catholics have been discouraged from joining the International Order of Good Templars and the Ancient Mystical Order Rosae Crucis.[52]

Roman Catholic Missions and Missionary Practice

When the sixteenth century dividing of Christendom began, the foreign missions of the medieval Western church in the non-Western world were under the patronage of the king of Portugal (Asia, Africa, and America as far as a line 370 leagues west of the Cape Verde Islands) and the crown of Spain ("the Indies," that is, the remainder of America). The foreign missions, like their European patrons, remained loyal to the Roman see.

The foundation of the missions-oriented Society of Jesus marked a new departure in Roman Catholic missions; so did the establishment of the Carmelite missionary seminary at Rome in 1613. The centralization of the direction of foreign missionary effort through the establishment of the Congregation for the Propagation of the Faith ("Propaganda") in 1622 was even more epochal.

The evangelization of pagan Africa had been begun in the mid-fifteenth century under Portuguese auspices.[53] By the early seventeenth century the demands of missionary expansion outstripped the resources of Portugal, and the Congregation for the Propagation of the Faith took over part of the task. Prior to the revival of missionary interest in the nineteenth century, the number of missionaries was too small for the task; accommodation to the indigenous cultures came too late; the recruitment of an indigenous priesthood lagged. Even in the nineteenth century, by the end of which Roman Catholic missions had been established throughout Africa, the link between the missionary effort and the colonial system was obvious. Nevertheless, by the mid-twentieth century the black Roman Catholic population in Africa exceeded 11 million.

The missionary effort in the Americas goes back to the end of the fifteenth century. It was carried on chiefly by the Franciscans, the Dominicans, and, from 1549 on, the Jesuits. Here too, the missionary enterprise and colonialism were linked together. But while the royal administrations all too often shamelessly exploited the native population, the latter found some of its most articulate champions among the missionaries: Bartholomew de las Casas (1474–1555) is a distinguished example. The Jesuit "Reductions" in South America in the seventeenth century were designed in the same spirit to gather the aboriginal population into missionary settlements beyond the reach of the authorities. In statistical terms the Roman Catholic missions in Latin America were a great success and a hierarchy was established in the sixteenth century. But the Christianity of the broad masses of the people was often only a thin phenomenological veneer behind which the aboriginal religion continued; the number of priests was always inadequate and some of the priests were vulnerable to the accusation of simony. Except in a relatively few places, Latin America ceased to be a missionary territory only in a technical sense. (The Roman Catholic missionary outreach into the areas that became the United States and Canada is discussed separately in the section on the Roman Catholic Church in these two countries.)

On the Indian subcontinent the seat of a vast diocese that included all the territory from the Cape of Good Hope to Japan was established at Goa in 1534. The Franciscans, Jesuits (beginning with St. Francis Xavier), Capuchins, and Carmelites provided the bulk of the missionaries in India. Initially conversions came with great ease; the missionaries baptized candidates with few demands upon them in the way of preparation, and in territories where the Portuguese crown had established its sway the favor or disfavor of the colonial administration was a freely used form of pressure. Continuing contact with the regnant Hinduism of the native population demonstrated the need for a fuller understanding of the indigenous belief systems. The Jesuit Robert de Nobili (1577–1656) became a "Christian Brahmin" in Madura and adhered faithfully to the social requirements of his Brahmin status as far as his conscience permitted, even to the point of avoiding contact with outcastes. Related to both Goa and Rome, he succeeded in vindicating his highly successful method of reaching the hitherto unreached leaders of the Hindu community, but after his death his methods were repudiated both by the Congregation for the Propagation of the Faith and by the Roman see itself. The work in the north of India was frustratingly slow, hindered both by popular unresponsiveness and by governmental intolerance. Almost fatal to the work in the whole subcontinent was the "rites controversy" that began between the Capuchins and the Jesuits in 1703/1704 and continued for over half a century, ending with the defeat of the Jesuits; accommodation was still the issue. The determination of the church and the colonial administration to Europeanize the native Christians had dire consequences. For the most part only the outcastes and the non-Hindu population embraced Roman Catholicism. The Roman Catholic Church never really penetrated the higher castes. As a result the nineteenth-century missionary revival lacked the cultural bridge that would have added greatly to the effectiveness of the Roman Catholic evangelistic outreach then and subsequently.

China in the sixteenth century was barred to most foreigners. Only ambassadors and their staffs, traders, and immigrants who admired China's culture and were ready to respect its laws could gain admittance. On this basis Matthew Ricci (1552–1610) entered the country at whose threshold his fellow-Jesuit Francis Xavier had died. Ricci was a mathematician, an astronomer, and a linguist as well as a priest. He donned the garb of a scholar, perfected himself in the Chinese language, mastered the Chinese classics, and after two decades of patient effort he became adviser to the emperor himself. To spare the feelings of Christian converts Ricci and his successors prudently pruned from the usages of the Roman Catholic Church the features that might offend Chinese sensibilities. In the mid-seventeenth century these concessions prompted the Dominican rivals of the Jesuits to render a report to the Congregation for the Propagation of the Faith that led to a condemnation of the Jesuit methods. Another "rites controversy" was thus precipitated. It ended in 1742 when Benedict XIV finally rejected the Jesuit accommodations. The Chinese emperor reacted with predictable hostility, the conversion of members of the learned class came to an end, and many of those who had accepted Christianity apostatized. The nineteenth century was an era of dedicated missionary effort and periodic persecutions; the Roman Catholic missionaries that entered China in increasing numbers laid the foundations for greater success in the twentieth century. The removal of the greatest psychological barrier to acceptance of the Roman Catholic faith—the official declaration in 1935 that the homage paid to Confucius was purely civil—resulted in new advances in the brief period that intervened before the conquest of China by the communists and the general repression of Christianity.

On the far eastern rim of Asia the history of the missions of the Roman Catholic Church through the eighteenth century is one of alternating persecution and success. In what became French Indochina the methods of accommodation that Ricci used in China found effective application. The use of carefully trained catechists was another helpful device designed to compensate for the serious lack of priests. In Thailand an early emphasis on recruiting an indigenous clergy proved rewarding.

In the islands beyond Southeast Asia, bitter persecution by Muslims, the political rivalries of the European colonial powers, a lack of coordination and even actual competition between the missionary orders combined to prevent the Roman Catholic Church from striking sufficiently deep roots to make it self-sufficient and able to weather the storms that struck it. The greatest measure of success came in the Philippines. Here the Roman Catholic Church was able to adapt itself in an unusual degree to the requirements of the indigenous population. By uniting scattered groups under a common religious and moral banner and by a tender concern for native feelings and institutions, the Philippines (with the exception of the Muslim islands in the far south) developed into a solidly Roman Catholic community.

The mission to Japan began auspiciously, but the favor that the Japanese shogun Nobunaga showed in 1562 had been replaced by virulent persecution and the death of the twenty-five martyrs of Nagasaki in 1597. The first years of the seventeenth century provided a brief breathing space, but in 1616 Christianity was forbidden and until 1854 the Roman Catholic community was compelled to exist—with remarkable tenacity and courage—underground. Again, part of the problem was the shortage of indigenous priests; although the first three Japanese priests were ordained in 1601, the first Japanese bishop was not consecrated until 1927.

In the predominantly Muslim Middle East, Roman Catholic expansion was largely linked with the political maneuverings of the European powers. The success of the Roman Catholic Church has largely been limited to communities on which Islam had exerted little influence. In the competition with Islam in black Africa, where the Roman Catholic Church has been securely entrenched it has resisted Muslim penetration, but where it has been weak it has frequently succumbed. On balance, the Roman Catholic Church has neither been able to halt the advance of Islam nor to succeed significantly in penetrating the Muslim world.

Characteristic of modern Roman Catholic missionary effort are its adaptation to the needs of the newly independent nations in which it has been working, efforts at accommodation to industrial and urban change, acceptance of the fact of religious and cultural pluralism, changes—even very radical changes—in the liturgy to take cognizance of local customs and feelings, encouragement of indigenous religious music and art, greater emphasis on the use of local vernaculars, recognition of the validity of existing indigenous philosophic and religious insights and efforts at their purification and elevation, more appropriate training of missionaries, the recruitment of high quality native priests and religious, stress on the lay apostolate among indigenous Christians, a realization both that the Roman Catholic Church's contacts with the non-Christian world cannot be restricted to professional missionaries and that these contacts involve receiving as well as giving.

Since the sixteenth century the Roman Catholic motive for evangelization has undergone a certain degree of change. The initial imperative for missionary efforts came from the conviction that faith in God and in Christ is an intrinsically necessary and absolutely essential means of attaining salvation. Increasingly another emphasis has recently grown up beside this one. It stresses God's universal will for the salvation of all human beings, from which it derives the tenet that in some way every human being must be able to become a member of the church historically and concretely. This, it is held, demands not only ascending stages of church membership that begin with baptism and progress to full fellowship with the Roman Catholic Church's eucharistic life, but also descending stages that begin with baptism and go down to a Christianity that is only implicit and nonofficial ("anonymous Christians").[54] The explicit Christian message communicated through missionary outreach is thus the articulation of the grace-given divine revelation that human beings always sense in the depths of their being as soon as they experience their limitless transcendence. In accepting himself fully, a human being also accepts this experience and this revelation through the operation of the grace of God and of Christ. This involves more than keeping the natural moral law. It involves God's impartation of the gift of authentic (even if inarticulate) faith, in ways known to himself alone, even to those whom the proclamation of the explicit gospel has not reached. All this does not dispense Christians from the task of evangelism, since they face two demanding obligations. One is toward those who do not know the essential truth about God's love with all the clarity that the gospel provides. The other is the glory of God, whose redemptive activity in Christ deserves to be known as such.[55]

On these premises missionary activity becomes an effort to emancipate individuals whom the evil one has caught up in his deceptions and who are serving creatures rather than the creator; to deliver those who are subject to utter hopelessness; to promote God's glory; and to obey Christ's command to preach the gospel to every creature.[56]

Roman Catholicism in the United States and Canada[57]

The first Roman Catholic Mass in what is now the United States of America was conducted in 1521 in Florida, discovered eight years earlier by Juan Ponce de León (ca. 1460–1521). A priest in the exploration company of Jacques Cartier (1491–1557) on the Gaspé Peninsula celebrated the first Mass in Canada.

Roman Catholic missionaries accompanied various Spanish and French explorers to the new world. Franciscans came to Florida in 1528; twelve missionaries came with Hernando de Soto (ca. 1500–1542) to Tampa Bay in 1539. The city of St. Augustine was founded in Florida and the oldest Roman Catholic mission in the United States was established there in 1565. Colonization of Canada by French Roman Catholics began with the foundation of Quebec in 1608 by Samuel de Champlain (ca. 1570–1635) and the establishment of Montreal in 1642. Earliest missionaries to Canada included Franciscan Recollects who arrived in Quebec in 1615, French Jesuits who came in 1625, and the Sulpicians who began work in 1640.

By 1600 Roman Catholic missionaries had entered what is now Alabama, Arizona, Arkansas, California, Florida, Georgia, Kansas, Mississippi, Nebraska, New Mexico, New York, North Carolina, Oklahoma, South Carolina, Tennessee, Texas, and Virginia. Early Roman Catholic missionaries in the new world include Claude Jean Allouez (1622–1689, French Jesuit), John Altham (1589–1640, English Jesuit), Louis Cancer de Barbastro (1500–1549, Spanish Dominican), Jacques Gravier (1651–1708, French Jesuit), Isaac Jogues (1607–1646, French Jesuit), Eusebio Francisco Kino (ca. 1645–1711, Italian Jesuit), John Lalande (d. 1646, French Jesuit brother), Antonio Margil (1657–1726, Spanish Franciscan), Jacques Marquette (1637–1675, French Jesuit), Zenobius Membre (1645–1687, French Franciscan), Juan de Padilla (d. 1542, Spanish Franciscan), Charles Raymbaut (1602–1643, French Jesuit), Junípero Serra (previously named Miguel José, 1713–1784, Spanish Franciscan), and Andrew White (1579–1656, English Jesuit).

Ecclesiastical organization of the Roman Catholic Church in Canada began with the appointment of Francois de Montmorency-Laval (1623–1708) as vicar apostolic of New France in 1658 and with the naming of Quebec as the first diocese in 1674.

Canadian Roman Catholics experienced new difficulties when England acquired Canada with its 70,000 French-speaking inhabitants through the Treaty of Paris in 1763. Anglo-French differences were exacerbated by Anglican-Roman Catholic antagonisms. Canadian Roman Catholics were accorded religious liberty through the Quebec Act of 1774, the Constitutional Act of 1791, and legislation approved by the queen of England in 1851. Antipathy toward Roman Catholics in Canada moderated as a result of the loyalty of the French-speaking populace to the crown during the American Revolution and the War of 1812.

In 1784, when there were approximately 25,000 Roman Catholics in a population of about 4 million in the newly established United States of America, John Carroll (1735–1815), a Jesuit who had been born in Upper Marlboro, Maryland, had been educated in France, and had returned to his homeland in 1774, was appointed head of Roman Catholic missions in the United States. In 1789 Carroll was appointed bishop of Baltimore with a diocese coextensive with the United States; he was consecrated to the episcopate in 1790 and elevated to the archepiscopate in 1808. The first Roman Catholic seminary in the United States was established by the Sulpicians at Baltimore in 1791. A school which became Georgetown University was opened at Georgetown, Maryland, in 1791; a secondary school for girls was begun in Georgetown in 1792. By 1840 Roman Catholics operated more than 200 elementary schools in the United States.

From 1830 to 1900 the Roman Catholic population in the United States and Canada rose significantly as a result of immigrations from Ireland, Germany, France, and eastern and southern Europe.

Roman Catholic bishops of the United States held seven provincial councils at Baltimore, Maryland, from 1829 to 1849. In 1846 they proclaimed the Blessed Virgin Mary patroness of the United States. In separate plenary councils at Baltimore the bishops in 1852 drafted rules for parochial life, matters of ritual and ceremonies, financial matters, and teaching of doctrine; in 1866 condemned current doctrinal errors and adopted rules for organization of dioceses, education and conduct of clergy, property management, parish duties, and general education; and in 1884 prepared the Baltimore catechisms, required establishment of parochial schools, initiated action to establish the Catholic University of America in Washington, D.C., and fixed six holy days of obligation to be observed in the United States.

Roman Catholicism was brought to western Canada through the missionary activity of Joseph Norbert Provencher (1787–1853) and was advanced there through the work of the Oblates of Mary Immaculate. Quebec became a metropolitan see in 1844. The First Council of Quebec was held in 1851. Laval University was inaugurated in 1854 and canonically established in 1876. In 1908 Roman Catholics in Canada were removed from mission status and from the jurisdiction of the Congregation for the Propagation of the Faith.

In the nineteenth century the Roman Catholic Church in the United States identified itself with the labor movement. James Gibbons (1834–1921), ordained to the priesthood in 1861, consecrated bishop in 1877, named archbishop in 1877 and cardinal in 1886, went to Rome to defend the Knights of Labor. The 1891 papal encyclical *Rerum novarum* included rejection of the theory that there should be no government interference in social and economic matters and held that poverty should be alleviated by charity and justice.

Toward the close of the nineteenth century United States Roman Catholics were accused of neglecting contemplative virtues in favor of practical virtues and of modifying doctrine to gain converts. In *Testem benevolentiae*, an apostolic letter to Gibbons from Leo XIII, doctrine is described as a divine deposit to be adhered to at all times, though adaptations may be made in Christian life to suit time, place, and national customs.

The Roman Catholic Church in the United States was removed from mission status in 1908 by the apostolic constitution *Sapienti consilio* of Pius X.

In the nineteenth and twentieth centuries opposition to Roman Catholicism in the United States was reflected in several organizations, the Know-Nothings in the 1850s, the Ku Klux Klan from 1866 on, and the American Protective Association of 1887. Opposition to Roman Catholicism was pronounced during the presidential campaign of Alfred E. Smith in 1928 and was intensified over the Roman question occasioned by the 1929 Lateran Agreement. The election of Roman Catholic John F. Kennedy as president of the United States in 1960 and the Declaration on Religious Freedom of Vatican Council II helped to decrease social and political opposition to Roman Catholicism.

The greatest concentration of Roman Catholics in Canada is in the eastern portion. The bilingual differences in the population are reflected in the church, for example, in the parallel structures of the Canadian Catholic Conference established in 1943. Quebec continues as the center of French cultural life. Roman Catholicism in Canada embraces other language groups besides French and English. There is a special metropolitan see with four eparchies for 255,000 members of the Eastern Rite.

Vatican Council II stimulated the process of change under way in Roman Catholicism in the United States and Canada in the second half of the twentieth century. The phenomena of change include different trends and emphases in theology, variations in interpretation and implementation of Vatican Council II directives, changes in the spiritual formation and life-style of the clergy, and conflicting views in dealing with such issues as race relations, poverty, peace, and ecumenism.

In 1975 representatives of the Roman Catholic Church in Canada joined representatives of the Anglican, Lutheran, Presbyterian, and United churches to announce an agreement according to which each church would recognize the validity of baptisms conferred according to the established norms of the others. The agreement was the product of a Joint Working Group of the Canadian Council of Churches and of the Canada Catholic Conference. Baptisms will be recognized when they are conferred with flowing water, by pouring, sprinkling, or immersing, accompanied by the invocation of the three persons of the Holy Trinity. Roman Catholics affirm that the agreement is an application of decisions of Vatican Council II.[58]

A number of major problems confront Roman Catholics in both the United States and Canada. The Roman Catholic parish school system has been threatened by decline in the number of priests and nuns to staff schools and by various financial pressures. Some institutions of higher education are also fighting for survival. There are problems relating to the requirement of celibacy. Liturgical reforms have created divisions that portend serious long-term aftereffects. The larger role played by laity may require revamping of the church's structure. Social and ethical issues relating to birth control and abortion are proving to be difficult and disturbing.

In the United States the National Conference of Catholic Bishops provides the bishops of the Roman Catholic church with a vehicle for exchange of views and insights and for common action. Offices are at 1312 Massachusetts Ave., N.W., Washington, D.C. A similar organization for Roman Catholic bishops in Canada is the Canadian Catholic Conference with offices at 90 Parent Avenue, Ottawa, Ontario. Roman Catholics in the United States number approximately 49 million in nearly 25,000 churches gathered in thirty-two provinces and 164 dioceses and archdioceses. In Canada Roman Catholics number almost 9,500,000 gathered in seventeen provinces and fifty-one archdioceses, dioceses, and eparchies.

NOTES

1. "A 'Profession of Faith' from Pope Paul VI," *St. Louis Review,* July 5, 1968, p. 5.
2. "See" is from the Latin *sedes,* "seat," in this the bishop's seat. "Diocese" is from the Latin transliteration of the Greek word *dioikesis,* originally a group of civil provinces of the Roman Empire that a vicar governed. Taken over by the church, it acquired its present meaning by the thirteenth century.
3. Until the time of Leo XIII these titular bishops were known as bishops *i[n]*

p[*artibus*] i[*nfidelium*] ("in the territory of the unbelievers"). A priest may be made a titular bishop as a reward for long and faithful service or to enable him to discharge an important office in the educational activity of the church (such as rector of a pontifical university) or in the administration of the church.

4. At the International Congress of Theologians meeting at Brussels in 1970, 149 (out of 173) participants voted in favor of a drastic revision of the manner in which popes are chosen.

5. Technically they are prothonotaries apostolic *ad instar participantium* ("equal to the [actual] participants"), that is, they could if necessary perform the duties of the seven members of the very ancient college of prothonotaries apostolic in Rome.

6. Impatience with the slow speed at which the Roman Catholic Church was renewing itself after Vatican II and a sense of frustration among some priests, religious, and laymen at the institutional church's failure to attack the inequities of modern society led to the establishment of Roman Catholic irregular "underground" churches. This happened especially in urban areas and in the vicinity of Roman Catholic campuses. Although led by Roman Catholic priests, these "underground" churches tended to be more inclusive in membership and more ecumenical in relation to other religious bodies. See, for example, the essays by Roman Catholics in Malcolm Boyd, ed., *The Underground Church* (New York: Sheed and Ward, 1968).

7. Tradition has created a graduated series of forms of address and reference for the different grades of ecclesiastical dignity: His Holiness for the pope; His Eminence for a cardinal (the title Cardinal is now inserted between the Christian name[s] of the prelate in question and his family name); His Excellency (and Most Reverend) for bishops and archbishops; Very Reverend for lower-ranking deans; Reverend for pastors and other clergy. Father is the form of address for priests, Mr. for deacons. In French-speaking areas of Canada *Monseigneur* is a designation for bishops and archbishops.

8. Co-responsibility is regarded as not only an aspect of papal-episcopal relations, but as something that affects every other group in the church as well—the theologians, the priests, the religious, and the laypeople.

9. "Consensus Statement of the Symposium on Co-Responsibility in the Church," April 3-5, 1970 (6-page lithoprinted document), p. 3. Among the thirty-eight participants were three Roman Catholic bishops, four foreign Roman Catholic theologians, a nun, a laywoman, and six non-Roman-Catholic experts.

10. Ibid., p. 4.

11. In the creeds of the West the phrase *sanctorum communio* originally meant "participation in the holy [things]," that is, the body and blood of Christ in the sacrament of the altar.

12. The teaching that the "poor souls" in purgatory can intercede for other members of the mystical body has been deemed at best a probable opinion, although Leo XIII in 1889 approved an indulgenced prayer (subsequently abrogated) invoking the help of the "holy souls" against bodily and spiritual perils. Since St. Gregory the Great in the sixth century the common opinion of Western Christian theologians has been that prayers for the damned in hell are useless.

13. In 1969 Paul VI divided the Congregation of Rites, which formerly had this responsibility, into the Congregation for the Divine Cult and the Congregation for the Causes of the Saints.

14. If the candidate was only equivalently beatified, evidence of three subsequent miracles accomplished by the candidate's intercession must be introduced.

15. The canonization process is often slow. The cases of some candidates proposed for the first time centuries ago still await decision. One reason is that the expense of the canonization process is very great. A major item is the cost of the actual canonization ceremonies in St. Peter's Church at Rome. In 1968 a report began to circulate that the Dutch Carmelites were discontinuing their efforts to secure the beatification of a member of their community, Titus Brandsma, whom the German nazis had killed in the extermination camp at Dachau during World War II. The monks, it was

asserted, had decided to divert the money set aside for the beatification process to the needs of people in developing countries. At that time some expert observers estimated the cost of the canonization process at up to $100,000. A Vatican spokesman fixed the costs prior to, but not including, the canonization ceremony itself at $40,000 (*America,* June 8, 1968, p. 743).

16. The first to propose a critical edition of the lives of the saints on the basis of authentic sources seems to have been Heribert Rosweyde (1569–1629), but he died before any of the material was published.

17. These have included such popular saints as St. Valentine; St. Christopher, patron of travelers; St. Barbara, patroness of artillerymen; St. George, patron of England and of soldiers; and St. Nicholas, the original of "Santa Claus." Among the others eliminated were seventeen early bishops of Rome. Some Eastern Orthodox churchmen regarded the elimination of SS. George and Nicholas and other saints especially venerated in the East as a deliberate Roman Catholic insult to their faith. Elimination from the liturgical calendar does not mean that the saints affected cannot be chosen as name-saints at baptism (and confirmation), as patrons of churches, or as intercessors by Christians who invoke their prayers.

18. See, for example, Donald Attwater, *A Catholic Dictionary,* 2nd edition New York: The Macmillan Company, 1956), pp. 201–202.

19. A typical and comprehensive diocesan religious education program is that set forth in September 1972 in "Guidelines for the Teaching of Religion" in the Archdiocese of St. Louis. Stated goals and objectives include "to assist in building up the reign of Christ" by teaching "the primacy of God from whom flows the duty and privilege [of the students] to serve their fellowmen"; "to present to [them] an authentic statement of the teachings and practices of the [Roman] Catholic Church"; to "offer an opportunity to learn who Jesus Christ is and what he teaches through the [Roman] Catholic Church, to accept church teachings, and to embrace and apply these to

one's own life"; "to appeal to the whole person: mind, will, memory, emotions, and imagination"; and to offer "opportunities of participating in some kind of out-of-class Christian activity." The doctrinal and moral content "must be faithful to the teaching of the ordinary magisterium" and is to reflect the principle that "the revealed word of God (the core of content) is unique" and that this word of God itself contributes "to the personal faith of the student." The doctrinal and moral content "must be accurate and clear," but it "cannot be isolated from liturgy, social action, or attitudinal formation." Methodologically teaching must respect "the dignity of the individual [student], his right to act freely," and "his age and level of human development." The structure of religious education involves the archbishop, the archdiocesan school board and the archdiocesan religious education office; the pastor of the parish; the elementary school principal, the chairman or coordinator of the parochial department of religious education, and the coordinator of the parish school of religion; and the parents. In Roman Catholic high schools the program additionally involves the principal of the secondary school, the chairman of the department of religion, and a corps of full-time religion instructors. Teachers, chairmen, and coordinators in Roman Catholic elementary schools, Roman Catholic high schools, and parish schools of religion must meet appropriate certification standards ranging from twelve undergraduate college-level semester-hours for teachers at the parish level to a master of arts degree in theology or religious education for the chairman of the religion department of a Roman Catholic high school (*St. Louis Review,* September 29, 1972, section 3).

20. This use of the word "religious" is intended to affirm that in the abstract the "religious life" is the highest of many forms that an authentically Christian life can take. It is not intended to say that life under a rule is the only genuinely Christian kind of life or that only monks and nuns are genuinely religious people.

21. "Nun," strictly speaking, describes a

female member of an order, "monk" a male member.

22. A "sister," strictly speaking, is a female member of a congregation.

23. The members of the Missionary Society of St. Paul the Apostle (Paulists) give a solemn undertaking in place of the usual vows.

24. To describe orders of nuns who share a common founder and (sometimes with modifications) a common rule with an order of male religious, the term "second order" is sometimes used. "Third order" is used in two senses: (1) A *secular* third order comprises men (normally laymen) and women who follow their ordinary secular callings but who try to bring into their daily lives some of the spirit of the cloister. Secular tertiaries are not bound by vows. The largest secular third order is that of the Franciscan Tertiaries. (2) A *regular* third order comprises tertiaries who enter communities in which they follow their respective rule under the ordinary simple vows.

25. For example, the impact of the newer Roman Catholic doctrine of the last things upon the Helpers of the Holy Souls, a nineteenth-century foundation the members of which undertake to pray, suffer, and work for the benefit of the souls detained in purgatory, or the impact of the decline in the cultic veneration of the reserved sacrament of the altar upon the Benedictine Sisters of Perpetual Adoration.

26. The 4th (1971) edition of the *National Directory of New Communities and Apostolates* (published out of 6901 Southwest Florence Lane, Portland, Oregon 97223) listed over fifty new Roman Catholic communities in the United States alone. These communities are of many different kinds and exhibit a wide continuum of ecclesiastical recognition. Typical of many is the "noncanonical nucleation of contemporary Christian women" who call themselves Sisters for Christian Community and whose stated "primary apostolic goal is to witness the uniqueness of Christian community." Each sister "creates the content of her own commitment formulation and decides the length of time of commitment according to her own vocational charisms." Instead of taking vows, each sister makes "a simple statement or promise to give witness to Christian community in a celibate state. Each sister is self-employed and self-supporting." Poverty "is not concerned with the quantity of money held but with the Christlike relationships and services it facilitates." Obedience conforms to the Thomist definition, "the conformity of the will to right reason as directed toward the common good." Decisions affecting the community are arrived at collegially (ibid., p. 15).

27. In 1943 *Mystici corporis Christi* made this analogy obsolete by describing the Holy Spirit as the soul of the church.

28. *Lumen gentium*, 8. *Dignitatis humanae*, 1, professed "its belief that God himself has made known to mankind the way in which men are to serve him and thus be saved in Christ and come to blessedness." It goes on: "We believe that this one true religion subsists in the catholic and apostolic church."

29. *Unitatis redintegratio,* 1 and 3. In "The 'Credo' of the People of God" (1968), Paul VI summarized his own views on the subject: "Recognizing also the existence outside the organism of the church of Christ [that is, the Roman Catholic Church] of numerous elements of truth and sanctification which belong to her as her own and tend to Catholic unity, and believing in the action of the Holy Spirit who stirs up in the hearts of the disciples of Christ love of this unity, we entertain the hope that the Christians who are not yet in the full communion of the one only church will one day be reunited in one fold with the one only shepherd" ("A 'Profession of Faith' from Pope Paul VI," *St. Louis Review,* July 5, 1968, p. 5).

30. This is a strictly Roman Catholic term without precedent in the vocabularies of non-Roman-Catholic denominations.

31. *Lumen gentium* 22.

32. In a case of urgent need (such as peril of death or the presence of persecution) the local bishop may authorize a non-Roman-Catholic without access to a minister of his own communion to receive the required sacraments at the hand of a Roman Catholic priest if the non-Roman-Catholic spontaneously asks for them, is rightly disposed,

and declares a faith in the sacraments in harmony with the faith of the Roman Catholic Church. A Roman Catholic has an equivalent privilege only if the non-Roman-Catholic minister "has been validly ordained."

33. See the four volumes published through 1970 in the series edited by Paul C. Empie and T. Austin Murphy, *Lutherans and Catholics in Dialogue* (Washington, D.C.: United States Catholic Conference, 1965————). (Vol. I, *The Nicene Creed as Dogma of the Church;* vol. II, *One Baptism for the Remission of Sins;* vol. III, *The Eucharist as Sacrifice;* vol. IV, *Eucharist and Ministry*); Warren Quanbeck, "Roman Catholic and Lutheran Relationships," in Vilmos Vajta, ed. *The Gospel and Unity* (Minneapolis, Minn.: Augsburg Publishing House, 1971), pp. 131-143; Warren Quanbeck, *Search for Understanding: Lutheran Conversations with Reformed, Anglican, and Roman Catholic Churches* (Minneapolis, Minn.: Augsburg Publishing House, 1972), pp. 87-117; Nils Ehrenström and Günther Gassmann, *Confessions in Dialogue: A Survey of Bilateral Conversations among World Confessional Families 1962–1971* (Geneva: World Council of Churches, 1972), pp. 15-31; Andre Appel and Jan Willebrands, eds., "Report of the Joint Lutheran/Roman Catholic Study Commission on 'The Gospel and the Church,'" reprinted from *Lutheran World* 19 (1972); J. Robert Wright, "Documentation and Reflection—The Graymoor Conference: Episcopalians and Roman Catholics View Their Future," *Anglican Theological Review* 54 (1972): 351-359; Herbert Ryan and J. Robert Wright, eds., *Episcopalians and Roman Catholics—Can They Ever Get Together?* (Denville, N.J.: Dimension Books, 1972). Of great importance in this connection is the "Windsor Statement on Eucharistic Doctrine," setting forth the shared belief agreed to by the International Anglican and Roman Catholic Commission of Bishops and Theologians and released on December 31, 1971; for the text, see *Worship* 46 (1972): 2-5.—See also Richard L. Davies and Ernest L. Unterkoefler, eds., *Reconsiderations: Roman Catholic/Presbyterian and Reformed Theological Conversations 1966–1967* (New York: World Horizons, 1967).

34. For example, the two works of John Jay Hughes, *Absolutely Null and Utterly Void: The Papal Condemnation of Anglican Orders 1896* (Washington, D.C.: Corpus Books, 1968) and *Stewards of the Lord: A Reappraisal of Anglican Orders* (London: Sheed and Ward, 1970).

35. See, for instance, Edward P. Echlin, *The Anglican Eucharist in Ecumenical Perspective: Doctrine and Rite from Cranmer to Seabury* (New York: Seabury Press, 1968). The Jesuit author sees a movement in the 240-year period from 1548 to 1789 toward an interpretation of the Eucharist among Anglicans that includes the ideas of a propitiatory sacrifice and a persisting real presence.

36. Some Roman Catholic theologians have argued that intercommunion need not await formal union between the Roman Catholic Church and other denominations. Historically, they insist, the Eucharist is not only a symbol of unity in faith already reached but also a means to obtaining such unity. They have on occasion even urged that the leaders of the Roman Catholic Church and of the denominations with which the Roman Catholic Church is engaged in discussions looking toward intercommunion begin by celebrating the sacrament of the altar jointly in order to help in creating the consensus of faith that both parties are seeking.

37. See Erwin Iserloh, "Luther in Contemporary Catholic Thought," in Hans Küng, ed, *Do We Know the Others? (Concilium: Theology in the Age of Renewal*, vol. 14) (New York: Paulist Press, 1966), pp. 5-15.

38. More responsible controversialists than the three named were the Dominican theologian Thomas de Vio de Gaeta (Cajetan) (1469–1534); the irenic Franciscan Caspar Schatzgeyer (1463–1527); John Gropper (1503–1559), who incurred the suspicion of heresy because of the concessions that he seemed to be making to the Lutheran movement; and George Witzel (1501–1573), a one-time supporter of Luther who subsequently abandoned him without ceasing to demand far-reaching reforms within the part of the medieval church that supported the papacy. As

the revised view of the sixteenth century has gained acceptance, these moderate defenders of the papal position have also acquired added respect and appreciation.

39. Among the able expositions of the revised Roman Catholic view of Luther and the Lutheran Reformation that have appeared in English are the works of Joseph Lortz, *The Reformation in Germany*, trans. Ronald Walls, 2 vols. (New York: Herder and Herder, 1968), *The Reformation: A Problem for Today*, trans. John C. Dwyer (Westminster, Md.: The Newman Press, 1964), and *How the Reformation Came*, trans. Otto M. Knab (New York: Herder and Herder, 1964); Harry J. McSorley, *Luther: Right or Wrong? An Ecumenical-Theological Study of Luther's Major Work, "The Bondage of the Will"* (New York: The Newman Press, 1969); Jared Wicks, ed., *Catholic Scholars Dialogue with Luther* (Chicago: Loyola University Press, 1970); John C. Olin, ed., *Luther, Erasmus, and the Reformation: A Catholic-Protestant Reappraisal* (New York: Fordham University Press, 1969); John M. Todd, *Martin Luther: A Biographical Study* (Westminster, Md.: The Newman Press, 1964); John P. Dolan, *History of the Reformation: A Conciliatory Assessment of Opposite Views* (New York: Desclee and Company, 1965). See also Robert E. McNally, *The Unreformed Church* (New York: Sheed and Ward, 1965).

40. Representative of a large and growing literature in this area are Henri Brouillard, *The Knowledge of God* (New York: Herder and Herder, 1968), a critique of Karl Barth's position on the "natural" unknowability of God; Jerome Hamer, *Karl Barth*, trans. Dominic M. Maruca (Westminster, Md.: The Newman Press, 1962); Colm O'Grady, *The Church in the Theology of Karl Barth* (Washington, D.C.: Corpus Books, 1968); René Marle, *Bonhoeffer: The Man and His Work*, trans. Rosemary Sheed (New York: The Newman Press, 1968); Heinrich Fries, *Bultmann, Barth, and Catholic Theology*, trans. Leonard Swidler (Pittsburgh, Penn.: Duquesne University Press, 1967); René Marle, *Bultmann and Christian Faith*, trans.

Theodore DuBois (Westminster, Md.: The Newman Press, 1968); Thomas O'Meara and Donald Weisser, eds., *Rudolf Bultmann in Catholic Thought* (New York: Herder and Herder, 1968); Carl J. Armbruster, Jr., *The Vision of Paul Tillich* (New York: Sheed and Ward, 1967); Donald J. Keefe, *Thomism and the Ontological Theology of Paul Tillich: A Comparison of Systems* (Leiden, Holland: E. J. Brill, 1971); and Thomas O'Meara and Celestin D. Weisser, eds., *Paul Tillich in Catholic Thought* (Dubuque, Iowa: The Priory Press, 1964).

41. At least until the Synod of Meaux (845) all bishops were regarded as "vicars of Christ," that is, wielders of divinely imparted authority. As late as the Council of Trent the Spanish bishops laid claim to the title, although the claim provoked acrimonious disputes in the council, fighting in the streets, and even bloodshed.

42. It is Roman Catholic teaching that the same infallibility is assured to the College of Bishops when it exercises the supreme teaching authority with the pope, for instance, in a general council.

43. Papal infallibility does not imply that the pope is personally sinless, that he is inspired in the sense in which the sacred Scriptures are inspired, or that he is the bearer of new revelations.

44. Three articles by Roman Catholics in the *Journal of Ecumenical Studies* 8 (1971), bear directly on the issue of papal infallibility: Leonard Swidler, *"The Ecumenical Problem Today: Papal Infallibility,"* pp. 751-767; John T. Ford, "Infallibility—From Vatican I to the Present," pp. 768-791; and Brian Tierney, "Origins of Papal Infallibility," pp. 841-864.

45. Roman Catholics concede, for instance, that political considerations were allowed to determine the omission of a passage that denounced the leveling of the charge of deicide (that is, the killing of God) against the Jews. Similar considerations made the document in its final form merely deplore (rather than condemn) anti-Semitism. It must not be forgotten that a considerable number of Roman Catholics are Arabs or live under Arab governments.

46. On the whole question of the relations of Roman Catholicism and Judaism, see Augustin Bea, *The Church and the Jewish People: A Commentary on the Second Vatican Council's Declaration on the Relation of the Church to Non-Christian Religions* (New York: Harper & Row, 1966). See also Jean Danielou, *Dialogue with Israel,* trans. Joan Marie Roth (Baltimore, Md.: Helicon Press, 1966), and Edward Zerin and Benedict Viviano, *What Catholics Should Know About Jews,* ed., Augustine Rock (Chicago: Priory Press, 1967).

47. See, for example, Eugene Hillman, *The Wider Ecumenism* (New York: Herder and Herder, 1968).

48. See, for example, Wiliam Johnstone, *The Still Point: Reflections on Zen and Christian Mysticism* (New York: Fordham University Press, 1970).

49. *Lumen gentium,* 16.

50. See, for example, Roger Garaudy and Quentin Lauer, *A Christian-Communist Dialogue* (Garden City, N.Y.: Doubleday & Company, 1968); Giulio Girardi, *Marxism and Christianity,* trans. Kevin Traynor (New York: The Macmillan Company, 1968); and chap. 3, "Non-Religious Humanism and Belief in God," in Edward Schillebeeckx, *God and Man,* trans. Edward Fitzgerald and Peter Tomlinson (New York: Sheed and Ward, 1969), pp. 41-84.

51. Jacques de Molay (1243?–1314) was the last grand master of the Knights Templars. When the order came under suspicion early in the fourteenth century de Molay invited Clement VII to investigate the charges made against the knights. In 1307 Philip IV of France ordered the arrest and examination of all Templars in his domains, including de Molay. De Molay confessed that at his entrance into the order he had had to abjure Christ. When the pope initiated his own investigation, de Molay and many of his knights withdrew their confessions, alleging that they had been procured through torture. Clement was persuaded to suppress the Templars and in 1314 three cardinals sentenced de Molay and other officials of the order to perpetual imprisonment. When they once more denied the confessions on which their judges had based this verdict, Philip's officers burned them at the stake as relapsed heretics the same afternoon. Many Roman Catholics saw in the choice of de Molay as the eponym of the Masonic boys' and young men's organization a deliberate effort on the part of Freemasonry to excite and perpetuate suspicion and antagonism against the Roman Catholic Church.

52. A number of secret societies have developed within the Roman Catholic Church as a kind of counterpart to those outside the denomination. These include the Order of the Alhambra, the Catholic Order of Foresters, the Catholic Workmen, the Ancient Order of Hibernians, the Knights of Columbus, and the Knights of Peter Claver.

53. But in 1452 Nicholas V allowed the Portuguese monarch not only to permit but even to take part in the slave traffic.

54. See Karl Rahner, "Anonymous Christianity and the Missionary Task of the Church," *IDOC-International,* North American edition, 4 April 1970, pp. 70-96.

55. See in this connection "Mission Theology for Our Times: Conclusions of the SEDOS [that is, Servizio di Documentazione e Studi] Symposium, Rome, March 27-31, 1969," in Pedro S. de Achutegui, ed., *Mission and Development: Ecumenical Conversations* (Manila, P.R.: Loyola House of Studies of the Ateneo de Manila University, 1970), pp. 158-163.

56. Traditionally Roman Catholic theology saw unbelief, in the sense of the Latin *infidelitas* as taking the form (1) of an ignorant lack of faith of the kind ascribed in 1 Timothy 1:13 to St. Paul prior to his conversion, or (2) of a guilty lack of faith arising out of general religious indifference, or (3) of "positive infidelity," that is, a deliberate and direct rejection of faith. Some contemporary Roman Catholic theologians see this differentiation as inadequate to an understanding of faith as the grace of faith with its accompanying enlightenment. God offers this grace, they argue, to all men in his desire for their salvation. The *free* refusal of this grace of faith entails guilt; in the case of human beings who have not yet achieved the kind of freedom that enables them to refuse the offer of the grace of faith, even if

they are atheists, there cannot be guilty unbelief at the level of what Karl Rahner calls "the ultimate depths of existence."

57. The material in this section was prepared by the editor primarily from material on Roman Catholicism in the United States written by the author for inclusion in *Lutheran Cyclopedia,* ed. Erwin L. Lueker (St. Louis: Concordia Publishing House, 1975).

58. *1976 Catholic Almanac,* ed. Felician A. Foy (Huntingdon, Ind.: Our Sunday Visitor, 1975), p. 459.

BIBLIOGRAPHY

BISHOPS, CARDINALS AND PRIESTS

Feuillet, Andre. *The Priesthood of Christ and His Ministers.* Trans. Matthew J. O'Connell, New York: Doubleday & Co., 1975.

Suenens, Leon Joseph. *Coresponsibility in the Church.* New York: Herder and Herder, 1968.

THE CHURCH

Butler, B. C. *The Idea of the Church.* Baltimore: Helicon Press, 1962.

Dulles, Avery. *The Dimensions of the Church: A Postconciliar Reflection.* Westminster, Md.: The Newman Press, 1967.

———. *Models of the Church.* New York: Doubleday & Co., 1974.

———. *Church Membership as a Catholic and Ecumenical Problem.* Milwaukee: Marquette University, 1974.

Küng, Hans. *The Church.* Trans. Ray and Rosaleen Ockenden. New York: Sheed and Ward, 1967.

———. *Structures of the Church.* Trans. Salvator Attanasio. New York: Thomas Nelson and Sons, 1964.

———. *Truthfulness: The Future of the Church.* New York: Sheed and Ward, 1968.

LeGuillou, M. J. *Christ and Church: A Theology of Mystery.* Trans. Charles E. Schaldenbrand. New York: Desclee Company, 1966.

McKenzie, John L. *Authority in the Church.* New York: Sheed and Ward, 1966.

Rahner, Karl. *The Church and the Sacraments.* Trans. W. J. O'Hara. New York: Herder and Herder, 1963.

———. *The Shape of the Church to Come.* Trans. Edward Quinn. New York: Seabury Press, 1974.

Riga, Peter J. *The Church Renewed.* New York: Sheed and Ward, 1966.

Schnackenburg, Rudolph. *The Church in the New Testament.* New York: Herder and Herder, 1965.

Tavard, George. *The Pilgrim Church.* New York: Herder and Herder, 1967.

THE COMMUNION OF SAINTS

Delehaye, Hippolyte. *The Legends of the Saints: An Introduction to Hagiography.* Trans. V. M. Crawford. Notre Dame, Ind.: University of Notre Dame Press, 1961.

Lamirande, Emilien. *The Communion of Saints.* Trans. A Manson. New York:

Hawthorn Books, 1963.

Molinari, Paul. *Saints: Their Place in the Church.* Trans. Dominic Maruca. New York: Sheed and Ward, 1965.

Sheppard, Lancelot. *The Saints Who Never Were.* Dayton, Ohio: Pflaum Press, 1969.

THE IMPACT OF THE ECUMENICAL MOVEMENT ON THE ROMAN CATHOLIC DOCTRINE OF THE CHURCH

Congar, Yves M.-J. *Ecumenism and the Future of the Church.* Chicago: Priory Press, 1967.

Dulles, Avery. *Revelation and the Quest for Unity.* Washington, D.C.: Corpus Books, 1968.

Hurley, Michael. *Theology of Ecumenism.* Notre Dame, Ind.: Fides Publishers, 1969.

Lambert, Bernard. *Ecumenism: Theology and History.* Trans. Lancelot C. Sheppard. New York: Herder and Herder, 1967.

Lash, Nicholas, ed. *. . . Until He Comes: A Study in the Progress Toward Christain Unity.* Dayton, Ohio: Pflaum Press, 1968.

McGovern, James O. *The Church in the Churches.* Washington, D.C.: Corpus Books, 1968.

Schlink, Edmund. *After the Council: The Meaning of Vatican II for Protestantism and the Ecumenical Dialogue.* Trans. Herbert J. A. Bouman. Philadelphia: Fortress Press, 1968.

Sheerin, John B. *A Practical Guide to Ecumenism.* Revised edition. New York: Paulist Press, 1967.

THE POPE

Brown, Raymond E., Donfried, Karl P., Reumann, John, eds. *Peter in the New Testament.* Minneapolis: Augsburg Publishing House, 1973.

Gratsch, Edward J. *Where Peter Is.* New York: Alba House, 1975.

Kirvan, John J., ed. *The Infallibility Debate.* New York: Paulist Press, 1971. Essays by Gregory Baum, George Lindbeck, Richard McBrien, and Harry J. McSorley on the issues raised by Hans Küng's *Infallible? An Inquiry.*

Küng, Hans. *Infallible? An Inquiry.* Trans. Edward Quinn. Garden City, N.Y.: Doubleday & Company, 1971. Among the many discussions of this controversial book, see John T. Ford, "Küng on Infallibility: A Review Article," *The Thomist* 35 (1971): 501-512; "Hans Küng's *Infallible? An Inquiry*: A Symposium," a series of essays by Avery Dulles, Michael A. Fahey, and George Lindbeck in *America,* April 24, 1971, pp. 427-433; and Gregory Baum's "Truth in the Church—Küng, Rahner, and Beyond," *The Ecumenist* 9 (1971): 33-48; and B. C. Butler, "The Limits of Infallibility," *The Tablet,* April 17, 1971, pp. 373-375, and April 24, 1971, pp. 398-400.

McCord, Peter J., ed. *A Pope for All Christians? An Inquiry into the Role of Peter in the Modern Church.* New York: Paulist Press, 1976.

Oakley, Francis. *Council over Pope? Toward a Provisional Ecclesiology.* New York: Herder and Herder, 1969. Chaps. 4-6 (pp. 105-190) discuss contemporary conciliarism in Roman Catholic theological thought.

Simons, Francis. *Infallibility and the Evidence.* Springfield, Ill.: Templegate Publishers, 1968.

THE PRIESTHOOD OF THE FAITHFUL

Brungs, Robert A. *A Priestly People.* New York: Sheed and Ward, 1968.

De Smedt, Emile-Joseph. *The Priesthood of the Faithful.* Trans. Joseph M. F. Marique. Glen Rock, N.J.: Paulist Press, 1962.

THE RELIGIOUS

Berkery, Patrick J. *Restructuring Religious Life: A Plan for Renewal.* Staten Island, N.Y.: Alba House, 1968.

Cegielka, Francis A. *All Things New: Radical Reform and the Religious Life.* New York: Sheed and Ward, 1969.

Gelpi, Donald L. *Functional Asceticism: A Guideline for American Religious.* New York: Sheed and Ward, 1966.

Huyghe, Gerard, Karl Rahner, and others. *Religious Orders in the Modern World: A Symposium.* Westminster, Md.: The Newman Press, 1965.

Klimisch, (Sister) Mary Jane. *The One Bride: The Church and Consecrated Virginity.* New York: Sheed and Ward, 1965.

Mulhern, Philip F. *Dedicated Poverty.* Washington, D.C.: Corpus Books, 1970.

RELIGIOUS EDUCATION AND CATECHETICS

Babin, Pierre. *Options*. New York: Herder and Herder, 1967. A highly praised and provocative inquiry by a leader in the new catechetics movement in which he canvasses the question, Is formal religious education desirable or even possible today? The author's sequel to this work, from the same press in the same year, is entitled *Methods*.

Flynn, Elizabeth W., and La Faso, John F. *Group Discussion as a Learning Process*. Paramus, N.J.: Paulist Press, 1972.

Fundamentals and Programs of a New Catechesis. Trans. Walter Van de Putte. Pittsburgh: Duquesne University Press, 1966. A summary report of the experiences of the Nijmegen Higher Institute of Catechetics of Holland.

McDermott, Timothy S. *Beyond Questions and Answers: The Creed for Today's Catholic*. New York: Herder and Herder, 1968. An effort to bridge the gap between the old catechisms and the new catechetics for the reassurance of older Roman Catholics.

Moran, Gabriel. *Vision and Tactics*. New York: Herder and Herder, 1968. A plea for free experimentation as the indispensable as a means to achieving the ideal of catechetical excellence.

Ranwez, Pierre. *The Dawn of the Christian Life: The Religious Education of the Young*. Trans. Edmond Bonin. Paramus, N.J.: Paulist Press, 1970.

Sloyan, Gerard S. *Speaking of Religious Education*. New York: Herder and Herder, 1968.

Van Caster, Marcel. *The Structure of Catechetics*. New York: Herder and Herder, 1965.

RELIGIOUS FREEDOM

Murray, John Courtney. *The Problem of Religious Freedom*. Westminster, Md.: The Newman Press, 1965.

———, ed. *Religious Liberty: An End and a Beginning—The Declaration on Religious Freedom, an Ecumenical Discussion*. New York: The Macmillan Company, 1966.

Sturzo, Luigi. *Church and State*. 2 vols. Notre Dame, Indiana: University of Notre Dame Press, 1962. The author traces the development of official church-state relations from Constantine the Great to the threshold of World War II.

THE ROMAN CATHOLIC CHURCH AND SECRET SOCIETIES

Whalen, William J. *Handbook of Secret Organizations*. 2nd printing. Milwaukee: Wis. Bruce Publishing Company, 1967.

ROMAN CATHOLIC MISSIONS AND MISSIONARY PRACTICE

Burns, Patrick J., ed. *Mission and Witness: The Life of the Church*. Westminster, Md.: The Newman Press, 1965.

Cotter, James P., ed. *The Word in the Third World*. Washington, D.C.: Corpus Books, 1968. The papers, comments, and discussions of the Woodstock Conference on Mission Theology of 1967.

PART V

CHURCHES DERIVED

FROM POST-TRIDENTINE

ROMAN CATHOLICISM

---

14. The Old Catholic Communion in Europe

The term "Old Catholic" describes a number of church bodies that either themselves separated at various times from the jurisdiction of the Roman see or have descended in one way or another from these seceding church bodies. They have retained in varying degrees distinctive doctrines and practices of the Roman Catholic Church, but in general they have rejected the authority of the bishop of Rome as of divine right, along with various decisions of the Council of Trent and of later Roman Catholic popes and councils that they see as contradicting at one point or another "ancient Catholic principles."

The oldest of these communities is the Church of Utrecht in the Netherlands, consisting of the archdiocese of Utrecht and the sees of Haarlem and Deventer, which has been separate from the See of Rome ever since 1724. The issue that provoked the breach was ultimately Jansenism, especially as the Convent of Port-Royal had propagated it.[1]

After Vatican Council I, a group of Roman Catholic Christians in Germany, Switzerland, and Austria refused to accept the council's definition of the dogmas of the infallibility and universal ordinary jurisdiction of the pope. Under the leadership of the church historian Ignaz von Döllinger they withdrew from the Roman Catholic Church, formed Old Catholic churches in their respective countries, and obtained episcopal orders from the Church of Utrecht.

In 1889 the Old Catholic churches and the Church of Utrecht adopted the Declaration of Utrecht as their common doctrinal basis. It accepts the teachings of the primitive church as the ecumenical councils down to A.D. 1000 define them, and affirms the sacrifice of the Mass and the real presence of Christ in the sacrament of the altar. It is silent about the propitiatory nature of the Mass and the doctrine of transubstantiation. It rejects the dogmas of the immaculate conception of the Blessed Virgin Mary and papal infallibility, the encyclicals *Unigenitus* (1713) against Quesnel and Jansenism and *Auctorem fidei* (1794) against the Synod of Pistoia (1785), as well as the *Syllabus* of modern errors (1864).

In 1907 the Polish National Catholic Church of America became a part of the Old Catholic communion with the consecration of Bishop Francis Hodur, its primate, by the Old Catholic archbishop of Utrecht and the Old Catholic bishops of Haarlem and Deventer.

In 1925 the Old Catholic communion formally recognized Anglican orders and in 1932 the European churches comprising the Old Catholic communion entered into full communion with the Church of England on the basis of the Bonn Agreement of 1931. Intercommunion with the overseas provinces of the Anglican communion and with the daughter-churches of the Church of England followed.

Over the years the Old Catholic communion has been engaged in conferences with representatives of the Eastern Orthodox communion looking toward intercommunion, but these have not been successful to date.

A new era in Roman Catholic–Old Catholic relations began in November 1966, when the Roman see withdrew unreserved subscription of the Formula of Submission (1665) of Alexander VII and of the encyclical *Unigenitus* (1713) of Clement XI as an indispensable precondition of a resumption of intercommunion.

Polish National Catholic Church of America

The heady wine of freedom that nineteenth-century Polish immigrants tasted in the United States affected not only their political but also their ecclesiastical outlook.

The revolt against the Roman Catholic Church began almost simultaneously in widely separated areas of the country.

In Chicago, the Reverend Antoni Stanislaus Kozlowski left a Roman Catholic assistantship to organize an independent Polish parish in 1895. Other congregations sprang up in imitation, formed a synod, and elected Kozlowski as bishop; he obtained Old Catholic consecration in Switzerland in 1897.

Another independent parish established itself in Buffalo, New York, in the same year. It called the Reverend Stephen Kaminski to be its parish priest and chose him as its bishop at a parish synod; Joseph René Vilatte consecrated Kaminski as his suffragan for the Polish Old Catholics in 1898.

In the 1890s the Polish members of the Roman Catholic Sacred Heart of Jesus parish of Scranton, Pennsylvania, began to have difficulties with their German pastor and their Irish bishop over the degree to which they might participate in the management of their parish affairs. Things went from bad to worse and in 1897 the dissident parishioners called a forceful, eloquent, widely read and strongly nationalistic[2] former assistant priest of the parish, the Reverend Francis Hodur, to shepherd them in the new church that they had begun to build. Later in the same year Hodur organized his flock as the first Polish National Catholic parish.[3] The following year he visited Rome in the hope of obviating a schism, but he failed in his mission.

In the Scranton area, too, the example of these independents quickly found imitators.

In 1904 a synod of delegates from twenty-four parishes in five states organized the Polish National Catholic Church in America (Polski Narodowy Katolicki Kościoł w Ameryce), decreed the use of Polish in worship, invited the cooperation of other Christian communities, repudiated the Roman Catholic Church's claim to be the sole interpreter of Christian teaching, and chose Hodur as bishop-elect. The Old Catholic archbishop of Utrecht consecrated him in 1907, with the Old Catholic bishops of Haarlem and Deventer as co-consecrators.

Most of Kozlowski's group joined the new body after their primate's death in 1907, and in 1914 the parish formerly headed by Kaminski (who had died in 1911) also affiliated with the Polish National Catholic Church.

In 1913 a parallel movement began among some Lithuanian congregations in Pennsylvania. It led to the formation of the Lithuanian National Catholic Church in America, which became an affiliate of the Polish National Catholic Church.[4]

A diocese has been erected for a number of Slovak parishes that have followed the Passaic (New Jersey) Slovak parish into the Polish National Catholic Church.

The Polish National Catholic Church acknowledges Holy Scripture, holy tradition, and the first four ecumenical councils as its foundation, but its official teaching still bears the imprint of Hodur's own thinking.[5] Chief is the Confession of Faith, which Hodur drew up and which the church adopted officially in 1913.[6] It must be regarded as a supplement to the so-called Apostles' and Nicene creeds, both of which are used in the denomination's worship. The short form of the Confession of Faith reads:

I believe in one God, the Father, the cause of all existence, Eternal Truth, Love and Justice.[7]

I believe in Jesus Christ, the Saviour and the spiritual Regenerator of the world; of one substance with God, begotten to humanity of the Holy Mother Mary.

I believe that this Nazarene Master, through His holy life, work, teaching, and martyrdom, became the glowing ember of a new life of mankind, a life taking its beginning, strength and fullness in knowledge of God, in loving Him, and in fulfilling His holy will.

I believe that the Holy Spirit, the Spirit of God, rules the world, and that from the Holy Spirit flows grace, which brings it to pass, that when a man cooperates with it in life he shall attain joy eternal in God.

I believe in the holy church of Christ, apostolic and universal. I believe that this church is the true teacher, both of individual man and of all mankind; that it is a steward of divine graces and a light in man's temporal pilgrimage to God and salvation.

I believe in the necessity of hearing the Word of God and the receiving of the holy sacraments.

I believe that all people, as children of God, are equal.

I believe that all people have equal rights to existence, but also sacred obligations toward God, themselves, their nation, and the whole of human society.

I believe in the ultimate justice of God, life beyond the grave, immortality, and eternal bliss in the union with God of all people, generations and times. Amen.[8]

A Catechism of the Polish National Catholic Church shows the influence of the Roman Catholic *Baltimore Catechism* at many points. It explicitly affirms the Trinity and the deity of Christ. It lists under daily prayers the Hail, Mary (with the concluding petition, "Holy Mary, Mother of God, pray for us sinners, now and at the hour of our death. Amen."[9]) Faith, "a divine virtue infused into our hearts by God by which we firmly believe in the truths which God has revealed," is "absolutely necessary for salvation."[10] Tradition is "the teachings and practices of the Apostolic Church, which complement the New Testament writings."[11] The church is the Body of Christ, with Christ as its head and all baptized people as members, as well as "a gathering of people professing the truths of Christ and using those means to salvation which He instituted."[12] The resurrection of the body means "that personal individuality is preserved beyond the grave."[13] Eternal punishment would contradict the wisdom, love and justice of God; "ultimately through the mercy and love of God, all mankind will be redeemed, purified, and saved."[14] The seven sacraments are "baptism with confirmation as its completion; the word of God;[15] penance; holy eucharist; extreme unction; holy orders; matrimony."[16] In the Eucharist the consecration of the bread and the wine marks "the sacramental change of bread and wine into the mystical Body and Blood of Our Lord Jesus Christ."[17] The sacrifice of the Mass differs from the sacrifice on the cross only in its presentation. On the cross Christ "was offered in a bloody manner and in the sacrifice of the mass he is offered in a mystical, unbloody manner. The mass derives all its value and merits from the sacrifice of the cross offered once and for all time."[18] The celebrant may offer the Mass "for the spiritual and temporal welfare of the living and for the eternal repose of the dead."[19] Christ is present "whole and entire under the forms of either consecrated bread or wine."[20] Holy Communion is normally administered to the congregation under the form of bread only, but it may be administered under both forms on occasions that the church indicates. In extreme unction "a sick person receives health and strength of soul and sometimes of the body."[21] Holy orders is "the sacrament by which men become priests and receive the power and grace to perform their sacred duties," including "the power to offer the sacrifice of the mass and to remit and retain sins" in Christ's name.[22] The minister of the sacrament of matrimony is the priest.[23]

The Polish National Catholic Church rejects the claim of the papacy to be the deciding authority in matters of faith and morals. It accepts the teachings of the first four ecumenical councils as having dealt with all essential matters of faith.

The rite of the Polish National Catholic Church is the Latin Rite of the nineteenth century translated into the vernacular. Its calendar has special feasts of the Poor Shepherds, the Polish National Catholic Church, the Remembrance of the Dear Polish Fatherland, Brotherly Love, and the Christian Family.

The Polish National Catholic Church has always been in communion with the Old Catholic Church of Utrecht from which it received the apostolic succession. In 1946 the Polish National Catholic Church and the Protestant Episcopal Church in the United States of America established intercommunion, and in 1958 the Polish National Catholic Church entered into official inter communion with the Anglican Church of Canada. With Polish National Catholic bishops taking part in consecrations of Protestant Episcopal and Canadian Anglican bishops as co-consecrators, an increasing number of members of these hierarchies have received consecrations that the Roman Catholic Church regards as valid even though irregular.

Lines of authority run upward from the parish through the seniorate (the equivalent of a deanery) and the diocese to the whole church. The chief officer of the church is the prime bishop.

The headquarters of the Polish National Catholic Church of America are in Scranton, Pennsylvania. It maintains close relations with an autonomous daughter synod in Poland which has its own hierarchy.[24] In the United States and Canada it reports 165 churches and missions with an inclusive membership of 285,000.[25] Services are held in both the English language and the respective European vernacular.

NOTES

1. An appreciation of the Port-Royal tradition of piety and theology is almost a hallmark of the Old Catholic movement.
2. "Hodur was full of the spirit of Polish Messianism as expounded by [Adam] Mickiewicz [1798–1866], an author whom he greatly admired" (Theodore Andrews, *The Polish National Catholic Church in America and Poland* [London: SPCK, 1953], p. 27). The Polish National Catholic Church's calendar commemorates Mickiewicz, Julius Sławacki and Zygmunt Kasiński, the "trio of Polish Messianic poets," along with John Hus, Jerome Savanarola, and Peter Waldo.
3. Roman Catholic pressure in Scranton and Lackawanna County was sufficiently strong to force the new body to use the name Polish Reformed Church in the articles of incorporation (ibid., p. 29).
4. Hodur consecrated Jonas Gritēnas as

bishop for the Lithuanian body in 1925. Upon the latter's death in 1928, the parishes (one in Scranton, a second in Wilkes-Barre, and a third in Lawrence, Massachusetts) that comprised the Lithuanian National Catholic Church were placed under the Reverend Michael Valadka of the Providence of God parish in Scranton as administrator; although the Lithuanian National Catholic Church continues to have legal existence, the three parishes, with about 1,800 members, function to all intents and purposes as part of the Central Diocese of the Polish body, whose confession of faith and theological principles the Lithuanian church carefully reproduced. See the thirty-fifth-anniversary volume, *Lietuvių Katalikų Tautinė Bažnyčia, Scrantono Parapija* (Scranton, Penn.: Providence of God Parish, 1949), especially pp. 72-73, 175-190.

5. This is most apparent in its doctrines of man and of the last things. The former stresses human dignity rather than human depravity and describes sin solely in terms of "actual sin." The stress on long-lasting rather than eternal punishment and the silence on purgatory may reflect a reaction against an overemphasis on hellfire in the popular Roman Catholic preaching with which Hodur was acquainted. See Andrews, pp. 51-53, 55.

6. For the full text as contained in the constitution, see Andrews, pp. 109-111; a slightly shorter variant version occurs in Paul Fox, *The Polish National Catholic Church* (Scranton, Penn.: School of Christian Living, 1956), pp. 112-113. For an English version of the founder's own commentary on this confession, see Franciszek Hodur, "Our Faith" (*Nasza Wiara*), trans. Theodore L. and Joseph C. Zawitowski (Fall River, Mass.: Theodore L. Zawitowski, 1966) (twenty-page mimeographed pamphlet).

7. The longer form of this article reads in part: "I believe in God Almighty, the Cause of all existence, a Being whose Spirit permeates the whole universe, and is the source of its life and evolution, physical as well as spiritual and moral. . . . God as Spirit of Life, Holiness, and Goodness influences chosen spirits of the peoples, who at given epochs in human evolution are the creative agents in the building of the Kingdom of God on earth. This immediate influence of God . . . is found in all nations and in all times, for the purpose of bringing life, evolution, and the attainment of the highest degree of culture to individual nations and states, and to humanity as a whole" (Andrews, p. 109).

8. *A Catechism of the Polish National Catholic Church* (Scranton, Penn.: Mission Fund, Polish National Catholic Church, 1962), p. 5. Very influential on the theological thought of the Polish National Catholic Church have been *Eleven Great Principles* which Hodur set forth in 1923. This document discusses the spiritual communion of Christ with the believers; the relation of the National Catholic Church to the kingdom of God on earth; salvation, the condition of entering the kingdom of God; leading a man into the kingdom of God; the church and its foundations; the word of God, the great sacrament of the church; the love of God and the inconsistency with it of the doctrine of everlasting punishment; nations as members of God's one family on earth; the kingdom of God as a federation of all free nations; religious rites in the vernacular; and the right of parishioners to own the property of the church.

9. Ibid., p. 3. The official sources of doctrine do not have a developed Mariology.

10. Ibid., pp. 9-10.

11. Ibid., p. 11.

12. Ibid., p. 22.

13. Ibid., p. 27.

14. Ibid., p. 34.

15. Through the sacrament of the word of God, Christians "learn to know the divine will of God, become strengthened in faith, are united with Christ our Lord, become better qualified to labor for the kingdom of God" (ibid., p. 59).

16. Ibid., p. 52.

17. Ibid., p. 47.

18. Ibid., p. 70.

19. Ibid., p. 73.

20. Ibid., p. 73.

21. Ibid., pp. 74-75.

22. Ibid., p. 76.

23. Ibid., p. 78.

24. When the prime bishop of the Polish National Church consecrated bishops

Tadeusz Majewski and Franciszek Koc in Warsaw in 1966, one of the co-consecrators was Bazyli Doroszkiewicz, bishop of Wrocław and Paznań in the Russian Orthodox Autocephalous Church in Poland. The other co-con-secrators were the bishop ordinary of the Polish National Catholic Church in Poland and two Mariavite bishops. This was the first time that an Eastern Orthodox bishop participated as co-consecrator in an Old Catholic con-secration.

25. This writer gratefully acknowledges the assistance of the Reverend Theodore R. Hanus, pastor of Peace Church, Scranton, Pennsylvania, in securing information about the Polish National Catholic Church.

BIBLIOGRAPHY

Andrews, Theodore. *The Polish National Catholic Church in America and Poland.* London: SPCK, 1953. A doctoral thesis by a priest of the Protestant Episcopal Church in the United States of America.

A Catechism of the Polish National Catholic Church. Scranton, Penn.: Mission Fund, Polish National Catholic Church, 1962 (ninety-six-page brochure).

15. Other Churches Claiming Old Catholic Orders

Early in this century various individuals put forth efforts at establishing Old Catholic missions in Great Britain and the United States. Late in 1907 a suspended English Roman Catholic priest, Richard O'Halloran, and two excommunicated monsignori approached an ex-Roman-Catholic priest who had served briefly as a curate in an Anglo-Catholic parish in London, Arnold Harris Mathew (1852–1919). Halloran informed Mathew that large numbers of Roman Catholic priests and congregations in England desired to withdraw from the Roman Catholic Church and become Old Catholics and that they had elected Mathew as their bishop. On the strength of these representations, which the Old Catholic leaders in Holland learned only later to have been false, the archbishop of Utrecht consecrated Mathew. In 1910 Mathew declared his tiny following autonomous and independent. In the years that followed he proceeded to consecrate a number of bishops, among them (in 1913) an Austrian nobleman, Rudolph Francis Prince de Landas Berghe et de Rache, Duc de St. Winock (1873–1920). With the outbreak of World War I the prince-bishop fled to the United States to escape internment in Great Britain as an enemy alien. On October 3, 1916, de Landas Berghe consecrated William Henry Francis (Brothers).[1] The following day, the prince-bishop consecrated a former Roman Catholic priest, Carmel Henry Carfora (1878–1958), as bishop of the Old Roman Catholic Church of America with the title of archbishop of Canada. When the prince-bishop returned to the Roman Catholic Church in 1919, Carfora established himself in Chicago as the "Most Illustrious Lord, the Supreme Primate of the North American Old Roman Catholic Church." In the course of his career he consecrated a considerable number of bishops, many of whom established themselves as heads of rival jurisdictions. When Archbishop Carfora died his church body claimed sixty-two churches and a membership of 84,435.[2] A schism followed upon the death of the supreme prelate.

The North American Old Roman Catholic Church (Brooklyn, New York)

Carfora's successor as primate-metropolitan, according to the *Yearbook of American Churches for 1959*, was the Most Reverend Hubert Augustus

Rogers, a black prelate whom William Ernest James Robertson of the African Orthodox Church had consecrated in 1937 and whom Carfora reconsecrated in 1942.

As far back as 1950, the North American Old Roman Catholic Church rejected the Church of Utrecht and its associated Old Catholic Churches in Europe because of their alleged heterodoxy. With the Second Council of Utrecht of 1763 the North American Old Roman Catholic Church affirms its reverence for the Holy See of Rome. But, it asserts, since the North American Old Roman Catholic Church, as a part of the continuing authentic Old Catholic Church, stands under the Roman see's unjust censure, the North American Old Roman Catholic Church must continue to exist as an autonomous body. It administers the seven sacraments according to the canons and prescriptions of the Roman Catholic Church and uses the usual sacramentals. It teaches devotion to the Blessed Virgin Mary and veneration of the images and relics of the saints, although it declares that it avoids superstitious excesses. It admits married men to the priesthood. It describes its teachings about the person of Christ, original sin, the eternal punishment of hell, and the necessity of faith for salvation as a reaffirmation of the Catholic position on these points. It asserts the real presence of Christ in the Blessed Sacrament and the spiritual efficacy of the sacrifice of the Mass for the living and the dead. Parochial services may be either in Latin or in the vernacular, but episcopal functions must be conducted in Latin.[3]

Secessions of some of its bishops during the early 1960s reduced its size. The jurisdiction reports five churches with an inclusive membership of 972. The headquarters are at Brooklyn, New York.

The North American Old Roman Catholic Church (Chicago, Illinois)[4]

In 1944 Hubert Augustus Rogers consecrated Cyrus A. Starkey for work among the Negroes of New York. The *Yearbook of American Churches for 1960* lists Starkey as one of the bishops under Rogers. Starkey's name is significantly absent from the next edition. The edition for 1962, like the subsequent editions, lists a second North American Old Roman Catholic Church that claimed sixty-four churches and 84,565 members and that had Starkey, listed as residing in Moorestown, New Jersey, as metropolitan-primate and the Most Reverend John E. Schweikert[5] of Chicago as his chancellor. Prior to his death in 1965, Starkey took the title primate of the Americas and Canada, with Schweikert as archbishop-coadjutor. Schweikert succeeded Starkey in December 1965. In 1967 he was elected presiding (arch)bishop of the church body; the newly established office does not carry with it primatial authority. The jurisdiction accepts the canons of the church of the patristic age as Old Roman Catholics throughout the world receive them. It admits married men to the priesthood only after careful consideration by the local ordinary. Its services and rites (except for the bestowal of holy orders) are in the vernacular. It does not actively seek union with any group.[6] A congregation of nuns maintains the Convent of Our Most Blessed Lady Queen of Peace in Chicago.[7] The jurisdiction reports 121 churches and 60,241 members. The headquarters are at 4200 North Kedvale Avenue, Chicago, Illinois.

The Old Catholic Church in America

This church body traces its history back to 1897, when the Old Catholic bishop of Berne, Switzerland, consecrated Antoni Stanislaus Kozlowski, a former Roman Catholic priest in Chicago, to head the Old Catholic mission to the dissident Polish Roman Catholics of North America. Kozlowski called his organization the Polish Old Catholic Church. When he died in 1907, most of the clergy of the Polish Old Catholic Church affiliated with the Polish National Catholic Church. For the next nine years Kozlowski's vicar general, Jan Francis Tichy, administered the few remaining parishes. In 1911 a group of former Anglican Benedictines at Fond du Lac, Wisconsin under William Henry Francis as their abbot, associated themselves with the Tichy group. On October 3, 1916, Rudolph Francis Prince de Landas Berghe et de Rache, whom Arnold Harris Mathew had elevated to the episcopate in 1913, consecrated Francis.[8] The new bishop's followers, organized as the Old Catholic Church in America,[9] elected him archbishop and metropolitan in 1917. In 1962 Francis led his church body into the Russian Orthodox Catholic Church in America (patriarchal exarchate) to become the latter's Western Rite administration.[10] In 1967 Francis withdrew from the exarchate's jurisdiction. He and his followers then revived the Old Catholic Church in America. Its theological posture is in the Old Catholic tradition. It claims to represent in North America the Old Catholic Church of the Mariavites of Poland. The archdiocesan chancery is at Woodstock, New York. It reports about forty centers in the United States and one in the Canal Zone; no accurate census of the membership exists.[11] Recent efforts to contact church officials have been unsuccessful.

North Amercian Province of the Old Roman Catholic Church

Carmel Henry Carfora consecrated Richard Arthur Marchenna in 1941. In 1950 the latter conditionally reconsecrated Gerard George Shelley.[12] In 1952 that branch of Archbishop Arnold Harris Mathew's Old Roman Catholic Church in Great Britain which adhered to Archbishop Bernard Mary Williams[13] elected Bishop Shelley as its primate upon Williams's death, with the title of archbishop of Caer-Glow, the ancient name of Gloucester. Bishop Marchenna and his followers had submitted to Archbishop Williams in 1950; the latter had thereupon constituted the group a missionary jurisdiction of the Old Roman Catholic Church. His successor elevated it to status of a province, with Marchenna as metropolitan-archbishop. In August 1964 Shelley named Marchenna his primatial coadjutor with right of immediate succession.

The Old Roman Catholic Church regards itself as a part of the Roman Catholic Church, juridically separated for the time being from the communion of the vicar of Christ in the person of the pope, whose primacy, infallibility, and right to govern the whole church it recognizes. It accepts the Creed of Pius IV, the Council of Trent, and the two Vatican councils. In its interpretation of the faith, polity, and practice of the Roman Catholic Church it associates itself with the "conservative" party in the latter denomination.

The province has seven churches and missions in Massachusetts, New York, New Jersey, Pennsylvania, Florida, and California, and three in Ontario, with a total membership of 800. The headquarters for the United States were at 1083 Broad Street, Newark, New Jersey, for Canada at 5 Manor Road West, Toronto.[14] Recent efforts to contact church officials have been unsuccessful.

Evangelical Orthodox Church in America
(Nonpapal Catholic Establishment, Diocese of the Western States)

In 1938 Wilhelm Waterstraat founded the Protestant Orthodox Western Church at Santa Monica, California. When he retired in 1940, his canonically elected successor, Frederick Littler Pyman (b. 1901), applied to Carmel Henry Carfora, metropolitan-primate of the North American Old Roman Catholic Church, for episcopal consecration. Carfora elevated Pyman to the episcopate on August 15, 1943, and simultaneously designated Pyman as regionary bishop of the North American Roman Catholic Church for the western United States of America. Pyman formally resigned the latter dignity and withdrew from the North American Old Roman Catholic Church in 1948, but continued to represent Carfora as episcopal visitor of a number of Old Catholic Franciscan religious communities in California. At the same time Pyman formally reorganized the Protestant Orthodox Western Church as the Evangelical Orthodox Church in America (Nonpapal Catholic Establishment), while acknowledging Carfora as the metropolitan-primate of the latter body in an "instrument of prelatial submission."

The Evangelical Orthodox Church holds the apostolic faith as summarized in the Apostles', Nicene, and Athanasian creeds, conforms to the positions taken by the church in the first seven ecumenical councils, accepts the Leipzig Interim of 1548,[15] and commends to its clergy for optional use the six chief parts and the morning, evening, and table prayers of the *Small Catechism* of Martin Luther. It accepts the entire Bible as the progressive revelation of God's nature and will; practices voluntary private confession and absolution; holds that the general confession and absolution in the liturgy conveys forgiveness and assurance to the truly penitent; rejects the pope's infallibility and supremacy over the whole church, but regards him as the first bishop among equals and concedes primacy in the Western Church to him; does not require celibacy as a precondition of ordination; and permits membership in fraternal orders, although it encourages its "members to apply Christian principles in their daily life and affiliations, so that they will voluntarily abstain from all that is incompatible with their religion."[16] The clergy support themselves by means of secular employment.

The headquarters are at St. Monica's House, San Jose, California. There are eleven churches and missions in California, Washington, Oregon, Arizona, and Nevada, with a total membership of 1,250. Recently three churches and two missions with a membership of 300 have been established in Maine, New Hampshire, and Pennsylvania. Pyman is now bishop emeritus. The Reverend Perry Ronald Sills serves under his jurisdiction.[17]

The Old Catholic Church in North America

According to the Most Reverend Grant Timothy Billett, six Old Catholic bishops and the priests of their respective jurisdictions established the Old Catholic Church in North America in 1950. The College of Bishops then elected Billett, whom the Most Reverend Earl Anglin James (Mar Laurentius) of Toronto, archbishop-metropolitan of Acadia and exarch of the Catholicate of the West in the Canadas, had consecrated bishop, as the primate.

The Old Catholic Church in North America stresses both its ecumenicity and its similarity to the Roman Catholic Church in worship and doctrine. It accepts the primacy but denies the infallibility of the pope, considers the apostolic succession vital in a valid Christian ministry, acknowledges seven sacraments, teaches transubstantiation, prays for the departed, and venerates and invokes the glorious and immaculate Mother of God, the saints, and the angels. Its worship is in the vernacular. Celibacy is not required of its clergy. Its expressed aim is neither division nor reformation, but reconstruction or restructure on canonical lines. It currently reports forty-eight churches with approximately 12,000 members. The primate resides in York, Pennsylvania.[18]

Old Roman Catholic Church in Europe and North America (English Rite)

In 1950 the Reverend Wilfrid Andrew Barrington-Evans and three other priests withdrew from the Old Roman Catholic Church (Pro-Uniate Rite), headed by the Most Reverend Bernard Mary Williams, and founded the Old Roman Catholic Church (English Rite), with Barrington-Evans as administrator. The following year Bishop D. L. T. Tollenaar of Arnhem, Holland, whose episcopal orders derived by way of Charles Leslie Saul and Benjamin Charles Harris from James Martin of the Free Protestant Episcopal Church of England, elevated Barrington-Evans to the episcopate.

In 1962 the Most Reverend Robert A. Burns, a former clergyman of the Protestant Episcopal Church whom Archbishop Carmel Henry Carfora had reportedly consecrated to the episcopate in 1948 and whom Archbishop Richard A. Marchenna had conditionally reconsecrated in 1961, withdrew from the North American Province of the Old Roman Catholic Church. Together with ten priests whom Carfora had ordained and who looked to Burns for leadership, the latter united in 1963 with Archbishop Barrington-Evans. The latter designated Burns archbishop of Chicago and metropolitan for America (including Canada, the United States, and Mexico). Primate since December 1974 is the Most Reverend Archbishop Francis Peter Sascione of Bloomfield Hills, Michigan.

Theologically the Old Roman Catholic Church in Europe and North America (English Rite) takes a position very close to that of the Roman Catholic Church in the period prior to Vatican Council II. In 1968 Burns joined Barrington-Evans and his coadjutor in reasserting the adherence of their jurisdictions "to the Christian faith as defined by the infallible authority of the Supreme Pontiff of the One, Holy, Catholic, Apostolic and Roman Church, without any difference or distinction, whether by way of augmentation or otherwise," and in pledging themselves to receive and conform to "all future definitions, pronouncements and decrees of the Supreme Pontiff on matters of faith and morals." The statement stresses that all the clergy of the Old Roman Catholic Church in Europe and North America (English Rite) must subscribe the oath against the errors of modernism set forth in 1910 in the *motu proprio* of Pius X, *Sacrorum antistitum*. The statement also expresses concern that in the post-Vatican II Roman Catholic Church "some abandonment or modification of certain articles of faith" may be in mind, and announces that the Old Roman Catholic Church "will not accept any decree, definition or pronouncement which abandons, alters, or modifies any article of the Christian faith previously declared by the [Roman] Catholic Church to be *de fide*."[19]

The North American Province of the Old Roman Catholic Church in Europe and North America (English Rite) claims fifty churches and missions and four dioceses in the United States and Canada, with an active membership of 65,290. Headquarters are at 2472 Mulberry Road, Bloomfield Hills, Michigan.

The Ontario Old Roman Catholic Church

In 1962 Richard Arthur Marchenna, metropolitan-archbishop of the North American Province of the Old Roman Catholic Church, consecrated William Pavlik (d. 1965) for the newly erected diocese of Ontario as bishop of All Canada. In 1963 the latter declared the independence of the Ontario Old Roman Catholic Church, and in 1964 consecrated Nelson D. Hillyer (b. 1912) as his coadjutor (with the right of succession). Upon Pavlik's death Hillyer took the title of archbishop of All Canada.

The Ontario Old Roman Catholic Church holds the dogmas set forth in the so-called Nicene Creed in its Western form (with the phrase "and the Son" in describing the procession of the Holy Spirit). It attempts "to deal with modern-day social problems in a realistic way and [tries] not to become involved with issues outside the realm of spirituality."[20]

The headquarters are at 5 Manor Road West, Toronto, Ontario. In addition to the Toronto church, there are two parishes in the United States (Niagara Falls, New York, and Erie, Pennsylvania). The total active membership is estimated at 300.

The Old Roman Catholic Church (Orthodox Orders)

In 1946 Carmel Henry Carfora consecrated Earl Anglin Lawrence James[21] (b. 1901) as bishop of Toronto. The next year Mar Georgius I (Hugh George de Willmott Newman), Old Catholic archbishop and metropolitan of Glastonbury and catholicos of the West, enthroned James *in absentia* as "His Eminence Mar Laurentius, Archbishop and Metropolitan of Acadia and Exarch of the Catholicate of the West in the Canadas." On February 19, 1965, according to the published statements of the Old Roman Catholic Church (Orthodox Orders), James consecrated Guy F. Claude Hamel (b. 1935), head of the Holy Congregation of St. Paul, to the episcopate.[22] In 1966, Hamel declares, the bishops of the Old Roman Catholic Church (Orthodox Orders), elected him patriarch, whereupon he assumed the style of His Holiness, Claudius I, Universal Patriarch.[23] James made an unsuccessful effort to return to power and was excommunicated. In 1968 Hamel announced an international council of his church body to be held in August 1970 ("Conclave 1970"). In this connection he published a list of eighty-eight North American and overseas bishops under "the college of twelve cardinals."[24] In 1969, after an intensive investigation by the Anti-Rackets Branch of the Ontario Provincial Police, Hamel was arrested and charged with perjury and fraud.[25] He was brought to trial in April 1970 and found guilty. A number of Hamel's prelates in the United States have affiliated with the Orthodox Old Roman Catholic Church, II. Responsibility for the remnants of the Old Roman Catholic Church (Orthodox Orders) appears to have devolved upon James again.

Although the Old Roman Catholic Church (Orthodox Orders) is theologically inclusive, it professes to be under the spiritual—but not administrative—jurisdiction of the Roman pope.

There does not appear to have been at any time an infrastructure at the parochial level corresponding to the elaborate hierarchical superstructure. How many active faithful there are—if any—cannot be determined.[26] During the regime of Hamel the headquarters of the church were at Domaine St. Paul, Cordova Lake, Havelock Post Office, Ontario, Canada. James's address is 460 Danforth Avenue, Toronto, Ontario.

The Orthodox Old Roman Catholic Church, II

The founder of the Orthodox Old Roman Catholic Church, II, Oliver W. Skelton II (b. 1927), began his priestly career in 1962 with ordination in the Old Catholic Church [of the West] (Philadelphia, Pennsylvania), then presided over by Maurice Francis Parkin, who later entered the Antiochian Orthodox Church of America. Skelton broke with Parkin and in 1964 Skelton incorporated the Orthodox Old Catholic Church, II, at 3369 South State Street, Salt Lake City, Utah.[27] In January 1965 he associated himself briefly with the Most Reverend Christopher Maria Stanley,[28] metropolitan of the Southeastern Province of the American Orthodox Catholic Church (New York, New York), took the religious name of Leo Christopher, and received conditional reordination and episcopal consecration at the hands of Stanley and of the Most Reverend John Joseph Frewensky of Athens, Georgia.[29] Skelton nevertheless continued to head the body that he had incorporated the previous year. By the end of 1965 he had withdrawn from the American Orthodox Catholic Church (New York, New York). Skelton proclaimed himself the metropolitan-primate and archbishop of his church body, established the Orthodox Old Catholic Chancery in the "metropolitan primatial residence" at 6744 North Broad Street, Philadelphia, Pennsylvania, and adopted the address Your Eminence. In 1966 Skelton linked himself with the Most Reverend Guy F. Claude Hamel (His Holiness Claudius I) of the Old Roman Catholic Church (Orthodox Orders). Skelton's association with Hamel was stormy, and ended, according to Skelton, with his resignation from the Old Roman Catholic Church (Orthodox Orders) in May 1969, shortly before Hamel's arrest for perjury and fraud. With a number of other cardinals and prelates of Hamel's group, among them the Most Reverend Leo Gregory Mancinelli and the Most Reverend Paul French,[30] Skelton reactivated the Orthodox Old Catholic Church, II, as the Orthodox Old Roman Catholic Church, II. He secured incorporation in California for it as an out-of-state nonprofit association in January 1970. He uses the style His Beatitude, the Most Reverend Mark I, Leo Christopher Skelton, D. D., Patriarch (Founder).[31]

The Orthodox Old Roman Catholic Church, II, regards itself as "the true apostolic orthodox Catholic Church founded by the Apostle St. Peter at Antioch in Syria, 38 A.D." Its biblical canon includes the so-called Old Testament apocrypha. It admits married candidates to the priesthood, but does not permit the marriage of ordained priests. It accepts as irreversible the dogmatic canons of the seven ecumenical councils. It uses both the Eastern and the Western rites.

The headquarters of the Orthodox Old Roman Catholic Church, II, were at 6237 Fountain Avenue, Hollywood, California. In 1970 there were eight organized parishes and missions in the United States; the patriarch (founder) estimated that these parishes and missions have a total active membership of 1,200. Recent efforts to contact him have been unsuccessful.

Ultrajectine Ordinariate, Holy Catholic Church
(Old Roman Catholic Church, Incorporated:
The [Roman] Catholic Legation [of Utrecht])

The history of the Old Roman Catholic Church, Incorporated, according to the Most Reverend Joseph William Damian Hough, its primate, began with the formation of a congregation of Oblates of St. Martin of Tours. The congregation nominated him titular bishop of Caesarea and auxiliary bishop of Los Angeles in the Old Roman Catholic Church in the course of the winter of 1964/1965. In April 1965 he incorporated the Roman Catholic Legation of Utrecht for the purpose of uniting all Ultrajectines (from Ultrajectum, the ancient form of Utrecht) in North America into a single synod. According to "The Apostolic Succession in the Ordinariate of America, Province of Utrecht, Holy Catholic (and Apostolic) Church," the Most Reverend Richard Arthur Marchenna, metropolitan of the North American Province of the Old Roman Catholic Church, consecrated Hough as titular bishop of the see of Treguier[32] and of the archsee of Caesarea on July 23, 1965. In July 1966 Hough incorporated the Old Roman Catholic Church in the United States. Later in the summer he withdrew from Marchenna's authority, and cooperation between the latter and the legation, of which Hough is the legatial prelate, ceased.[33]

The Ultrajectine Ordinariate of the Holy Catholic Church professes to share the position of the provincial synods of Utrecht and of the Formula of Utrecht of 1823.[34] While retaining local autonomy of jurisdiction, it declares that it recognizes the primatial status of the Roman see and maintains the same faith, the same sacraments, and the same discipline as other jurisdictions of the Western Church. It permits the ordination of married men to the ministry. Clergymen are expected to earn their own living in secular occupations and to give their services to the church voluntarily.[35]

The headquarters of the Ultrajectine Ordinariate, Holy Catholic Church, are at 1418 Second Street, Santa Monica, California; the Catholic Legation receives its mail at Box 269, Venice, California. The jurisdiction currently consists of congregations holding services in house chapels in various parts of Los Angeles county. No information is available about the size of the active membership other than that it is small.[36]

The Brotherhood of the Pleroma and Order of the Pleroma, Including the
Hermetic Brotherhood of Light (Formerly the Brotherhood and
Order of the Illuminati); Pre-Nicene Catholic (Gnostic) Church

In 1952 Dr. Ronald Powell (born 1919), a lay member of the Liberal Catholic Church in Australia, became the archon ("leader") of the Ancient Mystic Order of the Fratres Lucis (Italy), reportedly founded in 1948. In

England he legally changed his name to Richard Jean Chrétien Duc de Pala-tine, founded the Pre-Nicene (Gnostic) Catholic Church, and in 1953 was consecrated as its presiding bishop by Hugh George de Willmott Newman, Metropolitan of Glastonbury and Catholicos of the West.[37]

The Brotherhood and Order of the Pleroma (formerly the Brotherhood and Order of the Illuminati), of which de Palatine is the grand hierophant, undertakes to trace its genesis back through the English Freemason John Yarker, Junior (1833–1913), Helena P. Blavatsky, the medieval and post-Reformation mystics, the Paulicians and Cathari, Neoplatonism, Maniche-ism, Gnosticism, and the mystery religions of Egypt and Asia Minor, to Atlantis "before it was submerged by the waters in 9,564 B.C."[38]

The brotherhood describes *pleroma* ("fulness") as a Gnostic term mean-ing "divine world" or "universal soul." Its system, which it identifies with the Raja Yoga, the philosopher's stone of alchemy, and the "lost word" of Freemasonry, teaches the infinite oneness of God; the essential excellence of truth; the law of toleration of all men and women with reference to opin-ion; respect for all men and women with reference to character and conduct; entire submission to God's decrees as to fate; karma and reincarnation; chas-tity of body, mind, and soul; and mutual help under all conditions.[39] It holds that each human being is a trinity of spirit, soul, and body; each human being is in this way an aspect of the one man-god. The spiritual self is a spark of God, entombed within a coffin of fleshly matter but not dead. Each human soul is a cell in the body of the One, that is, of God; for the whole to be one, each cell must conquer the conditions which keep it apart from the One. The real self in each human being waits for discovery and recognition of the divine presence. Once a human being realizes that he is a divine soul, he must do battle with the "ruler of the body," conquer him, rise out of the tomb of the body, and ascend to the soul's original home.[40]

The Brotherhood of the Pleroma describes itself as limited to a maximum of seven hundred members worldwide; it claims an actual membership of about six hundred. After three years of probationary purification in the Brotherhood, the aspirant to illumination is deemed ready for membership in the Order of the Pleroma (The Hermetic Brotherhood of Light). As an *illuminato*, he is assured, he will be able to enter into a condition described as "a state of mystical sensitivity or receptivity" in which he retains the full use of his physical senses while his human consciousness allows a downpour-ing of the life and consciousness of the divine soul "within the soul vesture," so that the divine and human become as one in the physical body.

The North American headquarters of the Brotherhood and Order of the Pleroma are at Sherman Oaks (P. O. Box 5220), California. There are eight study groups in California, Illinois, New York, Michigan, Texas, and Alaska, with a total active membership of 470. Since 1967 the deputy leader of the Brotherhood of the Pleroma has been the regionary bishop of the Pre-Nicene Catholic (Gnostic) Church for the Americas and most of the study groups are combined with churches of the Pre-Nicene Catholic

(Gnostic) Church. The latter is a "closed rite," with membership confined to members of the Brotherhood and Order of the Pleroma.[41]

The Liberal Catholic Movement

Early in this century the forms of traditional Catholic sacramental worship of Archbishop Arnold Harris Mathew's Old Roman Catholic Church attracted the interest of a number of English Theosophists. By mid-1915 a majority of his priests were members of Mrs. Annie Wood Besant's Theosophical Society and the messianic Order of the Star of the East. When Mathews ordered them to abjure their Theosophical beliefs and discontinue their memberships in these organizations, half a dozen, under the leadership of James Ingall Wedgwood (1883–1951), the general secretary of the Theosophical Society in England and Wales from 1911 to 1913, declined to obey. Then Mathews announced his intended "unconditional submission" to the Roman see and informed his priests that he had "terminated the movement." Frederick Samuel Willoughby, whom Mathew had consecrated "to safeguard the episcopate" but subsequently suspended, consecrated two of the Theosophist priests to the episcopate. These two new bishops and their consecrator elevated Wedgwood to the episcopate on February 13, 1916. (Liberal Catholics regard this as the birthdate of their movement, even though the name Liberal Catholic Church was not adopted until later.) Later in 1916 Wedgwood went to Australia, where he consecrated to the episcopate Charles Webster Leadbeater (d. 1934), a long-active Anglican clergyman whom Mme. Helena Blavatsky had converted to Theosophy.

In spite of the Theosophical orientation of all the early leaders, Wedgwood stressed as early as 1919 that "a man can be a good member of the Liberal Catholic Church without having to give any allegiance whatsoever to the Theosophical Society or any approval of its characteristic doctrines" and that the Liberal Catholic Church "did not wish or intend to appeal solely or even primarily" to Theosophists.[42]

In 1919 Wedgwood and Leadbeater consecrated Irving Steiger Cooper (d. 1935), a frequent lecturer at Theosophical gatherings, as regionary bishop for the newly erected Province of the United States of America. Leadbeater succeeded Wedgwood as presiding bishop in 1923. In 1926 three more bishops were consecrated for the United States, including Ray Marshall Wardall (d. 1953).

Jeddu Krishnamurti, Mrs. Besant's protégé and the widely heralded forthcoming world teacher and vehicle of the new Messiah, renounced this dignity in 1929, disbanded the Order of the Star of the East, and went off on his own spiritual course. Increasingly since then the Liberal Catholic Church has stressed that it never had any official or organic connection with the Theosophical Society and that it has never sought to make acceptance of Theosophical doctrine a condition of membership. Thus Bishop Frank Waters

Pigott in 1929 deplored the "ill-advised enthusiasm for Theosophy" and indicated his desire for "the Church becoming wholly detached not only from the Theosophical Society but from Theosophical influences."[43]

In 1931 Charles Hampton (d. 1958) was consecrated bishop for the United States of America; in 1935 Edmund Walter Sheehan; in 1936 Buenaventura Jiménez (for Puerto Rico); and in 1939 John Theodore Eklund.

Difficulties arose within the Province of the United States during World War II. In 1943 Presiding Bishop Pigott suspended and later removed Hampton as regionary bishop for the United States and appointed Eklund as regionary bishop *pro tempore*. When Hampton's appeal to the General Episcopal Synod was rejected in 1945, he left the Liberal Catholic Church, but not before he had turned over the provincial leadership to Wardall.[44] In 1946 Pigott and Wedgwood consecrated Ernest Whitfield Jackson regionary bishop for Canada. In 1947 Eklund, by direction of the General Episcopal Synod, consecrated Newton Arnold Dahl and Walter James Zollinger, and Wardall, despite a cabled prohibition from Pigott, consecrated Edward Murray Matthews. The presiding bishop then dismissed both Wardall and Matthews and their supporters from the church. The property rights were litigated and in 1961 the Superior Court of Los Angeles County handed down a judgment declaring that the church headed by Matthews is the legitimate Liberal Catholic Church in the United States.[45] Efforts at rapprochement between the United States Province and the groups headed by Matthews are presently underway, and merger of the two groups is expected.

All three of the Liberal Catholic communities in the United States and Canada—the Province of the United States and the Province of Canada of the Liberal Catholic Church, the International Liberal Catholic Church with its affiliated Liberal Catholic Church, Diocese of New York, Incorporated, and the Liberal Catholic Church with headquarters at Miranda, California—have until recently used the same liturgy and subscribe to largely identical statements of principles.

The Liberal Catholic movement proposes to combine a sacramental form of worship, "with its stately ritual, its deep mysticism, and its abiding witness to the reality of sacramental grace," with intellectual liberty and respect for the individual conscience. For that reason it "permits to its members freedom of interpretation of the Scriptures, the Creed and the Liturgy," encourages among them "the freest play of scientific and philosophic thought," and erects "no barriers in the nature of standards of dogmatic belief."[46] It disavows a desire to proselytize and "welcomes people to regular and full participation in its services without asking or expecting them to leave their original Church."[47]

Liberal Catholicism affirms both the immanence and the transcendence of God, as well as the Trinity, although its literature discloses considerable divergence of opinion on the nature of the Trinity and on the mode of Christ's deity. The eucharistic liturgy incorporates the Nicaeno-Constantinopolitan

Creed of the Western eucharistic rite,[48] but authorizes the substitution of the "Original Nicene Creed" of A.D. 325 or of either of two Acts of Faith. The first reads:

> We believe that God is Love, and Power, and Truth, and Light; that perfect justice rules the world; that all His sons shall one day reach His Feet, however far they stray. We hold the Fatherhood of God, the Brotherhood of man; we know that we do serve Him best when best we serve our brother man. So shall His blessing rest on us and peace for evermore. Amen.

The second reads:

> We place our trust in God, the holy and all-glorious Trinity, who dwelleth in the Spirit of man. We place our trust in Christ, the Lord of love and wisdom, first among many brethren, who leadeth us to the glory of the Father, and is Himself the Way, the Truth, and the Life. We place our trust in the Law of Good which rules the world; we strive toward the ancient narrow Path that leads to life eternal; we know that we serve our Master best when we serve our brother man. So shall His power rest upon us and peace for evermore. Amen.[49]

Liberal Catholics hold that the Bible is inspired "in a general sense only." Baptism, administered with water and the usual trinitarian formula, grafts the candidate, whether an infant or someone older, into the mystical body of Christ, and in the pouring of water it "symbolizes both the washing away of sin and the downpouring of power from on high."[50] The Holy Eucharist is "a mystery-drama, re-enacting in time and space the primal cosmic Sacrifice of the Logos, the incarnation or descent into matter of the Second Person of the Blessed Trinity," in which by the words of consecration "the bread and wine in their natural substance become the Body and Blood of Christ . . . the special expression or manifestation of the Christ, the channel of His blessing for the nourishing of our souls."[51] The sacrament of absolution may follow either auricular confession or the general confession of the public service, in which the worshipers confess that they often "forget the glory of [their] heritage and wander from the path which leads to righteousness" and that they need to have God look with eyes of love "upon [their] manifold imperfections and pardon all [their] shortcomings."[52]

The church is the "blessed company of all faithful people." The different churches receive this blessing in proportion to the earnestness of their members and the extent to which they retain the sacramental channels of the divine grace and reflect what Christ intended his church to be. Liberal Catholics see the unity of the Liberal Catholic Church based not upon the profession of a common belief but upon a willingness to worship corporately through a common ritual.

The 1919 *Liturgy* expanded an experimental edition that had come out in 1918 and represented a collaboration between Wedgwood and Leadbeater. The latter is described as "one of the greatest occultists and trained clairvoyant seers of all time. Much of the investigating connection with the development of the Liberal Catholic Liturgy and Rite was done by the aid of his supernormal faculties."[53] A revised second edition of *The Liturgy* came out under Leadbeater's imprimatur. A third revised edition, still in general use among English-speaking Liberal Catholics, came out in 1942; the changes were minor and did not affect "either the teaching or the tone of the book."[54]

The preface of *The Liturgy* points out that the eucharistic rite, the core of the book, derives primarily from the Roman Missal, with "many sentences and collects from the Anglican Book of Common Prayer."[55] The preface also notes the deletion of all "expressions which indicate fear of God, of His wrath, and of an everlasting hell," as well as "expressions of servile cringing and self-abasement, abject appeals for mercy, even culminating in naive attempts to bargain with the Almighty," along with every vestige of "the jealous, angry, blood-thirsty Jehovah of Ezra, Nehemiah and the others—a god who needs propitiating and to whose 'mercy' constant appeals must be made." The present century's knowledge of Eastern religions, modern and ancient, the preface observes, has "dispelled the illusion that the Jews had any monopoly of divine truth and proportionately lessens the value of the Old Testament as an integral basis of the Christian faith."[56] The simplified calendar conforms to the Western Christian year; it includes the baptism (January 15), transfiguration (January 27), and presentation (February 2) of Christ; the annunciation (March 25), assumption (August 15), and nativity (September 8) of Our Lady; Corpus Christi; and commemorations of St. Alban, St. John Baptist, St. Peter and the Holy Apostles (June 29), St. Michael and All Angels, All Saints, and All Souls.[57]

The Liturgy also contains abbreviated versions of prime, vespers, and compline and orders for baptism, confirmation, matrimony, confession and absolution, unction and communion of the sick, a service of healing, the burial of the dead, holy orders (cleric, doorkeeper, reader, exorcist, acolyte, subdeacon, deacon, priest, and bishop), admission of members, singers, and servers, various blessings, the foundation-stone laying and the consecration of a church, as well as occasional prayers.

The Liberal Catholic bodies forbid their clergy to accept fees for the performances of sacraments and sacred rites. In general Liberal Catholic clergy and prelates are persons who either have independent means or who support themselves by means of secular employment.

The Liberal Catholic Church, Province of the United States and Province of Canada

After the schism of the 1940s, the United States segment of the Liberal Catholic Church on the North American continent that remained in communion with the General Episcopal Synod of London, England, incorporated itself in 1962 as the Liberal Catholic Church, Province of the United States of America. Its leaders included Bishops Dahl, Zollinger, Jiménez, and William H. Pitkin (consecrated in 1957). The General Episcopal Synod erected a parallel province in Canada under Bishop Jackson.

These branches of the Liberal Catholic Church pay deep homage to the "mother-nature of God," of which the "highest expression is the World Mother as represented by the holy Lady Mary." They believe "that there is a body of doctrine and mystical experience [which is] common to all the great religions of the world and which cannot be claimed as the exclusive possession of any" and find "evidences of the highest inspiration in other scriptures of the world [beside the Bible]."[58]

They also affirm that man is "himself divine in essence—a spark of the divine fire"; that the divinity that was manifest in Christ "is gradually being unfolded in every man"; that the evolution or spiritual unfoldment of a human being "takes place under an inviolable law of cause and effect" so that "his doings in each physical incarnation largely determine his experience after death in the intermediate world (or world of purgation) and the heavenly world and greatly influence the circumstances of his next birth."[59]

Although this branch of the Liberal Catholic Church and the Theosophical Society have a large overlap in membership, its leadership continues to stress that the Liberal Catholic Church was not established as a part of the Theosophical Society and that it has never intended to require its clergy or its laity to be Theosophists. At the same time, to ensure that those who join its ranks as communicants will not abuse the freedom that the Liberal Catholic Church affords "to try to steer us back to the older orthodoxies," only those "who are in general agreement with the Church's *Summary of Doctrine* are admitted to holy orders."[60]

This branch of the Liberal Catholic movement issued in 1967 a fourth edition of *The Liturgy according to the Use of the Liberal Catholic Church*, incorporating the changes which the General Episcopal Synod authorized in 1958. *A Shorter Form for the Celebration of the Holy Eucharist*, published in 1966, contains some of these changes. While the Niceno-Constantinopolitan Creed may still be used, the 1966 order does not print it out. Instead it has this as the Act of Faith II:

> We believe in one God, the holy and all-glorious Trinity, the Three who yet are One, the Father, Son, and Holy Ghost, coequal, coeternal;
>
> In God the Father, from whom do come the worlds and all that is therein, seen or unseen;
>
> And in God the Son most holy, alone-born from His Father before all aeons; not made, but springing forth; being of the substance of His Father, true God from the true God, true Light from the true Light, by whom all forms were made; who for us men came down from heaven and took the robe of matter, yet riseth thence again in ever greater glory to a kingdom without end;
>
> And in God the Holy Ghost, the Life-Giver, springing forth also from the

Father and the Son, equal with them in glory, who revealeth Himself through His angels.

We acknowledge one holy catholic and apostolic church, one communion of the saints, one baptism for the demission of sin; we look for the resurrection of the dead and the life of the coming age. Amen.

In the Commemoration of the Saints the celebrant may at his discretion add "our heavenly Mother" after the reference to "the holy Lady Mary."

The new rite retains the Trinitarian Benediction from the Book of Common Prayer that begins "The peace of God, which passeth all understanding." At the same time it restores for use at the celebrant's discretion with the permission of the regionary bishop an alternative benediction that is quite "theosophical in its import:

> May the Holy Ones, whose pupils you aspire to become, show you the light you seek, give you the strong aid of their compassion and their wisdom. There is a peace that passeth understanding; it abides in the hearts of those who live in the eternal. There is a power that maketh all things new; it lives and moves in those who know the self as one. May that peace brood over you, that power uplift you, till you stand where the One Initiator is invoked, till you see His Star shine forth.

The first two editions of *The Liturgy* made this blessing mandatory, the third omitted it altogether. The regionary bishops of both North American provinces have given permission for its use.[61]

The highest governing body of these provinces is the General Episcopal Synod, composed of the bishops at the head of the fourteen provinces (covering forty-five countries) of the worldwide body. The polity of the denomination is hierarchical in spiritual matters, but largely democratic in business matters. The Province of the United States has twenty-nine parishes and missions with 2,393 members. The Province of Canada has approximately six parishes and missions with 100 members. Headquarters are at Route 2 Krotona, Ojai, California.

International Liberal Catholic Church

In 1928 Bishop Wedgwood consecrated John Hubert Bonjer as his auxiliary for the Netherlands. In 1959 Bishop Bonjer formed an independent Liberal Catholic Church under the name Gemeenschap van het Heilig Sacrament and entered into communion with the Liberal Catholic Church presided over by Bishop Edward Murray Matthews. In 1962 the General Episcopal Synod of the Gemeenschap deposed Bishop Matthews from his offices in the international body and elected Francis Erwin as presiding bishop. Bishops Roberts, Daw, and Sheehan of Matthews's jurisdiction joined forces with Erwin. The church is incorporated as the International Liberal Catholic

Church in California with headquarters at Ojai, California; in Canada it bears the name the Liberal Catholic Church.

It affirms its disinclination to seek the source of its dogmas in Theosophy, and it has no teaching on reincarnation. It holds that man evolves from unconscious perfection through conscious imperfection to conscious perfection, and that the mission of the church is to help men, individually and collectively, to accelerate this evolutionary process.[62]

Several years ago it had four parishes and missions in California and eleven parishes and missions in Canada. The interracial and autonomous Liberal Catholic Church, Diocese of New York, Incorporated, with four parishes, is part of the International Liberal Catholic Church.

The highest international authority is the General Episcopal Synod, which supervises churches and missions in Holland and Belgium in addition to the North American churches and missions. The total number of participating members of the International Liberal Catholic Church in the United States (including the New York jurisdiction) and Canada is estimated at 3,000.[63]

Recent efforts to make contact with the church have been unsuccessful.

The Liberal Catholic Church (Miranda, California)

The Liberal Catholic Church (Miranda, California) is headed by Presiding Bishop Edward Murray Matthews. In an encyclical of 1959 the presiding bishop reiterated the right of the lay members of the church to "a full and unrestricted privilege of interpreting not only the traditional Creeds and Scriptures, but also the Church's Liturgy, all of which form a part of the Church's structure," but required the interpretation of its clergy to be "in its basic principles that which is agreed upon by . . . those of the Episcopal Order, namely the General Episcopal Synod."[64] The encyclical also required the clergy to accept and adhere to the principle that Christ is the source of all grace in the sacraments, that he is present in them, and that he himself instituted them for the spiritual welfare of mankind. It also declared that the Liberal Catholic Church over which Matthews presides "does not now nor has it ever at any time insisted or prescribed that the dogma or teaching of the principle known as Reincarnation, 'Christian' or otherwise, is a tenet of its belief and practices."[65] Because in earlier editions of the *Statement of Principles* those sections which acknowledged the influence of Platonism, Neoplatonism, Theosophy, Gnosticism, New Thoughts, psychical research, and kindred movements on the Liberal Catholic Church had been widely misunderstood, these sections were omitted in the 1963 edition of the *Statement of Principles*.

The suffraganates of New York and the West Indies and of Canada, erected in 1955, were terminated in 1962.[66] The headquarters were moved from Los Angeles, where they had been since 1917, to Bear Butte Road and United States Freeway 101, Miranda, California, in 1964. The presiding bishop estimates that 200 people from around the nation are associated with the group.[67] Merger efforts with the Liberal Catholic Church, Province of the United States and Province of Canada, are presently under way.

NOTES

1. In 1962 Francis was united with the Russian Orthodox Catholic Church in America (Patriarchal Exarchate) with the style of Very Reverend as head of the exarchate's Western Rite administration. He subsequently withdrew from the exarchate's jurisdiction.

2. "These figures cannot be accepted without question," wrote Henry R. T. Brandreth, *Episcopi Vagantes and the Anglican Church,* 2nd edition (London: SPCK, 1961), p. 27, of the substantially identical figures in the *Yearbook of American Churches for 1958.* A statistical survey of the period 1947–1967 at intervals is instructive. *The Yearbook of American Churches for 1947* lists thirty-nine churches with 57,500 members (an average of 1,218 per church) under Carfora. The edition for 1953 lists forty-seven churches with 85,500 members. The edition for 1957 lists sixty-four churches with 84,565 members. The edition for 1962 lists fifty-two churches with 71,521 members under Rogers and sixty-four churches with 84,565 members under Starkey. The edition for 1967 lists thirty churches with 18,500 members under Rogers (an average of 617 members per church) and forty-two churches with 88,788 members under Schweikert (an average of 2,114 members per church).

3. "Doctrinal Statement," in Carmel Henry Carfora, *Historical and Doctrinal Sketch of the Old Roman Catholic Church,* revised edition (Brooklyn, N.Y.: North American Old Roman Catholic Church, 1965), pp. 18-21.— According to the *Yearbook of American Churches* the North American Old Roman Catholic Church claims that the Eastern Orthodox archbishop of Beirut had received the North American Old Roman Catholic Church into union with the Eastern Orthodox Church in 1911 and that the Eastern Orthodox patriarch of Alexandria had done the same in 1912. Since these actions would have antedated Carfora's consecration, the statement clearly needs some qualification. Presumably the statement refers to an "Act of Union" that the Old Roman Catholic Church reportedly accomplished with the two Orthodox patriarchates in the years named (*An Account of the Old Roman Catholic Church . . . by the Research Staff of the Crux News Service* [Shickshinny, Penn.: Sovereign Order of St. John of Jerusalem, 1964], pp. [2]-[3]; see also Peter F. Anson, *Bishops at Large* [New York: October House, 1965], pp. 185-187. At all events, the North American Old Roman Catholic Church (Brooklyn, New York) is not in communion with any American branch of Eastern Orthodoxy recognized by the ecumenical patriarch in Istanbul.

4. This is still the official name of the body, but the Most Reverend John E. Schweikert states in a letter that the church prefers to use the name Old Catholic rather than Roman so that people will not entertain the idea that his jurisdiction is linked with the Roman Catholic Church.

5. Schweikert was consecrated by Zigmunt K. Vipartas, who in turn was consecrated by Carfora (letter from Archbishop Schweikert).

6. Arthur R. Green, *The Old Catholic Church* (undated pamphlet), p. 3. The author was Schweikert's vicar general. He has since become a clergyman in the Universal Fellowship of Metropolitan Community Churches.

7. This writer acknowledges gratefully the help of the Reverend John E. Groh, S.T.M., Ph.D., then pastor of the Church of the Divine Savior, Palos Hills, Illinois, who interviewed Archbishop Schweikert at this writer's request.

8. J[ustinus] Febronius, Fil[ius](pseudonym), *What Is Old Catholicism?* (New York: Old Catholic Church in America, 1939) (pamphlet), pp. 8-9.

9. Other names that this jurisdiction has used include the Old Catholic Church, the Catholic Church of North America, and the Orthodox Old Catholic Church in America.

10. *Yearbook of American Churches for 1963*, p. 78.

11. Letters from the Most Reverend Joseph A. MacCormack, archbishop-coadjutor and vicar general, the Old Catholic Church in America, and from the Most Reverend William Henry Francis, archbishop of the Old Catholic Church in America.

12. Ordained priest by Arnold Harris Mathew and consecrated bishop in 1949 by William Henry Francis (Brothers).

13. Born James Charles Thomas Ayliffe Williams. Mathew consecrated Williams as his perpetual coadjutor with right of succession in 1916, but Williams himself consecrated no successor.

14. Letter of the Most Reverend Richard Arthur Marchenna, J.C.D., O.S.J.; *Roman Catholic Directory (Ultrajectine)* 1967 (Newark, N.J.: Catholic Information Center, 1967). "Ultrajectine" in the title of the latter reference refers to the Latin form of Utrecht, Ultrajectum.—Included in the province since 1960 is the jurisdiction of the Most Reverend Emile F. R. Fairfield, 4011 Brooklyn Avenue, Los Angeles, California. Fairfield derives his episcopal orders from Carmel Henry Carfora by way of José Macario Lopes, whom Carfora consecrated as bishop of Pueblo (Mexico) in 1926 (letter from Archbishop Marchenna).

15. The Leipzig Interim was drafted at the command of Elector Maurice of Saxony by the theologians of his electorate under the leadership of Philipp Melanchthon and was promulgated by Maurice in December 1548. The elector designed it as an alternative to the Augsburg Interim of the same year, which Holy Roman Emperor Charles V was endeavoring to force upon the nonpapalist estates of the empire, but which the estates of Electoral Saxony categorically refused to approve. In its exceedingly irenic thrust it strove to avoid formulations that would gratuitously antagonize the emperor and his party, but its positive affirmations were broadly in harmony with the Augsburg Confession. In general, its ceremonial prescriptions merely canonized the existing conservative liturgical practice of most of the congregations in the electorate; the only real novelties from the Lutheran standpoint were the restoration of unction and of the Feast of Corpus Christi (the Thursday after Trinity Sunday kept in commemoration of the institution of the sacrament of the altar) as an ecclesiastical-civil holiday, but without the customary procession with the Blessed Sacrament. The Leipzig Interim (like the Augsburg Interim) ceased to be in force after the Treaty of Passau (1552). For the original text see *Corpus Reformatorum* 7: 259-264 (to be supplemented from columns 51-62, 217, and 219-220). "The Evangelical Orthodox (Catholic) Church (Nonpapal Catholic Establishment): A Concise Statement as to Its Doctrine and Establishment" (Santa Monica, Calif.: Migdol and Son, 1950) (28-page pamphlet), pp. 7-16, contains an English version of the Leipzig Interim. More generally accessible is the translation in Henry Eyster Jacobs, ed., *The Book of Concord, or, the Symbolical Books of the Lutheran Church* 2 (Philadelphia: G. W. Frederick, 1883): 260-272.

16. Ibid., p. 6.

17. Letters from the Most Reverend Frederick Littler Pyman, C.S.A., S.T.D., regionary bishop, diocese of the Western States, the evangelical Orthodox Church in America, San Jose, California.

18. Letters from the Most Reverend Grant Timothy Billett, Ph.D., D.D., York, Pennsylvania.

19. "Statement by the Bishops and Clergy of the Old Roman Catholic Church" (two-page typescript document dated February 14, 1968).

20. Letter from the Reverend Thomas McCourt, chancellor, the Ontario Old Roman Catholic Church.

21. On James, see *Laurentius I, Earl Anglin James: Curriculum Vitae* (Toronto, Canada: EAJ Peace Missions, 1965) (forty-page pamphlet); [*Holy*] *C*[*ongregation of*] *S*[*aint*] *P*[*aul*] *World News*, vol. 3, no. 2 (February 1966), p. 1, and no. 4 (April 1966), p. 1; Barbara Moon, "Prince of Degree Merchants," *McLean's Magazine*,

April 6, 1963, pp. 26-28; Peter F. Anson, *Bishops at Large* (New York: October House, 1964), pp. 245-246 and *passim;* "Action Line," *Telegram* (Toronto, Ontario, Canada), March 2, 1967. Among the many letterheads that James uses is that of "The World Jnana Sadhak Society," allegedly founded in 1956 by Bhabes Chandra Chaudhuri. The society is described as "a silent world fellowship of culture, wisdom, and unity." The legend on its seal is "Prajnanam Brahma (Wisdom is God)." James is listed as the dean of the organization.

22. *Encyclical "Veteris Romanae Ecclesiae"* (Havelock, Ontario: Domaine St. Paul, [1967]) (eight-page pamphlet), p. 7. In a letter dated August 25, 1970, James asserts: "I never consecrated Hamel." According to Hamel, he founded the Holy Congregation of St. Paul in 1958. The masthead of the *C. S. P. World News* described him as the "general superior" of the congregation; how many other members of the congregation had—if any at all—cannot be determined. Hamel came to Toronto in 1962. In 1964 William Pavlik (d. 1965), whom Richard Arthur Marchenna had consecrated as Old Roman Catholic bishop of Kitchener, Ontario, in 1962, ordained Hamel to the Old Roman Catholic priesthood, only to depose and excommunicate him two months later. Hamel was for a time a follower of the French antipope Clement XV (Michael Collin) of Clémery; *C. S. P. News*, vol. 2, no. 10 (October 1965), p. 1, described Clement as "the real McCoy." On October 21, 1962, Hamel claimed, Clement's "apostolic delegate, His Eminence, Cardinal M. Emmanual[!]," consecrated Hamel, "the mystical archbishop of [the] Congregation of St. Paul," to the episcopate; as late as the October 1965 issue of *C. S. P. News*, Hamel published a picture showing himself "receiving the mitre from the hands of Cardinal M. Emmanual" (ibid.). At the end of the year in which James reportedly consecrated Hamel, in December 1965, Hamel consecrated to the episcopate John Wilson. Wilson reportedly claimed to be "bishop of the Old Catholic Orthodox Church and head of St. Joseph's Mission for all of North America." In June 1966 Hamel

excommunicated Wilson. At the time a Toronto newspaper described the Old Cathoic Orthodox Church as a "one-man sect," identified its head (on the basis of Pennsylvania prison records) as a convicted car thief, and characterized his wife as "a self-styled nun who served 30 days in Mercer Reformatory in 1964 for stealing $110 from a cripple." (George Anthony, "It's a One-Man Sect: A Renegade Bishop Seeks $150,000," *Telegram*, June 10, 1966, pp. 1-2; see also Albert Warson, "Cleric on Bail: Mystery Surrounds Sect's Toronto Activity," *Toronto Globe and Mail*, December 29, 1965.)

23. *Disciplinary Canons and Constitution of the Congregation of St. Paul [and of the] Old Roman Catholic Church (Orthodox Orders)* (Cordova Lake, Ontario: Congregation of St. Paul, 1966) (thirteen-page pamphlet), which Hamel published at this time, acknowledges its indebtedness to *The Disciplinary Canons and the Constitution of the Orthodox Old Catholic Church, II* (Philadelphia: Dunrite Press, 1965) thirty-six-page pamphlet), that the Most Reverend Leo Christopher Skelton, founder-primate of the Orthodox Old Roman Catholic Church, II, had drafted and that he brought with him when he joined Hamel in 1966. At that time Hamel designated Skelton as primate of the Old Roman Catholic Church (Orthodox Orders) with the title of cardinal (*Disciplinary Canons and Constitution of the Congregation of St. Paul*, pp. 1, 2, 11), then replaced him "for health reasons" and stated that Skelton would retain "a small mission in the United States until his retirement" (*C. S. P. World News*, vol. 4, no. 1 [January 1967], p. 3). Four months later Hamel abolished the office of primate and announced Skelton's nomination to "the Sacred College of Cardinals" under the title of "Archbishop of Pennsylvania" (ibid., no. 5 [May 1967], p. 1). In 1969, according to Skelton, he withdrew from Hamel's jurisdiction, whereupon Hamel placed Skelton under major excommunication (ibid., vol. 6, no. 7 [July 1969], p. 5).

24. *C. S. P. World News*, vol. 5, no. 4 (April 1968), pp. 6-7. The roster of bishops listed each one only by a single name (Christian name or family

name) and state (or nation). The names included identifiable Protestant Episcopal, Old Catholic, and Eastern prelates in North America and abroad, living and dead, such as Boltwood, England; Billett, Pennsylvania; De Witow, New York; Growchowski[!], Pennsylvania; Heiler, Germany; Ilarion, Manitoba; Lichtenberger, New York; Ofiesh, Pennsylvania; and Pillai, New York. If a prelate complained at being included on Hamel's list, the latter could respond that the complainant was "not the only man of that name" (letter, Claudius I to Mr. Charles B. Breslow, Miami, Florida, dated April 27, 1968). (A list of "Old Roman Catholic Archdioceses and Dioceses" published in C. S. P. World News, vol. 6, no. 4 [April 1969], p. 7, was more specific as to names, but contained many obvious errors). To the list of members of the "holy synod of bishops," Hamel appended the names of twenty-eight members of a priestly "secretariat" which would serve at Conclave 1970; the present writer was interested in observing that the list included a "Father Piepkorn, Missouri." In 1969 the present writer received from Hamel an unsolicited "approved identification" made out in the name of "Rev. A. C. Piepkert[!], 801 Domun [!] Ave., St. Louis, Mo.," certifying him as a "missionary" of the Old Roman Catholic Church. Possibly because of the present writer's connection with Concordia Seminary, St. Louis, that institution received from Hamel in 1967 an unsolicited "charter of intercommunion." Other recipients of the "charter of intercommunion" were the Louisiana Psychological Association, the Anglican Orthodox Church, the New Apostolic Church of North America, and the Liberal Catholic Church (ibid., vol. 4, no. 4 [April 1967], p. 1). Among those whom Hamel elevated to the cardinalatial dignity in his church was Anton Szandor La Vey of San Francisco, California, head of the Church of Satan. La Vey in turn designated Hamel his "filial wizard" for Canada. (Frank Drea, "A Satanic Benediction for the Wildest Sect in Ontario," Weekend Telegram [Toronto, Ontario], May 23, 1970, feature section, pp. 1-2.)

25. Letters from Detective Sergeant Godfrey H. R. Cooper, Anti-Rackets Branch, Ontario, Provincial Police, Toronto, Canada, dated June 23, August 29, and September 24, 1969; " 'Pope Claudius I' Held on Fraud, Perjury Charges," Telegram, July 4, 1969. As early as 1966, Telegram had stated: "Hamel's dubious status in the community is recorded in one of the Toronto Better Business Bureau's thickest files. It takes two hands to lift it and a stronger constitution to read it" (Anthony, p. 2).

26. The roster of bishops published in anticipation of Conclave 1970 included a bishop or archbishop in each of the United States (C. S. P. World News, vol. 5, no. 4 [April 1968], p. 7). But in the Encyclical "Veteris Romanae Ecclesiae," p. 5, Hamel claimed to have had in the United States at that time (November 1967) a total of only thirty-nine churches and missions, two monasteries, and a major and a minor seminary. In estimating the number of his spiritual subjects in the United States he quoted the eighteen-year-old Yearbook of American Churches for 1949 in order to lay claim to 47,500 lay members. In 1968 the "patriarchal secretariate" claimed a worldwide membership of approximately 550,000 (C. S. P. World News, vol. 5, no. 8 [August 1968], p. 6).

27. Letter from the secretary of state, State of Utah. The ordinal II at the end of the church's name is explained as standing for "second movement."

28. Stanley also signed as Metropolitanus Christophorus, C. J. Stanley, D.D.

29. "Church Consecrates Bishop," Courier-Journal, Louisville, Kentucky, January 22, 1965.

30. Mancinelli joined Hamel in September 1966 and was immediately consecrated a bishop; he was named a member of the college of cardinals of the Old Roman Catholic Church (Orthodox Orders) the following month. French, also a cardinal, was archbishop of California in Hamel's organization.

31. Mancinelli, whom Skelton has designated as his successor, is the regional patriarch, United States of America, French the bishop of Long Beach. French describes himself as superior of the Society of Missionary Priests of the Sacred Heart; in 1970 he reported

a major and a minor monastery as well as an average attendance of about forty in his domestic chapel in Long Beach.

32. The Breton town of Treguier was the seat of a bishop from the mid-ninth century, when it was established by Nomenoë (d. 851), duke of Brittany, until the French Revolution. Most of its territory was incorporated in the neighboring diocese of St.-Brieuc after the Concordat of 1801/1802; since 1852 the bishops of St.-Brieuc have been authorized to add the name of Treguier to their diocesan title.

33. Letters from the Most Reverend Joseph Damian Hough, archiepiscopal legate, Ultrajectine Ordinariate, Holy Catholic Church.

34. For the text of the formula, see John Mason Neale, *A History of the So-Called Jansenist Church of Holland* (Oxford: John Henry and James Parker, 1858), pp. 351-352, reprinted in Claude Beaufort Moss, *The Old Catholic Movement: Its Origins and History* (London: SPCK, 1948), pp. 161-162. The formula is the statement that the bishops of the Church of Utrecht offered in 1823 to subscribe in place of the act of submission which the papal nuncio to Holland demanded. The formula declares the bishops' acceptance of "all the articles of the holy catholic faith"; their determination to teach no other "opinions than those which have been decreed, determined, and published by our mother, the holy church, conformably to holy scripture, tradition, the acts of ecumenical councils, and those of the Council of Trent"; their rejection of anything contrary to these opinions, especially of all heresies which the church has rejected and condemned; their detestation of every schism that separates them from the Roman Catholic Church and "its visible head upon earth"; their explicit condemnation of "the Five Propositions condemned by the Holy See, which are stated to be found in the book of [Cornelius Otto] Jansenius [1585–1638] called *Augustinus*"; their "fidelity, obedience, and submission in all things" to Leo XII and his successors "according to the canons of the church"; and their intention to maintain respectfully and to teach, in accordance with the same canons, the decrees and constitutions of the Roman see. The issue in 1823 was whether or not the Five Propositions were actually contained in Jansen's *Augustinus*; the bishops of the Church of Utrecht held that they were not, while the Roman see held that they were. Accordingly, the Roman Catholic Church deemed the submission of the bishops of the Church of Utrecht on all other points as not sufficient to warrant receiving them into communion with the Roman see. On the whole issue, see Moss, chap. 12, pp. 161-168.

35. An Account of the Old Roman Catholic Church, Ultrajectine Rite (Antiqua Romana Catholic Ecclesia) (Venice, Calif.: The Catholic Legation, 1968) (eight-page leaflet), pp. 5-6.

36. As archbishop of the "exarchal see of America, Malabar succession of Antioch," Hough claims to be the "canonical successor to Mar Julius 1866 and Mar Timotheus 1892, the original Old Catholic foundation in America, 'Western Orthodox' 1885." "Mar Julius" is the ex-Brahmin Roman Catholic priest Antonio Francisco-Xavier Alvarez (Alvares), who took the name Mar Julius I after Mar Paul Athanasius, the Non-Chalcedonian/Syrian Antiochene bishop of Kottayam, India, consecrated Alvarez in 1889 as "archbishop of the Independent Catholic Church of Goa and Ceylon," founded the year before. (The number 1866 refers to the year in which Bedros [Homs], who later became the Non-Chalcedonian Syrian patriarch of Antioch as Mar Ignatius Peter III and who in that office authorized the conscration of Alvarez, is alleged to have consecrated an ex-Roman Catholic priest, Julius Ferrete, as "bishop of Iona.") "Mar Timotheus" is Joseph René Vilatte, whom Alvarez in 1892 consecrated as archbishop-metropolitan of the "churches adhering to the Orthodox faith" in the "archdiocese of America." Vilatte in turn consecrated Frederick Ebenezer John Lloyd, a former presbyter in the Protestant Episcopal Church, as "bishop of Illinois" in the American Catholic Church in 1915. Lloyd consecrated Samuel Gregory Lines, also a former presbyter in the Protestant Episcopal

Church, as "bishop of the American Catholic Church (Western Orthodox) in the province of the Pacific" in 1923. On April 7, 1928 (or, according to another source, December 21, 1927), Lines consecrated to the episcopate Justin Joseph Andrieu Boyle (Ivan Drouet de la Thibauderie d'Erlon, *Églises et evêques catholiques non romains* [Paris: Dervy-Livres, 1962], p. 105; Henry R. T. Brandreth, *Episcopi Vagantes and the Anglican Church,* 2nd edition [London: SPCK, 1961], p. 63). The repeatedly made assertion that Boyle was a former Roman Catholic priest is reportedly untrue. Boyle later resumed legally his original name, Robert Raleigh (letter from the Most Reverend H. Adrian Spruit, archbishop, Province of the United States, Church of Antioch [Malabar Rite]. Under the name of Raleigh he founded "the Church of Antioch and the National Academy of Metapathics," Box 2, Agoura, California, incorporated in 1940. Other agencies which he also sponsored were the Mystical Prayer Shrine and St. Primordia's Guild. Upon Lines's death in 1965, Raleigh succeeded to the former's exarchal dignity. Whether or not he had any clerical or lay subjects cannot be determined. Early in 1969 Raleigh consecrated Hough as "archbishop of the Malabar Rite—St. Thomas Christians," with the right of succession in America upon Raleigh's death, which took place in April of the same year. Hough disclaims any connection with the Christian Academy of Metapathics, which seems to have functioned through the distribution by mail of "text manuscripts" to interested inquirers. For a powerful spiritual force to come and make an adherent's body the temple of the Holy Spirit, Raleigh declared, all that is necessary is that the mind and soul of the worshiper be "at-one with the holy ones." The seal on Hough's stationery is identical with that used by Raleigh, except that Raleigh's device bore the legend "patriarch's seal," while Hough's device bears the legend "exarch's seal." (Robert Raleigh, "The Better Way," undated [1963 or later] five-page typescript description of Christian Metapathics which Mr. James V. Geisendorfer, Minneapolis, Minnesota,

kindly shared with the present writer; letter from Joseph Damian Archbishop Hough, the Exarchal See of America, Malabar Succession of Antioch, Box 269, Venice, California; Henry R. T. Brandreth, *Episcopi Vagantes and the Anglican Church,* 2nd edition [London: SPCK, 1961], pp. 58, 62, 63, 70; Peter F. Anson, *Bishops at Large* [New York: October House 1965], pp. 36, 105-108, 125, 254, 256-257. Neither Brandreth nor Anson is apparently aware of the alleged consecration of Raleigh by Lines.) Another of Hough's letterheads describes him as president of Sequoia University, with administrative offices at 1418 Second Street, Santa Monica, California. Sequoia University is not listed in Part 3 (Higher Education) of the *Education Directory* published by the United States Office of Education.

37. Peter F. Anson, *Bishops at Large* (New York: October House, 1964), p. 492; Henry R. T. Brandreth, *Episcopi Vagantes and the Anglican Church,* second edition (London: Society for the Promotion of Christian Knowledge, 1961), p. 83 and n. 3. It appears that Powell was never a priest in the Liberal Catholic Church, as Anson and Brandreth state.

38. *Introductory Handbook, The Brotherhood of the Pleroma and the Order of the Pleroma, Including the Hermetic Brotherhood of Light* (London: B. C. M. Consortium, undated 33-page mimeographed booklet), pp. 6-8, 16-17.

39. Ibid., pp. 10, 29.

40. Ibid., pp. 18-25.

41. Letter from the Most Reverend Stephan A. Hoeller, deputy leader and bishop, The brotherhood of the Pleroma and the Order of the Pleroma. The curator of the James V. Geisendorfer Collection of Original Source Materials on American Minority Religious Groups has generously shared the materials in the Geisendorfer Collection on the Brotherhood of the Pleroma with the present writer.

42. James Ingall Wedgwood, *The Liberal Catholic Church and the Theosophical Society: Where They Agree and Where They Differ* (Los Angeles, 1919), pp. 3-4, quoted in Edward Murray Matthews, *Deceptio, Falsum et Dissimulatio: A Critique* (Los Angeles: St.

Alban Bookshop, 1959), appendix, p. iv.

43. Ibid., appendix, p. xi.

44. The General Synod did not recognize this action.

45. Memorandum decision, Superior Court of the State of California in and for the County of Los Angeles, Action No. 678,744, April 13, 1961, *Liberal Catholic Church* v. *Edward M. Matthews and others.*

46. "In the Liberal Catholic Church there is room for any degree of syncretism in religious thought," says Charles Samuel Braden, *These Also Believe* (New York: The Macmillan Company, 1951), p. 318.

47. "General Information," *The Liturgy according to the Use of the Liberal Catholic Church, Prepared for the Use of English-Speaking Congregations,* 3rd edition (London: St. Alban Press, 1942), pp. 7-8.

48. Notes explain *monogenēs* ("alone-born," "only-begotten," or "only") as meaning "born from a single principle, not a syzygy or pair," and *aiōn* ("age," "world") as "emanation" (ibid., p. 173.)

49. Ibid., pp. 174-175. The second Act of Faith, a Christian version of the "Three Refuges" of Buddhism, is rarely, if ever, used. Both Acts of Faith have been taken over into *The Liturgy and Ritual* of the Universal Spiritual Association.

50. Ibid., p. 252.

51. Ibid., pp. 177-178.

52. Ibid., p. 183.

53. Supplement to *Ubique*, February 1966, p. 11.

54. *The Liturgy*, p. 19.

55. Ibid., p. 16.

56. Ibid., pp. 10-11. The preface also takes note of the deletion from the *Gloria in excelsis* of "Lamb of God," a characterization that impresses "the virgin mind with . . . a sense of the ridiculous" (ibid., p. 13).

57. Ibid., p. 20.

58. *The Liberal Catholic Church: Statement of Principles and Summary of Doctrine,* 6th edition (London: The Liberal Catholic Church, 1959) (a nineteen-page pamphlet), pp. 5-6, 11.

59. Ibid., pp. 16-17.

60. Supplement to *Ubique* for February 1966, pp. 14-15.

61. *A Shorter Form for the Celebration of the Holy Eucharist . . . according to the Use of the Liberal Catholic Church* (London: St. Alban Press, 1966), inside cover, pp. 10-12, 19, 22. The benediction "May the Holy Ones" has been incorporated into *The Liturgy and Ritual* of the Universal Spiritual Association with minor changes as "A Master Class Invocation."

62. *The Statement of Policy [of the] International Catholic Church* (Ojai, Calif.: International Liberal Catholic Church, 1967) (eight-page mimeographed pamphlet), p. 2. The same document states: "Liberal Catholic clergy function as specialists in . . . the invocation and radiation of sacramental grace to comfort, to inspire, and to accelerate the unfoldment of the Eternal in man —individually and collectively. In that unfoldment man will become truly civilized, and will walk the earth in peace and good will" (p. 4). "The church . . . should seek in its membership people who are dissatisfied with the contemporary expression of Christianity and are searching for answers to and experiences of the deeper, inner phases of life—men and women who will enter upon and perseveringly tread the mystic way of the cross to progressively unfold the Christ Spirit within" (p. 8).

63. Letters from the Most Reverend Francis Erwin, presiding bishop, the [International] Liberal Catholic Church, and from the Right Reverend Thomas A. Feuss, suffragan bishop, Province of the United States, the [International] Liberal Catholic Church, 9 South Barclay Avenue, Margate City, New Jersey.

64. Edward Murray Matthews. *Freedom of Thought: An Encyclical* (Los Angeles: The Liberal Catholic Church, 1959) (seven-page pamphlet), p. 2.

65. Ibid., pp. 6-7.

66. *The Liberal Catholic Church: Statement of Principles and Table of the Apostolic Succession,* 8th edition (Los Angeles: The Liberal Catholic Church, 1963) (a twenty-page pamphlet), p. 19.

67. Communications from the Most Reverend Edward Murray Matthews.

BIBLIOGRAPHY

Braden, Charles Samuel. *These Also Believe: A Study of Modern American Cults and Minority Religious Movements.* New York: The Macmillan Company, 1951. Chap. 8, "The Liberal Catholic Church," pp. 308-318.

Cooper, Irving Steiger. *The Ceremonies of the Liberal Catholic Rite.* 2nd edition. London: St. Alban Press, 1964.

Leadbeater, Charles Webster. *The Science of the Sacraments.* 2nd edition. Adyar, India: Theosophical Publishing House, 1929. An exposition of the inner working of the Catholic sacraments "as observed clairvoyantly."

The Liturgy according to the Use of the Liberal Catholic Church, Prepared for the Use of English-Speaking Congregations. 3rd edition. London: St. Alban Press, 1942.

Matthews, Edward M. *Deceptio, Falsum et Dissimulatio: A Critique.* Los Angeles: St. Alban Bookshop, 1959. This brochure sets forth the events leading to the schism in North America from the standpoint of the Liberal Catholic Church (Miranda, California).

Wedgwood, James Ingall. "The Beginnings of the Liberal Catholic Church, February 13, 1916," ed. William H. Pitkin, supplement to *Ubique* (Lakewood, N.J.), February 1966, pp. 1-11.

16. The Renovated Church of Jesus Christ

Michel Collin was born at Bechy, Lorraine, France, in 1905. In 1933 he received ordination in the Congregation of Priests of the Sacred Heart of Jesus of St. Quentin. In 1935, Collin declared, Christ himself consecrated Collin to the episcopate, and in 1950 God the Father imparted to him the papal crown and consecration as the designated future successor of John XXIII.[1] The Renovated Church of Jesus Christ came into being, according to Collin, when he officially succeeded John under the name of Clement XV[2] on May 31, 1963, at Lourdes, France. Clement was crowned pope at Clémery, France, the site of his "Little Vatican," the Domaine de Marie Corédemptrice, on June 9, 1963.[3] In 1966, Clement states, Christ commanded him to submit to reconsecration by a former Old Catholic bishop who had joined the Renovated Church and whose line of episcopal succession included Bishop Jacques-Benigne Bossuet of Meaux, "so that 'weak souls' may have no excuse anymore not to recognize" Clement and his hierarchy on the ground that they lack apostolic succession. After receiving reconsecration himself, Clement in a solemn act (that is, mystically, without actually laying hands on them) reconsecrated all his bishops and reordained all his priests by affirming the consecration and ordination of each.[4] Clement claimed a worldwide following of about 25,000, of whom an estimated 1,000 are in Canada and the United States. A priest of the community acknowledges that 2,500 would be closer to the truth; "we are of no numerical importance," he writes.[5]

The Renovated Church of Jesus Christ declares that "it rests entirely on the pure and uncomplicated Gospel," taught "according to the traditional interpretation of the fathers of the church." It proclaims its opposition to "the errors and abuses, the laxity and the confusion, which have invaded the Roman [Catholic] Church and a large part of its clergy." It refuses to recognize the present leaders of the Roman Catholic Church as "the true representatives of God" and rejects Vatican Council II.[6] In spite of practical differences, the basic theology of the Renovated Church of Jesus Christ accords with the conservative theology of the Roman Catholic Church before Vatican II, with strong mystical, ascetic, apocalyptic, and Mariological thrusts.

In 1963 Clement XV called together the cardinals and bishops of the Renovated Church of Jesus Christ for a three-day council in Lyons, France. To make the sacraments more accessible to the faithful for their sanctification, this council directed a number of changes in the administration of the sacraments. The mother of a newly born infant is to baptize it immediately; a confirmatory baptism and the solemn entry of the child into the church takes place later. In all sacramental ministrations the reserved sacrament will be used in place of oil or chrism at all anointings. A member of the church may receive confirmation many times during his life; a priest whom the bishop delegates may administer confirmation. Auricular confession is not necessary to obtain forgiveness (although it is permitted); a priest will grant general absolution to those who have true contrition and a sincere purpose of avoiding sin and occasions of sin.

Children under the age of reason may receive Holy Communion. The faithful may receive Communion oftener than once a day; the eucharistic fast is not required. The sacrament may be reserved in "eucharistic homes," that is, homes of families belonging to the Renovated Church of Jesus Christ that are authorized to have the reserved sacrament. Priests may say Mass in any decent and suitable place, day or night. Prescribed fasts and abstinence no longer bind the offender under pain of grave sin, but every Christian must engage in voluntary mortification. Failure to assist at Sunday Mass is no longer a mortal sin, but the faithful must sanctify the day by prayer and retirement from "the frivolities of the world." Communion under both species is authorized except where it is too inconvenient so to administer it.

The priesthood is open to all religious who have made perpetual vows, regardless of sex, as well as to married persons. Most married priests will be "sacramental" priests, authorized only to administer sacraments. A second category of priests will receive additional faculties, such as the authority to preach and to direct souls. Men and women of all ages may be ordained as deacons and deaconesses, with authority to distribute Holy Communion.

Sacramental marriage must be contracted before a priest; marriages lawfully contracted before a minister of another church body or before a civil authority are valid, but not licit. Sick persons not in danger of death may receive holy unction (the sacrament of the sick) as a comfort and support to them in soul and body.

Modifications of common Roman Catholic formulas include suppression of "catholic" in the creed and the substitution of "thy son" for "the fruit of thy womb" and the addition of "and our mother" after "Mother of God" in the Hail Mary.[7]

The council directed the decentralization of the church and the establishment of a "vatican" for each nation.[8]

The Renovated Church of Jesus Christ is represented in North America by the Apostles and Disciples of the Infinite Love, Order of the Mother of God. Gaston Tremblay, a native of Rimouski, Quebec, reported that he founded the order in 1947 in response to Christ's command imparted to him in a vision. He took the religious name of Jean de la Trinité and in 1950 with two companions he established the first center of the Order at St.-Jovite, Quebec, seventy-five miles northwest of Montreal. By the end of 1966 the foundation, called the Domaine de la Magnificat, had grown to 170 members, and had established a number of branch centers.

The Apostles or religious—fathers, brothers, and sisters[9]—take vows of poverty, chastity, and obedience, and follow the thirty-three-point rule that Our Lady of La Salette reportedly dictated to Melanie Calvat in 1846.[10]

The Disciples, married or unmarried, commit themselves to poverty, chastity, and obedience as evangelical counsels according to their state in life, but they do not take vows. Married Disciples may live in the immediate vicinity of foundations of the order or elsewhere, but they must be model Christians in the world, fleeing "vanities and frivolous pleasures," such as television, smoking, games, and attendance at theaters and sports events. Women Disciples wear a special habit; male Disciples do not. Disciples live under a rule of their own and under the jurisdiction of the order. If they are married they are required to make their homes "centers of fervor"; wherever possible, they are expected to have the reserved sacrament in their homes ("eucharistic homes").[11]

Juvenists are children from six to fifteen years of age of both sexes who are receiving preliminary preparation for the religious life. They wear a simple habit.[12]

Early in 1967 tensions began to develop between Clement XV and the St.-Jovite community.[13] On January 6 Clement expelled Jean de la Trinité, prior-general of the Apostles of the Infinite Love, "for civil and religious irregularities" and Father Jean-Marie Brunet "for exaggeration contrary to the spirit of the gospel."[14] In April Clement anathematized Raphael of the Immaculate Heart of Mary, the order's bishop for the United States. The order in turn declined to accept any of Clement's further directives, which it described as "not inspired by Heaven, directives which would only destroy God's work."[15] With a view to effecting a permanent and public reconciliation Jean and Raphael, in response to what they believed to be a directive of Christ, went to Europe in November, but Clement refused to grant them a personal audience.[16] In September 1968 he once more publicly affirmed that the followers of Jean de la Trinité were in schism; a few days later he reportedly thought better of his action. In November 1968 a member of Clement's staff could write: "At the present hour Clement XV has entrusted all the powers of the apostolate to Father [Jean] and to the Monastery of St.-Jovite, according to the will of God and according to laws of each country. The Monastery of the Magnificat is exhibiting an exemplary and unparalleled piety."[17] The St.-Jovite leadership now asserts that "to assist and continue the work of [the mystical pope Clement XV] God raised up Gregory XVII [Father Jean de la Trinité], who by the divine will bears the title of Servant of the Holy Church of Jesus Christ."[18] In 1975 Gregory XVII issued a universal encyclical for Christian unity.[19]

In addition to its headquarters for Canada at St.-Jovite, the order has five other centers in Quebec. In addition to the 200 Apostles, Disciples, and children at these seven communities, there are an estimated 250 additional "eucharistic homes" in the United States and Canada.[20]

NOTES

1. *L'Élu du Ciel, Clément XV, Flos Florum, Fleur des Fleurs* (Nancy, France: Imprimerie Nancéienne, 1968?) (forty-page brochure), pp. 9, 18.—Late in 1963, a group of Clement's followers established themselves in Necedah, Wisconsin, where the Blessed Virgin Mary had reportedly appeared to Mrs. Mary Ann van Hoof in 1950. The mission closed after a few months. (Letters from the Reverend Gerald L. Herman, pastor, St. James's Church and St. Paul's Church, Necedah, Wisconsin, and Father Raphael of the Immaculate Heart of Mary, bishop for the United States in the Renovated Church of Jesus Christ.) On the first series of alleged apparitions of the Blessed Virgin Mary at Necedah, see Margaret Frakes, "Setting for a Miracle," *The Christian Century* 67 (1950): 1019-1021.

2. The officially still undivulged third part of the "secret of Fatima" allegedly identifies the second successor of Pius XII as Clement XV ("eucharistic letter" from Bishop Raphael of the Immaculate Heart of Mary, dated August 30, 1967).

3. *Magnificat: Spiritual Notes of the Apostles of the Infinite Love,* September 1966 (special edition), pp. 18-19.

4. "Eucharistic letters" from Bishop Raphael of the Immaculate Heart of Mary, dated July 7 and September 14, 1967.

5. Clement's claim was reported by *Time* (Canadian edition), January 27, 1967, p. 15; the priest of the community is Father Paul du Coeur de Jésus, O. D. M., whose acknowledgment is in a letter to the editor, May 20, 1976.

6. *Magnificat,* September 1966 (special edition), p. 18.

7. Ibid., pp. 34-40. Among the new feasts of the Renovated Church of Jesus Christ are: the Merciful Christ; the Sacred Head of Christ, Seat of Divine Wisdom; Mary, Our Lady of the Revelation, Who Is Eternally in the Thought of God; and Our Lady of Light. The Mass may take one of three forms: the liturgy of the day; the "Brief Mass" (offering, consecration, prayer for unity to Christ and Mary, Our Father, prayer to St. Joseph, Communion, post-Communion, blessing, and the Last Gospel); and the "Mass of the Last Supper" (three Gloria Patris; consecration; Communion; Our Father; Hail Mary; Gloria Patri; blessing. (Ibid.)

8. Ibid., p. 41.

9. The order remembers that "apostles of the latter times" were "foretold by the Most Holy Virgin and many Saints, especially by St. Louis-Marie [Grignon] de Montfort" (1673–1716), founder of the Daughters of Wisdom and the male Company of Mary, but Father Jean de la Trinité has cautioned readers of *Magnificat* that these apostles will be "not necessarily and exclusively those who wear the tunic of the Apostles of the Infinite Love, [but] those who will best live the Rule dictated by the Mother of God at La Salette" (ibid., p. 31).

10. Some of the Apostles are married couples who have by common consent decided to separate (and, if they have children, to commit them to the order for education). The voluntary separation of married couples in order to enter upon the religious life is, of course, not unprecedented, as the order points out (*Magnificat,* June 1967, pp. 29-44). Some of the examples that the order cites are of dubious historicity, but the reasonably certain cases of

mutual undertakings to live "as brother and sister" or to separate so that both parties may enter the religious life include St. Hilary of Poitiers (315?–367) and his wife; SS. Amator (d. 418) and Martha of Auxerre; St. Paulinus of Nola (d. 431) and Therasia; SS. Melania the Younger (383–439) and Valerius Pinianus of Rome; St. Wandrille of Fontenalle (d. 668) and his wife; St. Etheldreda of Ely (d. 679) and her husbands Tonbert and Egfrid; Count Madelgar (Vincent) of Hainault and St. Waltrude of Mons (d. 688); Witger of Lobbes and St. Amalberga of Maubeuge (d. 690); SS. Gundebert and Bertha of Reims (8th century); Duke Henry of Silesia and St. Hedwig (1174?–1243); Blessed Mary of Oignies (d. 1213) and her husband; Boleslaus V the Chaste, King of Poland, and Blessed Cunegund of Hungary (1224–1292); St. Elezear of Sabran (1285–1323) and Blessed Delphina of Glandeves (d. 1360); Eggard von Kürnen and St. Catharine of Vadstena (1322–1381); Blessed Joan Mary de Maille (1332–1414) and Robert de Sille; Francis and Catharine Coronel, the parents of Venerable Mary of Agreda (1602–1655); Pierce Connelly (who later returned to the Anglican communion, which he had abandoned for Roman Catholicism) and Mother Cornelia Connelly (1809–1887); the Slovenian Cistercian monk Martin Kajtna (1836–1923) and his wife; and the parents of Maximilian Kolbe (1894–1942), the nazi-concentration-camp martyr.

11. Married Disciples who live at one of the centers of the order have their children educated in the school that the order maintains at St.-Jovite.

12. *Magnificat,* September 1966 (special edition), pp. 19-25.

13. In January 1967 the order received international publicity when the social welfare court of St.-Jérome (about twenty-five miles northwest of Montreal), within whose jurisdiction St.-Jovite lies, ruled that the children of the Domaine of the Magnificat were exposed to physical and moral danger and directed that eighty-two children be placed elsewhere. The small number that the authorities were able to find at the Domaine of the Magnificat were put in foster homes in and near St.-Jérome. The members of the community spirited most of the children away and they escaped the police searches. The community devoted the 112-page July-August 1967 issue of *Magnificat* to a rehearsal of the community's experiences at the hands of some of the Roman Catholic clergy in the province, the provincial Department of Social Welfare, and the lower courts. In February 1968 the Superior Court of Quebec quashed and annulled the lower court's order. The following month the St.-Jérome social welfare court directed the return of seven children of United States nationality whom social welfare officials had removed from the Domaine of the Magnificat in the summer of 1967 (*Magnificat,* March 1968, p. 106).

14. *Telegram,* Toronto, Ontario, January 18, 1967, 2.

15. "Eucharistic letter" from Bishop Raphael of the Immaculate Heart of Mary, dated April 20, 1967.

16. Letter from Bishop Raphael of the Immaculate Heart of Mary.

17. Communication from Father Ange du Magnificat, bishop of the Holy Church of Jesus and Mary, Vatican de Marie Corédemptrice, Clémery par Nomeny, Meurthe-et-Moselle, France.

18. *Magnificat,* October 1968 (special edition), p. 310. In the lead article of this issue Father Jean designates himself "Brother Jean de la Trinité, Bishop-Servant of the True Church of Jesus-Christ" ("Message to Christianity," ibid., p. 273). Another article in the same issue, "A New Clergy," has this sentence underlined: "The essential condition for being a priest of God in the new times will be to be a true servant of God" (ibid., p. 312).

19. *Peter Speaks to the World: Universal Encyclical for Christian Unity* (St.-Jovite, Quebec: Monastery of the Apostles, 1975), 407 pages.

20. Letter, Sister Marie Anne of the Child Jesus, Monastery of the Magnificat, St.-Jovite, Quebec, and communication from Bishop Raphael of the Immaculate Heart of Mary. However, the figures may be inflated; in response to a recent letter to confirm their accuracy Father Paul du Coeur de Jésus, O.D.M., wrote: "We are of no numerical importance."

Index

Abris, 4

Absolution, 8, 9, 47, 110, 112, 113, 114, 136, 144n, 289, 298, 312

Acolytes, 19, 47

Addai, Saint, 4, 9

Adoptianism, 130

Aedesius, Saint, of Tyre, 24

Aix-la-Chapelle, Council of (809), 130, 144n

Albigenses, 131, 144n, 173

Alleluia, Singing of, 34, 108, 112

Ambrose, Saint, 120, 158

Ambrosian Rite, 165

Analogy of being, 213

Anchorites, 9

Ancren Riwle, 155

Aneed, Anthony, 90, 91–92

Angels, 15, 93, 122, 216–217, 232n, 290

Annihilation, 154

Anointing, 15, 19, 44, 47–48, 136

Anselm, Saint, of Canterbury, 121ff., 161, 227

Ansgar, Saint, 170

Anthony, Saint, of Egypt, 21, 168

Anthony, Saint, the Greek, 34

Antichrist, 108–109, 115n, 174

Anti-Modernist Oath, 204

Anti-Pelagian, 166

Apocrypha, Old Testament, 9, 27n, 39

Apostles' Creed, 55n, 93, 151–152, 163n, 214, 244, 281, 289

Apostolic succession, 8, 16, 38, 43, 112, 141, 241, 290

Arc of Light. See Mary, Virgin

Archbishops, 47, 242

Archdeacons, 8

Archpriests. See Vicars general

Arianism, 24

Arles, Council of (314), 138

Arles, Council of (813), 144n

Articles of Constance, 134

Asceticism, 38

Athanasian Creed, 55n, 93, 149–151, 162n, 214, 289

Athanasius, Saint, 21, 34, 42, 129

Augsburg Interim, 304n

Augustine, Saint, 120–121

Auraham of Kashkar, 6

Autun, Second Council of (ca. 670), 162n

Awa I, 5

Baptism, 4, 8, 15, 18, 19, 34, 44, 51, 105n, 110, 112, 113, 114, 128, 131, 133, 135, 136, 159, 180, 266, 282, 298, 312

Barsoma, 5

Bartholomew, Saint, 4, 16

Basel, Council of (1431), 134, 144n, 155

Basil, Saint, of Caesarea, 34, 40, 45, 54n, 120, 168

Bawai the Great, 6, 8

Beards, 34, 114

Beatification, 245

Benedict, Saint, of Nursia, 168, 169

Bernard, Saint, of Clairvaux, 169

Bible, 19, 21, 25, 27n, 39, 48, 76, 79, 93, 95, 105n, 113, 119, 120, 123, 127, 131, 132, 136, 143n, 174, 179–180, 198n, 204, 208n, 218–219, 232n, 281, 282, 289, 293, 298; Peshitta, 9

Biblical Commission, 204, 205, 208n, 224

Biblical criticism, 220

Biblical movement, 204–205

Biblicism, 128

Biel, Gabriel, 127, 129

Birth control, 47, 95, 194

Bishops, 8, 16, 19, 33, 43, 47, 102, 119, 128 129, 136, 141, 157, 158, 181, 241, 266n–267n

Bologna, Council of. *See* Basel, Council of (1431)

Borromeo, Charles, Saint, 183

Bowing of the head, 133

Bread, 34, 106n, 108, 126, 133, 134, 135

Brethren of the Common Life, 169

"Cadaver Council" (897), 145n

Caesarius, Saint, of Arles, 168

Caesaropapism, 54n

Calixtines. *See* Unity of the Brethren

Callistus, Saint, 145n

Canon law, 46, 49, 171–173

Canons regular, 168–169

Capuchins, 183, 260

Cardinals, 242

Carsiaca, Council of (853), 143n

Carthage, Council of (256), 139, 140

Cassian, John, 168

Cathars, 131, 144n, 173

Catholic, 196n

Catholic action, 207, 208, 209n

Catholic Congress, Mechelen, Belgium (1909), 209n

Catholicism, 99

Catholicoi, 19

Celibacy, 8, 16, 19, 25, 34, 47, 75, 95, 100, 102, 103, 105n, 110, 111, 158, 174, 181, 195, 249, 287, 290, 293, 294, 312

Celtic Rite, 165

Cenacle, 9

Cenobites, 167

Censorship, 181

Chalcedon, Council of (451), 13, 16, 17, 22, 24, 31, 121, 139, 140

Chaldean Rite, 7

Châlon-sur-Saône, Council of (813), 144n

Chastity, 249

Chemnitz, Martin, 182

Chiliasm, 121

Chrismation, 8, 15, 19, 44–45, 113, 135. *See also* Confirmation

Christian morals, 132

Christology, 3, 4; Church of the East, 5, 6, 7, 8, 10n, 11n; Syrian Orthodox Church, 13; Armenian Church, 18, 19; Coptic Orthodox Church, 22; Ethiopian Church, 24; Eastern Orthodox, 42; Holy Orthodox, 76; African Orthodox, 93, 99, 105n, 113, 119, 122, 123, 124, 125, 129, 150–

151, 152, 204, 226–232, 234n, 235n, 282, 287

Christotokos. See Mary, Virgin

Chrysostom, John, Saint, 34, 40, 45, 54n

Church (Doctrine of), 3, 4, 8, 9, 18, 42, 51, 93, 105n, 119, 121, 131, 151, 152, 204, 239–241, 251–254, 269n, 282, 298

Church and state, 34, 36, 37, 120, 130, 131, 173, 190

Church architecture, 49

Church buildings, 25, 131

Church music, 35

Church year, 48, 57n

Circumcision, 25

Clement, Saint, of Alexandria, 21

Clementine Constitutions, 172

Clergy, 19, 25, 33, 94, 102, 105n, 110

Codex juris canonici, 190

Collegiality, 243, 255

Commission for Studies on Justice and Peace, 194

Common Extravagants, 172

Communion of saints, 94, 244–247

Conciliarism, 173, 174

Concordantia discordantium canonum, 172

Concordat of Worms (1122), 130, 142

Concubinage, 110, 130, 158

Confession, 9, 46–47, 131, 132, 136, 144n, 156, 289, 298, 312

Confession of Faith (Polish National Catholic Church), 281–282

Confessors, 158

Confirmation, 15, 19, 44, 135, 180, 312. *See also* Chrismation

Congregation for the Causes of the Saints, 245, 267n

Congregation for the Divine Cult, 267

Congregation for the Doctrine of the Faith, 194, 195

Congregation for the Propagation of the Faith, 183, 259, 260, 261, 265

Congregation of Rites, 245, 267n

Congregation of the Index, 186

Congregations, 249

Conrad of Gelnhausen, 173

Consecration, 115n

Constance, Council of (1414–1418), 128, 133–134, 144n, 155, 175

Constantinople, Council of (381), 3, 7, 15, 17, 139

Constantinople, Council of (553), 4, 27n, 31, 140

Constantinople, Council of (680–681), 4, 31, 140

Constantinople, Council of (869–870), 130, 145n

Consubstantiation, 126, 154

Contrition, 136

Convergence of opposites, 128

Coptic calendar, 23

Coptic Rite, 23

Co-responsibility, 243–244, 267n

Corpus Christi (Festival), 155

Corpus juris canonici, 172, 173

Corpus juris civilis, 172

Corredemptrix. *See* Mary, Virgin

Council of the Laity, 194

Counter-Reformation, 182–184, 197n

Creation, 3, 123, 125, 215–216

Creationism, 223

Creed, 26n, 108, 148ff.

Creed of the 150 Fathers of Constantinople. *See* Nicene Creed

Cross, 108, 131

Crusaders, 130

Cum permissu superiorum, 213

Cur Deus homo?, 122

Cyprian, Saint, 119

Cyril, Saint, of Alexandria, 21, 31, 34

Cyril, Saint, of Jerusalem, 34

Dabtaras (lay clerks), 25

Dance (in worship), 25

Deacons, 8, 19, 43, 47, 157

Decalog, 9, 15, 19, 58n

Declaration on the Relation of the Church to Non-Christian Religions, 257

Declaration of Indulgence (1687), 198n

Declaration of Indulgence for Tender Consciences (1672), 198n

Decree (*Decretum*) of Gratian. *See* Concordantia discordantium canonum

Decree on Ecumenism, 251, 252

Defensor, pacis, 173, 175n

Demons. *See* Satan

Denys, Saint, of Milan, 158

Desert Fathers, 21

Devil(s). *See* Satan

Devotio mderna, 169, 174

Diamper, Synod of (1599), 14

Diaphorites, 13, 25n

Dictatus papae, 142

Diodore of Tarsus, 6

Divorce, 47, 94

Dogma and revelation. *See* Revelation and dogma

Donation of Constantine, 141

Donation of Pepin, 140

Donatists, 173

Doorkeepers, 19

Dvin, Synod of (505/506), 16

Easter, 132, 139, 155, 156

Eastern Orthodoxy, 132, 206, 280

Eastern Rite, 37, 50, 53n, 98, 102, 199n, 253, 265

Ecumenical Council, Eighth (869–870). *See* Constantinople, Council of (869–870)

Ecumenical Councils, Seven, 38, 39, 53n, 79, 93, 95, 99, 102, 113, 130, 279, 281, 283, 289, 293

Ecumenical movement, 50–51, 206–207, 251–254, 270n

Edessa. *See* Urfa

Edict of Justinian, 22, 31

Edict of Nantes, 197n

Election, 174

Elevation, 155

Emser Punktation, 198n

End times, 43

English Rite, 165

Ephesus, Council of (431), 4, 5, 15, 16, 17, 121, 160

Epiklesis, 33, 45, 46, 86n

Episcopal visitors. *See* Vicars general

Episcopalism, 198n

Episcopate, 19

Ethiopic Rite, 27n

Everlasting life, 4, 8, 15, 18, 125, 151, 152

Evolution, 215

Ex cathedra, 188, 255

Ex opere operato, 154, 180

Examen Concilii Tridentini, 182

Excommunication, 155–157

Exorcists, 19

Extravagants of John XXII, 172

Faith, 9, 41, 94, 95, 113, 124, 125, 127, 129, 136, 159, 174, 214, 282, 287

Faithful departed, 9, 19, 43

Fasting, 9–10, 23, 34, 46, 48, 174

Fathers of the church, 95

Febronianism, 186

Ferrara, Council of (1437). *See* Basel, Council of (1431)

Ferrara, Council of (1438), 24, 135, 228

Ferrete, Julius, 90, 91
Filioque (and the Son), 15, 33–34, 41, 51, 85n, 93, 95, 108, 153, 163n, 292
Florence, Council of (1439), 14, 24, 33, 37, 135, 144n, 179, 197n
Foods (clean and unclean), 25
Forgiveness of sins, 4, 18, 44, 105n, 127, 130–131, 132, 151, 152
Francis, Saint, of Sales, 183
Frankfurt-am-Main, Imperial Council of (794), 130
Friuli, Council of (796), 130
Frumentius, Saint, 24

Gallican Rite, 165
Gallicanism, 186, 197n
Generationism, 223
Gerson, John le Charlier de, 127, 128, 144n
Gnosticism, 119
God, 3, 7, 18, 40–41, 100, 121, 124, 126, 128, 151, 152, 213–215
Good and evil, 120
Grace, 15, 19, 26n, 35, 41, 121, 123–124, 125, 126, 127, 128, 129
Gratian Decree (*Decretum*) of. *See Concordantia discordantium canonum*
Gregorian calendar, 48, 66, 78, 102
Gregorian chant, 205
Gregory of Rimini, 127, 128
Gregory, Saint, of Nazianzus, 34, 140
Gregory, Saint, of Nyssa, 34
Gregory, Saint, the Illuminator, 16, 26n, 27n

Healing, Ministry of, 76, 95, 101
Heaven, 18, 43
Hell, 43, 133, 287
Hermits. *See* Solitaries
Hesychasm, 55n
Holy Communion, 9, 12n, 15, 19, 33, 34, 39, 44, 45–46, 47, 56n, 85n–86n, 95, 100, 101, 102, 105n, 108, 110, 112, 113, 114, 119, 120, 126, 128, 129, 131, 132, 133, 134, 135, 153–155, 165–167, 174, 175n, 180, 181, 205, 279, 282, 287, 298, 312
Holy Land, 132
Holy leaven, 8, 9
Holy Spirit, 3, 4, 7, 8, 15, 18, 19, 24, 33, 38, 42, 76, 93, 100, 129, 132, 135, 151, 152, 159, 214, 240–241
House churches, 102
Human beings, 33, 41, 42, 121, 122, 125, 126, 127, 128, 129

Humanae vitae, 194
Hus, John, 175
Hymns and hymnals, 94
Hypostasis, 3, 5, 10n, 13, 24, 40, 41, 149, 162n, 222, 226, 228

Ibas of Edessa, 31
Iconoclastic controversy, 32, 33, 34, 130
Iconodules, 32, 34
Images and icons, 9, 19, 25, 27n, 32, 43, 49, 94, 95, 97, 108, 112, 113, 130, 132, 158, 159, 181, 287
Immortality of the soul, 137
Impanation. *See* Consubstantiation
Imprimatur, 213
Imprimi potest, 213
Incarnation, 3, 4, 13, 15, 24, 31
Index of Prohibited Books, 204
Indulgences, 34, 113, 130, 132, 157, 159, 163n, 174, 181
Inerrancy, 219–220
Inquisition, 186
Inspiration, 219
Integralism, 208n
Intinction, 154–155
Investiture controversy, 130, 142, 144n
Irenaeus, Saint, of Lyons, 119, 170

Jacobite, 14
James I, 4, 45
Jansenism, 185, 197n–198n, 279
Jerome, Saint, 120, 143n, 157
Jerusalem, Synod of (1692), 95
Jesus Prayer, 57n
Jews, 257, 271n–272n
John of Paris, 173
John, Saint, of Damascus, 34, 35, 38, 40, 123
John, Saint, of the Cross, 183
Joseph, Saint, 234n–235n
Josephinism, 186
Judgment, 3, 4, 8, 18, 94, 105n, 133, 151, 152
Julian calendar, 48, 66, 102, 114
Justification, 15, 94, 95, 113, 125, 180

Kauma, 15, 26n
Knights Templars, 133

Laity, 19, 43, 45, 67
Last things, 121, 123, 135
Lateran Council (649), 140, 160
Lateran Council (1443), 136

Lateran Council, Fifth (1512–1517), 137, 146n
Lateran Council, First (1123), 130
Lateran Council, Fourth (1215), 131, 154
Lateran Council, Second (1139), 131
Lateran Council, Third (1179), 131
Latin Rite, 11n, 50, 75, 85n, 165, 190, 199n, 205
Lausanne, Council of. *See* Basel, Council of (1431)
Lay movement, 207–208
Learned ignorance, 128
Lectors, 8
Leipzig Interim, 304n
Leo, Saint, 158
Liberal school, 204
Liber extra, 172
Liber sextus, 172
Liturgical movement, 205–206, 208n–209n
Liturgy, 8, 9, 16, 21, 23, 25, 35, 45, 47, 48, 57n, 84, 94, 97, 102, 114, 133, 165ff., 181, 204, 283, 298–299, 300
Lollards, 174
Luther, Martin, 129, 163n, 254, 271n, 289
Lutheranism, 36, 37, 45, 51, 52, 54n, 56n, 58n, 99, 163n, 180, 181, 182, 199n, 205, 304
Lyons, First Council of (1245), 132
Lyons, Second Council of (1274), 132, 143n

Magdeburg Centuries, 145n
Malabarese Rite, 7, 95, 104n
Malankarese Rite, 14
Manichaeans, 173
Mari, Saint, 4, 9, 31
Mark, Saint, of Ephesus, 21, 39, 40
Marriage, 15, 19, 47, 57, 110, 113, 114, 130, 132, 136, 137, 143n, 181, 282, 312
Married clergy. *See* Celibacy
Marsilius of Padua, 173, 175n–176n
Martin, Saint, of Tours, 158, 168
Martyrs, 44, 158
Mary, Virgin, 4, 5, 7, 8, 9, 11n, 15, 18, 25, 27n, 34, 43, 55n, 93, 105n, 113, 125, 127, 134, 151, 152, 158, 160–162, 187, 191, 199n, 200n, 212, 222, 226, 228–232, 234n, 235n, 279, 282, 287, 290, 300, 312
Maximalists, 230
Maximus, Saint, the Confessor, 34, 40
Mayence, Council of (813), 144n
Mayence, Council of (829), 144n

Melkites, 14, 22, 25n, 85n, 92, 106n
Merit, 41
Metropolitans, 8, 47
Military service, 95
Millennium, 121
Minimalists, 230
Missions, 11n, 50, 170–171, 259–263, 272n–273n
Modernism, 203–204, 208n
Möhler, Johann Adam, 189, 207
Molinism, 185
Monasticism, 16, 21, 36, 47, 57n, 112, 167–170, 181
Mongols, 6, 14
Monophysite, 25n
Monotheism, 122
Monothelitism, 31, 55n, 140
Montanists, 173
Mother of Christ. *See* Mary, Virgin
Mother of Emanuel. *See* Mary, Virgin
Mother of God. *See* Mary, Virgin
Mother of Light and Life. *See* Mary, Virgin
Mother of the Church. *See* Mary, Virgin
Mozarabic Rite, 165
Music, 70
Muslims, 6, 14, 17, 22, 24, 34, 35, 50, 132, 257, 261, 262
Mysticism, 128

Neoplatonism, 121, 124, 128
Neoscholasticism, 189
Neri, Philip, Saint, 183
Nestorians, 5, 9, 17, 25n, 31, 99, 104n, 121, 140
Nicaea, Council of (325), 3, 7, 15, 17, 32, 49, 54
Nicaea, Council of (786–787), 4, 31–32, 54n, 55n, 130, 145n
Nicene Creed, 3, 10n, 34, 39, 100, 152–153, 184, 214, 239, 281, 289, 292, 298
Niceno-Constantinopolitan Creed, 3, 7, 18, 93, 95, 297–298, 300
Nicholas of Cusa, 127, 128
Nicholas, Saint, of Rome, 32
Nihil obstat, 213
Niobites, 25n
Nominalism, 122, 127, 128, 129, 174
Non-Chalcedonian Christians, 4, 13ff., 31, 35, 51, 53n, 85n, 91, 136, 307n
Novationists, 173

Obedience, 249, 269n

Oblation of the body and blood of Christ, 8
Old Believers, 37
Old Roman Creed, 151
One Hundred Articles Council (1551), 113
Orange, Second Council of (529), 129, 143n
Orate Fratres, 206
Orders, 19, 94, 126, 130, 132, 133, 136, 157–158, 169, 181, 249, 282, 313
Ordination, 19, 47, 102, 111, 113, 131, 144n, 157
Oriental Rite, 199n
Origen, 21, 120
Our Father, 9

Pachomius, Saint, 34, 168
Pachonium, Saint, 21
Palamas, Gregory, Saint, 35, 40, 55n
Papacy, 36, 51, 76, 97, 102, 113, 127–128, 130, 132, 133, 134, 135, 139, 173, 174, 180–181, 187–188, 254–256, 271n, 279, 283, 287, 289, 290, 291, 292, 294, 311
Paris, Council of (825), 130
Paris, Council of (829), 144n
Partav, Synod of, 27n
Pastor aeternus, 188
Patriarchs, 8, 19
Patrick, Saint, 168
Pauline theology, 128
Paulinus, Saint, of Trier, 158
Pavia, Council of (998), 144n
Penance, 19, 46, 122, 132, 135, 180, 212, 282
Perfection, 133
Persians. *See* Sassanians
Peter d'Ailly, 127, 128, 144n
Peter, Saint, 4
Philanthrōpia, 42
Photius, Saint, 32, 39, 55n, 130
Pilate, Pontius, 4
Pilgrimages, 174
Pisa, Council of (1409), 133
Pisa, Second Council of (1511), 136
Pleroma, 295
Polity, 38
Pontifical Biblical Institute, 205, 208n
Poverty, 249, 269n
Prayer, 9, 15, 19, 26n, 48, 165–166
Prayers for the dead, 43, 94, 131, 290
Preaching, 38, 181
Predestination, 94, 121, 128, 129, 143n, 185, 217

Presbyter, 157
Priesthood, 8, 16, 19, 109, 110, 112, 113, 126, 287, 312
Priesthood of the faithful, 250–251
Priests, 8, 19, 43, 47, 110, 113, 128, 131, 132, 181, 242, 243
Primates, 19
Probabilism, 197n
Prophets, 4
Providence, 216
Psalms, 108, 112
Purgatory, 34, 43–44, 105n, 113, 121, 133, 135, 143n, 154, 157, 163n, 174, 181, 212

Quietism, 185–186

Raskol, 37, 109
Readers, 19, 47, 114
Real Presence, 94
Reason, 123, 124, 125
Reform Catholicism, 208n
Reformation, 179
Reformed Theology, 99
Religious, 248–250, 268n–269n
Religious art, 38
Religious education and catechetics, 25, 248, 268n
Religious freedom, 247–248
Reservation, 155
Resurrection, 4, 8, 18, 125, 151, 152, 282
Revelation and dogma, 218–223, 233n
Rheims, Council of (813), 144n
Roman Catholic, 196n
Roman Rite, 165
Rosary, 161, 231

Sabbath, 15, 25, 34
Sacramentals, 123
Sacraments, Church of the East, 8; Syrian Orthodox Church, 15; Armenian Church, 19, 26n; Eastern Orthodox, 44ff.; African Orthodox, 94; Church of Antioch, 95, 101, 105n, 120, 123, 124, 126, 131, 133, 135, 180, 287, 290
Sacred College of Cardinals, 242, 305n
Sacrifice of the Mass, 129, 131, 181, 279, 287
Saints, 9, 15, 19, 32, 43, 87n, 94, 96, 137, 158–160, 164n, 174, 195, 245, 267n–268n, 290
Salvation, 3, 15, 19, 41, 42, 43, 105n, 113, 121, 122, 125, 126, 127, 129, 136, 151, 159, 282, 287
Saracens, 131, 132

Sardica, Council of (343?), 129
Sarpi, Paul, 182
Sassanians, 5
Satan, 216, 217, 232n
Scholasticism, 121–124, 129
Scotus, John Duns, 126–127, 234n
Second Heaven. *See* Mary, Virgin
Secret societies, 258–259, 272n, 290
Secretariat for the Promotion of the Unity
    of Christians, 199n
Secular institute, 249
Semipelagianism, 197n
Shimun-bar-Sabbai, 5
Sign of the life-giving cross, 8, 9, 44, 108,
    112
Simony, 130
Sin, 15, 19, 41, 42, 46, 105n, 119, 121, 123,
    125, 127, 128, 133, 156–157, 174, 180,
    223–226, 234n, 287
Sirmium, Council of (358), 145n, 163n
Society of Jesus, 36, 181, 183, 186
Soissons, Council of (744), 144n
Solitaries, 9, 167
Souls, 15, 112, 135, 137, 223, 233n
Spiritual healing, 76
Spoleto, Council of (1849), 198n
Studites, Theodore, Saint, 35, 40
Subdeacons, 8, 19, 47
Suenens affair, 200n
Syllabus of Errors, 186, 187, 198n, 203,
    247, 280
Symeon, Saint, the New Theologian, 35, 40

Te Deum Laudamus, 148–149, 162n
Templars, 133
Tertullian, 119
Thaddeus, Saint, the Apostle, 4, 16
Theatines, 183
Theodore of Mopsuestia, 5, 31
Theodoret of Cyrrhus, 31
Theological seminaries, 181
Theōsis, 42
Theotokos, 5, 32, 43, 48, 49, 55n, 113, 160,
    228
Theresa, Saint, of Avila, 183
Thomas Aquinas, Saint, 124ff., 189, 211ff.
Thomas de Vio, Saint, called Gaetano, 183
Thomas, Saint, 4
Thomism, 189, 211
Toledo, Third Council of (589), 129, 152
Toul, Council of (860), 143n
Tours, Council of (813), 144n
Tradition, 38, 113, 220–221, 281, 282

Traducianism, 223
Transformist view, 222
Transubstantiation, 94, 101, 126, 131, 133,
    174, 180, 279, 290
Treaty of Passau, 304
Trent, Council of (1545–1547; 1551–1552;
    1562–1563), 143n, 179ff., 198n, 220,
    239, 279, 289
Trinity, 9, 11n, 40, 46, 105n, 119, 120, 122,
    123, 125, 128, 149, 214, 222, 282, 297
Tritheism, 122
Truth, 128

Ultramontanism, 186, 188, 198n
Unam sanctam (1302), 142
Unction, 8, 113, 174, 180, 282, 312
Unctionists, 24
Unionists, 24
Unity of the Brethren, 175
Unleavened bread, 133
Urfa (Edessa), 4, 5
Usury, 133
Utraquists. *See* Unity of the Brethren

Valence-sur-Rhône, Council of (855), 143n
Vartapet, 27n
Vatican Council (1869–1870), 40, 186,
    187, 203, 256, 279, 289
Vatican Council (1962–1965), 51, 184,
    191–194, 206, 207, 211, 214, 220, 222,
    230, 240, 243, 246, 247, 248, 249, 250,
    251, 252, 253, 255, 256, 257, 258, 265,
    266, 267n, 289, 291, 311
Vercelli, Synod of, 153
Vestments, 34, 68, 94, 102, 132
Vicar of Christ, 142
Vicars general, 8
Vienne, Council of (1311–1312), 133
Vilatte, Joseph René, 90–91, 92, 94, 95,
    96, 97, 103n
Vincent de Paul, Saint, 183
Vows, 249

Waldensian Movement, 99, 131, 174
War, 121, 131
Western Rite, 56n, 64, 68, 85n, 92, 95, 96,
    98, 199n
Whoever Wishes to Be Saved. *See*
    Athanasian Creed
Will, 129
William of Occam, 127, 128, 144n
Wilna, Conference of (1599), 99

Women as priests, 100
Words of institution, 33
Works, 41, 94, 105n, 113, 128, 129, 159
World Council of Churches, 194, 195
Worldliness, 131

Worship, 38, 94, 95, 133, 165ff.
Worship (Periodical). *See* Orate Fratres
Wyclif, John, 174–175

Zoroastrianism, 5